T0386100

THE GENERALS' WAR

TWENTIETH-CENTURY BATTLES
Edited by Spencer C. Tucker

THE GENERALS' WAR

OPERATIONAL LEVEL COMMAND ON THE
WESTERN FRONT IN 1918

Major General David T. Ząbecki
US ARMY, (Ret.)

Foreword by General Anthony Zinni
USMC, (Ret.)

Indiana University Press

This book is a publication of

Indiana University Press
Office of Scholarly Publishing
Herman B Wells Library 350
1320 East 10th Street
Bloomington, Indiana 47405 USA

iupress.indiana.edu

Manufactured in the United States of America

Cataloging information is available from the
Library of Congress.

ISBN 978-0-253-03701-5 (hardback)
ISBN 978-0-253-03782-4 (ebook)

Second printing 2020

Cover illustration credits: Top front (*left to
right*): Ludendorff, photograph via George
Grantham Bain Collection, Library of
Congress Prints and Photographs Division
[LC-B2-5240-7]; Haig, photograph by
Elliot and Fry; Foch, photograph by
Melcy; Pershing, photograph via Library
of Congress Prints and Photographs
Division [LC-USZ62-13554]; Hindenburg,
photograph by Nicola Perscheid;
Pétain, portrait by Marcel Baschet.

FOR MY GRANDDAUGHTERS

Amy Franciszka Ząbecki

&

Wren Valentina Ząbecki

CONTENTS

FOREWORD

My FATHER SERVED IN THE American Expeditionary Force during World War I. He was a young Italian immigrant to the United States and was drafted into the U.S. Army, deploying to France in 1918 as a mechanic in an aviation squadron. A number of his friends in our neighborhood also served in France, and some who immigrated after the war had served in the Italian army on the Austrian front. I grew up listening to their war stories with rapt attention. I had my father's uniform, helmet, war souvenirs, and a priceless photo album of pictures he took of dogfights, downed aircraft, and fellow Doughboys. I came along much later in my parents' lives, so my friends had fathers who served in World War II. I had cousins who also served in that war in the Pacific and Europe as well as a brother who served in the Korean War. It was a considerable advantage, in my mind, to be able to hear the stories about three very different conflicts and to hear them from men who were "in the trenches." My prized toys at that time were sets of miniature soldiers that gave me endless pleasure as I fought imaginary battles in my backyard.

No one in my family had been an officer, so I didn't think much about things like strategy, operations, or tactics at that time of my life. It all seemed to me that there was a group of infallible generals at the top who made brilliant decisions. Besides, I never heard any of the hardened veterans in my neighborhood, and there were many, speak ill of their battlefield leaders. I assumed that serving in the military was a rite of passage to manhood and that I would serve at some point. I did. For thirty-nine years I served in the United States Marine Corps and became one of those generals who I realized were not as infallible as I thought.

My first war was Vietnam. It was a war that I experienced in a very up-close-and-personal way in two tours of duty there. In my first tour as a lieutenant, I was an adviser to the Vietnamese Marines. I went to language school prior to my assignment, wore the uniform of the Vietnamese Marines, lived in the villages, rarely saw other Americans, and operated throughout the country. That experience gave me a unique view of the conflict, one that differed greatly from my brother officers who served in U.S. units and saw the war through that prism. On my second tour as an infantry company commander, I gained a totally different perspective before being severely wounded and evacuated. These experiences had me questioning the generals and political leaders who appeared to me to be totally out of touch with the realities of that battlefield and in those villages. It seemed we had it wrong at every level and were winning battles through the sheer courage and tenacity of our troops and not through any strategic, operational, or tactical brilliance. Our generals were formed and forged in World War II and Korea. This war seemed to befuddle them.

As my peers and I became more experienced, educated, and hardened, we grew more critical and reflective about what we went through. The study of military history caused us to realize that wars, campaigns, and battles of the past were complex affairs, and those who led or planned for them were human: sometimes brilliant, sometimes flawed, sometimes lucky, and sometimes unlucky. An honest, in-depth study of wartime leaders pulls away the flawless, heroic images we project for the folks back home and for our posterity and reveals men of varying degrees of skill, intelligence, character, and judgment. Wars produce heroes and legends. They also produce scapegoats and reveal incompetence.

Much has been written about generalship. The model general is expected to be strategically brilliant, deeply caring about his troops, charismatic, and a bit flamboyant. During World War II, we focused on the generals, arguably, more than in any other conflict before and after. MacArthur, Marshall, Bradley, Eisenhower, Patton, Montgomery, Rommel, and others became well known to the world.

I was asked to do an assessment of our operations in Iraq and Afghanistan in 2009 and 2010. I arrived in Afghanistan during the tenth year of our involvement in that region and realized that we had ten commanders there in those ten years, seven commanders of U.S. Central Command, and five chairmen of the Joint Chiefs of Staff. A similar record of turnover at the top had occurred in Iraq. There was a revolving door through which many top generals passed at a rate unlike in any other war. It struck me that favorable media attention, durability, trust from the political leadership, and repeated success (although not perfect success) on the battlefield were the keys to generals having a positive historic reputation.

World War I did not seem to have the heroic generals that World War II did. Possibly the way that war was conducted, or played out, contributed to that. World War I came at a point in history when new, highly advanced technology met old military thinking in terms of tactics, operations, and strategy. Slugging it out in miserable trenches did not capture the imagination as much as dashing generals leading decisive sweeps and maneuvers against enemy lines or admirals orchestrating great naval battles and island-hopping campaigns. High-casualty frontal assaults against fortified lines seemed like unimaginative slaughter. The overreliance on firepower versus maneuver received criticism from military analysts and historians, and blame fell to the generals. After World War I, a plethora of military historians and theorists wrote critically about the war and drew strategic and operational lessons that were to be applied in World War II with varying degrees of success. One of the most important questions coming out of the "war to end all wars" was how to make competent generals. Marshall's experience in World War I gave him a great perspective on what was required, and he applied what he learned in selecting his generals two decades later as he served as the Allies' "architect of victory," in Churchill's words.

We can still learn a great deal from studying the leadership in World War I, for a number of reasons. As in all wars, the generals offer a great opportunity for comparison. Their character, education, experience levels, personal views on operational concepts, and perception of the battlefield are among interesting aspects to consider. It is also important to understand them in the context of their times and events. History has a way of reframing generals in either a positive or negative way that belies their true role. David Zabecki made an excellent choice in analyzing Foch, Pétain, Haig, Pershing, Hindenburg, and Ludendorff. This group lends itself to great comparisons and contrasts. As a general and historian, Dave brings a unique perspective to this analysis. He examines these leaders from every professional and personal aspect of their lives and careers in a manner that gives us an insight into who they were and why they thought, decided, and acted the way they did.

We have never devised a foolproof method of making ideal generals. I have often lectured about the different types or kinds of generals who have served the United States. I call my talk "The Four Georges": George Washington, George McClellan, George Marshall, and George Patton. They had unique personalities and approaches to their profession, and something was to be learned from each of them. In the same way, no conflict, intervention, or war should go unexamined or unstudied. All aspects are important, especially the leadership. The leaders of World War I do not get the attention in this respect, perhaps because the Second World War followed so closely and the generals and admirals of that war seemed far more interesting to historians and the public. That is unfortunate, since there is so much to learn from studying them. Fortunately, Dave Ząbecki has given us a superb analysis of these men of World War I.

Anthony C. Zinni
General, USMC (Retired)

ACKNOWLEDGMENTS

I WISH TO EXPRESS MY deep appreciation to several people for their generous help during the research and writing of this monograph. Major General Mungo Melvin, Colonel Douglas Mastriano, and Professor Michael Neiberg read various portions of the draft text and offered sage advice. Professor Holger Herwig read the entire manuscript closely and offered many excellent suggestions. I am particularly indebted to Professor Sir Hew Strachan for his thoughts on the postwar relationship between Field Marshal Haig and Prime Minister Lloyd George. My wife, Marlies Schweigler, translated Foch's 1918 directives from French into English, a task far beyond my meager linguistic capabilities. Professor Donald Frazier produced the excellent maps; this is the fifth book of mine for which he has been the cartographer. Finally, I owe two gentlemen some very special thanks: Professor Spencer Tucker, the series editor of the Twentieth-Century Battles series, and Robert Sloane, editor in chief emeritus of Indiana University Press. Without their extended patience and faith in the project, this book would have never seen the light of day. I, however, am solely responsible for any errors of fact, omission, or interpretation.

David T. Ząbecki
Freiburg, Germany

TABLE AND MAPS

Table

MAPS

follow page 124

Map 9
Battle of Amiens (8–14 August 1918)

Map 10
Allied Offensives (4 July–9 September 1918)

Map 11
German Defensive Lines (1918)

Map 12
Closing to the Hindenburg Line (9–26 September 1918)

Map 13
Allied General Offensive (26 September–11 November 1918)

Map 14
Meuse-Argonne Offensive (26 September–11 November 1918)

PLATES

Field Marshal Paul von Hindenburg

General of Infantry Erich Ludendorff

Marshal of France Ferdinand Foch

Marshal of France Philippe Pétain

Field Marshal Sir Douglas Haig

General of the Armies John J. Pershing

Major General Fritz von Lossberg

General of Infantry Hermann von Kuhl with the First Army staff of
    Colonel General Alexander von Kluck

General of Division Charles Mangin

Field Marshal Sir William Robertson

Field Marshal Sir Henry Wilson

General Peyton C. March

General Tasker H. Bliss

Lieutenant General Hunter Liggett

Foch's tomb, Hôtel National des Invalides, Paris

Pétain's tomb, Ile d'Yeu, France

ABBREVIATIONS

AEF   American Expeditionary Force

AOK   Armee Oberkommando, headquarters of a numbered field army (used in notes section)

BEF   British Expeditionary Force

G-2   intelligence section, general staff (U.S.)

G-3   operations section, general staff (U.S.)

GHQ   general headquarters

GQG   Grand Quartier Général, general headquarters of the French Armies of the North and Northeast

Hgr   Heeresgruppe, army group (used in notes section)

Ia   General Staff Officer, Operations (German) (used in notes section)

Ic   General Staff Officer, Intelligence (German) (used in notes section)

OHL   Oberste Heeresleitung, headquarters of the German Supreme Command

PMR   permanent military representative to the Supreme War Council

QMG   quartermaster general

SWC   Supreme War Council (Allied)

THE GENERALS' WAR

ONE

GENERALSHIP IN THE GREAT WAR

The truth is, no study is possible on the battlefield. One does there simply what one can in order to apply what one knows. Therefore, in order to do even a little, one has already to know a great deal, and to know it well.

Marshal Ferdinand Foch, Principles of War

The hour after an attack begins is a trying time at headquarters. There is nothing for a general officer to do but sit with folded hands. . . . He had done everything he could before H Day, or if he has not, it is too late now. He can do nothing now until the first reports come in.

Lieutenant General Hunter S. Liggett, A.E.F. Ten Years Ago in France

NO GENERAL, AS THE OLD saying goes, ever wakes up in the morning and decides he is going to lose a battle, or indeed a war. Yet for every general who loses a battle, he has a counterpart on the other side who wins the fight. This has been a constant of warfare, from long before Leonidas met Xerxes at Thermopylae in 480 BC to Norman Schwarzkopf's encounter with Saddam Hussein during Desert Storm in 1991. World War I, however, is seen somewhat differently by history, or at least by popular history. From the four years of "mud and blood" carnage, the likes of which the world had never seen, the myth of "lions led by donkeys" still holds great sway one hundred years later. The troops on all sides were courageous and patriotic, but they were blindly led to the slaughter by heartless and incompetent "butchers and bunglers"

1

who lived in châteaux, far from the front lines. The generals ate well and drank champagne while their troops lived in rat-infested trenches and endured unrelenting shelling from enemy artillery until they were committed to senseless frontal attacks, only to be massacred en masse.

World War I today is seen quite differently by the general publics of the four nations this study concerns itself with. The Great War exists only dimly in the American consciousness, even though the United States emerged from that war as one of the great powers of the twentieth century. Germans today also pay little attention to World War I, although the war does have somewhat greater resonance in France. In all three countries, there is far more interest in World War II, or in earlier conflicts, such as the Napoleonic wars and the American Civil War. Accordingly, relatively few military historians in those three countries specialize in the 1914 to 1918 period. This is not the case in the United Kingdom. For the British, the Great War is still *the* war. The eleventh of November passes in Germany each year without the slightest recognition. In the United States, it has been transformed from Armistice Day into Veterans Day, a national holiday to recognize all veterans of all wars. In the UK and many Commonwealth countries, however, Remembrance Day is the most significant national observance of the year. For the British, the Great War still looms very large, and many British historians continue to write books and produce new research about it. It is important to keep in mind, however, that most British scholarship concentrates on the British Expeditionary Force (BEF).

One hundred years on, British military historians continue to grapple with questions: Why was the First World War such a gridlocked bloodbath? Did it have to be that way? Could it have been fought differently? And if so, why wasn't it? For many years, two basic schools of thought dominated, and in the past thirty-five years or so a third school has emerged. The internal factors school emphasizes the structural weaknesses and the inbred culture of the Edwardian army, which produced incompetent and callous commanders and poorly trained staff officers. The external factors school focuses on things that generally were beyond the control of the BEF, including the exponential expansion of the British army during the war, new war fighting technologies that no one could ever have anticipated, political interference, and a very tough opponent that fielded one of the best armies in history.[1] The recent and third school attempts to strike a balance by integrating both the internal and external factors and also stresses the defects in prewar British military doctrine, especially a lack of understanding of combined-arms warfare.[2] Much of that third school model can also be applied to the experiences of the French, and especially to the Americans.

Nonetheless, the internal factors school continues to have a great deal of resonance in British thinking. Yet, for all the appealing and apparent clarity of the "butchers and bunglers" view, it was not nearly that simplistic. World War I was a war unlike any other ever fought. It was a war of "future shock." Newly emerging technologies in weaponry, communications, and later mobility rendered all the old tactics and mechanics of war fighting obsolete. All the past experience, doctrine, and theory no longer worked. Nor did the new dynamics of war fighting remain static between 1914 and 1918. They evolved quite rapidly, constantly changing the harsh realities of the battlefield. Thus, the senior military leaders on all sides, including the Germans, spent most of the first three years of the war trying to keep up with and come to terms with the new technologies—how most effectively to use them and how best to counter them in the hands of the enemy. As historian Tim Travers put it so aptly, "The story of the Western Front was really the attempt of senior officers to come to mental grips with a war that had escaped its pre-ordained boundaries and structures."[3] Unfortunately, when you are in the middle of fighting a war, trial and error is the only viable mechanism for such a process.

By the start of 1918, many of the most important lessons had been learned and internalized, albeit at a terrible price. However, none of the separate national armies—German, French, British, American—learned exactly the same lessons at the same pace. And for all its emotional appeal, the "Château General" fable does not quite hold up to close scrutiny. Because of the relatively primitive communications systems of the time, the higher the level of command, the farther back from the front the commander had to be to exercise effective command and control across the span of his front. That, of course, changed as communications technologies improved during the course of the war, but the communications systems of 1918 were still very primitive compared with those of 1939–45. Nonetheless, seventy-eight British, seventy-one German, and fifty-five French generals were killed in action or died of wounds during the Great War.[4] Historian Richard Holmes estimated that some three hundred British generals were wounded in action.[5]

This, then, is a study of World War I senior-level generalship in 1918 on the Western Front. The starting point for any such analysis must be a working definition of generalship itself. The art of generalship—and it is very much an art rather than a science—involves far more than the command of large formations of troops. It also has to do with forming, organizing, equipping, and training an army; transporting forces to a theater of operations and sustaining them logistically throughout their deployment; collecting, processing, and analyzing intelligence on the enemy; planning operations and committing the forces to battle; and directing and coordinating their actions once committed. The classic German military theorist Major General Carl von Clausewitz grouped these diverse activities of generalship into two primary categories: preparation for war and the conduct of war proper: "The knowledge and skills involved in the preparation will be concerned with the creation, training, and maintenance of the fighting forces. . . . The theory of war proper, on the other hand, is concerned with the use of these means, once they have been developed for the purpose of war. All that requires from the first group is their end product, an understanding of their main characteristics."[6] Clausewitz went on to argue that very few generals are equally skilled in both broad categories. History bears him out.

There is no such thing as a wartime general who does everything perfectly all of the time. Generals are flesh-and-blood human beings. They all at one point or another rate some degree of legitimate criticism for their actions and decisions. But such judgments always are made after the fact. Most of us cannot possibly imagine what it is like to be responsible for the lives of thousands, even hundreds of thousands, of one's own countrymen or to have to make decisions under extreme pressure, in the environment of the fog and friction of war, with partial, incorrect, or even intentionally deceptive information upon which to base those decisions. And even if the general does everything right, his troops will still wind up suffering casualties while killing and wounding huge numbers of the enemy. It is just this mass expenditure of human life in war that results in the tendency to classify generals into neatly self-contained categories: heroes (cult generals such as World War II's Erwin Rommel), villains (World War I's "butcher and bunglers"), or fools (World War I's "donkeys"). Virtually no World War I general is today considered in the hero class. Yet every battlefield general in history can be included simultaneously in all three of those categories to one degree or another. As the distinguished historians Will Durant and Ariel Durant once noted, "History is so indifferently rich that a case for almost any conclusion from it can be made by a selection of instances."[7]

Specifically, the focus of this study is on the operational level of war, that level between the tactical and the strategic. While strategy focuses on winning wars at the national level and tactics focuses on winning battles and engagements on the battlefield, the operational art deals with the design, management, synchronization, sustainment, and command and control of campaigns that connect tactical results to strategic objectives. Prior to the nineteenth century, during the era of much smaller armies, a distinct set of military activities above the tactical was known as "grand tactics." But the mass armies that first appeared during the Napoleonic wars and the range and lethality of weaponry that increased rapidly throughout the 1800s presented entirely new and different military problems and required completely different ways of thinking about warfare. The body of military theory that emerged from that process came to be known as "the operational art." At the start of World War I, the concepts were still imperfectly understood, although the Germans were the most advanced in this process.

This analysis, therefore, will concentrate on the six senior-most Western Front battlefield commanders of 1918, those generals in charge of the operational level of the war:

- Field Marshal Paul von Hindenburg, chief of the general staff of the German Field Army (Feldheer)
- General of Infantry Erich Ludendorff, first quartermaster general of the German army
- Marshal of France Ferdinand Foch, general-in-chief of the Allied armies
- Marshal of France Philippe Pétain, commander in chief of the French Armies of the North and Northeast
- Field Marshal Sir Douglas Haig, commander in chief of the British Expeditionary Force
- General of the Armies John "Black Jack" Pershing, commander in chief of the American Expeditionary Force

Despite today's broad rejection in most academic circles of the "Great Man" school of history, these six generals had the biggest influence on the outcome of the campaigns of 1918 and, ultimately, of the war. Each naturally was a creature of his own national army and the culture of that institution. But in the end, it was those senior-most generals who made the decisions, and it is impossible to understand the Western Front in 1918 without studying them.

The study of 1918 must start in November 1917, when two meetings, one on the German side and one on the Allied, set the stage for the final twelve months of the Great War. The Allied Rapallo Conference of 5–7 November resulted from the Italian disaster at the Battle of Caporetto two weeks earlier. The problems encountered in the redeployment of British and French troops from the Western Front to shore up the Italians exposed a clear need for some sort of inter-Allied coordinating body, which the Allies still did not have after three years of war. The resulting Allied Supreme War Council was a political body rather than a combined military command structure, but it was the first step that ultimately led to the establishment of such a command and the appointment of Foch as the Allied generalissimo in the spring of 1918.

Meanwhile, the Germans on 11 November convened a planning conference at Mons, Belgium, under the leadership of Ludendorff as first quartermaster general.[8] Time was not on Germany's side. The Allied naval blockade had pushed Germany's civilian population to the brink of mass starvation. The United States had entered the war on the Allied side that April; American troops were now starting to flow into Europe, and it was only a matter of time before they would tip the manpower balance decisively in favor of the Allies. But Russia had recently dropped out of the war, and the Germans had a very narrow window of opportunity to transfer a large number of divisions from east to west, giving them a temporary but very real superiority in the correlation forces. If the Germans could mass their forces at the right time and place and hit the Allies fast and hard enough, they just might win the war on the battlefield before the Americans could make a difference. The purpose of the Mons Conference was to decide where, when, and how to strike.

As 1918 progressed, the endgame of World War I increasingly became an operational-level struggle between Ludendorff and Foch. The key points that will emerge from a close study of the Western Front in 1918 include the following:

- World War I was a twentieth-century war fought by nineteenth-century men. From the most senior field marshal to the most junior platoon leader to the privates on the front lines, they all had to climb a very steep learning curve, and they had to climb it rapidly. By 1918 they were finally learning how to fight this new form of war.
- The fighting from March to November 1918 consisted of two large-scale campaigns. Between 21 March and 17 July, the Germans conducted five

massive offensives against the Allies and had planned in detail a sixth, which they never got the opportunity to launch. From 18 July to 11 November, the Allies assumed the offensive and finally brought the war to its conclusion.

· The decisive period of 1918 was not the last 100 days, when the Allies were on the offensive following the 8 August British attack at Amiens, but rather the 118-day period from 21 March to 17 July, when the Germans were on the offensive.[9] When the Germans failed to take the critical British rail hubs at Amiens and Hazebrouck in March and April respectively, the operational balance tipped against them. When Ludendorff ordered his forces to continue south from the Vesle River on 28 May, the German army quickly exceeded its operational as well as its strategic culminating point, and Germany lost the war on the battlefield. It would, however, take more than five additional months of fierce fighting for the Allies to bring the war to a conclusion. During that period, the Germans had no reasonable hope of turning the situation around.

· Although Ludendorff arguably was the most brilliant tactician of the war, he had a special blind spot for the operational level and virtually no understanding of the strategic. The five German offensives of 1918 did not constitute a coordinated, integrated, and sequentially phased operational campaign but rather five huge, costly, and largely unconnected tactical actions. After the failure of the first offensive in March 1918, each subsequent offensive was a reaction to the failure of the one before it.

· Rail lines were the key to the 1918 campaigns. The Allies and especially Foch continually targeted the German rail network. The Germans, although generally sensitive to their own rail network, failed to focus sufficiently on the significant vulnerabilities in the shallow and fragile Allied rail system. When the third German offensive in May pushed from the Chemin des Dames ridge south to the Marne River, the Germans were left holding a large and ultimately indefensible salient that had no major rail lines leading into it. The outcome was inevitable.

· Rather than attacking vital Allied vulnerabilities, Ludendorff repeatedly tried to win with force-on-force attacks. Although the Germans did have a temporary force superiority early in 1918, it was not large enough for that kind of strategy.

· Despite much of what has been written in the last hundred years, the Germans in May, June, and July 1918 never tried to take Paris. The three German offensives during that period were diversions. The Allies certainly were supposed to believe that Paris was under attack, and they did so. But the German intent was to force them to withdraw the large French reserves from behind the British in Flanders. After that, the Germans would launch a sixth precisely planned but never executed offensive designed to knock Britain out of the war. Once that happened, the Germans expected the French to collapse before enough Americans could arrive. As all the surviving German operations orders, war diary entries, and message traffic make quite clear, Paris itself was never the objective.

· Hindenburg is the most enigmatic of the war's senior commanders. Although Ludendorff largely ran the war in the west from July 1916 on, Hindenburg was more than the mere figurehead he today appears to be. The German command system was significantly different from that of the Allies. The relationship between a German commander and his chief of staff—or the chief of staff of the German army and his vice chief of staff, in the case of Hindenburg and Ludendorff—was a far closer partnership than in any other army of the time. Thus, it is impossible to consider one or the other alone. They must be analyzed as two components of the same unit.

· The two key French generals of 1918, Foch and Pétain, were very different. Pétain was by far the better tactician, but he was cautious and pessimistic at the operational level. Foch had serious shortcomings as a tactician, but at the operational level he was the best general of the war. Fortunately for the Allies, they were the two right generals in the right positions at the right time—Pétain as commander in chief of the French army and Foch as the overall Allied commander. They were very similar to Generals Dwight D. Eisenhower and George Patton in 1944–45 in that neither could have done the other's job half as well.

· Foch today remains largely underrated. As Elizabeth Greenhalgh has noted, "Most historians dismiss the First World War version of supreme command as of little value, and Foch's role in the victory as minimal." But as she then goes on to argue, "The conditions of [Foch's] appointment and the constraints under which he worked were very different from those that governed General Dwight D. Eisenhower a generation later."[10] Foch's role in the Allies' final victory was anything but minimal, and the precedent of his appointment to the supreme command and the lessons derived therefrom were the essential foundation for the successful British-American combined command of World War II. Foch's August–November 1918 operational strategy of concentric attacks across a broad front was essentially the same as Eisenhower's Broad Front Strategy of late 1944. Unlike the uncoordinated German offenses during the first half of 1918, the Allied attacks during the second half were synchronized and systematically timed.

· Much fair, but also unfair, criticism has been heaped upon Sir Douglas Haig over the course of the last eighty years. For almost twenty years following the war, Haig generally was held in high esteem by the British public. That changed radically in the mid-1930s, when wartime prime minister David Lloyd George started publishing his *War Memoirs*. He castigated the entire British general officer corps and made Haig his special scapegoat in what became a generally successful effort to deflect criticism from his own role in the war. Like General William Westmoreland in America's Vietnam War, Haig became a lightning rod for almost everything that went wrong during World War I, including those things over which he really had no control. He was hardly a stellar battlefield general and was a rather unimaginative tactician, but by 1918 he had become a competent and effective operational-level commander. He also had a significant influence on Foch's concept for the Allied General Offensive of the final two months of the war. Even Lloyd George himself admitted in 1918 that the British really did not have a viable replacement for Haig.

· In America, Pershing has long had a reputation as one of the country's greatest generals. His reputation among the British, French, and Germans, however, has always been rather low and much closer to the actual mark. Pershing was a brilliant organizer of the AEF. He also was an efficient trainer—but not an effective one. Unfortunately, he trained his troops for the wrong things. Pershing came late into the war, infused with the belief in American national exceptionalism and an unstinting faith in superior American marksmanship and the power of the bayonet. Ignoring the experiences of the previous three years, he believed that the tired and dispirited Europeans hiding in their trenches could never stand up to the robust and fresh American Doughboys. Accordingly, he discounted the effects of new weapons like machine guns, trench mortars, artillery, and aircraft, pushing his troops forward in relentless frontal attacks.

· When Pershing continually referred to the effectiveness of the German infiltration (stormtroop) tactics of 1918 as justification for his advocacy of "open warfare" training, he completely misread the similarities. Pershing's misinterpretation of the World War I battlefield was a major factor in the U.S. Army suffering a staggering 117,700 dead and 204,000 wounded in just a little more than seven months of major combat operations.

One hundred years after the end of World War I, there is still much to learn from studying it, especially the last year of the war. The Great War changed the way that wars have been fought ever since. The basic outlines of the war fighting mechanics it introduced are still with us today. As Major General Jonathan Bailey has written, "The new thinking of 1917–18 formed the seedbed for the new techniques of fire and manoeuver practiced in the Second World War."[11] And far beyond.

TWO

FUTURE SHOCK ON THE
1914–1918 BATTLEFIELD

Nothing is more dangerous in war than to rely on peace training; for in modern times when war is declared, training has always proved out of date. Consequently, the more elastic a man's mind is, that . . . is[,] the more it is able to receive and digest new impressions and experiences, the more commonsense will be the actions resulting.

> *Major General J. F. C. Fuller,* Generalship: Its Diseases and Their Cure

We had to learn our lessons in the pitiless school of war.

> *General Sir Noel Birch, in Tim Travers,* The Killing Ground: The British Army, the Western Front and the Emergency of Modern Warfare

THE CALCULUS OF WAR

The process of war fighting is like an algebraic equation made up of constants, independent variables, and dependent variables. In land warfare, the constants include weather, terrain, and the human factor. The psychology of opposing groups of men living in harsh conditions and continuously facing death is the same today as it was in the days of the Roman legions. The effectiveness of leadership will always bear on the outcome of the battle. Good weather generally favors the attacker; bad weather, the defender. Conversely, darkness generally favors the attacking force, but only if it is well trained. Although battles must be fought differently in open areas, heavily wooded areas, or urbanized areas, the physical problems presented by each of those types of terrain change very little over time. The force of gravity still confers an advantage on the side that holds the high ground.

The key independent variable in warfare is technology. Improvements in weaponry, mobility, and communications have made warfare faster-paced and more lethal. The dependent variable is tactics. As the weapons and means of communications and transportation change, the tactics must adapt accordingly. Up through at least the 1950s, generations of American grade-school children were taught that the reason the colonists prevailed in the War of American Independence was that they were smarter than their British opponents. While the British stood in nice straight rows and wore red coats, making them easy targets, the Americans hid behind rocks and trees and picked them off with well-aimed shots. That all sounded good, but it was complete nonsense. Because of the short ranges and inaccuracy of the smoothbore muskets of the eighteenth century, the only way to achieve any sort of fire effect was through massed and disciplined volley fire. The British were masters of that tactic, and the Americans kept losing until a former Prussian officer named Friedrich von Steuben taught them how to fight the same way. Nonetheless, the legend of American rifle marksmanship cast a very long shadow over the battlefields of 1918.

THE TECHNOLOGICAL REVOLUTION IN MILITARY AFFAIRS

The years between 1914 and 1918 made up the greatest period of change in the history of warfare. If an infantry battalion commander of 1914 were picked up and set down in a battalion command post of late 1918, he would be completely bewildered by what was going on around him. The battalion staff would be doing and coordinating things he could never have conceived of in his wildest imagination. But if a battalion commander of late 1918 made a similar fast-forward trip to late 1944, he would recognize much. Most of the weapons and technologies he had known in 1918 would have improved vastly, and a few new things would have appeared, but the basic structure of managing a battle would still be there.

By 1914 the last major war on the European continent had been the Franco-Prussian War of 1870–71. The only other large-scale war in the world since then had been the Russo-Japanese War of 1904–5. In retrospect, that war should have given very clear warnings about what the next major European war might be like, but most military leaders and planners tended to dismiss as a fluke any war between an Asian and a European country, especially when the Asian side won. Although a small handful of military thinkers around the world did pay serious attention to the Russo-Japanese War, most dismissed it as the result of gross Russian incompetence and internal corruption.

When the Great War started in 1914, the military commanders on all sides found themselves fighting with and against new weaponry for which all their experience and training had not prepared them. Alone, the logistics required to maintain armies of that size in the field for a period of years were totally unprecedented in military history. Nor did the new war fighting technologies of 1914 remain static. Over the course of the next four years they improved and expanded exponentially, and completely new classes of weapons came into the fight. By 1918 the changes that the commanders of 1914 had considered only vaguely, if at all, included these:

- airships (zeppelins)
- observation balloons
- observation and liaison aircraft
- bomber aircraft
- fighter aircraft
- ground attack aircraft
- aerial photography and stereoscopic photo analysis
- motor vehicles
- massive fuel requirements
- tanks
- artillery-delivered weaponized gas
- gas masks and chemical decontamination
- large-scale medical and casualty evacuation systems
- medical X-rays
- radio
- telephones
- machine guns
- submachine guns
- semiautomatic and automatic rifles
- semiautomatic pistols
- rifle grenades
- "rapid-fire" artillery (breech-loading guns with recoil systems)
- artillery mechanical time fuzes
- artillery "super-quick" point-detonating fuzes

- massive ammunition requirements
- indirect artillery fire direction
- meteorological artillery corrections
- sound and flash ranging
- dual-effect artillery projectiles (combined blast and fragmentation effect)
- antiaircraft guns
- anti-tank guns
- Stokes-type trench mortars (later classified as infantry mortars)
- flamethrowers
- wire tapping by induction
- signals intelligence
- deceptive wireless transmissions
- radio direction finding
- submarines
- depth charges
- magnetic sea mines
- sonar
- landing craft
- ship-launched aircraft
- propaganda films

Many of these technologies did exist in rudimentary form before 1914, of course, but no one had any real experience with them in actual warfare. Machine guns had been around for about twenty years, but in the absence of any major combat experience they were considered specialist weapons, possibly useful in the defense but of little use in the offense. The growth of the types of military aircraft between 1914 and 1918 typifies the expansion of technology. Experiments with military aircraft started around 1907 in some countries, but in 1914 primitive military aircraft were used primarily for observation. By 1918 all sides were operating bomber, fighter, and observation and liaison aircraft. In late 1917 the Germans introduced the world's first purpose-built ground-attack aircraft.

One final point to consider, however, is that there is really no such thing as an obsolete weapon—obsolescent, yes, but not truly obsolete. In the right circumstances, any weapon ever invented can still have some sort of effect. A soldier killed in Vietnam by a Viet Cong crossbow was just as dead as one shot with an AK-47. Many soldiers in World War I were killed during trench raids with such primitive weapons as entrenching tools, nail-spiked clubs, and trench knives with brass knuckle–like handguards.

By World War II, all of the above war fighting technologies had improved significantly in terms of power, range, and effect, but their actual applications were essentially the same. Additional new technologies did shape the 1939–45 period of warfare, but the list is smaller, and many of the new weapons were essentially technological improvements or expansions of the World War I weapons. Jet aircraft, transport aircraft, and helicopters, for example, were three new classes of combat aircraft added to the four that existed at the end of 1918. Even electronic warfare, which played such a significant role in World War II, had begun to take shape and influence the outcome of battles during the Great War. World War II advances included these:

- parachute infantry
- glider infantry
- penicillin
- artillery proximity fuzes
- self-propelled artillery
- radar
- electronic guidance systems
- electronic vectoring
- jet aircraft
- helicopters
- transport aircraft
- guided missiles (the German V-2)
- cruise missiles (the German V-1)
- autoloading antiaircraft artillery
- infrared sights
- gyroscopic gun stabilization (tanks and naval)
- acoustic and pressure sea mines
- guided torpedoes
- nuclear weapons

THE THREE PARADIGM SHIFTS

This virtual explosion in war fighting technologies between 1914 and 1918 did more than require drastic revisions in battlefield tactics. Writing in a 1996 monograph published by the British Strategic and Combat Studies Institute,

Major General Jonathan Bailey argued that World War I was "a military revolution which was the most significant development in the history of warfare to date, *and remains so*" (original emphasis).[1] Drawing on the work of Thomas Kuhn, historian Tim Travers applied the concept of the paradigm shift to the study of the Great War.[2] The *Cambridge Dictionary* defines a paradigm shift as "a time when the usual and accepted way of doing or thinking about something changes completely."[3] Paradigm shifts do not happen often, but the soldiers of 1914–18 experienced and had to cope with three simultaneous and interconnected radical departures from long-standing war fighting thought and practice.

The first of the three great paradigm shifts centered on mechanization, the change from animal and human muscle power to machine power. But that transformation did not occur evenly across the spectrum of war fighting technologies. The two principal elements of combat power at the tactical level are firepower and maneuver. Since the dawn of warfare, these two elements have been in a constant tug-of-war with each other as technology evolved, with neither element gaining the upper hand over the other for very long. By 1914, however, firepower mechanization was far ahead of maneuver mechanization. Innovations such as breech-loading artillery with stable recoil systems, magazine-fed rifles, and machine guns dramatically increased the volume, range, and lethality of firepower.

Maneuver, defined as battlefield movement to gain positional advantage, was still largely limited to muscle power at the start of the war. By the end of 1918 the battlefield applications of the internal combustion engine were finally beginning to mature, with the appearance of the tank and the increased use of motor vehicles. The horse had dominated warfare for thousands of years, but between 1914 and 1918 it almost completely disappeared from the battlefield. Armies would continue to use horses through World War II, but by then the storied war steed of history had been reduced to little more than a painfully slow auxiliary source of transport power. The extended period of imbalance between firepower and maneuver lasted from about the 1890s through the 1920s, although the gap between the two progressively narrowed. But from 1914 to mid-1918, the overwhelming dominance of firepower was the main cause of trench warfare. As historian Sir Hew Strachan has noted, "Artillery was the key weapon of trench warfare."[4] Thus, the names of such World War I battles as Verdun, the Somme, and Passchendaele have become bywords for mass slaughter and the worst horrors of modern war.

At the operational level of war, the primary task is the application of the available time, space, and forces. Military mobility at the operational level functions somewhat differently from battlefield maneuver at the tactical level. At the tactical level, the prime movers in 1914 were horses and human feet. At the operational and strategic levels, however, the prime mover was the railroad, which had well-developed military applications since the 1860s. The American Civil War of 1861–65 was the first major conflict where the railroad was used to make large-scale troop movements over long distances and also carry large quantities of supplies. The Germans made superb use of railroads during the Franco-Prussian War, and by 1910 the single largest department of the German Great General Staff was dedicated to the detailed planning of rail movements. Railways made possible rapid movement of large masses of troops and equipment, which correspondingly shortened transit times and reduced feeding and billeting requirements. Troops and horses arrived in relatively fresh condition, and improved logistical support made possible the sustainment of mass conscript armies in the field.

It was this great disparity between tactical and operational/strategic mobility that made trench warfare so static. Attackers could almost always penetrate into the enemy's defensive lines, but actually breaking through was almost impossible. As attackers advanced, they inevitably outran the range of their own artillery support. The poor battlefield mobility combined with the terrain torn up by heavy artillery fire made it difficult if not impossible for the attackers' own guns to move forward rapidly and also for their logistics system to keep the lead echelons supplied adequately. Thus, the attack inevitably slowed down and eventually reached culmination. Outside the tactical attack zone, meanwhile, defenders could use the rail networks in their rear and lateral sectors to reinforce the threatened zone with troops, ammunition, and more artillery. In the end, the attackers' poor tactical mobility was no match for the defenders' much greater operational mobility. No side ever made an actual breakthrough on the Western Front, although the Germans came very close in March 1918.

The importance of rail at the operational level also meant that the targeting of an enemy's key rail nodes could produce significant second-order effects on the tactical level. That is precisely what shaped much of the two major campaigns of 1918. This will be addressed in some detail in the subsequent chapters that address those battles. In general, however, Foch had a far greater appreciation of his enemy's rail vulnerabilities than did Ludendorff.

The second paradigm shift was the change from two-dimensional to three-dimensional warfare. The introduction of military aviation took war fighting into the third dimension. The long-held military concept of dominating the high ground assumed an entirely new meaning. The establishment and maintenance of air superiority exerted a significant, if not decisive, influence on ground operations. Not only did aircraft extend the range of observation, but as the war progressed the airplane also evolved as a platform for delivering firepower from above. Cover and concealment now had to be overhead as well as all around. Military leaders now had to think and plan in all three dimensions rather than the traditional two—albeit contoured—dimensions. And although tunneling and mining had long been a technique in land-based warfare, the advent of the submarine added a new subsurface dimension to naval warfare.

It can be argued that the third major paradigm shift was the product of the first two, but it forced military commanders to think in completely new ways. Until World War I, battles almost always had been fought and decided at the line of contact between the two armies or on the immediate flanks. In World War I, however, longer-range artillery, aerial observation and targeting acquisition, and the perfection of the techniques of indirect fire—the ability to engage and hit targets far beyond the visual range of the gun crew—added the element of depth to the battlefield and vastly increased the space over which battle was prosecuted. The battle zone expanded far beyond the line of contact, and the battle-in-depth has been a characteristic of warfare ever since. Commanders now had to fight and coordinate three simultaneous battles: (1) the close battle to tactical depth along the main line of contact; (2) the deep battle of interdiction against the enemy's base areas, logistics and communication nodes, and reserve forces; and (3) the rear battle to defend against and neutralize the enemy's deep battle efforts.[5] During 1917 and 1918, German *Fernkampfartillerie* (literally, long-distance battle artillery) groups were among the first units to appear on the battlefield with a primary purpose of what we today would call deep battle.

Depth is one of the primary elements that distinguishes the operational level of war from the tactical. Depth extends not only in space but also in time. Rather than a campaign centering on a single decisive battle, campaigns became a series of battles extended in time and built on sequential effects. By 1918 this had become something quite different from the prolonged battles of attrition of 1916 and 1917. Depth in both time and space also requires far greater logistical support and sustainment. The difference in the levels of logistical requirements is another key distinguisher between the tactical and operational levels. World War I was the most massive military logistical effort to that time and has since been surpassed only by World War II.

At the strategic level, the deep battle extended to striking directly the enemy's homeland and industrial base. That made World War I the first total war in the modern sense. The respective armies of nations were no longer at war only with each other; entire nations and all their resources and populations were now directly in the fight. Aerial attack against cities, which was such a horrific characteristic of World War II, first started in World War I.

THE VAST NEW SCOPE OF WARFARE

The vast scope of World War I military operations was something no military commander of 1914 had any experience with. For the previous forty years, the armies of Germany, France, Britain, and the United States had engaged primarily in colonial police actions and frontier skirmishes. Relatively few regular officers and troops participated in Germany's colonial wars in Africa between 1887 and 1908. Both France and Britain fought a number of campaigns in their far-flung empires of the period. Britain's biggest war immediately prior to World War I was the Second Boer War of 1899–1902, which largely was fought either on horseback or on foot. Some 347,000 British troops took part in that struggle, a mere 9 percent of the number that would serve in the Great War. The U.S. Army's primary field experience in the years following the Civil War were limited to the remote Indian campaigns on the western frontier, the brief fighting in Cuba during the Spanish-American War, and the small Mexican Punitive Expedition of 1916–17. The U.S. Army, which totaled some 4 million troops in 1918 (roughly half of them in Europe), had only 120,000 regular soldiers in April 1917. Thus, for the first time in their respective histories, both Britain and America sent the main force of their armies overseas in a major war to confront the main strength of a first-rate opponent in the war's principal theater.[6] In fact, until the United States did so, no country in all history had tried to deploy a 2-million-man force 3,000 miles from its own borders.

The general staffs of some countries had planned for large-scale warfare, continuously revising those plans to accommodate the changing strategic realities. Perhaps the most famous of those war plans was the Schlieffen Plan of

1905, as modified by General Helmuth von Moltke (the Younger) just prior to the outbreak of the war. France's equivalent in 1914 was called Plan XVII. Britain and America, on the other hand, had developed no such plans. The British and American armies did not even have general staffs until 1904 and 1903, respectively. Although the British and French general staffs conducted a series of joint talks between December 1905 and May 1906, no firm military commitments or war plans resulted. It was not until 12 August 1914, eight days after Britain declared war on Germany, that the British political and military leaders decided exactly where on the Continent the small six-division British Expeditionary Force would deploy. On the far side of the Atlantic, U.S. president Woodrow Wilson in 1914 specifically forbade the U.S. Army General Staff from doing any planning for war with Germany. The president even went so far as to tell Acting Secretary of War Henry Breckinridge to relieve any officer of the general staff involved in such planning and order him out of Washington.[7] Wilson believed that even contingency planning was an act of aggression and a violation of America's stated neutrality. In 1917 and 1918 the soldiers of the AEF would pay a heavy price for that blindness.

Also never seen before in war were the numbers of troops and the size of the forces. Field Marshal Alfred von Schlieffen's plan called for the mobilization and deployment of almost 3 million men. In contrast, General Helmuth von Moltke (the Elder) had only 280,000 soldiers against Austria and Bavaria in 1866. At Waterloo in 1815, the Duke of Wellington had only 60,000 troops. Prussian war minister General Karl von Einem warned that never in history had a single commander tried to command the twenty-three corps that Schlieffen's plan called for.[8] Yet, that was precisely the task facing the Elder Moltke's nephew in August 1914. As the war progressed and the force sizes increased, all sides were compelled to introduce for the first time in history army groups, a command and control echelon between the numbered field armies and the supreme headquarters.

Communications are the essence of command and control in battle. As recently as one hundred years earlier, a single commander such as Wellington at Waterloo could stand at his centrally located command post and see most of the action. Battlefield distances were relatively short, and orders could be sent by signal flags, signal lights, or mounted messenger with relative speed. But by 1914, a single senior commander's physical span of control could measure fifty to sixty miles, sometimes more. Field telephones provided rapid communications, but the phone wires were extremely vulnerable to the hazards of the battlefield. Radio then was primitive and unreliable. Hence, messengers were still the primary means of transmitting orders and information. The commander, thus, was mostly tied to his command post, which was the central node of the various and complementary communications systems. He could no longer see the battlefield personally. Were he to go forward to do so during the battle, he would then be effectively relinquishing command while he was out of position. And in any event, he could only see a small slice of the battlefield at any given time. By World War II, radio, other forms of electronic communications, and rapid mechanical transport systems such as armored vehicles and aircraft made it possible for the commander to move forward and still retain effective command and control. The commanders of the Great War, however, had no such luxury.

Tactical actions are the building blocks of operations. No operational plan can ever work unless it is well grounded in solid tactical principles. It is therefore necessary to have some understanding of the radical revolution in battlefield tactics during the Great War before one can make sense of the operational-level campaigns of 1918.

FIRE, MANEUVER, AND COMBINED ARMS

Most of the major armies entered World War I with modified versions of the linear tactics that had been standard since Napoleon's day. In the years immediately prior to the start of the Great War, the prevailing tactical doctrines stressed combat operations consisting of vast sweeping maneuvers and meeting engagements. No one really planned for the long and drawn-out static war on the scale that World War I turned into, but some military thinkers did have something of a sense of the battlefield problems that increases in firepower capabilities would cause. While some believed that the new technologies would reinforce the inherently superior strength of the defense, others argued that the decisive power of the offense would increase. Right from the first weeks of the war, the density of forces and the force-to-space ratio along the German, French, and Belgian borders made any sort of extensive maneuvering almost impossible. After the opposing forces spread out to establish two facing front lines running from the Belgian coast to the Swiss border, the absence of open flanks made impossible any replication of the grand encirclement or turning movement battles of military history. And once the expansive and lethal firepower started sweeping the surfaces of the intervening ground, the troops on both sides quickly realized the near impossibility of survival above ground. They started digging.

Many professional soldiers, however, continued to cling to the belief that an aggressive spirit was the only chance the attacker had of overcoming the greater firepower. The cult of the offensive was especially strong in the French army, with its doctrine of *attaque à l'outrance*, advocated by Colonel Loyzeaux de Grandmaison and Ferdinand Foch, at the time a brigadier general. As Grandmaison wrote, "For the attack only two things are necessary: to know where the enemy is and to decide what to do. What the enemy intends to do is of no consequence."[9] According to Lieutenant Colonel Pascal Lucas writing after the war, "Our officers had absorbed the theory of the offensive to the point where it had become a disease."[10] Firepower and its advocates, like then-colonel Philippe Pétain, were largely ignored. The cult of the offensive had become a substitute for any real body of tactical doctrine.[11]

Initially the commanders on all sides regarded the static trench lines and fixed fortifications as some unnatural and temporary phenomena. They spent the first three years of the war trying to develop some method of breaking through the enemy's defenses and restoring the "natural conditions" of maneuver warfare, also called "open warfare." They failed, however, to recognize the realities of that first paradigm shift in warfare. Rather than a cataclysmic clash between two opposing forces of blood, muscle, and bayonets, war had become a protracted struggle between armies consisting ever increasingly of machines, and man's most important function became the operation and servicing of those lethal engines. But most of the first three-fourths of World War I was essentially an effort to prevail with manpower in history's first truly mechanized war.[12]

Even more significantly, the new weapons technologies required, to a heretofore unprecedented degree, the coordination among the various arms—infantry, artillery, cavalry, and finally air. In the years immediately prior to 1914, the individual arms often trained with no real consideration of the others, as if they would be fighting their own separate wars. But World War I ended forever the days when large infantry units could carry battles on their own. By the end of 1917 the foundations of true combined arms warfare had started to emerge, with infantry, artillery, armored fighting vehicles, and airplanes complementing each other's strengths and compensating for each other's weaknesses. The result was a tactical multiplier effect, and the operations of 1918 brought it all together in a form that any modern soldier of today would recognize instantly.

In one way, the new artillery made it more complicated to coordinate fire support for the infantry. The guns' still-limited mobility and the relatively primitive communications systems of World War I made close-support fire increasingly difficult as the infantry advanced farther forward from their lines of departure. Radio was still in its infancy. The telephone worked reasonable well in defensive situations, but in the attack, requests for fire and fall-of-shot adjustments had to be sent by messenger, which sometimes took hours. One solution was to move the artillery fire forward on a precise schedule, controlled by phase lines on the map. That eventually evolved into the creeping barrage, with the infantry advancing closely behind the moving wall of fire. The main drawback to that approach was that now the infantry advance was wholly subordinated to the artillery schedule.[13] That, in turn, reinforced the use of rigid linear tactics. Ignoring the military effects of terrain in order to follow the artillery, the frontline infantry commanders came to have less and less control of their immediate tactical situations. By the middle of the Great War, the infantry had almost completely forgotten how to maneuver. The rigidity of the artillery-infantry tactics also centralized tactical decisions at ever-higher command echelons. But that resulted in slower response times because the communications technologies were inadequate for the greater degree of centralization. By the middle years of the war, attack planning virtually had been reduced to fixed sets of mathematical formulas—so many heavy guns per meter of front in the primary attack sector, so many machine guns, so many riflemen, so many rounds in the artillery preparation, and so on.

In the days before the advent of the motor vehicle, cavalry was the primary source of high-speed tactical maneuver on the battlefield. The Germans were quick to grasp that the days of horse cavalry were over, at least on the Western Front. Early in the war they disbanded almost all their cavalry divisions and used the horses for much-needed transport. The troopers were converted to infantry. The British, on the other hand, held onto their cavalry divisions until the end, hoping to use them as the exploitation force for the breakthrough that never came. Historian John Terraine criticized the Germans severely for launching attacks on the Western Front without cavalry to exploit any success.[14] Others have argued similarly that if the Germans had had a mobile exploitation force during their first great offensive in March 1918, the war might have turned out much differently when a wide gap opened in the Allied lines on 26 March. Such an exploitation force in those days, however, could accomplish its mission only if it was already positioned close to the point of any possible breakthrough. But on 26 March 1918, that fleeting gap occurred at a point far removed from the point of the intended German main effort. Besides, the Germans simply did not have the horses in 1918. Because of their vast inferiority in motor vehicles relative to the Allies, the Germans were forced to use every available horse for transport.

TANKS

More than one hundred years after the war, there is still wide disagreement about the significance of the tank. It was either the most potentially decisive weapon of World War I, or it was the most overrated. The Germans certainly were far slower than the Allies to recognize the possibilities of the new weapon system, an error they compensated for with a vengeance during World War II.

The British first committed tanks to battle at the Somme on 15 September 1916. They were used in small numbers and produced some initial surprise effect, which then wore off rather quickly. The French used tanks for the first time on 16 April 1917, but the results were disappointing because of the poor terrain. Ludendorff and other senior German commanders concluded from such ambiguous results that the tank was little more than a nuisance weapon that could be countered with the right tactics. The Germans, however, began to reconsider the tank after the British committed them en masse for the first time at Cambrai on 20 November 1917. And after the Allies counterattacked on 18 July 1918, spearheaded by 759 tanks, German General Staff officer Colonel Albrecht von Thaer wrote in his diary, "Even Ludendorff should now understand the power of the tank."[15]

Nonetheless, the arguments have continued on both sides of the tank question. Major General J. F. C. Fuller argued that the Germans would have won during their March 1918 offensive if they had focused all their manufacturing resources on the production of field guns and tanks.[16] Even General Hermann von Kuhl wrote that the 1918 offensives would have succeeded "if 600 tanks had cleared the way for our infantry."[17] Conversely, Major General Hubert Essame asked why, if the tank alone had been such a panacea for victory in 1918, the Germans in the spring of that year penetrated so much deeper without them than the Allies did with them in the summer and fall of that same year.[18]

John Terraine pointed out that the number of tanks the Allies could mass for the first day of an attack meant very little, no matter how great the initial results might have appeared. What mattered was how many tanks they could keep in action during the second and subsequent days. Even by the end of 1918, the tank was notoriously mechanically unreliable. And the more experience the Germans got against tanks, the more effective their anti-tank defenses became. General Charles Mangin's French Tenth Army had 346 tanks available for its 18 July 1918 counterattack against the Germans southwest of Reims. Of that number, only 225 got into action, and 102 were knocked out before the day was over. On 19 July the Tenth Army mustered 195 tanks, 50 of which were knocked out. By the third day the French had only 32 tanks left. The experience was similar for the British counterattack at Amiens on 8 August 1918, what Ludendorff called the "Black Day of the German Army." The British had 414 operational tanks on the first day, 145 on the second day, 85 on the third day, and 38 on the fourth day. By 12 August the British could put only 6 tanks into action.[19] Such attrition rates raise serious questions about just how effective an exploitation weapon the tank might have been even if the Germans had mass numbers of them. The fact remains, however, that the Germans did not have tanks in 1918.[20]

There also is an argument that the British forfeited strategic surprise when they committed tanks piecemeal in small numbers and too prematurely on the Somme in September 1916. Strachan dismisses this as nonsense, pointing out that the tank then was a very imperfect and evolving weapon system. Nobody knew with any certainty how the tank would function in combat, and the only way to get that experience was to use it. Besides, the tank was only moving into full production when the war ended in late 1918.[21] Such judgments in the light of perfect hindsight are typical of the criticisms that have been heaped upon the commanders of World War I over the years.

ARTILLERY

Artillery was the biggest killer on the World War I battlefields. As Ian V. Hogg wrote, "The war of 1914–1918 became an artillery duel of vast proportions."[22] It did not start out that way, however. The basic theoretical foundations for indirect fire, counterbattery fire, and meteorological corrections were understood by 1914, but the actual applications were slow, cumbersome, and considered to have no practical applications in fast-moving maneuver warfare. Almost all the belligerents entered the war with two basic categories of guns—field artillery and siege artillery (called foot artillery in the German army). The two branches were hardly on speaking terms with each other. Field artillerymen focused on speed and élan and considered themselves the elite among the gunners. Horse-drawn light guns were trained to charge into action at some critical moment, fire off a few rounds of direct fire over open sights, and then limber-up and gallop off to some other decisive point on the battlefield. The gunners of the slow, heavy, and plodding siege artillery were considered good only for set-piece destructive fire against heavy fortifications, such as the reduction of the Belgian frontier fortresses in August 1914.

Once static trench warfare set in, artillery almost by default became the primary means of prosecuting the war. But like all the other combat arms, artillery had to grope its way through the first years of the war, while gunners on all sides tried by trial and error to find the most effective way to use their guns. In a remarkable series of articles published in the 1920s in the *Journal of the Royal Artillery*, Lieutenant Colonel Alan F. Brooke—later Field Marshal Lord Alanbrooke, chief of the British Imperial General Staff during World War II—identified four general phases of artillery evolution that all sides went through between 1914 and 1918: inadequacy, experimentation and buildup, destruction, and neutralization.[23]

The period from 1914 through the early part of 1915 was one of inadequate fire support. Most of the world's armies in the first decade of the twentieth century regarded artillery as primarily an auxiliary arm whose mission was to assist the infantry in the attack. Some military theorists were writing about closely coordinating infantry and artillery actions—what we today take for granted as combined arms warfare—but at the practical level there was little effort to do so. During the early months of the war, that lack of understanding of what the other arm was doing produced dismal results on the battlefield, with artillery firing all too often on its own infantry.

When trench warfare set in, the field guns initially deployed directly on the front lines with the infantry, because direct fire required the gun crew to see the target. But the field guns very rapidly proved to be far too vulnerable to the enemy's infantry fire, especially the enemy's machine guns. Thus, the guns were forced off the front lines and into covered positions well to the rear. That, of course, reduced their effective range, but more significantly it forced the field gunners to use—or in most cases, to learn—indirect fire control techniques.

The mobility of 1914 field guns also meant that they had to be light. The German 77mm, the Russian 76.2mm, the American 3-inch, the British 18-pounder, and the famous French 75mm were effective against troops in the open, but their light shells were not at all effective against troops well dug into reinforced positions. For the most part they also were guns, rather than howitzers. Guns have a high muzzle velocity but also a relatively flat trajectory, which made it hard to hit targets in defilade, such as those immediately behind hills. Howitzers have a much lower muzzle velocity, but their trajectory is more arched, making it easier for them to hit masked targets. Unlike guns, howitzers also are capable of high-angle fire, which drops the projectile on the target from almost directly above.

Britain and France started the war with very few howitzers or heavy artillery. The Germans entered World War I with a significantly higher ratio of howitzers and heavy guns, because they paid closer attention to at least the artillery lessons of the Russo-Japanese War. Thus, the heavier siege artillery came into its own very early in the war. The heavier guns had the hitting power and the greater ranges needed for trench warfare. The siege and foot artillery guns also had the calibrated sights and fire control systems necessary, and the heavy gunners were trained on indirect fire.

As the military leaders on all sides began to understand the problems they were facing, most of 1915 was a period of artillery experimentation and build-up. All sides vastly increased the production of howitzers and heavier guns, but initially the more immediate problem was of artillery ammunition shortages. French war plans, for example, estimated an average consumption of 100,000 rounds per month, but the actual monthly average for 1914 was close to 900,000 rounds. By 1916 the French were shooting 4.5 million rounds per month. Throughout most of 1914 and 1915, tactical plans were held hostage to the supply of artillery ammunition.[24]

The growing importance of artillery made it necessary to attack directly the enemy's artillery, and until bomber and ground attack aircraft became more developed by the end of the war, artillery was the only way to do that. But aside from the rather vague concept of the "artillery duel," there was very little systematic counterbattery doctrine before the war. The 1913 French Field Service Regulations specifically forbade French artillery from engaging in artillery duels.[25] By the end of the war, designated artillery groupings would be task-tailored specifically for the counterbattery mission.

Prior to the war there was very little real centralized command and control of artillery above the divisional level. The Royal Artillery entered the war with no experience in fire planning and control above the level of the artillery battalion. In most armies of 1914, corps-level artillery existed only as a pool of assets, to be allocated among the divisions as the mission required. By 1918, artillery planning cells were in operation even at the army group level. When the war ended, the Royal Artillery had more soldiers than the Royal Navy had sailors.

More guns, heavier guns, and the ammunition needed to feed them moved artillery into its destruction phase of 1916–17. During this period of tactical stagnation, the main function of artillery became the destruction of defensive positions and the annihilation of enemy troops—destroy the attacking enemy before the attackers reached friendly lines, and destroy the defending enemy before attacking friendly troops reached the hostile positions. That, in turn, increased exponentially the rates of ammunition consumption. The prevailing philosophy of this period became "The artillery conquers; the infantry occupies."[26] The dominance of artillery naturally gave rise to counterbattery operations against the enemy's artillery, where the destruction principle based on rigid mathematical formulas also prevailed.

The key offensive fire support technique during this period became the artillery preparation, intended to "soften up" the enemy prior to the infantry assault. But as the war went on, the artillery preparations increasingly grew longer and longer, lasting days and then weeks. The extensive preparations, however, actually caused more problems for the attackers. The longer the preparation lasted, the more time the defenders had to reinforce their threatened sector and to initiate countermeasures. The massive artillery fire also tore up the intervening ground the attackers had to cross, slowing down both the infantry and the forward movement of the attackers' artillery necessary to support any advance in depth. The massive preparations also caused an enormous logistical drain that slowly bled the national economies of the belligerents.

By late 1917, artillery started to move into its final phase of neutralization. As leaders on all sides continued to struggle to find both firepower and maneuver solutions to the tactical deadlock, the major innovations in fire support started to develop on the Eastern Front. The key to the new thinking was the idea that artillery fire was more effective when its tactical effect was neutralization rather than destruction. The basic idea behind neutralization was that it was not necessary to destroy completely the enemy prior to the infantry attack; rather, just disrupting and dislocating it to the point where it could not defend effectively, and only long enough for the attacking infantry to get on top of it, was enough. When neutralization fire was later combined with the new infantry tactics that were developing on the Western Front, the result was a more effective form of many of the prewar tactical concepts.

The most influential artillery tactician of the war was Colonel Georg Bruchmüller, an obscure, medically retired German officer recalled to active duty for the war. General Max Hoffmann called Bruchmüller "an artillery genius,"[27] and Ludendorff called him "one of the most prominent soldiers of the war."[28] Starting on the Eastern Front as early as 1915 and culminating in the 1917 Battle of Riga, Bruchmüller experimented with various fire support methods centering on neutralization. At the Battle of Lake Narotch in April 1916, Bruchmüller became the first artillery officer in the German army to plan and coordinate fires above the divisional level.

Bruchmüller understood the counterproductive nature of the long, destruction-oriented preparations. Thus, while the preparations in the west were lasting weeks, Bruchmüller planned and executed preparations in the east lasting only a few hours, yet achieving better effect. His preparations were not long, but they were incredibly violent—designed not to obliterate a defending enemy but to stun it senseless. The British came to call such preparations "hurricane bombardments." In Bruchmüller's own words, "We desired only to break the morale of the enemy, pin him to his position, and then overcome him with an overwhelming assault."[29]

Bruchmüller was the driving force behind some of the war's most important fire support innovations. He was one of the first to organize artillery preparations into distinct phases, with each phase intended to accomplish a specific tactical purpose. Because it had no direct blast effect, artillery-delivered gas was an ideal neutralization weapon, and Bruchmüller carefully matched the effects of various types of gas—lethal and nonlethal, persistent and nonpersistent—against specific types of targets to achieve precise effects. One of his greatest innovations was a system of task-tailored artillery groups, each with a specific mission to perform during the battle—infantry direct support, counterbattery, deep interdiction, and special heavy destructive fire against carefully selected enemy communications and command and control nodes. Bruchmüller also was one of the earliest advocates of centralized fire planning but decentralized execution based on close coordination with the infantry. He even invited infantry commanders to review and comment on his fire plans, something almost unheard of prior to 1917.

After the Germans captured Riga and effectively knocked Russia out of the war, Ludendorff transferred Bruchmüller to the west to control the artillery of the Eighteenth Army for the March 1918 offensive. Shortly after arriving on the Western Front in November 1917, Bruchmüller quickly became the principal champion of a newly developed technique to "predict" artillery registration corrections based on the careful measurement of local weather conditions and the muzzle velocity characteristics of each gun tube in a battery. The system developed by Captain Erich Pulkowski is essentially the same as that used by all the NATO armies today, although all the calculations are now done by computer.

Bruchmüller was not the only artillery innovator of the war, of course, nor did he personally develop all of the techniques he used so effectively. He did, however, perfect many of them on the battlefield, and he was the first to make them all work in a comprehensive system.[30] French artillerymen, for the most part, were always several steps behind the Germans. They were slow to accept a return to neutralization and to understand the value of surprise. Several British gunners, on the other hand, had been advocating many of the same principles as the war progressed. Foremost among that group were Lieutenant General Sir Noel Birch, Major General Sir Herbert Uniacke (known in Royal Artillery circles as "the British Bruchmüller"), and Brigadier General H. H. Tudor. The British attack at Cambrai actually predated the Germans in the use of a system to predict artillery corrections without registering. Technical errors in the application, however, produced mixed results.

THE DEFENSIVE

The Germans also pioneered the most important innovations in infantry tactics, although most of the development work took place on the Western Front. Once Hindenburg and Ludendorff in July 1916 were transferred to the Western Front to assume overall command at Oberste Heeresleitung (OHL), Ludendorff immediately embarked the German army on an all-encompassing review and revision of its tactics in modern war. The German army had been on the defensive on the Western Front almost continuously since late 1914 (with the notable exception of the Verdun Offensive), and its defensive tactics and techniques had evolved considerably. Defense, then, was the first area addressed. On 1 December 1916, OHL published the German army's new defensive doctrine as *Principles of Command in the Defensive Battle in Position Warfare (Grundsätze für die Abwehrschlacht im Stellungskrieg).*[31] An analysis of offensive doctrine came next, and following a thirteen-month study, OHL on 1 January 1918 issued *The Attack in Position Warfare (Der Angriff im Stellungskrieg).*[32]

At the start of the war, defensive tactics were based on establishing rigid positions with the bulk of combat power concentrated in the forward trenches. The concept is known as forward defense. And as taking ground in the offense cost more and more human lives, it seemed sacrilegious to yield even a few inches of it in the defense. The defensive credo became one of holding "at all costs," regardless of the tactical situation. Typical of the nineteenth-century notions of honor and manliness, military commanders believed that allowing troops to withdraw under pressure, even a tightly controlled deliberate withdrawal, would somehow be an endorsement of mass cowardice. In the face of modern firepower, however, the rigid, forward defense was suicidal. It placed the bulk of the defender's forces in densely packed positions, where they were just so many clear targets for the enemy's artillery.

While he was chief of the General Staff at OHL, General Erich von Falkenhayn pursued a ruthless strategy of exploiting the Allies' tactical doctrine of conducting rigid defenses with the bulk of their forces packed into the forward trenches. Oddly enough, Falkenhayn himself followed the same defensive doctrine, insisting that German commanders hold the front line at all costs. Consequently, the Germans troops paid a high price in blood during the great Allied offensives in Champagne in 1915, the Somme in 1916, and Arras in 1917. But in the process, local German commanders and staff officers developed increasingly more effective defensive methods. Colonel Fritz von Lossberg was one of the most prominent of those defensive tacticians.

Called alternately "der Abwehrlöwe" ("the Lion of the Defensive") and "Ludendorff's Fireman" by his contemporaries in the German army, Lossberg served throughout the war as the chief of staff of one corps, five different field armies, and two army groups on the Western Front. Whenever the Allies launched a major offensive, OHL transferred Lossberg to the point of immediate danger, with orders to do whatever necessary to bring the situation under control. With almost a free hand, Lossberg played the key role in the transformation of German defensive tactics on the battlefield, which were later adopted as official doctrine.

The new doctrine can best be described as flexible defense, or flexible defense-in-depth. It rested on three key principles: flexibility, decentralized control, and counterattack. While the command and control of the Allied attacks became centralized at ever-higher levels, German commanders in the defense had an impressive amount of autonomy. A frontline battalion commander had the authority to withdraw from forward positions under pressure as he saw necessary. More important, he had the authority to order the remaining battalions of his regiment (echeloned to his rear) into the counterattack when he judged the timing right.

The Germans recognized two distinct types of counterattacks. The hasty counterattack (*Gegenstoss*) was immediate and violent, designed to hit the attacking enemy immediately, before the attackers had a chance to consolidate their newly won position or move up reinforcements. Locally planned and executed, the *Gegenstoss* was launched on the initiative of the frontline battalion commander. The deliberate counterattack (*Gegenangriff*) was centrally planned and more methodically prepared. It was only used when a *Gegenstoss* had failed or was unfeasible.

The Germans organized their deep defensive positions into three zones. The outpost zone (*Vorfeldzone*) was 500 to 1,000 meters in depth and manned with sparsely positioned early-warning posts. The battle zone (*Kampffeld*) was up to 2,000 meters deep. And the rearward zone (*Hinterzone*) was where the reserves and counterattack units were held, often in deep, reinforced bunkers. The leading edge of the battle zone was the main line of resistance (*Hauptwiderstandslinie*), with three or more successive trench lines. Between the battle zone and the rearward zone came another line of multiple trenches that served as the protective line for the artillery. The Germans also decreased the strength of the forward positions. While the French were putting two-thirds of their combat strength into the first two lines, the Germans put only 20 percent into the same positions. The Germans even came to regard their forward-most trenches as useful only in quiet periods. During an artillery bombardment prior to an Allied attack, the forces in the rear would move into their deep, protected bunkers to ride out the storm. The troops in the thinly held outpost line would slip out of their trenches and take cover in nearby shell-holes—while the Allied artillery pounded the empty trenches.[33]

By the latter half of 1917, the Germans started distinguishing between two types of divisions with different tactical functions. The defensive positions in the line were manned by "trench divisions" (*Stellungsdivisionen*). Farther back in the operational rear, the Germans positioned their "attack divisions" (*Angriffsdivisionen*) to conduct the larger-scale, deliberate counterattacks. When the Germans went over to the offensive in 1918, this distinction played a key role, with an entire attacking corps moving up into a sector of the line that had been held by a single trench division.[34]

By the start of 1918, the Western Allies had little experience in defending. As they faced the inevitable German offensives they expected for that spring, they made some efforts to adopt their own defenses based on their previous experiences against the Germans. The British attempted to establish the deep three-zone defenses, but they understood the system imperfectly, and their troops were not trained to fight that way. Thus, the British suffered heavily during the first two offensives in March and April. When the German main effort shifted to the south, the French still tried to execute a rigid forward defense during the third German offensive in May. By the time of the fifth German offensive in July, however, the French finally had mastered the principles of deep and flexible defense, and the Germans found themselves hoist with their own petard.

THE OFFENSIVE

Attaque à l'outrance proved far from the panacea the French had believed it to be in 1914. By mid-1917, many Allied commanders started to realize that decisive penetration was just not possible under the current conditions and especially against the new German defensive system. As British major general R. C. Money summarized the tactical problem, it was "how to surprise, overrun, and penetrate a well-sited defense system some four miles deep, the front edge of which was only a short distance from one's own, protected by massive wire entanglements and covered by the flanking fires of machine guns and a wall of fire from artillery and mortars of all calibers sited in depth."[35]

Pétain, among others, advocated limited objective attacks, designed to eat away at an enemy's position in small chunks—what the British later called "bite and hold." Other tacticians, however, were thinking bolder ideas. In May 1915, French captain André Laffargue wrote a pamphlet suggesting that specially trained teams of skirmishers precede main attacks. Armed with light machine guns and grenades, these teams would infiltrate into the German lines ahead of the main attack, locate and neutralize the German machine guns, and even penetrate deeply enough to attack the German artillery positions. The British and French largely ignored Laffargue's pamphlet, but the

Germans captured a copy during the summer of 1916, translated it, and issued copies to their frontline units.[36] Laffargue's pamphlet, of course, advocated many of the tactical techniques that later came to be associated with German stormtroop tactics or, more correctly, infiltration tactics.

On the German side of the line, Captain Willy Rohr was one of the earliest leaders in the development of the new offensive tactics. In August 1915 Rohr took command of the recently formed assault detachment (*Sturmabteilung*) on the Western Front. Under Rohr, the assault detachment conducted very successful counterattacks using nonlinear methods drawn from the traditional tactics of the German *Jäger* (light infantry) units. The basic unit for such operations was the assault squad (*Stosstrupp*). Armed with grenades, automatic weapons, trench mortars, and flamethrowers, their tactics and techniques were very similar to those suggested by Laffargue.[37]

Rohr's detachment eventually grew into a *Sturmbattalion*. After the initial attacks at Verdun, the Fifth Army started using Rohr's battalion as a training unit during the lulls in the fighting. In May 1916, Falkenhayn directed selected Western Front units to spend fourteen days training with Rohr's battalion. When Ludendorff arrived at OHL later that year, he expanded the program. By January 1917 each German field army had an assault company. By the end of 1917 each field army had an assault battalion that functioned as a training cadre.[38]

These special assault units became known as stormtroops (*Stosstruppen*). The storm battalions were one of the earliest forms of a true combined arms task force. Typically, their structure included three to four infantry companies, a trench mortar company, an accompanying artillery battery, a flamethrower section, a signal section, and a pioneer section.[39] Meanwhile, by March 1917 the standard German infantry squad was restructured around a four-man light machine gun team as the fire element and a seven-man team as a maneuver element.[40]

By 1917 Rohr's infiltration tactics became the official counterattack doctrine on the Western Front. In September 1917 the Germans at Riga on the Eastern Front made their first attempt to apply the tactics to a large-scale offensive operation. Instead of the typical attack formations of rigid lines, the German Eighth Army of General Oskar von Hutier attacked in fluid leaps and bounds, with one element moving forward while another element provided fire cover. Then the two elements reversed roles and leapfrogged each other.

The forward-most units completely bypassed the defenders' strong points, isolating them and leaving them for heavier follow-on forces to eliminate. Reserves were used only to reinforce success rather than thrown in where the attack was faltering.

Riga was also the first time the new infantry tactics were combined on a large scale with the new artillery tactics developed by Bruchmüller. The Germans also used similar tactics during their successful attack at Caporetto the following month. The new tactics, or more precisely their results, shocked the Western Allies. The French, in particular, looked for a single tactical mastermind as the source of the new tactics and settled on Hutier. Thus, they erroneously dubbed the new German tactics "Hutier tactics." The German counterattack at Cambrai on 30 November 1917 was the first large-scale use of stormtroop tactics on the Western Front. The twenty-division counterattack was almost as successful as the British mass tank attack ten days earlier.

The new doctrine envisioned the attack in two main phases: first, a methodical assault against the enemy's organized positions, which required detailed preparation and centralized control, and then an aggressive continuation of the attack to prevent the enemy's ability to reorganize and respond. The second phase was characterized by decentralized execution and initiative on the part of the subordinate commanders. This phase began in the enemy's intermediate zone, beyond the range of the creeping barrage. In the attack, as opposed to the defense, the higher echelons maintained tighter control of the follow-on forces.[41]

Depth and speed were the two keys to success. The flanks of the attacking elements would be secured by speed and depth. The immediate objective of the attack was to penetrate as far as possible into the enemy positions, at a minimum reaching and overrunning the enemy's artillery positions on the first day. The new doctrine stressed infantry-artillery coordination and the need to move artillery forward to sustain the attack. Artillery neutralization fire was emphasized over destruction. The intent was to disrupt the enemy's communications and bypass and isolate the enemy's strong points. The new doctrine marked a key conceptual shift from destruction to large-scale disruption—which is one of the basics of the operational art.[42]

While the Allies attacked in successive waves, in order to relieve the pressure on their lead units, the Germans continued to press the attack with the lead units in order to maintain momentum. This, of course, burned out the lead units quickly, and within the framework of sequential operations it was counterproductive and had serious consequences for the Germans after March 1918.[43]

The Germans considered the division the basic unit capable of conducting independent battlefield operations. In 1916 they reconfigured all their divisions from the square to the more flexible triangular structure. As noted above, they started distinguishing between trench and attack divisions in 1917. The *Angriffsdivisionen* started out as counterattack units and eventually evolved into the principal assault units for the 1918 offensives. During the 1918 offensives, the best trained and best equipped of the attack divisions were further classified as mobile divisions (*Mob. Divisionen*).[44] Essentially, they became entire stormtroop divisions, but their standards and training were not as high as original assault battalions. Divisions were converted by being pulled out of the line and put through three to four weeks of special training at Sedan or Valenciennes.[45] Only half the heavy machine-gun units of the *Angriffsdivisionen* were horse-drawn because of the shortage of animals. By March 1918, only 56 out of 192 German divisions on the Western Front were classified as attack divisions. Ludendorff later came to regret the decision to have two different divisional structures.[46]

ADAPTATION IN WARFARE

As British historian Sir Michael Howard once wrote, it is almost impossible for armies to get things right at the outset of any war. This was especially true for the First World War, where the vast technological changes created complexities that soldiers and commanders never before had to face. Thus, it was far more important to adapt and change to the new battlefield realities between 1914 and 1918. As Sir Michael also noted, "In these circumstances when everybody starts wrong, the advantage goes to the side which can most quickly adjust itself to the new and unfamiliar environment and learn from its mistakes."[47] Adaptability, self-assessment, and the management of change within an army are primary responsibilities of that army's generals. The way in which the six major commanders in this study both drove and managed change and adaptation in their respective armies was a major factor in the outcome of the final year of the Great War.

THREE

THE STRATEGIC SITUATION
AT THE END OF 1917

Superiority of numbers in a given engagement is only one of the factors that determine victory. The forces available must be employed with such skill that even in the absence of absolute superiority, relative superiority is attained at the decisive point.

Major General Carl von Clausewitz, On War

All men can see these tactics whereby I conquer, but what none can see is the strategy out of which victory is evolved.

Sun Tzu

GERMANY

By the time Ludendorff and the army group and army chiefs of staff met at Mons on 11 November 1917, Germany's strategic situation was bleak at best. For one thing, the combined populations of the four Central Powers (Germany, Austria-Hungary, Bulgaria, and Turkey) was 144 million. The combined population of the Entente Powers was 690 million, including colonies. Germany's coalition partners were weak and getting weaker all the time. Despite the specifically designed intention of the Schlieffen Plan, Germany for the last three years had been fighting a two-front war, the dreaded nemesis of German strategists since at least the days of Frederick the Great. When Russia finally was knocked out of the war that September, that problem eased somewhat, but only temporarily. American's entry into the war brought the problem back in another dimension. Since 1914 Germany had been fighting two enemies (France/Britain and Russia) separated in space. From 1918 on the country would be fighting two sets of enemies (France/Britain and America) separated in time.[1]

The Schlieffen Plan was supposed to be the master formula for Germany to avoid that two-front war. Assuming that the Russians would take far longer to mobilize than the French, the strategy was to deploy only a small holding force to the east, launch the main attack in the west, crush the French rapidly, and then turn to the east to deal with the Russians. Such a plan turned on Germany's central position on the European continent and its ability to exploit interior lines. The attack in the west was designed as a massive turning movement. The German main battle line, heavily weighted on the right and pivoting on the left, would penetrate toward the Channel coast and sweep around the west of Paris. Then the two jaws of the German wings would slam shut, crushing the French army in between.

But as the old paraphrase from Moltke the Elder goes, no plan ever survives first contact with the enemy. One of the fatal flaws inherent in the Schlieffen Plan was that the required balance of forces, time, and space meant the Germans would have to violate Belgian neutrality to make it all work, and that inevitably would bring Britain into the war. And in this case, the Russians mobilized much faster than anticipated. When East Prussia was threatened, the chief of the German Great General Staff, Helmuth von Moltke the Younger, felt compelled to withdraw some forces from the German right and redeploy them to the east. As the deployment in the west unfolded, the German First Army on the right wing passed to the east of Paris as a gap opened between it and the Second Army on its immediate left. When the small British Expeditionary Force probed cautiously at first into that gap, it further disrupted the German operational scheme. The Allies regrouped, and the Schlieffen Plan died at the Battle of the Marne in early September 1914.

Much ink has been spilled over whether or not Moltke the Younger fatally weakened the Schlieffen Plan by continually tinkering with what Alfred von Schlieffen had drawn up in his famous 1905 memorandum. In the first place, the strategic and political conditions of 1914 were not those of 1905. All war plans must be adjusted periodically as the situation changes, and that was one of the primary functions of the German General Staff. The problems, however, ran far deeper. As Gerhard Gross has noted, "The German Army lacked the mobility required to turn its theoretical planning into reality. The General Staff had underestimated the interdependence between the time pressures at the operational-strategic level and the mobility of the troops required for the execution of operations. They thus failed to recognize that mobility was not only the most important, but the decisive factor in the conduct of operations."[2]

Following the Battle of the Marne, both sides tried to outflank the other, steadily moving toward the north, in what came to be called the "Race to the Sea." That series of maneuvers ended with the bloody First Battle of Ypres in October–November 1914. The subsequent period of trench warfare on the Western Front lasted until March 1918, as the Germans then went over to the general defensive in the West and concentrated on defeating Russia in the East. Commanding the German Eighth Army in the east, Hindenburg with Ludendorff as his chief of staff handed the Russians a devastating defeat at the Battle of Tannenberg in late August 1914, about a week before the German defeat at the Marne. The Eighth Army then followed up with a similar victory at the First Battle of the Masurian Lakes, just about the same time the Battle of the Marne was fought. Hindenburg and Ludendorff became German national heroes and their names household words. Hindenburg's status would remain such beyond the final German defeat in November 1918. Ludendorff's star, however, started to fade before the Armistice.

The Germans went on the offensive in the West only once during that period, when in February 1916 they attacked at Verdun. For most of the last one hundred years that battle has been regarded widely as an attempt by General Erich von Falkenhayn, then the chief of the German General Staff, to destroy the French army through attrition. However, recent scholarship by German historian Olaf Jessen suggests that what the Germans actually attempted was a flanking movement on a grand scale, somewhat like what Frederick the Great did at Leuthen in 1757.[3] But by the time the battle ended in December, it was a failure for the Germans on all three of the levels of warfare—tactical, operational, and strategic. In the middle of the Verdun debacle, Hindenburg and Ludendorff were transferred from the Eastern Front in July 1916 and assumed overall command of the German army at Oberste Heeresleitung. It took them several more months to bring the Verdun operation to an end because the French kept counterattacking to retake the ground they had lost during the first months of the battle.

In the middle of all that, Ludendorff initiated his comprehensive overhaul of tactical doctrine, completely changing the way the German army fought on the battlefield. Hindenburg and Ludendorff also presided over one of the shrewdest operational moves of the war. The frontline trace in the west had moved relatively little either way since the beginning of 1915, but the current German positions were not optimal defensively. Hindenburg and Ludendorff decided to pull the German positions in France back to a line based on more defensible terrain, eliminating vulnerable salients and making the overall line much straighter and shorter. In so doing, the Germans gave up more than 1,000 square miles of territory, but they shortened their overall line by 25 miles and freed up fourteen divisions. Those troops then could concentrate on training on the new tactics. The new positions also became the line of departure for the offensives of 1918.

The construction of the new German line was the greatest military engineering feat of World War I. The Germans called it the Siegfriedstellung (Siegfried Position). The Allies came to call it the Hindenburg Line.[4] The Siegfriedstellung took four months to build, employing some 540,000 reservists, French civilians, and Russian POWs. The three-hundred-mile line consisted of up to five successive lines in depth, each with three or more roughly parallel sets of trench lines, reinforced with barbed wire, land mines, machine-gun emplacements, strongpoints, and deep and reinforced bunkers, all backed by artillery and trench mortars. It took 1,250 supply trains of forty cars each to bring forward the necessary concrete and steel. And remarkably, the Germans managed to keep the activity largely concealed from the Allies.[5] Lieutenant General Wilhelm Groener, who replaced Ludendorff at OHL in the last weeks of the war, called the withdrawal to the Siegfried Position Ludendorff's greatest achievement.[6]

Once the new emplacements were built, the actual withdrawal was planned in detail and code-named Operation ALBERICH. On 9 February 1917 OHL gave the frontline units the warning order to prepare for the withdrawal. The movement started on 16 March and concluded just four days later. As the Germans withdrew, they also executed a scorched-earth action over the intervening ground. The move caught the Allies completely by surprise and disrupted many of the Allied offensive plans for 1917.[7]

By the end of 1917, all of Germany's coalition partners were weak, requiring Germany to prop up especially Austria-Hungary. Three years of war had wrecked the German economy. The British maritime blockade brought the German civilian population to the verge of mass starvation during the infamous "Turnip Winter" (Steckrübenwinter) of 1917. Some historians have suggested that the Royal Navy played the decisive role in the war by completely breaking the morale of the German nation. Richard Holmes, however, argues that although the blockade increased Germany's growing sense of desperation, it no more broke the country's morale than strategic bombing did during World War II.[8]

Nonetheless, the German army was drawing on the country's last manpower reserves and planning on calling up the conscription class of 1919 a year early. And Germany's archaic, rigid, and authoritarian political, social, and economic systems were strained to the breaking point. By the time of the 1917 Mons Conference, Hindenburg and Ludendorff were the virtual dictators of Germany, a function for which they had absolutely no competence. Nor did they have the time. Every hour they devoted to wrestling with Germany's intractable domestic and diplomatic problems detracted accordingly from their ability to manage the military operations. Almost exactly one year after the Mons Conference, the five-hundred-year-old Hohenzollern Dynasty of Brandenburg-Prussia collapsed as the kaiser abdicated and went into permanent exile in Holland. Thus, at the start of 1918, Germany had one final fleeting window of opportunity to win the war on the battlefield, or at least to establish a far stronger position for negotiation. But it was a long shot at best.

FRANCE

France too suffered severely. Most of the Great War was fought on French soil, wreaking untold destruction on the territories in the battle zone. At the start of 1918 the Germans held a huge part of northwestern France, including the vital Briey coalfields to the west of Metz. By mid-July 1918, Germany would hold even more French territory.

As the Schlieffen Plan failed for Germany, so did Plan XVII fail for France. At the start of hostilities three-quarters of the French army was staged south of Verdun. Plan XVII, a product of the *offensive à l'outrance* theorists, called for a main attack by four French armies. Two armies each would advance north and south of the Metz-Thionville fortresses, which Germany had seized from France in 1871. The southern armies would capture the former French provinces of Alsace and Lorraine. The northern armies would attack through southern Luxembourg and into Germany proper through the Saarland. Then the two wings would swing in toward each other to form gigantic pincers. Depending on the German movements, the northern French force also had the option of advancing toward the northeast through Luxembourg and Belgium.

Ironically, the French strategic planners largely disregarded the possibility that Germany would violate Belgian neutrality, although Plan XVII had an option for France to do just that.

Plan XVII was based on the assessment that the Germans did not have sufficient forces to drive across Belgium. The German regular army, in fact, was not large enough for something like that. Yet despite ample intelligence indicators to the contrary, French planners rejected any possibility that Germans would commit their mobilized reserve corps to the front lines. That is exactly what they did.[9] Thus, Plan XVII was based on three key assumptions, all of which proved false: (1) the deployable French force would be equal to or superior to the Germans, (2) Germany would not violate Belgian neutrality, and (3) the German main effort would come through the Ardennes and not through the Low Countries.[10] As historian Douglas Porch has written, "The tragedy of the French Army was that its leaders were committed to an aggressive strategy which was beyond their tactical powers."[11]

Aside from vague slogans about "liberty and justice," France did not develop clearly defined war aims until July 1916.[12] Meanwhile, between 1915 and April 1917 the French army was ground down by launching relentless and nonproductive massive assaults against the well-dug-in German positions. From February to December 1916, the French were forced to defend against the German attack at Verdun, which the Germans designed specifically as a massive battle of attrition, a huge meat grinder to bleed the French army dry. It almost worked. Four days into the German attack the French were on the verge of collapsing. As almost an act of desperation, Pétain was called in to command the fortified region of Verdun. After reorganizing and quickly stabilizing the defense, Pétain then developed a system of rotating divisions rapidly in and out of the battle zone. That ensured that French troops were always more rested than the German divisions opposing them. Pétain called it his *"noria"* system—named for a mill wheel's continuous chain of buckets.[13] Fortunately for the Allies in the long run, the Germans had miscalculated badly, and they suffered almost as many casualties as the French.

In April 1917, the disastrous "Nivelle Offensive" north of the Marne River came closer to breaking the back of the French army than even Verdun. That offensive had been planned based on the existing German positions prior to the Germans' withdrawal to the Siegfriedstellung. But after the Germans had conducted their withdrawal, the French plans were revised only superficially. The attack, which was widely touted as the one that would end the war, was a complete disaster. General Robert Nivelle should have known better. Most of his generals, especially Pétain, were against going ahead with the attack. The Nivelle Offensive is one case where the judgment of history is crystal clear.

In late April and early May, widespread mutinies rippled throughout the French army, triggered by the senseless bloodletting of the Nivelle Offensive. Amazingly, German intelligence never fully identified just how fragile and weak the French army was at that point. Meanwhile, Pétain, one of the few French senior generals universally respected and trusted by the *poilus*, assumed overall command, and with a light but firm hand he slowly restored order and methodically rebuilt the French forces. He initiated a massive rearmament program with the emphasis on artillery, aircraft, tanks, and chemical munitions. Pétain also adopted a temporary strategy of limited war (*stratégie des gages*). In his General Directive Number 1, issued on 19 May 1917, he wrote, "We should not launch great attacks in depth, with distant objectives. These attacks are long in preparation, costly in effectives—for the attacker generally suffers more than the defender—and they do not benefit from surprise."[14] America finally had entered the war just six weeks earlier, and Pétain's concept of "equilibrium of opposing forces" was based essentially on waiting for the Americans.[15]

BRITAIN

World War I ended Great Britain's period of "splendid isolation." Whoever controlled the Belgian coast controlled the English Channel, and whoever controlled the Channel threatened the maritime perimeter of the British Isles. Such was the center of gravity of the United Kingdom's national security strategy during the era when capital warships were the world's ultimate global weapon systems. Yet, ships of the line and later the Dreadnought-class battleships were not invulnerable. They depended on secure ports, reliable fueling and provisioning stations, and secure coastlines in narrow waterways. For the Royal Navy, the Channel was one of the most critical of those maritime choke points. If a friendly or a neutral power controlled the Belgian coast—and in 1914 Belgium was neutral—then the Channel was relatively secure. But if a hostile power threatened to occupy Belgium, then for generations of British policy makers the United Kingdom's only recourse was to war.

That was the situation when Britain declared war on 4 August 1914, when German troops crossed the Belgian border. The immediate problem was where on the Continent—or even if—to deploy what few ground forces the British had immediately available. But although the Royal Navy was the greatest fleet in the world, Britain's small army of one cavalry and six infantry divisions was little more than a colonial police force. Although the British and French conducted a series of joint staff talks between December 1905 and May 1906, no firm military commitments resulted. Many British military and political leaders believed that in the case of war, Britain's support of France would be primarily maritime rather than the deployment of a significant land force on the Continent.

On 5 August, the day after the declaration of war, an ad hoc war council met to decide what to do. After debating the options of landing either at Antwerp in Belgium or in France, the final decision was to land at Boulogne, where the BEF finally entered the Continent on 14 August. That was fortunate for the Allied cause. If the BEF had landed at Antwerp, it most likely would have been cut off by the Germans and isolated. But as soon as the BEF took the field, it was defeated at the Battle of Mons on 23 August, defeated again at the Battle of Le Cateau two days later, and then pushed back to almost the Seine River by 5 September. The following day, the BEF's I Corps under Haig started advancing back toward the north-northeast, probing into the gap that had opened up between the German First and Second Armies. Despite the lingering myth that the BEF "thrust into the gap," Haig proceeded cautiously and even dithered, while French commander in chief General Joseph Joffre cajoled and ordered him to advance aggressively.[16] By 8 September elements of the BEF crossed to the north bank of the Marne, but the Germans had already started their withdrawal to the Aisne River. Haig's role in the battle remains controversial.[17]

During the first months of the war, meanwhile, the Royal Navy established a maritime blockade of Germany, putting the Reich under severe economic pressure. Germany in turn retaliated by launching unrestricted submarine warfare against Britain. That naval campaign almost brought the United Kingdom to its knees economically, but in the end it also brought America into the war against Germany.

Unlike France and Germany, Britain entered the war with a very small standing army. The British Expeditionary Force eventually grew to sixty divisions, but that took several years. The BEF went through four distinct phases of growth. The original BEF of 1914 consisted of only 100,000 long-term professional soldiers. They called themselves the "Old Contemptibles," because Kaiser Wilhelm had once called them "a contemptible little army." But the heavy fighting of 1914 quickly ground that force down. In 1915 the British government was forced to call up and deploy 268,000 territorial (reserve and home defense) troops to reinforce the survivors of the original BEF. But as the realization set in that the war would be a long one, Secretary of State for War Lord Herbert Kitchener called for volunteers on a large scale. Throughout 1915 and into 1916, the hastily recruited, trained, and deployed divisions of the "New Army," also called "Kitchener's Army," fought bravely, but they suffered high casualty rates because of their low level of training and the relatively inexperienced leadership of their likewise hastily recruited officers. Britain finally was forced to resort to conscription from 1916 to 1918. During the same period, the British Dominions of Canada, Australia, New Zealand, and South Africa also sent divisions to France.[18]

Britain, then, had to fight the war while simultaneously trying to recruit, train, equip, and deploy an army that grew to ten times the original starting force. Soldiers cannot be trained in just a few days or weeks. Officers and noncommissioned officers take even longer to train, and it can take well up to twenty years to develop a well-seasoned senior commander. Britain did not have that time. They had to produce officers, staff officers, and senior commanders very rapidly. It can hardly come as any surprise, then, that many officers and commanders who were thrust instantly into positions of high responsibility made mistakes, even serious mistakes. Britain started the war with only a couple hundred officers who had completed the Staff College, and during the first nine months of the war some half of that number were killed or permanently crippled.[19]

In July 1916, in an effort to relieve pressure on the French at Verdun, the BEF launched its offensive on the Somme, which along with Verdun became one of the three great bloodbaths on the Western Front. And after the mutinies of April–May 1917 brought the French army to the verge of collapse, the BEF carried the main weight of the war against Germany until well into 1918. The BEF's Third Battle of Ypres (Passchendaele), from July to November 1917, was the third of the gigantic slaughter battles in the west.

Yet, for all the sense of horror that the very name Passchendaele conjures up to this day and the bitter condemnation heaped upon the British generals for fighting such an apparently mindless battle, there was an undeniable strategic effect. In 1929, retired German lieutenant general Hermann von Kuhl, who held a doctorate in history, wrote, "Today, now that we know the precarious state . . . the French Army was in during the summer of 1917, there can be no doubt of the fact the English tenacity bridged the crisis in France. The French Army had time to recover its strength, and the German reserves were drawn to Flanders. The sacrifices of England for the Entente paid off."[20]

By the end of 1917 the British were facing their own manpower crisis. In order to maintain the number of divisions in the field, the BEF was forced to reduce the strength of its divisions from 12 battalions to 9, resulting in the disbanding of 141 battalions.[21] The weaker divisions would be a key factor in the almost decisive setbacks the British suffered in March and April 1918. The French were not the only ones anxiously waiting for the Americans.

FOUR

THE COMMANDERS IN CHIEF

"Good-morning, Good-morning!" the General said
When we met him last week on our way to the line.
Now the soldiers he smiled at are most of 'em dead,
And we're cursing his staff for incompetent swine.
"He's a cheery old card," grunted Harry to Jack
As they slogged up to Arras with rifle and pack. . .
But he did for them both by his plan of attack.

Siegfried Sassoon, The War Poems

They only call me in catastrophes.

Marshal Philippe Pétain, quoted in Tommy: The British Soldier
on the Western Front, 1914–1918

THE CASUALTY COUNTS OF WORLD WAR I horrify us today, and future generations will think likewise. But as Barbara Tuchman describes in such rich detail in her book *The Proud Tower,* the world before 1918 and the world today are two different places. Not only the generals but virtually all people who came of age in the late Victorian period looked at the world much differently than we do today. As the distinguished military historian Sir Michael Howard once wrote, "The casualty lists that a later generation was to find so horrifying were considered by contemporaries not an indication of military incompetence, but a measure of national resolve, of fitness to rank as a Great Power."[1]

Leo Tolstoy was one of the earliest challengers of the Great Man approach to the study of history. In his novel *War and Peace,* he suggested that generals do not influence the outcome of battles in any way at all.[2] Georges Clemenceau, the wartime premier of France, questioned the very relevance of military leadership when he reportedly said, "War is too important to be left to the generals." On the other hand, James Longstreet, a Confederate States lieutenant general during the American Civil War, saw it much differently when he wrote, "The power of battle is generalship."[3] Almost always fighting outnumbered, Longstreet commanded in enough battles to give him considerable authority on this topic. And with all due respect to Tolstoy, what would the Grande Armée have been without Napoleon? As J. F. C. Fuller once noted, "Remove Napoleon from his command during the 1796 campaign, and the probabilities are that the Austrians would have won the war."[4]

In his now classic book *The Face of Battle,* John Keegan noted, "But because the decisions and acts of a commander apparently contribute more to the outcome of a battle than the decisions and acts of any single group of his subordinates, it does not follow that what he does is more important than what *all* his subordinates do, nor that his behavior is more a valid subject of study that theirs."[5] True enough. A general cannot single-handedly win a battle, but he can single-handedly lose one. During the Great War, Winston Churchill once said of Admiral Sir John Jellicoe, commander of Britain's Grand Fleet, that he was "the only man on either side who could lose the war in an afternoon." Any close analysis of the battles of 1918 will show quite clearly that a great deal turned on the decisions of both planning and execution made by the seniormost commanders. There is much to learn from the study of those decisions, the men who made them, and the conditions under which they carried out their duties as they saw them.

None of the senior-most commanders on the Western Front when the war started would be in place three years later. In Germany, General Helmuth von Moltke the Younger, the nephew of the great field marshal Helmuth von Moltke the Elder, was the chief of the Great General Staff. Upon mobilization, he became the chief of staff of the German Field Army (Feldheer). He was the German army's de facto commander, although Kaiser Wilhelm was the titular commander in chief. Moltke did not remain in place long. In September 1914, following the German failure at the Marne, Moltke was sacked and replaced by General Erich von Falkenhayn. A little more than two years later, and as the result of the German failure at Verdun, Falkenhayn was replaced by Field

Marshal Paul von Hindenburg, with General of Infantry Erich Ludendorff as his vice chief of staff. When the war started, Hindenburg had been retired from active duty since the end of 1912. In late August 1914, he was recalled to active duty and assigned command of the Eighth Army in East Prussia, after Moltke sacked General Maximilian von Prittwitz for his apparent intent to abandon East Prussia to the Russians. Ludendorff, meanwhile, had started the war as the acting commander of an infantry brigade. He led the successful assault on the key fortifications at Liège, Belgium, which were a major obstacle to the German advance. Ludendorff was decorated with the Pour le Mérite and reassigned to the Eighth Army as Hindenburg's chief of staff. The two men had never met before, but they instantly formed a solid partnership that lasted to the final month of the war. Collectively, they were called "The Duo," and also "H-L." On the Western Front they remained in their respective positions for the final twenty-seven months of the war.

At the start the war the French army was commanded by General Joseph Joffre, an engineer officer whose combat experience was all in colonial warfare. He was a huge, bulking physical presence, unflappable under pressure. He became a national hero for checking the Germans at the Battle of the Marne in September 1914, but as the war drug on, he came under increasing criticism in Paris. The Battle of Verdun finally led to Joffre's downfall; he was relieved in December 1916. General Robert Nivelle commanded the French army for only five months. He was sacked in early May 1917 following the disastrous failure of the "Nivelle Offensive" north of the Marne. That finally brought Philippe Pétain to the French supreme command as general-in-chief of the Armies of the North and Northeast. Pétain had started the war as a brigade commander, but by May 1916 he was in command of an army group.

Ferdinand Foch's rise was even more meteoric. He started the war as a corps commander, and within five months he was the commander of a provisional army group, coordinating the operations of the French and British on the Allied northern flank. Three years later his experience with the British, and theirs with him, would pay great dividends. Falling out of political favor at the end of 1916, Foch languished in a number of "special assignments." As a consequence of the failure of the Nivelle Offensive, Foch was appointed chief of the general staff of the French army. In that position he was the senior military adviser to the French government, but he had no actual command authority. In the spring of 1918 Foch was appointed the Allied generalissimo in response to the crisis resulting from the German offensives. Pétain was the

French commander in chief for eighteen months and Foch the Allied genera-lissimo for eight.

In August 1914, the small six-division British Expeditionary Force was com-manded by Field Marshal Sir John French. With the BEF organized into two corps, Lieutenant General Sir Douglas Haig was one of the corps command-ers. As the BEF rapidly expanded in size to an army group, Haig in Decem-ber 1914 assumed command of the British First Army. Despite his last name, French was anything but a Francophile. He and Joffre had a great deal of dif-ficulty getting along. When French was relieved of command in December 1915, Haig assumed command of the BEF. At thirty-five months, he was the longest-serving commander in chief on the Western Front.

In August 1914, John Pershing was the commander of an infantry brigade in the American far west. In 1916 and 1917 he commanded the Mexican Punitive Expedition. The United States, meanwhile, had remained neutral for almost the first three years of the war, finally declaring war on Germany in April 1917. Five weeks later President Woodrow Wilson appointed Pershing the com-mander of the American Expeditionary Force. Along with a small advanced party, he arrived in France that June to start the planning and coordination for the buildup and training of the AEF. That October Pershing was promoted from major general to full (four-star) general—the first in the U.S. Army since Philip Sheridan in 1888. When the U.S. First Army was established in August 1918, Pershing assumed command of it while simultaneously commanding the AEF. When the U.S. Second Army was established that October, Persh-ing relinquished command of the First Army to General Hunter Liggett, and from then until the end of the war Pershing functioned as an army group com-mander. Pershing was the AEF's commander in chief for seventeen months, but most of that time was devoted to planning, administration, logistics man-agement, and training. American forces did not begin fighting under his direct command until the start of the Saint Mihiel Offensive on 12 September 1918.[6]

REPUTATIONS ONE HUNDRED YEARS ON

As summarized in Table 4.1, the six Western Front warlords of 1918 had wide-ly varying backgrounds and personalities. The judgment of history still has not been settled on these six. For three of them, history's judgment rests far more heavily than the records of their wartime commands alone would merit. Pétain is rightly remembered as the savior of France on two separate occa-sions, Verdun in the winter and spring of 1916 and again in the spring of 1917 immediately after the mutinies. But he is even more remembered as the man who as the chief of the French State (Vichy) from 1940 to 1944 sold out France to the Third Reich. Hindenburg was the "Wooden Titan" ("der Nagelsäulen"), Germany's only true national hero during the war.[7] He also was the last president of the doomed Weimar Republic and the man who appointed Adolf Hitler chancellor of Germany in January 1933. The debate still continues on Ludendorff. He was either the greatest military genius of the war, or he was the man whose strategic ineptitude and personal military and political overreach resulted in a complete loss of focus that cost Germany the war. He also was an early supporter of the Nazis, put on trial right along with Hitler for participating in the infamous Beer Hall Putsch of November 1923.

Haig is the only one out of the six to be branded as a "Château General." Despite that enduring image, Haig, as one of his most recent biographers Gary Sheffield points out, spent most of his afternoons out visiting different parts of the BEF's front, and during major battles he commanded primarily from his headquarters train, as close to the front as possible.[8] Unfortunately, that was not the case in March 1918, when Haig appears to have been completely out of touch with what was happening on his right flank initially. Unlike the Allied armies, the near reverential status of German General Staff officers shielded Hindenburg and Ludendorff from such criticism. The average *Landser* on the front line probably knew little of Ludendorff, while Hindenburg was the august father figure of the German army. By the end of the war he even supplanted the kaiser as the patriarch of the nation. Foch had too much of a reputation as a fighter, and every *poilu* knew that Pétain was more careful with their lives than anyone else. Pershing never commanded in combat long enough to acquire any significant negative repute with the Doughboys. Somewhat like Hindenburg, Pershing was the great father figure of the AEF. For many Americans, he remains so today.

Foch, Pershing, and Haig all get generally good marks for their postwar activities. Foch did rub the political authorities the wrong way by being an outspoken critic of the Versailles Treaty, but history generally sides with him on that issue. Pershing after the war reorganized and modernized the entire staff structure of the U.S. Army, and Haig worked tirelessly on behalf of British veterans, which contrasts with his wartime reputation for disregard for the welfare of the troops. But Foch and Pershing have very mixed reputations based on their war records. Foch remains highly regarded in France, but in many other countries he is considered little more than a coordinator and a

TABLE 4.1. The Warlords of 1918

	Foch	Pétain
Months in supreme command	7	18
Current judgment of his WWI command	High in France, mixed elsewhere	"Savior of France"
Postwar taint	None	Vichy
Reputation as "Château General"	No	No
Reputation of deep concern for the troops	No	Yes
Military responsibility in 1918	Western Front	Western Front
Political power/responsibility	No	No
Overriding military concept	Continuous offensive	"Fire kills"
Micromanager	No (by 1918)	No
Significant changes in war-fighting concepts from start of war to 1918: tactical	Limited	Incremental
Significant changes in war-fighting concepts from start of war to 1918: operational	Yes	Incremental
Accepter of risk	Yes	No
Technology adaptive	Fair	Excellent
Family military background	No	No
Son or son-in-Law KIA in WWI	Yes x 2	No
Branch	Artillery	Infantry
Pre-WWI combat experience	No	No
Corps or above experience at start of war	Yes	No
War college/staff college graduate	Yes	Yes
War college/staff college instructor	Yes	Yes
Prewar general staff service	Yes	Yes
Prewar military theorist	Yes	Yes
Close prewar contact with foreign armies	Yes	No
Knowledge of contemporary enemy military theory	Good	Good
Foreign language	German (good)	No
Military supporters/allies	Joffre, Haig, H. Wilson	Pershing
Military critics/rivals	Pershing, Pétain	Foch, Nivelle
Political supporters	Clemenceau	Clemenceau
Political critics	Clemenceau	Clemenceau
Left memoirs/diary	Yes	No

Hindenburg	Ludendorff	Haig	Pershing
27	27	35	3
"Wooden Titan"	Very mixed	"Chief Butcher and Bungler"	High in America, low elsewhere
Hitler as chancellor	Nazi Party early support	None	None
No	No	Yes	No
Yes	No	No	No
Both fronts	Both fronts	Western Front	Western Front
Yes	Yes	No	No
German military as state within a state	Tactics over operations and strategy	Breakthrough and cavalry exploitation	Rifle marksmanship and open warfare
No	Yes	No (by later 1918)	Yes
No	Yes	Somewhat	No
No	No	Incremental	No
Yes	Yes	Limited	Yes
Poor	Good	Fair	Poor
Yes	No	No	No
No	Yes x 2	No	No
Infantry	Infantry	Cavalry	Cavalry
Franco-Prussian War	No	Colonial wars	Frontier and colonial wars
Yes	No	Yes	No
Yes	Yes	Yes	Yes
No	Yes	No	No
Yes	Yes	Yes	Yes
No	No	No	No
No	No	No	No
Fair	Very good	Poor	Poor
No	No	French (good) German (fair)	French (fair)
		Robertson, Foch	Bliss, Pétain
Hoffmann, Falkenhayn	Rupprecht, Kuhl, Groener, Falkenhayn	H. Wilson, French	L. Wood, March, Haig, Foch
		George V, Lord Derby	W. Wilson, Baker
Kaiser, Bethmann Hollweg	Kaiser, Bethmann Hollweg Prince Max	Lloyd George, Milner	Lloyd George, Clemenceau
Yes	Yes	Yes	Yes

figurehead rather than a real supreme commander in 1918. Many Americans still believe Pershing to be one of their greatest generals of all time, but many European historians rate him quite low as a military commander whose main contribution to the final Allied victory was to bring 2 million men to Europe. And then there is Haig, the "butcher-and-bungler-in-chief," the most vilified general of the war. But for a good fifteen years after the war the British generally held him in high regard, just a step below Wellington and Marlborough. That started to change after his death in 1928. But now, after some eighty years of ignominy, there are signs that the historical verdict on Haig is beginning to swing in the other direction.

POWERS AND RESPONSIBILITIES

The scope of their powers and responsibilities were not all the same. The four Western Allied commanders were focused on the Western Front only, and Haig, Pétain, and Pershing were responsible only for their respective national sectors. Hindenburg and Ludendorff were responsible for managing and coordinating both fronts, or even three fronts, counting the propping up of Austria-Hungary against Italy. None of the Allied commanders had any directly political responsibilities or powers, although they all interacted with their respective national political leaders—some of whom were supportive and some of whom were decidedly hostile.

By late 1918, Hindenburg and Ludendorff were the virtual dictators of Germany, trying to manage the country's economy, diplomacy, political system, and social structure, all while commanding the military operations. Neither was remotely qualified for these nonmilitary functions, but they assumed those powers almost by default, as Germany's rigid and fragile national institutions collapsed around them. Although the two worked in close coordination on operational matters, Ludendorff functioned virtually alone in the political sphere but always in Hindenburg's name.[9] In 1916 Ludendorff forced through the "Hindenburg Program," which was supposed to rationalize war production and increase the output of armaments. Later that year he also pushed through the Auxiliary Service Law, greatly restricting the freedom labor movement. Both programs effectively ended civil government in Germany, and in the end both caused more chaos than they were designed to eliminate. All the time and effort devoted to nonmilitary issues, of course, only detracted from the focus on military operations.

Both France and Germany started the war with large standing armies, robust reserve forces, established tactical doctrine, and standing, if flawed, war plans. Britain's small six-division army was little more than a colonial police force, and the even smaller U.S. Army was basically a frontier constabulary. By 1918 the BEF had expanded to sixty divisions, including Dominion formations from Canada, Australia, and New Zealand. The American army grew even more, from a force of a little more than 200,000 to about 4 million, with half that number in France. Those forces had to be recruited, trained, equipped, and transported overseas. Although Haig and Pershing were not solely responsible for those functions, they were heavily involved. Pershing commanded the largest number of soldiers in the field in American history, until Dwight Eisenhower in 1944–45, and Haig commanded the largest British army in the field ever.

MILITARY CONCEPTS

These generals all were guided by very different overriding military concepts. Before the war, Foch was one of the leading advocates of the *attaque à l'outrance* school. Pétain, as one of the French army's few exponents of the supremacy of modern firepower, was a pariah. His maxim was "Fire kills" (*le feu tue*). Actually, Foch's views on modern warfare were more sophisticated than his persistent advocacy of the offensive might indicate. He believed that adequate artillery support and capable commanders were absolutely essential to the success of any offensive.

Like Ludendorff in 1916 and 1917, Pétain completely revolutionized French tactical doctrine once he took command in the spring of 1917. Between 19 May and 20 December 1917, he issued a series of four general directives that finally jolted the French army into the twentieth century. Up to that point, France had fought war essentially with its infantry, and Pétain's objective was to build a combined arms force of artillery, infantry, tanks, and aircraft. Pétain's General Directive Number 4 of 20 December 1917 codified his doctrine of defense-in-depth.[10] Foch, however, never embraced that concept, arguing that mounting the major defensive effort from the second defensive position made counterattacks impossible. Pétain continually had to pressure his subordinate army commanders to establish deep defensive zones. As Douglas Porch noted, "The debate over tactics in 1917–18 can be almost seen as a clash of wills between the pious, spiritual Foch, and the agnostic, pragmatic Pétain."[11]

Ludendorff was not a slave to any particular tactical ideology. The only thing that mattered to him was whether or not a technique worked. He was the driving force in the German army's tactical virtuosity in 1917 and 1918. Hindenburg does not appear to have had any particular war fighting focus. Hindenburg was perfectly willing to give Ludendorff an almost free hand in planning and managing battles, while his priority was the German army itself, its reputation, its image, and its status as Germany's "state within a state." After the war, Hindenburg relentlessly defended the army against the ineptitude of the politicians. In his November 1919 testimony to the Reichstag, Hindenburg insisted that the German army had not lost the war; rather, it had been betrayed by disloyal elements at home.[12] Thus, Hindenburg became the principal author of the infamous *Dolchstosslegende*—the "stab-in-the-back myth."

Like almost all of the British generals of 1914, Haig embraced a concept of a human-centered battlefield and resisted the notion of one dominated by weapons and machines. He was slow to accept that the mechanics of modern warfare had changed radically. Until well into 1918, Haig continued to search for the ever-elusive operational breakthrough. While most of the armies dismounted their cavalry, the BEF retained a large number of mounted troops to have on hand for exploitation of the breakthrough when it finally occurred. Haig was right that the exploitation of any breakthrough would require a high mobility force, but he failed to grasp that the warhorse could no longer survive on the modern battlefield.

When Pershing reached Europe in the spring of 1917, he simply refused to accept the lessons of the almost three years of fighting. Ignoring the realities of modern firepower, Pershing, right up to the end of November 1918, continued to place all his faith in American rifle marksmanship and "open warfare," which all too often meant frontal attacks.

ADAPTABILITY AND RISK

Ludendorff and Pétain were the only true independent thinkers of the six. On the tactical level, Pétain probably had the best understanding of the potentials of the new technologies. Ludendorff reorganized the German infantry squad around the M-08/15 light machine gun, and he constantly pushed for more and better aircraft and artillery. He did, however, have a serious blind spot for the tank. Foch too was one of the earliest senior commanders of the French army to recognize that many of the prewar assumptions were no longer valid, and he was among the earliest of the senior French commanders to understand the value of intelligence in ensuring that the enemy would be reacting to him rather than the other way around.[13] But Foch still remained an advocate of continuous offensive, although he quickly accepted the reality of the strength of modern firepower. In 1912, Foch had written that the military value of aviation was "zero," but by 1916 he had become convinced of its importance.[14] And despite what he frequently heard from Haig, Foch never really accepted the almost decisive contribution that the Royal Navy made in the war against Germany.

Despite being tarred as such for many years, Haig not a technophobe. As John Paul Harris notes, "Most historians seem now to accept that, whatever his other faults, Haig was very open to technological innovation, that the British army on the Western Front was highly experimental and innovative, and that the British pushed the available military technology to its limits in the war's final year."[15] Haig was an early and stanch supporter of the tank, but as noted, he clung to the horse for too long. He did, however, have a blind spot for artillery, never quite understanding the necessity to concentrate rather than disperse his guns.[16] Haig also was a product of the cultural norms of the prewar British army, which stressed traditional values such as discipline, courage, and high morale. Unlike the German General Staff system, the British army at the start of the war did not have institutionalized procedures for collecting and analyzing lessons learned and modifying methods accordingly. Criticism and even disagreement with superiors were equated with disloyalty, and Haig discouraged discussion and constructive criticism. As a result, most of the tactical innovations in the British army developed at the level of the divisions and only slowly percolated up the chain of command—and even then were sometimes not quite understood fully at the level of BEF General Headquarters.[17]

Despite his own General Staff background, Hindenburg never stopped believing that the *Charakter* of the German soldier and his officers was more important than any weapons—a philosophy closely related to France's *attaque à l'outrance* and Britain's human-centric battlefield. Pershing never believed that trench mortars and machine guns could be any serious hindrance to well-led infantry in the attack. If the attack failed to advance on schedule, then the weakness must be in the leadership. During the final twelve months of the war Pershing sacked two corps commanders, six division commanders, at least four brigade commanders, and the commander of the AEF's lines of communications.[18]

The generals differed considerably in their levels of personal adaptation to the new forms of war fighting. Foch and Ludendorff, who were really the two primary opponents in 1918, changed the most, but on different levels of war: Foch adapted and changed the most on the operational level; Ludendorff, on the tactical. By 1918 Foch had adapted somewhat to the new tactics, but Ludendorff continued to ignore the operational level. In response to a prodding question for Crown Prince Rupprecht of Bavaria during a planning conference in February 1918, Ludendorff blurted out, "I can't abide the word operations. We'll make a hole. The rest will follow. That's the way we did it in Russia."[19]

Pétain essentially made only incremental changes in his basic tactical thinking, but that was because he started the war far ahead of almost everyone else in that respect. Even before the first shot was fired, he had a significantly clear picture of what ground combat would be like. And as the war progressed, his operational thinking did develop, but not to the degree of Foch's. Haig's tactical and operational thinking both improved somewhat, perhaps more on the operational level. By the second half of 1918 he had evolved into a relatively competent operational commander.

Hindenburg does not seem to have changed his operational or tactical thinking much during the war, but right at the start his training and experience should have given him the best grasp of the operational art of any of the six. By the middle of 1918 Foch had surpassed even him. Pershing did not change his thinking significantly on either level, but a direct comparison to the other five is somewhat unfair, considering the relatively short time he spent in command during the war. Pershing entered the war with ideas little different from Haig's in 1914–15. What might Pershing's thinking have been if the war had continued into the spring of 1919, assuming he managed to remain in command?

Pétain was less willing to accept risk than the others. He was careful and methodical, but he almost never made a mistake on the battlefield. He did, however, have a tendency toward extreme pessimism when things were going wrong. Foch at times bordered on the reckless. While in command of XX Corps during the Battle of Morhange-Sarrebourg in August 1914, Foch disobeyed orders to withdraw and instead continued attacking and counterattacking. Morhange was a bloody disaster. Foch's mentor, Joffre, buried the subsequent charges of Foch's disobedience because he was impressed with Foch's determination and spirit. As Belgium's King Albert once said of Foch, "That man could make the dead fight."

Hindenburg and Ludendorff accepted risk in the best traditions of the German General Staff. Although vastly outnumbered on the Eastern Front in August and September 1914, their defeat and virtual destruction of two Russian field armies at the Battles of Tannenberg and First Masurian Lakes remains one of the operational masterpieces of modern warfare. Hindenburg also was imperturbable under pressure, but not so Ludendorff. German wartime chancellor Theobald von Bethmann Hollweg once said that Ludendorff was "only great at a time of success," and when "things go badly he loses his nerve."[20] During the final months of the war Ludendorff cracked under the pressure, suffering a nervous breakdown.

Haig was rather adverse to risk. Writing in his diary on 25 February 1918, he stated his resistance to earmarking any of his divisions to the putative Inter-Allied General Reserve: "Rather than run such a risk at this time I would prefer to be relieved of my command."[21] Pershing ran risks, but considering his blind faith in "open warfare," there can be some doubt as to the degree of risk he was accepting in his own mind.

PERSONAL BACKGROUNDS

Aside from the fact that they were all general officers, no common thread connects the six commanders in chief of 1918. Only Hindenburg came from a traditional military family, although Foch lost both his son and his son-in-law in the war, and Ludendorff lost both of his stepsons. Hindenburg was a Prussian aristocrat and a descendant of Martin Luther. Haig too was from the upper classes, the scion of a wealthy Scottish distilling family. Ludendorff was a Prussian Junker, but not having the noble "von" in his name, he was on a somewhat lower level than Hindenburg. Foch was the son of a lower-level civil servant. He was a lifelong staunch Catholic and his brother was a Jesuit priest, facts that put him at a disadvantage early in his military career in the anticlerical Third Republic. Pétain came from solid peasant stock. Although his family was Catholic, he was not overly religious himself. Pershing was the son of a midwestern businessman. His primary motivation for attending West Point was the free education.

Pétain, Hindenburg, and Ludendorff were infantry officers. Haig and Pershing were cavalrymen. Foch was an artillery officer. Considering their respective branches, the expectation would be that the attitudes of Foch and Pétain toward firepower versus maneuver would be just the opposite of what they were in 1914. Foch, Pétain, and Ludendorff had never heard a shot fired in anger before the war. Haig did have considerable experience in Britain's co-lonial wars, including the Boer War. Pershing probably had the most prewar combat experience. He participated in operations against the Plains Indians and fought in the 1890 Battle of Wounded Knee. He served in Cuba during the Spanish-American War, fighting at the Battle of San Juan Hill. In 1905–6 Pershing was one of the official American military observers of the Russo-Japanese War. One of his German counterparts was Captain Max Hoffmann, who in 1914 would be Hindenburg and Ludendorff's chief of operations at Tannenberg and later the chief of staff of the German Command on the East-ern Front (Oberost). From 1909 to 1913 Pershing was the commander of the Department of Mindanao during the Philippine Insurrection. He command-ed the Mexican Punitive Expedition at about the same time that the European armies were fighting it out on the Somme. Hindenburg was the only one of the six with any previous experience in large-scale European warfare. As a young lieutenant, he served in the 1866 Austro-Prussian War, where he was wound-ed. Four years later he served in the Franco-Prussian War.

Hindenburg retired from active duty as a general of infantry in 1912. Dur-ing his long career, he was never promoted for outstanding service, advancing instead through the normal progression of seniority. He never had a reputa-tion for a high level of intellectual attainment, yet he did qualify as a General Staff officer, graduating with honors from the Kriegsakademie in 1876. Gen-eral Staff officer qualification in the nineteenth-century German army was brutally competitive. Following an entrance exam with strictly rank-ordered results, some 140 to 160 officers entered the Kriegsakademie each year. Only about 100 finished. That group then faced another competitive examination for General Staff posting, with only about 30 being accepted. Those select-ed underwent a two-year probationary period serving on the Great General Staff, followed by a final selection screening. Only about a half-dozen officers per year made the final cut.[22] Many graduates of the Kriegsakademie later re-turned as instructors, but Hindenburg did not.

Ludendorff was widely considered one of the "brains" of the German army, but his intellectual activity focused narrowly on military matters. He served for two years as an instructor at the Kriegsakademie and became the German army's master of tactical warfare on a grand scale, but as Holger Herwig wrote of him, "The truth is that Ludendorff never rose above the intellectual level of a regimental colonel commanding infantry."[23] Writing in 1928, the Brit-ish military critic Basil H. Liddell Hart said, "On Ludendorff the verdict of history may well be that he was the Robot Napoleon."[24] Neither Hindenburg nor Ludendorff spoke a foreign language.

Prior to 1914 both Foch and Pétain were widely regarded as important military theorists, albeit with almost opposite points of view. Foch served as an instructor at and later became commandant of the École Supérieure de la Guerre. In 1903 he published his military theories in the book *The Principles of War*. Pétain served as an instructor at the French School of Fire (École de Tir) and taught tactics at the cavalry school at Saumur. Until 1910 he was a professor of applied infantry tactics at the École Supérieure de la Guerre, where his heretical opinions were not at all welcome. Pétain spoke only French, but Foch had a good command of German.

In the early 1890s Pershing was a professor of military science and tactics at the University of Nebraska, where he also earned a law degree in his spare time. In the late 1890s he was an assistant instructor of tactics at West Point, and in the early 1900s he graduated from one of the first classes of the newly established U.S. Army War College. Before he went to France, Pershing had only a very rudimentary knowledge of French, but he worked hard to improve it.

Quite unjustly, Haig has been saddled with a reputation for being one of the dumbest senior generals of the Great War. Prime Minister David Lloyd George considered him stupid because he was somewhat inarticulate verbally. Haig, however, wrote clearly and effectively. He was an introvert. Contrary to common belief, many generals are introverts while at the same time they have what traditionally is called a type A personality. Pétain, Hindenburg, and Ludendorff almost certainly were introverts. Foch may have been the only real extrovert of the lot.

Very few European senior officers at the turn of the century were university graduates. Haig did attend Oxford but never received his degree, a fact later used to argue for his low intellectual attainments. Actually, Haig did pass all his final examinations, but because he missed a term owing to illness, he did not have the minimum required residence time to qualify for the degree.[25] He then attended the Royal Military College at Sandhurst, where he graduated first in his class of 129. (Sandhurst was not and still is not a four-year degree-granting institution like West Point but rather a yearlong officer training school.) In 1895 Haig graduated from the British army's Staff College, at a time when such training was not necessary for promotion to the senior ranks. Many if not most turn-of-the-century British officers took pride in affecting a posture of gifted amateurism and looked with great disdain on the deadly serious professionalism of German officers. Haig, however, was a soldier who thought about and studied his profession. He spoke French well and had a good command of German, and as a schoolboy he won a prize for Latin.

POLITICAL SUPPORTERS AND CRITICS

Soldiers are supposed to be apolitical, but all generals to some degree must deal with their nation's political leaders. The higher the general's rank, the greater the degree of interface. Commanders in chief, therefore, must deal with heads of government and heads of state on a routine basis. But in Germany, where the army was a "state within a state," there was almost a firewall between soldiers and statesmen, except at the very top level. Normally only the chief of the Great General Staff dealt directly with the chancellor and the kaiser, although officers frequently saw the kaiser when he came around to give out awards and decorations. That neatly compartmentalized system started to unravel after Hindenburg's and Ludendorff's stunning victories on the Eastern Front in 1914 and Hindenburg was promoted to field marshal. Kaiser Wilhelm II, who had a very insecure personality, at first liked to associate himself with Hindenburg. The implication was that the kaiser was still Germany's Supreme Warlord (Oberster Kriegsherr). But Wilhelm soon came to view the field marshal's popularity with the people as a direct threat to his own position. Meanwhile, the kaiser loathed Ludendorff as an upstart bourgeoisie. Ludendorff rates only one passing mention in the kaiser's memoirs.[26] By the end of the war the kaiser feared Hindenburg, who ironically remained steadfastly loyal to the end to the office of the kaiser, although he thought very little of Wilhelm personally.

Hindenburg and Ludendorff had a contentious and even hostile relationship with Germany's wartime chancellors: Theobald von Bethmann Hollweg; Georg Michaelis; Georg Graf von Hertling; and Prince Max von Baden. When Hindenburg and Ludendorff assumed overall command at OHL on 20 August 1916, Ludendorff demanded that Germany immediately and ruthlessly mobilize all of the country's national resources for the war effort. Supported by Hindenburg, Ludendorff increasingly meddled in political affairs, ultimately leading to the "Silent Dictatorship." Ludendorff, however, refused to consider the idea of an outright military dictatorship, despite at one point having the chancellorship almost thrust upon him.[27] Nonetheless, by the final months of the war Ludendorff held almost total political power in his hands, marginalizing the kaiser, the chancellor, and the Reichstag. Disingenuously, Ludendorff later quibbled in his memoirs, "Unfortunately, the government did not state clearly and emphatically in public that it, and not General Luden-dorff, was governing."[28]

As relations with Bethmann Hollweg continued to deteriorate, Ludendorff went so far as to order German commanders not to talk to the chancellor during his visit to the front in June 1917.[29] The final straw came the following month when the Reichstag started debating the Peace Resolution. Hinden-burg and Ludendorff forced Bethmann Hollweg to resign by threatening the kaiser with their own resignations. Wilhelm gave right in to The Duo because he feared the consequences. The kaiser with the backing of OHL appointed Michaelis as chancellor, but the Reichstag nonetheless passed the Peace Reso-lution a couple of days later. Michaelis was forced out of office three months later and replaced by the aging Hertling. From that point on, Ludendorff and Hindenburg (in name at least) were the virtual dictators of Germany until October 1918.

Despite its history, France had a long tradition of anti-militarism. Relations between France's political elites and military had been on thin ice since the traumatic and drawn-out Dreyfus Affair of 1894–1906 that split the nation down the middle. Once Alfred Dreyfus was finally exonerated, leftist elements in the French government launched a massive purge of right-leaning officers in the army. As a devout Catholic, Foch was under a cloud for a long time. Right at the start of the war Joffre's star should have set with the failure of Plan XVII, but then the subsequent "Miracle of the Marne" restored him as a French na-tional hero. As the war progressed, he assumed near dictatorial powers over the French army. Joffre refused to countenance any involvement in or even questioning of military operations by French civilian authorities. President Raymond Poincaré started losing confidence in Joffre by March 1915, but it took the shock of Verdun to bring Joffre down finally.[30] On 3 December 1916 Joffre was relieved of command but simultaneously made the Third Republic's first marshal of France. When Joffre fell, Poincaré personally ordered the relief of Foch as commander of the Northern Army Group. Foch then was assigned to plan potential operations in the event that Germany violated Swiss neutral-ity. Fortunately for France and the Allies, Foch was not forced into retirement like so many other French generals who were sacked.

Pétain was the most logical candidate to succeed Joffre, but Prime Minis-ter Aristide Briand instead selected General Robert Nivelle. A fluent English speaker (his mother was British), Nivelle was popular with the British and therefore seen as an asset to the coalition. But when the much-ballyhooed

Nivelle Offensive failed that April, Pétain finally was put in command of the French Armies of the North and Northeast. His most pressing task was to deal with the catastrophic consequences of the mutinies. Two days after Pétain's assignment, Foch was brought back from obscurity and named chief of the general staff of the French army. Although he had no actual command authority like the German chief of the General Staff had, at least Foch was back in the center ring.

That November Georges Clemenceau formed a new government and remained France's prime minister until January 1920. Clemenceau started out as a staunch supporter of both Foch and Pétain, although Pétain's concept of flexible defense horrified Clemenceau, who opposed giving up any more French ground to the Germans.[31] In May 1918, the Germans launched the third of their great offensives, which appeared to be headed for the gates of Paris itself. Among the widespread panic in the capital, many French deputies on 4 June demand the relief and courts-martial of both Pétain and Foch.[32] Clemenceau defended them vigorously, saying, "We must have confidence in Foch and Pétain, those two great chiefs who are so happily complementary to each other."[33] Nonetheless, Anthony Clayton noted that Clemenceau "on occasion exhibited the average French politician's paranoia that any successful general would develop into a Bonaparte."[34]

As the war progressed, however, relations between Clemenceau and his two senior-most generals deteriorated. And as Pétain's sense of pessimism grew, Clemenceau in March 1918 finally backed Foch as Allied supreme commander. Clemenceau once told Poincaré, "Pétain, who has his faults, belongs more in the second rank than in the first."[35] When the Allies went on the offensive after 18 July and started going from success to success, tensions began to grow between Clemenceau and Foch over what Foch considered civilian meddling in strictly military affairs, particularly those dealing with the Allies, where Foch believed Clemenceau had no constitutional authority. Matters finally came to a head when the two clashed over issues of policy and strategy during the period from the signing of the Armistice to the signing of the Versailles Treaty.[36] Their feud continued well after the war.

Haig had connections with the highest levels of the British government. He had established a good personal relationship with King Edward VII when the latter was still the Prince of Wales. Haig's wife was a maid of honor to Queen Alexandra. After Edward's son became King George V, Haig continued to maintain personal contacts with the royal family. At the king's invitation,

Haig regularly wrote to him directly throughout the war, bypassing the prime minister and the secretary of state for war. Haig, however, was not the only senior officer with that privilege.[37]

One of Haig's most important political supporters was Edward George Stanley, Lord Derby, who served as undersecretary of state for war from July to December 1916 and then as secretary until April 1918. His successor at the War Office, Lord Alfred Milner, did not hold a high opinion of Haig as a general, but he grudgingly recognized there were no better options to replace him. In September 1918 Milner said that Haig was being "ridiculously optimistic" when he projected that the war was going to end that year.[38] Haig, of course, proved right.

Herbert Asquith, the prime minister from April 1908 to December 1916, generally took a hands-off approach to the details of military operations. His successor, David Lloyd George, was an entirely different matter. Lloyd George disliked and distrusted generals as a rule, and his relations with Haig became extremely bitter. During a September 1916 visit to France, when he was still secretary of state for war, Lloyd George asked senior French generals their opinions of British generalship. Haig later wrote in his diary, "Unless I had been told of this conversation personally by General Foch, I would not have believed that a British Minister could have been so ungentlemanly as to go to a foreigner and put such questions regarding his own subordinates."[39]

The Nivelle Offensive irrevocably poisoned relationships between Lloyd George and his generals. The prime minister fell completely under the spell of the smooth-talking Nivelle, with his superb command of English. Lloyd George came to believe that Nivelle was head-and-shoulders above the pedestrian pack of British generals. At a meeting of French and British military and political leaders at Calais on 27 February 1917, Nivelle asked Lloyd George to put the BEF under his command for the upcoming offensive, effective 1 March. Lloyd George saw this as an opportunity to gain tighter control of the British generals. Haig and General Sir William Robertson, the chief of the Imperial General Staff, objected vehemently. They told the prime minister that they would rather face court-martial than "betray the army."[40]

The final agreement was that Haig would be subordinate to Nivelle temporarily, only for the duration of the offensive. Haig also retained the right of direct appeal to London if he thought any of Nivelle's orders were a threat to the overall safety of the BEF. When the offensive failed dismally, Lloyd George's high-profile support of Nivelle weakened his political position significantly with respect to Haig. Lloyd George later claimed that he had been attempting to establish Allied unity of command. But the arrangements worked out at the Calais Conference were a complete failure, discrediting for many months to come any idea of a unified command structure.[41] Curiously, despite Haig's alleged disdain for most politicians, he greatly respected and even admired Clemenceau.

By the time he was appointed commander of the AEF, Pershing was no stranger to the intersection of the political and military worlds. The father of Pershing's late wife was Senator Francis E. Warren of Wyoming, himself a recipient of the Medal of Honor from the Civil War.[42] Warren also was chairman of the Senate Committee on Military Affairs. In 1906 President Theodore Roosevelt promoted Pershing from captain directly to brigadier general, over the heads of 835 more senior officers. Some people at the time suspected that the promotion was the result of political connections rather than merit, but Pershing was not the only officer of the period who received fast-track promotions. Most of Pershing's contemporaries in the U.S. Army thought that the advancement was well deserved.

When America entered the war in the spring of 1917, there were two primary candidates to command the American forces in France, Pershing and General Leonard Wood. But although Wood had earned the Medal of Honor during the Indian Wars and had served as chief of staff of the army from 1910 to 1914, he was already in his late fifties and had a reputation for insubordination. Secretary of War Newton D. Baker decided for Pershing, and President Woodrow Wilson immediately confirmed the appointment. Pershing's father-in-law at that point was no longer on the Military Affairs Committee, but he was still an influential senator. The first point at which Pershing heard that he was under consideration for command was when he received a telegram from Warren saying, "Wire me today whether and how much you speak, read, and write French." Again, there was the appearance of political influence, but Baker steadfastly maintained that Warren "had no part, and sought no part in the selection of General Pershing for the overseas command."[43] All the historical evidence confirms that Warren had no direct influence in Pershing's rapid rise in rank or selection for command.

Pershing and Baker met with President Wilson on 24 May 1917, during which the president provided only the most cursory guidance about maintaining the AEF's structural integrity as an American army. Wilson and Pershing did not meet again until after the end of the war. Baker told Pershing, "I will give you only two orders—one to go to France and the other to come home. In the meantime, your authority in France will be supreme."[44] Thus, Pershing received virtually unstinting support from his own political masters. The political leaders of Britain and France, however, regarded the American commander in chief much differently.

Immediately upon his arrival in Europe, Pershing was wined, dined, and feted. The glow wore off fairly quickly, though. Initially, Lloyd George and Clemenceau became exasperated with Pershing's intransigence over using U.S. troops as filler replacements in the British and French armies. Once the AEF started conducting its own large-scale operations in September 1918, Clemenceau became even more hostile toward Pershing. During the early stages of the Meuse-Argonne campaign, Clemenceau became so outraged by what he saw as the incompetence of the American high command that he more than once ordered Foch to write to President Wilson demanding Pershing's removal. Wilson and Baker could not help but be aware of the political-level criticism directed at Pershing, but they supported him to the end. Had the war dragged out into mid-1919, as many believed it would, Pershing's position may have grown more tenuous.

THE POLITICAL AND THE STRATEGIC

The military and the political spheres intersect at the strategic level of war. In democracies, ideally, the ultimate strategic decisions are made by a nation's civilian leaders, after receiving and evaluating the expert advice of their senior military advisers. The process is always subject to a certain amount of dynamic tension, but throughout World War I it essentially worked as it should have for the three Western allies.

For France and America, there was relatively little tension at the strategic level. The political and military leaders were all in agreement that the overriding strategic imperative was to defeat the German army on the Western Front. It could not have been otherwise for France, with the Germans occupying a large swath of French soil and the French themselves wanting to reclaim Alsace and Lorraine. The Western Front also was the almost exclusive focus of the Americans. Although the United States did declare war on Austria-Hungary in December 1917, eight months after the declaration of war on Germany, only a single U.S. infantry regiment fought in Italy against the Austro-Hungarians, and then only during the last weeks of the war. The United States never did declare war on Turkey. As a result, the Americans did not have a seat at the table when after the war France and Britain presided over the dismemberment of the Ottoman Empire and redrew the national boundaries of the Middle East—the consequences of which are still with us today.

The strategic picture was not quite as clear for the British, who found themselves in their first confrontation with a major European power since the Crimean War of 1854–55. As an island nation, the British saw geopolitics somewhat differently than the Continental powers. Even before the first BEF troops landed in Europe, the British camp had divided into "Easterners" and "Westerners." The fault line ran through both the political and the military circles. The Easterners argued that the best way to defeat Germany was not through a direct force-on-force clash on the Western Front but rather by attacking the flanks and rear of the Central Powers by defeating Germany's weaker allies. Hence, the British campaigns in Gallipoli and Saloniki in 1915, both of which were dismal failures. The Westerners argued that such peripheral campaigns violated the principle of unity of effort, which had to be directed at the primary enemy. Throughout the war, Haig, staunchly supported by Robertson, was the leading Westerner. Lloyd George was the leading Easterner. In 1917 and 1918 the disagreement on overall strategy between Haig and Lloyd George became increasingly bitter. Winston Churchill was another leading Easterner. As British prime minister during World War II, Churchill was still a strong advocate of the "indirect approach" of attacking Germany through the southern flank of Europe's "soft underbelly." It proved no softer in 1942–45 than it had in 1915–18.

For the Germans, who started the war with a weak civil government that virtually evaporated as the war progressed, the military leadership completely dominated the political on all questions of strategy. But the Germans too had their own Easterner versus Westerner divide. After the Schlieffen Plan failed and the Russian army mobilized far faster than the German General Staff had estimated, the immediate threat to the Reich was in the east. After Hindenburg and Ludendorff won stunning victories at Tannenberg, and shortly thereafter at Masurian Lakes, they quickly became Germany's leading Easterners. General von Falkenhayn, who succeeded Moltke the Younger as chief of staff at OHL, continued trying to win the war in the west by outmaneuvering the French and the British. When that failed, Falkenhayn broke with all German operational tradition and tried to defeat the French through his grinding campaign of attrition at Verdun. Up through the middle of 1916, Hindenburg and Ludendorff agitated continuously for the transfer of sufficient forces to the east to defeat the Russians decisively, after which the Germans could turn around and deal with the French and British. But when Hindenburg and Ludendorff came west to replace Falkenhayn at OHL in July 1916, it did not take The Duo long to transform themselves into Westerners.

MILITARY ALLIES AND RIVALS

As in all hierarchal organizations, people moving up the ladder acquire collections of allies, competitors, and antagonists. Such relationships can grow very complex in peacetime armies, and the networks become quite large by the time an officer reaches the general officer ranks. Generals, as a rule, do not play well together. Any military officer who rises to the general officer ranks is almost certainly decisive, self-confident, aggressive, and competitive. He is unlikely to have much patience for local office politics, the stroking of sensitive personalities, or for slow and careful consensus building. Actual war fighting allows no such luxuries. But that is not to suggest that they have no feelings for war's cost in human life. They understand only too well their own responsibilities for such lives. One result of that burden is that almost all generals develop their own ways of doing things. Thus, when two or more generals meet face to face, their respective staffs devote some time to setting up and preparing the encounter for success with the minimum amount of friction. In today's parlance, staff officers call it "managing the elephants." No staff officer wants to get trampled by an angry elephant—especially his own elephant.

Part of the key to making sense of inter-general relationships is the command and staff structure of a particular army. The three Western armies were relatively similar; the Germans were different. The Franco/Anglo/American system was command-centric; the Germans were (and still are in today's Bundeswehr) staff-centric. In a command-centric structure the commander tells the staff what his intent is and the end he wants to achieve and states any constraints. Then the staff works out the various course-of-action options and presents the results of the analysis to the commander for final decision. In a staff-centric system, the staff working under the chief of staff identifies various possible end states, develops and war-games the various courses of action, and then presents the final recommendation. The commander accepts the primary recommendation, accepts it with modifications, or decides for an alternate course of action. The third decision is very rarely taken.

The staff-centric system makes the chief of staff a far more important player than he is in a command-centric system. Thus, the responsibilities and authority of a German chief of staff were much greater than those held by his command-centric counterpart. Rather than a strictly defined superior/subordinate relationship, this association was always more collegial in the German military. The chief of staff always had the right and even the responsibility to argue with his commander—albeit behind closed doors—right up to the point of decision. But once the decision was made, everyone got behind it. A German chief of staff was almost, but not quite, a deputy commander. Thus, the chief of staff was the motor of the German command and staff system, while the commander was its governor. In the case of Hindenburg and Ludendorff, the field marshal was not the micromanager that Ludendorff was. One of Hindenburg's strengths was that he knew what not to do.[45]

Another peculiarity of the German system was the concept that assignment (or function) overrode rank.[46] The Germans routinely appointed officers to command and staff positions far above the actual rank they held. Once in the position, however, the officer functioned with the full authority of the position, regardless of the nominal ranks and pay grades of his functional subordinates. Corps chiefs of staff, who may have been lieutenant colonels, routinely passed orders unchallenged to general officers commanding subordinate divisions. As a general of infantry, Ludendorff himself never wore more than three stars, yet in 1918 he issued orders to field marshals commanding army groups. Such a situation would be unthinkable in the British, French, or American armies.

At the national level of the various armies, the role of the chief of staff was a little more ambiguous. In Germany, the chief of the Great General Staff in Berlin became the chief of staff of the Feldheer upon mobilization. Constitutionally, the kaiser alone held *Kommandogewalt*, making him the commander in chief. The monarch might have been a capable field commander in the days of Prussia's Great Elector (Friedrich Wilhelm) or Frederick the Great (Friedrich II). Wilhelm II had all the fancy uniforms for the job but not much else. Thus, the chief of staff of the Feldheer was the functional commander, and his first quartermaster general (vice chief of staff) was his effective chief of staff. But from mid-1916 on, Ludendorff's position was even more powerful. When they were transferred to the Western Front, Ludendorff was offered the title of "second chief of the General Staff." He instead opted for the title of first quartermaster general, but he demanded from the kaiser and received "joint responsibility in all decisions and measures that might be taken."[47] It was an unprecedented level of authority conferred upon a staff officer.

In the Allied armies, the national chiefs of staff had little or no direct command authority. The British chief of the Imperial General Staff was the principal adviser to the government, as was the chief of the general staff of the French army. In America the position of the chief of staff, which had been established only as recently as 1903, was still not clearly defined. Thus, by 1918 Pétain, Haig, and Pershing were commanders in their own right, but only of their respective forces in the field in Europe.

After the Battles of Tannenberg and First Masurian Lakes, Hindenburg and Ludendorff were held in high esteem within the German army. But as the old saying goes, "No man is a hero to his valet." In the case of the early battles on the Eastern Front, that valet was Colonel Max Hoffmann, the brilliant operations officer of the Eighth Army. When Hindenburg and Ludendorff met for the first time in August 1914 on the train taking them to assume command in the east, they worked out the basic outlines of their plan. But Hoffmann, as the acting chief of staff until they got there, had come up with almost exactly the same plan and on his own initiative had set things in motion even before Hindenburg and Ludendorff arrived. Hoffmann continued to work under them until they went to OHL in 1916, whereupon he took over as the chief of staff of Oberost. But Hoffmann always looked somewhat askance at The Duo. A few years after the war, when touring the field at Tannenberg, Hoffmann told a group of cadets, "This is where Hindenburg slept before the battle; this is where Hindenburg slept after the battle; and this is where Hindenburg slept during the battle."[48] Conversely, Hoffmann's name does not even appear in Hindenburg's memoirs, and Ludendorff gives him only passing mention.

As noted above, once Hindenburg and Ludendorff became national heroes, tensions started to build between them and General von Falkenhayn. As the rivalry became increasingly bitter, The Duo finally maneuvered Falkenhayn out of office. Hindenburg was the first Prussian theater commander in history to demand the removal of a chief of the General Staff and threaten to resign to back up his demand.[49]

For the most part, Hindenburg was revered within the German army; Ludendorff was grudgingly respected. Despite his abrasive personality, Ludendorff was recognized early in his career as one of the smartest and most effective rising officers of the General Staff. He was not the only one, however. Wilhelm Groener, his closest competitor, succeeded Ludendorff as first quartermaster general in October 1918. The many critics Ludendorff acquired over the years included Crown Prince Rupprecht of Bavaria and his army group chief of staff, General Hermann von Kuhl. As Rupprecht noted in his war diary, "Ludendorff is certainly a wonderful organizer, but not a great strategist" (*aber kein grosser Stratege*).[50] By the time Ludendorff was sacked by the kaiser on 26 October 1918, few in the German army were sorry to see him go.

Joffre was a staunch supporter of Foch, and when Joffre fell from grace Foch went into temporary exile. Joffre never liked Pétain, but in February 1916 he recognized that he needed him at Verdun. Once the situation stabilized, Joffre two months later had Pétain "kicked upstairs" to take command of Army Group Center, bringing in Nivelle to replace Pétain as commander of the Second Army. General Sir Henry Wilson, who in early 1918 became chief of the Imperial General Staff, was a longtime personal friend of Foch and supported his selection for the supreme Allied command in the spring of 1918. Haig and Foch respected each other, albeit from a bit of a distance. Nonetheless, Haig too supported Foch's appointment, and the two worked together rather effectively until the end of the war. Pershing and Foch had difficulty getting along, although in September and October 1918 Foch shielded Pershing from Clemenceau's fierce political attacks. On the other hand, Pershing and Pétain developed a close personal relationship, and after the war Pershing called Pétain "the greatest general of the war."[51] The irony here is that Pershing's tactical thinking was much closer to Foch's.

Foch was the only World War I general who dealt regularly with all the Allied military leaders, which meant that from March 1918 on he had to choreograph three prima donnas—Pétain, Haig, and Pershing. Haig started out as a micromanager, but by 1918 he had learned to delegate more to his subordinate army commanders and trust their judgment. Pershing was certainly a micromanager. Foch also could be a micromanager when he was dealing directly with French subordinate commanders, at times going around Pétain to issue direct orders.[52] Pétain and Foch had a complex relationship. Earlier in the war they generally were mutual supporters, although their tactical opinions were significantly different. Pétain always was skeptical of Foch's overconfidence but nonetheless had a grudging respect for him. When Foch was appointed Allied commander in chief, Pétain accepted the situation without umbrage.[53] But from May 1918 a rift between them started growing. During the final months of the war, Clemenceau increasingly found himself acting as an arbiter between his two senior-most generals. Pétain later complained that Foch was playing politics and that "he wants people to say that he is 'offensive,' and that I am 'defensive.'"[54]

Pétain did not get along well with the British. He developed a strong Anglophobic streak following what he regarded as the BEF's failure to support his 4th Brigade at the Battle of Guise on 29 August 1914.[55] Sir John French, the first commander of the BEF, was really a poor choice for the job. Haig had been French's chief of staff in South Africa during the Boer War, but he nonetheless doubted that French had either the even temperament or the level of military knowledge necessary for high command. Haig was right, and he used his political leverage to get French replaced with himself. Once in command of the BEF, Haig continually had to walk a tightrope through the various internal intrigues within the British army. In his book *The Killing Ground: The British Army, the Western Front and the Emergence of Modern Warfare, 1900–1918*, Tim Travers offers a detailed discussion of the tensions and conflicts among the ranks of the senior British generals.

One of Haig's harshest critics was General Sir Henry Wilson, a very politically oriented officer who earlier in the war had been one of Haig's corps commanders. Haig's closest military ally was General Sir William Robertson, chief of the Imperial General Staff. Known throughout the British Army as "Wully," he was the first—and so far only—British soldier to rise through the ranks from private to field marshal. Early in the war Haig and Robertson formed a personal alliance to get Sir John French replaced as BEF commander. By September 1917, however, cracks were starting to appear in the Robertson-Haig alliance. Robertson's operational concepts were far more pragmatic than Haig's. As early as February 1915, when he was still the chief of staff of the BEF, Robertson issued a memorandum arguing that a decisive breakthrough of the German defenses on the Western Front was impossible. Instead, Robertson believed that the BEF should pursue methodical, set-piece operations, heavily supported by artillery. Later, when Robertson was the chief of the Imperial General Staff, Haig increasingly grew to resent the former's operational advice as interference.[56] As Gary Sheffield has written, "Haig myopically saw Robertson's broad strategic grasp, a major asset to the Allies, as a weakness."[57] Nonetheless, until early 1918, Haig, Robertson, and Lord Derby formed a solid triumvirate that kept much of the political heat off Haig. The BEF commander's life got much more complicated when Wilson replaced Robertson as chief of the Imperial General Staff in early February 1918 and Milner replaced Derby as secretary of state for war that April. Ironically, and much to his discredit, Haig did almost nothing to support or defend Robertson when the ax finally fell on him.[58]

Pershing's most important military ally was General Tasker Bliss, who was chief of staff of the U.S. Army from September 1917 to May 1918, during the period of America's massive military buildup. Bliss saw his job as doing everything possible to support the commander in the field. He never considered himself to be Pershing's military superior. Bliss's replacement, General Peyton March, saw things quite differently. As the U.S. Army's senior-ranking general officer, all other general officers were subordinate to him, including and especially Pershing. The AEF commander refused to admit subordination to another American general. Pershing believed the chain of command ran directly from him to Secretary Baker to President Wilson. The chief of staff of the army's job was to give the AEF commander what he wanted when he wanted it. The bitter Pershing-March feud extended well into the postwar years. Bliss, meanwhile, was sent to Europe as the American permanent military representative to the newly established Supreme War Council. Bliss did not always agree with Pershing but supported him loyally, especially during the amalgamation controversy. Ironically, when Pershing became chief of staff of the army in 1921, he immediately set to work to strengthen the position and confirm it as the senior-most military officer in the chain of command.

FIVE

THE YANKS ARE COMING

So prepare, say a prayer,
Send the word, send the word to beware.
We'll be over, we're coming over
And we won't come back till it's over over there.

"Over There," George M. Cohan

In many respects, the tactics and techniques of our Allies are not suited to American characteristics or the American mission in this war. The French do not like the rifle, do not know how to use it, and their infantry is consequently too entirely dependent upon a powerful artillery support.

Colonel Harold Fiske, AEF Assistant Chief of Staff for Training,
"Memorandum for the Chief of Staff. Subject: Training"

IN JULY AND AUGUST 1914, the system of interlocking alliances combined with rigid mobilization plans plunged Europe into war as if on autopilot. But the citizens and soldiers of those countries went to war for an array of other reasons. The overriding imperatives for the French were revenge for 1871 and the recapture of Alsace and Lorraine. Germany fought to claim its "place in the sun" and recognition as a great power. The strategic importance of the Belgian coast notwithstanding, many average Britons believed that they were taking up arms "to rescue gallant Belgium." The American popular casus belli was even more idealistic. When they entered the war in 1917, the Americans believed they would be fighting the "war to end all wars" and to "make the world safe for democracy." More than one hundred years on, Americans still have an almost religious faith that the universal spread of Western-style democracy is the solution to most of the world's problems.

It was much more complicated than that, of course. If not for German strategic and diplomatic incompetence, America just might not have ever entered the war. The Americans had a traditional and strong inclination toward isolationism, and the large German ethnic population in the United States actually produced a significant level of sympathy for Germany during the war's early years.[1] The country's large Irish ethnic population likewise generated little sympathy for Great Britain. But Germany's unrestricted submarine warfare campaign quickly turned many Americans against Germany, especially after a U-boat sank the RMS *Lusitania* in May 1915, resulting in the deaths of 1,198 passengers and crew, including 124 Americans. Then in January 1917, British intelligence intercepted and leaked the infamous Zimmermann Telegram, sent by the German foreign ministry proposing a military alliance between Germany and Mexico in the event of America entering the war against Germany. German foreign secretary Arthur Zimmermann had written, "We propose an alliance on the following basis with Mexico: That we shall make war together and together make peace. We shall give general financial support, and it is understood that Mexico is to reconquer the lost territory in New Mexico, Texas, and Arizona."[2]

With the resumption of unrestricted U-boat warfare on 1 February 1917, Germany believed it could force Britain to surrender within five months. Although it was almost a certainty that America would enter the war, OHL regarded the United States as a strange, disorganized, undisciplined, and distant place, with almost no army and governed by an idealistic political crank sitting in the White House. Moreover, the German navy was confident that it could sink any U.S. troop ships. The chief of the admiralty staff, Admiral Henning von Holtzendorff, went so far as to tell the kaiser, "I give your majesty my word as an officer that not one American will land on the Continent."[3] And even if U.S. troops did make it across, Ludendorff estimated that America could not put an effective army into the field in Europe until well into 1919. He largely discounted the American military impact on the war, and he failed to account for the economic impact over and above any actual military production. In this case, the German navy sunk only a single U.S. troop ship.

Ludendorff's assessment of the military situation was not wholly unfounded. America was quite unprepared for war. The U.S. Army at that point was only the seventeenth largest army in the world, ranking behind Portugal. Roughly one-third of the standing army consisted of cavalry and artillery in fixed coastal defenses. By the end of the war the size of the army had grown to 3,700,000, with slightly more than half that number in Europe. But its training and equipment left much to be desired. The day the United States declared war on Germany, the regular U.S. Army had only 128,00 troops, backed up by the National Guard with some 182,000 troops. During peacetime, the National Guard was a militia force under the control of the various state governors. Its degree of training and readiness varied greatly, and the regular army tended to look down on it as a poor distant cousin. Tensions between regular army and National Guard senior officers continued throughout the war—and well beyond.

America in 1913 had a larger economy than France, Britain, and Germany combined—minus their colonies. The United States also produced more steel than all three combined. By 1918 the Allies' total oil requirement was 9.5 million tons, 6.6 million of which America supplied. The United States that year also supplied enough foodstuffs to feed 18 million Frenchmen for a year. America was not, however, the "Arsenal of Democracy" that it would so famously become during World War II, when it supplied some two-thirds of all Allied military equipment. American industry in 1917 was not geared for war production. Aside from American-made rifles, U.S. Doughboys in World War I were equipped largely with French artillery, tanks, and aircraft. But during the last eighteen months of the war America did supply France with enough raw steel to produce 160 million artillery shells.[4] Sealift was a special problem. In 1917, America had only 1 million tons of transatlantic shipping, less than Norway, and the same gross tonnage as it had in 1810.[5] Much of the hastily raised American Expeditionary Force would cross the Atlantic in British bottoms, but the negotiations for this were difficult and protracted. A great deal of Pershing's time during 1917 and well into the start of 1918 was taken up with the shipping problem.

In May 1917, America had only 1,308 troops in France. By November 1918 the American force had grown to 2,057,675. Through late 1917 and 1918, America had the same problem that Britain did at the start of the war—having to "grow" officers, staff officers, and senior commanders virtually overnight. At the start of 1918 Britain had been at it for more than three years, while America was only starting the process. By the time the war ended ten months later, American leaders could not possibly have had the level of technical and tactical competence of the British, much less the French and especially the Germans. They simply had neither the training nor the experience. But by November 1918 the AEF had come farther and faster than either the Germans or the other Allies had thought possible. That did not, however, stop the French and the British from heaping criticism—some of it justified, some of it not—on the Americans right until the war's very end.

What standing military doctrine the U.S. Army had was based on the recent small war experiences of the Spanish-American War, the Philippine-American War, and the 1916 Punitive Expedition in Mexico. Any ideas of larger-scale warfare were still rooted in the concept of a U.S. Civil War meeting engagement. Only 379 officers had attended the recently established staff school at Fort Leavenworth or the Army War College in Washington. Pershing was the only American officer who had ever commanded a force larger than a brigade in combat. Like the British army of 1914, the U.S. Army of 1917 clung to a human-centric notion of the battlefield and paid little attention to the emerging military technologies of the period. An infantryman was a rifleman, nothing more or less. Hence the focus on "open warfare." The M-1903 Springfield was a splendid battle rifle, but American doctrine placed more weight on its long-range accuracy than on its rate of fire.[6]

The U.S. Army paid little real attention to what was happening on the European battlefields between 1914 and 1917. The military journals of the period continued to place heavy emphasis on the rifle and the bayonet. The American *Field Service Regulations* manual was updated in 1918, but even that edition paid little heed to tanks, aviation, or chemicals and underemphasized artillery, machine guns, and the importance of motor transportation.[7] The political atmosphere in Washington only reinforced the blinders worn by the military. In 1915, when President Wilson read in a newspaper that a group of officers at the U.S. Army War College (then in Washington) were developing war plans for potential engagement in the European conflict, the president ordered Acting Secretary of War Henry S. Breckinridge to investigate. If the story proved to be true, Wilson ordered Breckinridge to exile the offending officers from Washington.[8]

America had not fought a war with allies since 1783.[9] And although America declared war on Germany, and later on Austria-Hungary in December 1917, it refused to sign the 1915 Treaty of London, which was the legal basis of the Entente. Rather than an Allied power, America declared itself an "associated power." President Wilson personally ordered that America field an independent army. As soon as he landed in Europe, then, Pershing made it clear that the Americans would not serve as a replacement pool of company- or battalion-sized augmentations for French and British divisions. Despite Secretary of War Newton Baker's earlier comment to Pershing about giving him "only two orders," Baker on 26 May 1917 sent the AEF commander a very specific letter of instruction, which included this paragraph:

> 5. In military operations against the Imperial German Government you are directed to cooperate with the forces of the other countries employed against the enemy; but in so doing the underlying idea must be kept in view that the forces of the United States are a separate and distinct component of the combined forces, the identity of which must be preserved. This fundamental rule is subject to such minor exceptions in particular circumstances as your judgment may approve. The decision as to when your command, or any of its parts, is ready for action is confided to you, and you will exercise full discretion in determining the manner of cooperation. But, until the forces of the United States are in your judgment sufficiently strong to warrant operations as an independent command, it is understood that you will cooperate as a component of whatever army you may be assigned to by the French Government.[10]

Pershing's firm stance on this issue was a source of constant friction throughout the war. At the height of the crisis of the first major German offensive in March 1918, however, Pershing did offer temporary amalgamation of American units.

As the manager of America's industrial mobilization, President Wilson was largely a failure. Being reluctant to get involved in "purely military matters," Secretary of War Baker also failed to manage the expansion of the army. The War Department was in a state of constant chaos until General Peyton C. March became the chief of staff of the U.S. Army in late May 1918.[11] And although March was generally a strong and effective manager, he and Pershing had very different ideas about who worked for whom.

Despite March's efforts, the initial stateside training of hundreds of thousands of new soldiers was generally poor at best. There was too great a shortage of training camps, equipment, and qualified instructors. The level of training of the troops arriving in Europe was so low that Pershing was forced to add three additional months of training once those units reached France. During the course of the war Pershing also set up more than twenty AEF schools in France. One of the most critical was a general staff college established at Langres.[12] There was, however, one fairly bright spot in an otherwise cloudy picture. As historian Timothy Nenninger has noted, the most astonishing aspect of the American nineteen-month rapid buildup was the training and commissioning of some 200,000 officers, "most of them competent."[13]

The AEF organized very large divisions. At 28,000 troops each, they were twice as big as the European divisions, which made them cumbersome to maneuver and difficult to control. The Americans really had little choice in the matter. The AEF simply did not have the pool of experienced senior commanders and staff officers. If the AEF had organized twice as many divisions averaging 14,000 troops each, those units would not have had the command structures necessary to operate, because the United States did not have the necessary number of experienced generals and trained staff officers. Major General James Harbord, Pershing's first AEF chief of staff, also argued that the Americans had to have very large divisions to sustain continuous attack and force the enemy out of the trenches and into "open warfare."[14] Nenninger, on the other hand, has argued that the large divisions were far more suitable for conditions of trench warfare, as opposed to smaller and more nimble formations that could maneuver more easily on an open battlefield. The large divisions, therefore, created something of a tactical ambiguity between the AEF's doctrine and its structure.[15]

In late May 1917 Pershing and his small AEF advanced party staff sailed for Europe on the RMS *Baltic*. They spent the entire crossing planning the organization and deployment of the main force. A planning team headed by Lieutenant Colonel Fox Conner, Pershing's assistant chief of staff for operations (G-3), recommended the Lorraine sector, between the Argonne Forest and the Vosges Mountains. The question of which ports the AEF would use made it impossible for the Americans to assume a position in the line between the French and the British. The availability of France's western ports centering on St. Nazaire and the existing rail network made the Saint Mihiel sector the optimal location.[16] Conner further recommended the elimination of the Saint Mihiel salient, just south of Verdun, for the AEF's first major operation.

Pershing and his staff arrived in London to something of a hero's welcome. Crossing the Channel, they were received even more enthusiastically in Paris. However, the good feelings did not last long. Almost as soon as he got to Europe, Pershing was complaining to Washington about the French and British wanting to take control of American forces before America had even fielded an army. He also expressed his frustration about what he considered the lack of coordination between French and British.[17] He was right about that. Even by late 1917 there was very little synchronization of tactical and operational ideas between the two principal Western Allies.[18] That meant that French and British instructors assigned to the AEF were teaching the Doughboys different combat methods, and even then the primary focus of the instruction was on trench warfare rather than on Pershing's "open warfare" dogma. Before Pershing even got to Europe, Haig recorded in his diary on 3 May that Pétain wanted the Americans to send individuals over to France to enlist in the French army. Pragmatically, Haig thought there was very little chance of that happening.[19]

Pershing and Pétain met for the first time on 16 June 1917. They quickly forged a close personal bond, even though their views on modern war fighting were radically different. Later that month Pershing asked Pétain to allocate the Lorraine sector to the AEF. Pétain agreed immediately.[20] By the following month, however, Pershing rejected Pétain's concept of limited-objective attacks. Ignoring the experiences of the past three years of war, Pershing wrote, "The theory of winning by attrition, with isolated attacks on limited fronts, which was evidently the idea of the British General Staff, did not appeal to me in principle."[21] Later in August, Pershing started objecting to French training support because of the emphasis on trench warfare methods. "In order to avoid the effect of the French teaching it became necessary to take over and direct all instruction ourselves," the general wrote. "For the purpose of impressing our own doctrine upon officers, a training program was issued which laid great stress upon open warfare methods and offensive action."[22]

On 1 September Conner, accompanied by Pershing's aide Captain George S. Patton, went to Chaumont to set up AEF General Headquarters. Initially, however, Pershing's headquarters was overstaffed and top-heavy. Some fifteen heads of departments, bureaus, and services were based there, in addition to the five principal divisional chiefs of the general staff. Also present were miscellaneous elements, such as a press bureau and various welfare agencies, including the American Red Cross. Because of his tendency to micromanage, Pershing at first dealt with many of these entities directly, which consumed great amounts of his time.[23]

Early that same month Pershing had his first major run-in with French prime minister Georges Clemenceau over the use of individual American troops as fillers. The AEF commander flatly refused Clemenceau's demand that he put American troops into the line immediately, with or without training. The following month Pershing clashed with the U.S. War Department over the assignment of general officers to the AEF. In a cable to Secretary Baker he complained about the system of making general officer assignments solely on the basis of seniority. Many of those older senior officers were well past their prime and were both physically and psychologically incapable of handling the stress of brigade or divisional command. Pershing quite correctly argued that combat command assignments should be given to younger officers strictly on the basis of proven ability.[24]

The first American combat division in France was the U.S. 1st Division. Composed, on paper at least, of mostly prewar regular soldiers and units, it supposedly required far less preparation and training than the mobilized National Guardsmen and the new draftees. In fact, though, the 1st Division was a scratch unit, hastily pulled together from whatever was available. On 21 October 1917, the 1st Division entered the trenches in a quiet sector between Nancy and Luneville. Pershing, meanwhile, continued his running battle with the War Department over the lack of emphasis on "open warfare" in the stateside training of the new units. When a new training manual was issued early in December, the AEF commander objected bitterly about the statement "In all the military training of a division, under existing conditions training for trench warfare is of paramount importance."[25] Despite the AEF's experiences in October and November 1918, Pershing never changed his opinion. In his postwar memoirs he wrote, "Most of our officers were firm believers in the soundness of our [that is, Pershing's] doctrines, although a few continued to defer to the opinions of the French instructors, who were generally committed to the theory that only trench training was necessary."[26] But training in trench warfare did not necessarily mean exclusive reliance on passive defense. A detailed understanding of the realities of trench warfare was a fundamental precondition for planning and executing successful attacks against such heavily fortified and deeply echeloned positions. During the last months of the war the AEF paid a heavy price for that lack of general knowledge.

By the end of 1917, meanwhile, Pétain signaled a subtle shift in his own operational thinking based on the increasing American presence. In his General Directive Number 4 of 20 December he wrote, "The Entente will not recover superiority in combat effectives until the moment the American Army is capable of putting a certain number of large formations into the line. Until then, under the pressure of unavoidable wastage, we ought to adopt a waiting strategy with the idea . . . of going over to the offensive again as soon as we can."[27] In a further implementing instruction to the basic directive, Pétain also noted that the techniques of static and open warfare should no longer be considered mutually exclusive. Both methods in the future would be required, with forces switching from one posture to the other as the situation required.

Early in December British prime minister David Lloyd George entered the amalgamation controversy by proposing that the United States send over separate companies and battalions to fill out British units. Pershing continued to stand his ground, with the support of Washington. On 18 December, Baker cabled Pershing that he and President Wilson "do not desire loss of identity of our forces, but regard that as secondary to the meeting of any critical situation by the most helpful use possible of the troops at your command."[28] The problem with this ambiguous response was what exactly the definition of a "critical situation" was and who got to decide.

Pershing had solid reasons for resisting amalgamation, especially at the level of the individual soldiers. He continually pointed out the problems of language in serving with the French; innate Irish American hostility toward the British; the damage to national pride by the discounting of America's contribution to the war and its reduced role in the subsequent peace conference that would result from America not having had a distinct army of its own in the field; and the inevitable public outcry that would result if Americans suffered disproportionately large numbers of casualties while serving under foreign commanders.

But as Pershing's biographer Donald Smythe pointed out, amalgamation made perfect sense to the Allies, considering the AEF's chronic shortage of experienced senior commanders and trained staffs. Even temporary amalgamation could have been worked to the AEF's advantage if managed properly. Raw recruits would train faster and more effectively if teamed with veterans, and American casualties would be lower in the long run. By not waiting until the AEF developed the requisite number of higher staffs, America's weight just might have been brought to bear sooner against the Germans, possibly shortening the war.[29]

The amalgamation issue was tightly linked to the shipping problem. As previously noted, America simply did not have the sealift capacity to move large forces across the Atlantic, and Britain's already stressed merchant fleet was coming under increasing pressure from the renewed German U-boat campaign. Amalgamation of combat units would reduce the requirement for support forces, which ultimately made up 45 percent of the AEF. Pershing continued to wrestle with the shipping problem throughout the remainder of 1917 and into the first months of 1918. On 2 December he wrote to Baker and March requesting some support on the issue. On 10 January Pershing and General Tasker Bliss, the American military representative to the newly established Supreme War Council, met with the British chief of the Imperial General Staff, General Sir William Robertson, who tried to convince them to bring over 150 separate infantry battalions to feed into the BEF. The three met again in Paris on 25 January, where Pershing rejected Robertson's plan and instead insisted on enough shipping to transport six complete American divisions. Bliss initially was inclined to support the British proposal, but in the end he loyally backed Pershing.[30] The Allied leaders continued to argue various solutions to the combined shipping and amalgamation problems through the summer of 1918.

SIX

TWO CONFERENCES IN NOVEMBER 1917

Although the object of setting up the Council was to ensure the better coordination of military action, the members of the Council were ministers and therefore it was a political and not a military body. Consequently, it did nothing to improve the system of military command.

Field Marshal Sir William Robertson, From Private to Field Marshal

The submarine war had not up to date produced those economic results which the Chief of the Naval Staff had expected, and which I, relying on the opinions of the experts, had hoped for.

General of Infantry Erich Ludendorff, My War Memories, 1914–1918

THE ALLIED SUPREME WAR COUNCIL,
RAPALLO, 5–7 NOVEMBER

Through the end of 1917 the Germans had the major advantage of fighting under a unified command on the Western Front. The Allies had no such unified command, with coordination between the French, the British, and the Belgians alternating at times from good to almost nonexistent. The British government's original instructions to the commander in chief of the BEF about the maintenance of an independent army were not dissimilar to the instructions Pershing received almost three years later. When Joseph Joffre was commander in chief of the French army, he frequently had great difficulty achieving operational coordination between the French and the British. When he was succeeded by Robert Nivelle, matters became far worse.

Throughout the first three years of the war, various military and civilian leaders recognized the unity of command problem. In preparation for the Third Battle of Champagne (the Nivelle Offensive) in April 1917, Nivelle had the basically correct idea when he demanded that the BEF be subordinated to him when the British attacked at Arras in support of his main effort against the Chemin des Dames. British prime minister David Lloyd George supported Nivelle enthusiastically, while Haig and Chief of the Imperial General Staff Sir William Robertson protested vehemently. In the end, a compromise solution was reached where the operational subordination was limited and temporary. When the Nivelle Offensive failed miserably, one result was increased and widespread skepticism over the practical feasibility of any sort of unified Allied command. It also weakened Lloyd George's position in his running dispute with Haig and Robertson.

Foch never lost faith in the idea, which was firmly rooted in his own experience in late 1914 and early 1915 as the de facto commander of an ad hoc army group on the Allied left wing, where he coordinated the operations of French, British, and Belgian forces.[1] After Foch returned from administrative exile in May 1917 and was appointed chief of the general staff of the French army, he continued to push for the establishment of unified command. On 27 July 1917 Foch submitted a memorandum to the representatives of the Allied governments meeting in Paris, recommending unity of action through the establishment of "a permanent inter-Allied military organ, whose function would be to prepare the rapid movement of troops from one theater to another."[2]

French prime minister Paul Painlevé suggested to Lloyd George that Foch be designated chief of an Allied general staff. Lloyd George demurred. He preferred instead the establishment of a permanent Allied war council. Painlevé subsequently submitted the idea of an Allied council to the French Council of Ministers. They preferred an Allied generalissimo, whereupon Painlevé advised the ministers that the establishment of an Allied council would be the first step in the creation of a unified command under Foch.[3]

Despite their advantage of a unified command on the Western Front, the Germans for the first three years of the war fought under the handicap of a two-front war. Their primary ally in the east, Austria-Hungary, was more often than not a serious drain on resources. More than once the Germans were forced to redeploy major forces from the west to the east to prop the Austro-Hungarians up. The Habsburg Empire itself was fighting two main enemies, the Russians to the east and the Italians to the southwest. The war in northwestern Italy was actually a third front for the Central Powers. But after Russia was effectively knocked out of the war when German forces took Riga on 3 September 1917, the pressure in the east eased considerably. Ludendorff then seized the opportunity to shore up Austria-Hungary against Italy before then turning Germany's full attention against the Allies in northwest Europe.

Ludendorff established a new field army, the Fourteenth, consisting of seven German and eight Austro-Hungarian divisions. Most of the artillery was German. The resulting Twelfth Battle of the Isonzo, more popularly known as the Battle of Caporetto, started on 24 October. It was a crushing defeat for the Italians, who by the time the battle ended on 7 November lost 10,000 men dead, 30,000 wounded, 265,000 taken prisoner, and 3,152 guns. It was now the French and the British who were compelled to redeploy major forces to reinforce a faltering ally. Early that November a force of five British and six French divisions arrived in northern Italy from the Western Front.

On 28 October, during a meeting with Painlevé and the French War Committee, Foch and Pétain clashed over which of them should command the Allied relief mission to Italy. Pétain thought he should go, as a precursor to folding the Italian army under his overall command. Foch argued that as the chief of the general staff, he should be the one to go. Foch was the logical choice. Prior to becoming chief of the general staff, he had spent most of the preceding April in Italy on a special assignment to coordinate the plans for reinforcing the Italians in the event that the Germans and Austrians did attack in force. As much as anything it had been a busy-work assignment to keep Foch in relative isolation; but all of a sudden, the crisis actually had erupted, and Foch was the one who knew best the plans, the ground, and the Italian forces and leadership.[4]

Foch spent only a short time in Italy, but he quickly and effectively managed the deployment of the relief force. When the French divisions were organized into the Tenth Army under General Denis Duchêne, Pétain tried to have it placed under his overall command, which Foch successfully prevented.[5] Foch returned to France in early December and was replaced in Italy by General Marie Émile Fayolle, who continued reporting directly to the French minister of war rather than to Pétain. Foch, however, failed to convince the British to put their divisions in Italy under Fayolle's overall command. Foch and Pétain had so far maintained a respectful if arms-length relationship, but from that point on the friction between the two increased.[6]

Caporetto jolted the Allied political leaders into rethinking the need for an inter-Allied coordinating body. Lloyd George took the lead on 30 October, proposing establishment of a joint council.[7] He also saw it as a way to circumvent Robertson as chief of the Imperial General Staff and to restrict Haig's freedom of action. Two days later both the French and British governments accepted the idea in principle and agreed to convene a conference on the matter at Rapallo, Italy. On 4 November, the day before the opening of the conference, Lloyd George and Haig met in Paris. The British prime minister asked Haig for his opinion on the establishment of such a council. Haig was against it, but Lloyd George told the BEF commander that the Allied governments had made the basic decision already. Pershing also was skeptical. Before the meeting he told Lloyd George that the Supreme War Council (SWC) would be of little value, but what the Allies really needed was a supreme commander. Pershing, in fact, was afraid that the prime ministers intended to assume direct control of military operations.[8]

The conference met on 5–7 November. The SWC as formed was composed of the prime ministers of Britain, France, and Italy, plus a working representative from each government. The council had the mission of "watching over the general conduct of the war. It prepares recommendations for the decisions of the governments, assures the execution, and renders reports about them to the respective governments."[9] The council's real function, however, was to tighten civilian control over the military by establishing a body above the general staffs of the member nations. Although Edward House was President Wilson's personal representative, America as an associated rather than an Allied power did not participate in most of the political deliberations.[10] Committees were established for finance, food, munitions, transportation, and naval warfare—especially anti-submarine operations. Henceforth, the council would meet at Versailles.

Each country also had a permanent military representative (PMR), who was not a voting member of the council but rather a military technical adviser. The field commanders were specifically barred from serving as a PMR. The French initially appointed Foch; the British, General Sir Henry Wilson; the Italians, General Luigi Cardona; and the Americans, General Tasker Bliss.[11] Cardona had started the war as the chief of staff of the Italian army, but he recently had been sacked as a result of the Caporetto debacle. Haig had expected Robertson, his key supporter in London, to be appointed. He was not at all happy with the actual appointment. Wilson and Foch were friends of long standing, but Wilson was one of the most opportunistic political intriguers in the British army. There was bad blood between him and Haig and Robertson. Further rubbing salt into the wound, Wilson would report directly to the British War Cabinet rather than to Robertson as chief of the Imperial General Staff. Robertson walked out of the meeting in protest. Wilson was the only PMR who did not report to the chief of staff of his respective army.[12]

There was, however, a major problem with Foch serving as the French military representative on the council and simultaneously as chief of the general staff of the French army. Lloyd George objected, pointing out that it had been agreed that the military representatives would hold no other official position and that he therefore had not appointed Robertson. What the British prime minister really wanted was a strategic agent with the authority to overrule his chief of the Imperial General Staff.[13] The French finally agreed that Foch would relinquish the chief of staff position, but they stalled for a time.

On 29 November Clemenceau, at the suggestion of Foch, replaced him as PMR with General Maxime Weygand, who was Foch's longtime chief of staff. That allowed Foch to remain chief of staff of the French army. Weygand, however, was one of the most junior general officers in the French army. He was promoted from general of brigade (one-star equivalent) to general of division (two-star equivalent) to assume the position, but that still left him far junior in rank to the other PMRs. The British considered the whole thing as a maneuver to make the PMR committee little more than a mouthpiece of the French general staff.

After the war, historian Basil Liddell Hart wrote, "During the first months of its existence the members of the Supreme War Council spent more time pulling wires than in pulling together."[14] Lloyd George, supported by Henry Wilson, wanted to shift Allied war efforts away from the Western Front, in the naive believe that Germany could be defeated indirectly by knocking its allies out of the war. Wilson thought the Germans would attack toward the Black Sea before attacking in France. Haig thought those ideas were absurd, and Foch agreed with him. The Americans, who were not at war with the Ottoman Empire, also opposed operations outside France. Clemenceau, meanwhile, formed a new government on 16 November, shoring up his political support at home. He likewise continued to increase gradually Foch's military influence. On 18 November, Pétain in a statement to the French War Committee supported the appointment of a supreme commander for the purpose of unity of command.[15] He apparently offered no recommendation as to whom that supreme commander should be.

The SWC held its second meeting at Versailles on 1 December. Eleven days earlier, on 20 November, the British had launched an initially successful attack at Cambrai, heavily supported by tanks. But then the Germans counterattacked and rapidly erased most of the British gains. The SWC had to face the reality that the German army was not even close to being defeated in the field. On 3 December Haig told the BEF's army commanders that he was suspending his plans to launch another offensive in the spring and that the situation now necessitated "our adopting a defensive attitude for the next few months."[16] Despite the near unanimous assessment that the Germans would launch a major offensive just as soon as the spring weather permitted, Lloyd George managed to win over the SWC to the strategy of offensive operations against the Turks and Germans in Palestine while waiting for a buildup of tanks, planes, guns, and U.S. forces for a major Western Front offensive in 1919. At that point, virtually no one among the Western Allies believed that the war would end in 1918.

Foch sent a note to the SWC on 6 January 1918, outlining what he saw as the three primary tasks in dealing with the anticipated German spring offensive: (1) husband reserves for the counterattack, (2) use the bare minimum of forces in halting the enemy, and (3) determine the best time and place to counterattack. Foch also argued that these three functions could not be carried out adequately by the national commanders in chief because they were focused solely on the situation in their own specific sectors. Nor could a deliberative body like the SWC take the necessary decisive action. All that was required could be done only by an overall supreme commander—and, of course, the current chief of the French general staff was the most qualified general officer for that position. Two days later Pétain responded with a note arguing that although an operational-level Allied counteroffensive was essential, no such operation would be possible in 1918 until after the Americans had arrived in force and were ready.[17]

THE GERMAN PLANNING CONFERENCE, MONS, BELGIUM, 11 NOVEMBER

The Germans had managed to limit and mostly contain the British offensive at Third Ypres in the latter part of 1917, but their army was very badly shaken. And although the Germans had likewise been able to eliminate almost all of the gains made by the British surprise attack with tanks at Cambrai, OHL was forced to conclude that it could no longer afford to stand on the strategic defensive against the Allies in the west. Germany was running out of time. As Ludendorff later wrote in his memoirs, "In late autumn 1917 OHL was confronted by the decisive question: Should it utilize the favorable conditions of the spring to strike a great blow in the west, or should it deliberately restrict itself to the defensive and only make subsidiary attacks, say in Macedonia or Italy?"[18] Answering his own question, he continued, "The American danger rendered it desirable to strike in the west as early as possible; the state of training of the Army for attack enabled us to contemplate doing so about the middle of March."[19]

Ludendorff convened an operational planning conference on 11 November, at the headquarters of Army Group Crown Prince Rupprecht of Bavaria, in Mons, Belgium. Neither Rupprecht himself nor any other commander was present. Hindenburg did not even mention the meeting in his memoirs. The only participants were chiefs of staff and other senior General Staff officers. The decision to attack already having been made, their task was to analyze the attack options relative to the three principal elements of the operational art: time (when to attack), space (where to attack), and force (the order of battle based on the enemy forces and the available friendly forces).[20]

Rupprecht's brilliant chief of staff, General Hermann von Kuhl, recommended attacking in the north, in the direction of Bailleul–Hazebrouck. The objective would be to cut the BEF in half and then defeat it in detail. The key constraint was the condition of the ground in the Lys River valley, which had a very high water table. Typically, the ground would not be sufficiently dry to support military operations until April. Ludendorff was inclined to attack in the north, but he insisted on attacking no later than the end of February.

The chief of staff of Army Group German Crown Prince Wilhelm, General Friedrich von der Schulenburg, advocated an attack against the French center on both sides of Verdun, arguing that while Britain most likely could survive a major military setback, France would be broken by one. Ludendorff, however, thought that there was no incentive for the British to send reinforcements to the French at Verdun, which meant that the Germans still would have to fight the British later in Flanders. Ludendorff then suggested an attack by Rupprecht's Army Group in its southern sector: "It would seem that an attack near St. Quentin offers promising prospects. After reaching the line of the Somme between Péronne and Ham it might be possible, by resting the left flank on the

Somme, to advance the attack still farther in a northwestern direction, and thus eventually roll up the British front."[21]

Kuhl did not like that option. The ground in the Somme sector dried out far earlier in the spring than it did in Flanders, but the southern option had two significant drawbacks: the Germans would have to attack over the terrain that had been devastated by the 1916 Somme battles and by their own scorched-earth withdrawal to the Siegfried Position during Operation ALBERICH in 1917, and the left wing of such an attack would come into contact with the French and draw in their reserves that much faster.

Ludendorff made no final decision at Mons. The planners mooted several other options, but the two primary ones were Operations ST. GEORG, centered on Hazebrouck and the Lys valley in the north, and ST. MICHAEL, centered on St. Quentin and the Somme valley, along the juncture between the British and French armies. Ludendorff ordered the army group and army general staffs to analyze in detail the various options and develop the courses of action, especially in light of the lessons from the Allied offensive to that point in the war. The German planners had already concluded that the Allied offensives had failed because of a lack of adequate diversionary attacks. Ludendorff, however, decided that the Germans did not have sufficient forces to mount such major diversionary attacks. The great German offensive in 1918, the Kaiserschlacht, would be a single massive battle of annihilation. Rupprecht, however, later wrote that Ludendorff was vastly underestimating the resilience of the BEF.[22] As historian Correlli Barnett has pointed out, Ludendorff in effect was trying to run the Schlieffen Plan all over again—a gamble under acute time pressure, making use of a temporary superiority that was not really overwhelming.[23]

For the next several weeks the estimates and staff studies went back and forth between OHL and the various subordinate headquarters. By the start of December, Ludendorff had pretty much decided on the MICHAEL option, but he still wanted to see the fully developed staff studies before making it final. On 12 December, Ludendorff's chief operations officer at OHL, Lieutenant Colonel Georg Wetzell, produced his own staff study that called into question the direction in which Ludendorff was heading. Wetzell argued that neither MICHAEL nor GEORG would be able to achieve decisive results by themselves. He concluded, "Therefore, we will succeed in gaining truly decisive results only by a skillful combination of multiple attacks having highly reciprocal effects." Wetzell proposed a two-phase operation against the British "using the railways for the rapid transfer of [German] troops."[24]

Ludendorff did not adopt Wetzell's plan. He was already too determined on conducting a grand battle of annihilation—*Vernichtungsschlacht*—rather than a sequenced operation with cumulative effects. Wetzell was proposing an operational plan of attack, while Ludendorff was fixated on a tactical one. Nonetheless, Wetzell's assessment almost certainly influenced Ludendorff's decision to continue contingency preparations for an attack in Flanders should the attack in the St. Quentin sector fail. As we shall see, the major operational errors Ludendorff committed during the planning and especially during the execution of Operation MICHAEL doomed to failure any follow-on attack in Flanders. As the British official history of the war put it, "Fortunately for us, Lieut.-Colonel Wetzell's proposals were not accepted, although, in the end, after the first offensive had come to a standstill, Ludendorff, bearing them in mind, did order the second act—too late."[25]

Ludendorff held a second major planning conference with the army group chiefs of staff at Kreuznach on 27 December 1917.[26] He still made no final decision, but Ludendorff said that the balance of forces in the west would be in Germany's favor by the end of February, making it possible to attack in March. At the conclusion of the conference, OHL issued a directive to the army groups to plan and start detailed preparations for the key options, with the completed plans due on 10 March 1918.[27] Rupprecht's Army Group was directed to plan GEORG II in the Ypres sector; GEORG I in the Armentières sector; MICHAEL I in the direction of Bullecourt–Bapaume; MICHAEL II north of St. Quentin toward Péronne; and MICHAEL III south of St. Quentin toward Le Fére.

By late January, German intelligence was starting to get indicators that the British were extending their southern wing, taking over the sector of the French line that would be attacked by MICHAEL III. In theory, that would make the German task a little easier. The attack would now hit only the BEF rather than both the British and the French, and it also would hit the seam of the two armies, making it easier to divide them.

Ludendorff made his decision at a final planning conference at Aresens on 21 January 1918.[28] Setting the tone for the entire meeting, Ludendorff signaled the key to his whole thinking when he said, "We talk too much about operations and too little about tactics."[29] Explaining the basis for his decision,

Ludendorff ruled out GEORG as too dependent on the weather. A late spring in the area might delay the start of the attack until May, which was far too late for Ludendorff. He also said he thought it necessary to take Mont Kemmel and the southern Béthune Hills, which added to the difficulty of the operation.

MICHAEL on both sides of St. Quentin was the decision: "Here the attack would strike the enemy's weakest point, the ground offered no difficulties, and it was feasible for all seasons."[30] Ludendorff planned to have eight-five to ninety divisions in reserve in the west by the end of March. He saw the problems with the MICHAEL option, but he also saw the advantages of splitting the British and the French. He noted, "The center attack seemed to lack any definite limit. This could be remedied by directing the main effort between Arras and Péronne, toward the coast. If the blow succeeded the strategic result [*strategischer Erfolg*] might indeed be enormous as we should separate the bulk of the English army from the French and crowd it up with its back to the sea."[31] Crown Princes Wilhelm and Rupprecht, and their chiefs of staff Schulenburg and Kuhl, all pushed Ludendorff to establish a specific operational objective for the attack. Ludendorff shot back his infamous response, "I can't abide the word operations. We'll make a hole. The rest will follow. That's the way we did it in Russia."[32]

Three field armies were committed to the MICHAEL attack. The Second Army, commanded by General Georg von der Marwitz, would conduct MICHAEL II in the center; the Seventeenth Army, commanded by General Otto von Below, would conduct MICHAEL I on the right; and the Eighteenth Army, under General Oskar von Hutier, would conduct MICHAEL III on the left. All three attacking armies were then subordinate to Army Group Crown Prince Rupprecht, but Ludendorff also announced that that he was transferring the southern-most Eighteenth Army to Army Group Crown Prince Wilhelm. Rupprecht vehemently objected to such a blatant violation of the principle of unity of command.[33] There has been much speculation since that Ludendorff's motives were political, giving the kaiser's son a role in the great battle. It is more likely, however, that Ludendorff wanted to insert a split at the army group echelon to give OHL (himself) more of a direct role in the management of the battle. Ludendorff told Rupprecht's Army Group to continue making preparations for GEORG, but the Germans would attack in Flanders only if MICHAEL failed.[34] But failed to do what? That question was never answered.

SEVEN

THE GATHERING STORM

We can now deploy our entire strength in the West. To be sure, that is our last card.

> *Colonel Albrecht von Thaer,* Generalstabsdienst an der
> Front und in der O.H.L.

I was only afraid that the enemy would find our front so very strong that he will hesitate to commit his Army to the attack with the almost certainty of losing very heavily.

> *Field Marshal Sir Douglas Haig, in Gary Sheffield and John Bourne,*
> Douglas Haig: War Diaries and Letters, 1914–1918

VITAL ARTERIES AND JUGULARS

Almost everything that happened on the battlefields of 1918 tied back ultimately to the respective enemies' rail lines. The European roads of 1914–18 were incapable of carrying the necessary traffic to support the huge armies on the Western Front. As noted in Chapter 2, the railroads during World War I were the primary means of operational mobility and virtually the only means of strategic mobility on land. During the German Wars of Unification and ever since, the Germans were the masters of using rail for the transportation and deployment of troops.[1] Logistical sustainment, however, was quite another matter and was always one of the German army's major weaknesses. As historian Gerhard Gross has noted,

The World War also exposed another weakness of the German Army's operational thinking. In the tradition of Friedrich II, the logistics and transportation elements of German operational planning were designed for warfare close to the borders, a function of the central position of the German Reich. Neither in the west nor in the east had the pre-war operational plans extended beyond an area of approximately 400 kilometers from the German borders.[2]

If the enemy's key rearward rail lines could be cut, it would drastically reduce their ability to sustain their forces in the field. They simply would run out of ammunition, fuel, food, and replacements—both men and equipment. The loss of the rail lines also would make it far more difficult to withdraw major forces under pressure. By the end of the first year of the war, the Western Front was sandwiched between two principal east-west lateral rail systems.

The Allied rail network was thin and fragile in the north but far more robust south of the Marne. The majority of the main lines in the south ran east-west, while those in the north ran north-south. Immediately south of the Marne the main line ran from Paris to Épernay and then to Nancy. If that line was cut, there were adequate work-arounds to the south. A parallel line ran directly from Paris to Nancy. Even farther to the south, rail lines ran from the AEF's ports at Brest and St. Nazaire to Tours and thence to Chaumont, south of Verdun. In the BEF's sector the lines ran from Paris north via Amiens and Hazebrouck to the Channel ports. The German front lines there were much nearer to the coast, giving the British far less depth in their rear. Virtually everything that sustained the British army in the field entered the Continent through three major ports in the north (Dunkirk, Calais, and Boulogne) and three major ports in the south (Rouen, Le Harve, and Dieppe). The quartermaster general's staff (Q-Staff) of the BEF organized the logistics flow into a northern and a southern line of communications, with Amiens being the dividing point.[3]

The BEF's two major forward marshaling and switching yards at Amiens and Hazebrouck were the choke points of its entire rail system. Virtually everything that came in through the three northern ports had to go through Hazebrouck; everything that came in through the three southern ports had to go through Amiens. Furthermore, Amiens was the hub of the BEF's forward railway operations. Almost everything that ran between the forward railheads had to go through Amiens or be taken back to the regulating stations near the base ports.[4] Some 80 percent of the north-south traffic went through or around Amiens. In early 1918, the north-south traffic in the British sector averaged 140 trains per day. The network had a maximum surge capacity of 212 trains per day.

The loss of Amiens would result in the BEF losing two of its double-track lines across the Somme. Losing Abancourt, 40 kilometers southwest of Amiens, would result in the loss of all three lines. That would leave only the completely inadequate single-track coastal railway.[5] As Haig's Q-Staff estimated, if the Allies lost Amiens, all possible bypasses could handle only ninety trains per day. If Abancourt fell as well, the only remaining north-south link would be the single-track Dieppe–Eu–Abbeville line, which ran along the coast. It had a capacity of only eight trains per day.

As early as the spring of 1916, the BEF's logistics system was on the verge of collapsing under its own weight. In September of that year, it took 1,934 tons of supplies per mile of front per day to sustain the BEF.[6] In mid-1916 the British Fourth Army alone required seventy trains per day of all types. That September the British brought in the civilian rail expert Sir Eric Geddes to rationalize the system. He succeeded in staving off the collapse, but the system remained fragile and stressed until the end of the war.[7] In April 1918 the British ran an average of twenty-four ammunition trains alone to the front every day.[8]

In 1918 the German army had six great trunk line railways running from Germany to the Western Front. The high-capacity supply and communications network was composed of the following lines, with their key nodes from north to south:

1. Cologne–La Chappell–Liège–Namur–Compiègne–Paris Railway; double-tracked with a connecting line from La Chappel to Brussels–Lille and Arras, with a second connecting line from Liège and Brussels to Bruges and Ostend.
2. Cologne–Sedan–Mézières–Laon–Soissons–Paris Railway, with one connecting line from Soissons to Château-Thierry, a second between Mézières and Namur, and a third between Laon–Amiens.
3. Coblenz–Trier–Metz–Verdun Railway.
4. Mainz–Sarrelouis–Metz Railway, and from there the all-important north-south line running from Metz to Liège.
5. Mainz–Sarreguemines–Nancy Railway.
6. Mannheim–Nancy Railway, fed by the Wissembourg–Strassburg–Colmar line running north-south along the Rhine.[9]

Behind the German lines facing the British in the north, the two key rail junctions were Berlaimont and Roulers.[10] Running north-south between Metz and Liège, the main German rear-most lateral line had a capacity of three hundred trains per day. A roughly parallel lateral line closer to the front ran from Metz through Mézières to Valenciennes. In the south, Mézières was the major choke point closest to the French and American lines.

The Germans were naturally sensitive to their own rail network, but they failed to focus sufficiently on the significant vulnerabilities in the Allied rail network. This largely was a function of Ludendorff's obsession with the tactical level over the operational. In all the German operations orders for March and April 1918, any emphasis on the targeting of Allied rail was for the purpose of blocking troop movements rather than strangling the enemy by cutting off their logistics flow. Thus, during the first two of the German offensives, the Germans attempted direct force-on-force battles, for which they really did not have the necessary superiority in the correlation of forces. The critical Allied vulnerable points of Amiens and Hazebrouck were never designated as primary objectives. During the course of both battles, OHL did order the capture of both rail centers, but only as something of a consolation prize after it became clear that the main schemes of maneuver had failed. And by the time it did shift its attention to Amiens and Hazebrouck, it was too little, too late.

The Allied commanders, on the other hand, continually targeted the German rail network, despite its robustness and depth. During the Battle of the Somme in 1916, the Allies' deep operational objective was the major German railway complex between Cambrai, Le Cateau, and Maubeuge, fifty miles behind the German front line.[11] The Allies also established a train-watching network in occupied France and Belgium, run by French, British, and Belgian intelligence. The Germans had no equivalent intelligence network.[12] By the time the Allies went over to the offensive in July 1918, Foch saw clearly that Mézières was the jugular of the German forward logistical network.[13]

BRACING FOR THE DELUGE AS PÉTAIN AND FOCH SPAR

At the start of 1918, Pétain was planning his principal campaign to recover Alsace, but one he planned to launch in 1919. Pétain calculated that he needed a little more than 1 million troops on the Western Front, but he had only about 750,000.[14] Haig wanted to resume the attack in Flanders. Meanwhile, the gap between Pétain and Foch continued to widen. The two disagreed fundamentally on how to deal with the coming German offensive. Foch insisted on meeting the Germans with a powerful Allied counteroffensive. Pétain was preparing for an elastic defense-in-depth. But there was a great deal of resistance to

Pétain because the old Grandmaison doctrine of holding onto every inch of sacred French ground was still alive and well in some quarters. In retrospect, it seems clear that if Foch had prevailed, the very slim reserves that existed at that point would have been squandered prematurely, leaving the Allies in a much weaker position to counterattack in July, after the Germans had reached operational culmination.[15]

Early that January Foch complained to Prime Minister Clemenceau that Pétain should be planning offensives to counter the anticipated German offensives rather than just sitting passively on the defensive. Clemenceau conveyed the concerns to Pétain. Writing on 8 January, Pétain responded, "The American effort cannot make itself felt in the battle before 1919, and until then Franco-British forces will have to be husbanded with a prudence which leaves only the smallest possible part to chance."[16] He concluded, "To sum up, the battle of 1918 will be a defensive one on the Franco-British side, not through absolute choice of the command, but from necessity. Our lack of means is the cause. It is better to realize it now and get organized accordingly."[17] Foch nonetheless continually criticized Pétain's defensive and offensive doctrines to French political leaders, hoping to see him replaced by General Fayolle.

On 24 January Pétain issued a directive detailing his concept of the defense-in-depth:[18]

1. Divisions should deploy in two echelons.
2. The mission of the first echelon is to slow the enemy and buy time.
3. The main battle zone of the division should be several kilometers back, beyond the range of enemy artillery. Most of the divisions' heavy weapons should be deployed in this zone.
4. Smaller-caliber artillery, anti-tank guns, and mortars should be deployed directly behind the main battle zone.
5. Heavier artillery should be deployed farther back.

HAIG'S ENEMIES, FRONT AND REAR

Since the mutinies in April, the French had been pressuring the British to extend their lines farther to the south, thus freeing up French divisions. David Lloyd George agreed over Haig's objections. Pétain wanted Haig to extend his right flank fifty kilometers to the south. In the end, Haig agreed to extend thirty kilometers, to just south of the Oise River. The boundary between the British Fifth Army and the French Third Army would also be the junction between the British and the French. The two forces started their moves in early

January. The trenches and defensive positions the Fifth Army found in its new sector were incomplete, poorly constructed, and not organized in any depth. The British troops started digging, but they did not have anywhere near the manpower necessary to build proper defenses before the German blow fell.[19]

As 1917 came to a close, Haig finally accepted that a quick resumption of the offensive in Flanders was out of the question. The major German attack was coming, and the British would have to defend against it. But the BEF had little experience in defensive warfare. For the better part of the last three years they had been on the offensive. On 14 December BEF General Head-quarters (GHQ) issued general instructions for the defensive. The echeloned defense-in-depth would be organized into forward, battle, and rear zones. The British thus adopted the structure of the German system, but they failed to understand how to make it work. On the southern end of the British line, the Third and Fifth Armies deployed up to one-third of their strength in the forward zone. The Germans, on the other hand, routinely kept two-thirds of their troops in the rear zone for maneuver and counterattack. Thus, when the blow did fall, the British troops in the forward-most lines were decimated by the German preparatory fires. Nor did the troops understand the system. As one anonymous regular noncommissioned officer complained at the time, "It don't suit us. The British Army fights in line and won't do any good in these bird cages."[20]

In January, Lloyd George sent Maurice Hankey, secretary of the British War Cabinet, and South African general Jan Christian Smuts to France with the mission of finding a viable replacement for Haig. They concluded that there was no one. That same month Haig told Lloyd George that the war could possibly end in 1918 because of the economic, manpower, and other internal conditions in Germany.[21] Lloyd George saw Haig's optimistic assessment as additional evidence of his unfitness for high command.

Haig and Lloyd George also clashed in early 1918 on the issue of man-power and replacements. As of 1 January, the BEF was 605,000 troops below strength. At the same time, there were some 607,000 trained troops capable of frontline service in the United Kingdom. Haig was promised only 100,000 replacements, supposedly because the rest had to be held back for homeland defense in the event of a German invasion. On 10 January, the severe man-power shortages forced the BEF to reduce the strength of its divisions from 12 battalions to 9, resulting in the disbanding of 141 battalions.[22] When the

German blow finally fell on 21 March 1918, the BEF had insufficient frontline infantry to mount an effective defense, and the British soldiers paid the price.

After the war, Lloyd George actually admitted that he had held back the British replacements to prevent Haig from launching another costly and ineffective offensive in Flanders. Writing in 2005, historian Andrew Suttie noted that the British manpower shortage in 1918 was abundantly clear to both the soldiers and the politicians. They also knew that a major German attack was coming. Why then did the government not reinforce the BEF when the means were available? As for Lloyd George's justification, Suttie also points out, "It should not be forgotten that Haig persisted with his costly operations in Flanders only with the sanction, explicit or tacit, of the Government led by Lloyd George himself. He and his Government, therefore, were as responsible as anyone for the state of the BEF in March 1918. Nowhere in [Lloyd George's] *War Memoirs* is there a hint of an acknowledgment of this responsibility."[23]

PERSHING DIGS IN HIS HEELS

Nine months after America declared war, the AEF had only 175,000 troops in France, making up only four combat divisions. They were all in various states of training, none ready for commitment to the line. When Pershing and Pétain met on 23 December 1917, the French commander in chief tried to convince his American counterpart to allow smaller American units to be amalgamated into French formations. Pershing would agree only to regiments serving with the French for periods of no more than one month.[24]

When Pershing met with Haig and Pétain in mid-January, they tried to convince Pershing that he would not be able to field an independent American army as long as he did not have competent and trained divisional commanders and adequate artillery. The French and the British already had sufficient artillery in France. By the end of that month Pershing finally agreed to the transport of six infantry divisions from America, without their organic artillery. Secretary of War Baker endorsed Pershing's decision.[25] In March the Supreme War Council also ratified the decision. The Allies would provide the artillery, aircraft, and heavier weapons.

Meanwhile, although Pétain was the French commander generating the most pressure on the amalgamation issue, the relationship between Pershing and Foch turned sour rapidly. In his memoirs Pershing complained, "Foch never seemed interested when I talked to him of our problems, and I doubt whether at the time he ever thought, knew, or cared much about our organization, or our questions of transportation and supply. He was essentially a student and teacher of history and strategy."[26]

THE ELUSIVE GENERAL RESERVE

Tied closely to the issue of an Allied supreme commander was the establishment, command, and control of an Allied General Reserve. That was the single-most contentious issue the SWC wrestled with—an issue that was never resolved. Pétain and Haig heatedly opposed the idea, and Haig threatened to resign if any British troops were withdrawn from his direct command.

On 2 February 1918, the SWC issued Joint Note 13, calling for the establishment of such a general reserve in anticipation of a German spring offensive. Foch and General Wilson supported the idea and the council approved it. The SWC's Joint Note 14 also created the Executive War Board to control the General Reserve. That body consisted of the PMRs plus Foch as the president.[27] The functions of the Executive War Board were to[28]

1. determine the specific strength and composition of the General Reserve and national contributions,
2. determine the basing of the General Reserve,
3. coordinate and direct the transportation of the General Reserve,
4. determine and issue the orders for the commitment of the General Reserve, and
5. determine time, place, and strength of the counteroffensive.

The component forces would be administered and trained by national commanders in chief but could not be committed without orders from the Executive War Board.

Pétain lobbied fiercely against the command and control of such a force coming under Foch and the Executive War Board.[29] Pershing generally supported the concept of the General Reserve, but he was skeptical of the Executive War Board. Haig grumbled into his diary that Foch was becoming a de facto "Generalissimo."[30] General Robertson fought against the General Reserve to the last. Finally, to Lloyd George's delight, Robertson resigned as chief of the Imperial General Staff; and to Haig's chagrin, Wilson replaced Robertson on 9 February. As the new chief, Wilson told Lloyd George that Haig would fight the coming defensive battle well and that "the time to get rid of him was when the German attack was over."[31] Wilson's position as PMR at

Versailles was filled by General Sir Henry Rawlinson, who had commanded the Fourth Army at the Somme.

On 6 February, General Maxime Weygand, on behalf of the Executive War Board, issued a memorandum informing the Allied commanders in chief that Foch intended to form a general reserve of some thirty divisions: thirteen or fourteen French; nine or ten British; and seven Italian. That would constitute one-seventh of the total Allied forces available.[32] At this point the Americans were not included in the plan. Pétain and Haig protested, both citing the need to retain their own strong reserves to deal with the impending German offensive. Pétain and Haig then started to work together to circumvent Foch by establishing a bilateral mutual support plan directly between the French and British armies.

Their two staffs met on 21–22 February to work out the details. If the Germans attacked the British, Pétain agreed to commit six divisions, constituting the French Third Army, which would concentrate by the fourth day at either Montdidier–Noyon, Amiens, or between St. Pol and Doullens, as the situation required. In the case that the French were attacked, Haig agreed to concentrate six to eight of his divisions south of Soissons, between the Aisne and the Marne.[33]

On 2 March, Haig sent the Supreme War Council a note flatly refusing to commit any of his divisions to the General Reserve, citing his mutual support agreement with Pétain.[34] Facing a stone wall, the Executive War Board five days later reported to the SWC its inability to form a general reserve. The board further recommended that the matter be referred to the respective Allied governments.[35]

Meeting in London on 13–15 March, the SWC failed to resolve the issue.[36] Lloyd George was reluctant to apply direct pressure on Haig because of the coming German offensive. Foch demanded that the SWC force the issue, but in the end both Lloyd George and Clemenceau decided to support their respective commanders for the time being. The Allied General Reserve was a dead letter, which Foch bewailed as a disaster.

HAIG SPREAD THIN

As the spring approached, Haig had more than his share of problems. The British held 126 miles of front lines with four field armies. In the north, General Sir Herbert Plumer's Second Army held the BEF's most sensitive and vulnerable sector. The British back was virtually against the sea in the north, and the key British ports were almost within German artillery range. In the south the Fifth Army, under General Sir Hubert Gough, held the BEF's weakest sector; the southern part of that line was the ill-prepared defensive ground the British recently had taken over from the French. To the immediate south of the Second Army, General Sir Henry Horne's First Army was fairly solidly emplaced. Immediately north of the Fifth Army, the Third Army under General Sir Julian Byng was in significantly better shape than Gough's Fifth Army. The Third Army had fourteen divisions to defend a twenty-eight-mile front. The Fifth Army had twelve divisions for forty-two miles. There was, however, far greater depth behind the Fifth Army than anywhere else in the British line.

Gough was convinced that the main German blow would fall in his sector. On 1 February he sent an estimate of the situation to BEF General Headquarters, pointing out his small number of forces and the poor state of his southern defenses. He requested more engineers and labor troops. Three days later GHQ's instructions to Gough ordered him to maintain contact with the Third Army on his left, no matter what happened. From that message Gough also concluded that he was supposed to fight east of the Somme but also be prepared to fall back to the river line. In that case, he was to establish a bridgehead in the vicinity of Péronne and an emergency line along the river. No additional labor forces, however, were available for the construction of such a line.[37] Gough on 12 March once more sent a message to GHQ, pointing out the precariousness of his position. As late as 19 March he tried to have two of the BEF's general reserve divisions deployed closer to his lines, but he was rebuffed by GHQ.

Given the BEF's manpower shortages, Haig could not be strong everywhere. Gough's force-to-space ratio was extremely risky, and even though the vital rail center at Amiens was in Gough's sector, it was still a good forty-five miles from the presumptive German line of departure. If Haig reinforced the Fifth Army, it could be only at the expense of the forces covering Arras and Artois and the weakening of Plumer's northern command. In the worst-case scenario, Haig at all costs had to keep open his routes of withdrawal to the northern Channel ports.[38] Historians continue to debate the actual intent behind Haig's deployment of his forces in March 1918. The British official history suggests that he intentionally accepted risk in the south based on the depth to the Fifth Army's rear. Tim Travers, on the other hand, argues that this is an ex post facto justification and that Haig's deployments were based on his assumption that the German main effort would hit closer to his center, in the vicinity of Arras. The rationalization of trading space for time in the south also ignores the very real risk of the Germans splitting the French and the British.[39]

Haig nonetheless was confident—too confident. On 2 March, he made his famous comment in his diary about worrying that the Germans would hesitate to attack him because the BEF's defenses were too strong. By 14 March the French general staff had identified 188 German divisions on the Western Front. It estimated that there were two possible sectors for the German attack: in the British sector between the Oise and Arras, and in the French sector centered on Reims. The former was the more likely.[40]

STEEL WIND RISING

On 24 January, OHL issued the initial warning order, assigning the army boundaries.[41] A supplemental order further stated, "The MICHAEL offensive is to rupture the enemy front with the line La Fére–Ham–Péronne as its objective; thereafter, the offensive is to be advanced, in conjunction with Operation MARS, beyond the line Péronne–Arras."[42] That meant that the Seventeenth and Second Armies would pivot to the north in an effort to roll up the British. MARS was designed as a local attack against Arras to facilitate the pivot. To launch MARS, however, OHL would have to regroup and redeploy significant amounts of artillery. The Germans assembled fifty attack and seventeen trench divisions for MICHAEL. Preparations were to continue for Operation GEORG, which was to be ready to go by the beginning of April. But only thirty-five divisions would be available for GEORG, which was redesignated KLEIN-GEORG ("Little Georg").

The main effort of MICHAEL was on the northern wing of the Second Army and the southern wing of the Seventeenth Army. The single-most important immediate objective was to pinch out the British-held Flesquières salient, which straddled the inner boundary of the two armies. Ludendorff had made it very clear that the success of any subsequent large-scale operation depended on cutting off what the Germans called the Cambrai salient on the first day.[43] Even by this stage, however, there was no clear operational purpose, aside from achieving some sort of tactical success in the first phase to provide a basis for some sort of vague second phase.

OHL held another planning conference at Mons on 3 February. Ludendorff once again emphasized the primacy of tactics by stating, "It is the impression of OHL that the preparation phase for the attacks places too much emphasis on surprise and too little on tactical effect."[44] Four days earlier he had told Crown Prince Rupprecht much the same thing when he said that a "painstaking preparation of the attack was more important than its surprising execution."[45] On 8 February OHL issued a second warning order, which contained mostly tactical planning guidance resulting from the 3 February conference.[46] OHL issued the main operations order for MICHAEL on 10 March.

> His majesty commands:
> 1. The MICHAEL attack will take place on 21 March. Units will break into the enemy's first positions at 0940 hours.
> 2. The Group of Armies of Crown Prince Rupprecht will, as their initial important tactical objective, reduce the Cambrai salient now held by the British, and thereafter advance to the north of Omignon Creek to the line Croisilles–Bapaume–Péronne and the confluence of Omignon Creek and the Somme. In the event that the attack of the right wing makes favorable progress, the Seventeenth Army will advance it beyond Croisilles. The group of armies has the further mission to push forward in the direction of the line Arras–Albert; to hold with its left wing on the Somme at Péronne; and by shifting its main effort to the right wing, to force the British back across the front of the Sixth Army, thus releasing for the advance additional forces hitherto engaged in positional warfare. To this end, all divisions now in the rear of the Fourth and Sixth Armies will be committed should the contingency arise.
> 3. The Group of Armies of the German Crown Prince will first of all gain the line of the Somme and the Crozat Canal to the south of Omignon Creek. In the event of the Eighteenth Army making rapid progress, it will capture the passages across the Somme and the Canal. In addition, the Eighteenth Army will be prepared to extend its right wing to Péronne. The Group of Armies will reinforce the left wing of the Eighteenth Army with divisions from the Seventh, First, and Third Armies.[47]

The Seventeenth Army had the most difficult mission. The reduction of the Cambrai salient required it first to advance to the southwest on Bapaume. After that, it had to turn northwest to reach the line Arras–Albert. The Seventeenth Army's maneuver would be restricted on its right by Arras and the high ground around Monchy. General von Kuhl asked OHL to reinforce the Seventeenth Army at the expense of the Eighteenth, but OHL refused.[48]

The Second Army's mission was somewhat easier. Initially it had to attack to the west. As soon as the Seventeenth and Second Armies reached the line of Croisilles–Bapaume–Péronne, the Second Army would continue its advance toward Albert, anchoring its left flank on the Somme. From that point, its mission would be to follow and support the Seventeenth Army in rolling up the British.

The Eighteenth Army had the easiest mission. After reaching the Somme, it would extend its right wing as far north as Péronne. The operations order contained no follow-on mission for the Eighteenth Army after it reached the line of the Somme and the Crozat Canal. The sole purpose of its attack was to capture the river crossings and the canal to block any French reinforcements from the south. Although Amiens was in the Eighteenth Army's sector, it was not a designated objective.

During January and through the middle of March, German preparations, security measures, and the assembly of forces constituted a masterpiece of military staff work. The plan established the requirements for extension of road networks and narrow-gage field rail networks; extension of communications nets for the various headquarters, the artillery, and aviation; establishment of routes of approach, march tables, assembly areas, and divisional zones of action; establishment of command posts and observation posts; establishment of forward airfields and the pre-positioning of required tentage; and establishment of artillery and trench mortar firing positions and the pre-positioning of the ammunition.[49]

During the final four weeks just prior to that attack, the forces were moved up and emplaced in the following order of priority: first, corps headquarters, artillery headquarters, and communications units; second, divisional staff advanced parties, artillery staffs, engineer staffs, ammunition trains, and motorized trains; third, artillery units, air defense units, labor and road construction companies, aviation companies, and balloon detachments; and fourth, divisional combat units, horse depots, bridge trains, subsistence trains, medical units, and field hospitals.[50]

At this point, strategic surprise was impossible to achieve, but the Germans went to extreme measures to achieve operational surprise. German troops and even subordinate-level commanders were kept ignorant of the actual plan for as long as possible. To ensure the strict adherence to security procedures, OHL established a network of special security liaison officers with broad enforcement powers. The security restrictions mandated that no orders or information was to be disseminated to the trenches; no movement was to be made during daylight; and all detraining had to take place as far to the rear as possible. In addition, special controls were established on all incoming and outgoing personal mail; telephone discipline was strictly enforced; all new positions required overhead concealment; route discipline was to be enforced to avoid cross-country vehicle tracks observable from the air; and increased air activity was to be avoided in the planned attack sector.[51]

The Germans faced an enormous challenge in totally converting three field armies from defensive to offensive configuration and posture in a very short period of time. In each army a special corps headquarters was established to coordinate training. The fifty-six attack divisions had to be brought up to full strength for men, horses, and transportation equipment, most often at the expense of the trench divisions. Starting in late December 1917 the attack divisions were all withdrawn from the front and billeted far to the rear, where they received four weeks of rest, rehabilitation, and training. For the infantry units, a myriad of details had to be worked out and coordinated, including, but not limited to, assignment and transportation of light trench mortars and light machine guns; assignment of accompanying artillery; assignment of grenadiers (a critical specialty); ammunition basic loads; infantry ammunition wagons; hand grenades and flares; reduction of the infantryman's basic pack; composition of combat trains and field trains; draft animals for the train vehicles; and boards, bridging sections, and other material for crossing shell holes and obstacles. Between 15 February and 20 March the Germans ran 10,400 full-length trains, moving men and equipment from the rear echelons to the front.[52] On 15 March Herbert Sulzbach, a lieutenant in the Eighteenth Army's 5th Artillery Regiment, wrote in his diary, "We get the first secret orders for the attack, and again and again you have to gaze in wonder at this careful work that the staff people are putting in, working things out right to the last detail."[53]

The artillery preparations were especially important and time- and labor-intensive. OHL massed 6,608 guns and 3,534 trench mortars for MICHAEL. The distribution of those guns, however, remains questionable to this day. The Seventeenth Army had 2,234 guns and 1,197 trench mortars; the Second had 1,751 guns and 1,080 trench mortars; but the Eighteenth had 2,623 guns and 1,257 trench mortars. If the Eighteenth Army had only a tertiary mission, why then was it more heavily weighted with firepower? True, the Eighteenth had a greater sector width than the other two armies, but the dedication of that much firepower for a screening operation is still difficult to understand. One possible explanation is that OHL tried as much as possible to supply the estimates submitted by the individual armies. The Eighteenth Army's chief of artillery was Colonel Georg Bruchmüller, who just six months earlier had been

Hutier's chief gunner at Riga. Bruchmüller knew exactly what he needed, and both Hutier and Ludendorff knew that Bruchmüller was the German army's best gunner.[54]

On 20 March OHL issued the launch order for the next day, informing the subordinate commands that the kaiser himself had come to the front to assume personal command.[55] That same day Ludendorff, in a telephone conversation with Kuhl, talked about his concept for the exploitation and follow-on objectives in the event that MICHAEL was a major success. The Eighteenth Army would move toward the line Bray–Noyon; the Second Army on Doullens–Amiens; and the Seventeenth Army in the direction of St. Pol. But that, however, would be a divergent attack, and there was still no indication of targeting Amiens as a key Allied rail center. Ludendorff stressed that such a divergent operation would be feasible only if the Allies were defeated along the entire front. Even then, it would depend on whether the necessary forces were available at that point.[56] That, of course, would represent a significant change in the original operational concept. And in this case, that it is almost exactly what Ludendorff tried to do—but without first achieving his stated conditions for success. Once again, Ludendorff was allowing the tactical possibilities to blind him to the operational realities.

EIGHT

MICHAEL AND GEORGETTE: LUDENDORFF VERSUS HAIG

Even with the advantage of numbers on our side, it was not a simple matter to decide on an offensive in the west. It was always doubtful whether we should win a great victory. The course and results of the previous attacks of our enemies seemed to offer little encouragement.

Field Marshal Paul von Hindenburg, Out of My Life

With our backs to the wall and believing in the justice of our cause, each one of us must fight on to the end.

Field Marshal Sir Douglas Haig, quoted in James E. Edwards, ed.,
Military Operations: Belgium and France 1918

MICHAEL: 21 MARCH–5 APRIL 1918

On the evening of 20 March a heavy fog settled in on top of the British Third and Fifth Army positions. At 0440 hours the next morning, the Germans opened up with a five-hour-long artillery preparation. It was history's greatest artillery bombardment to that time, and the thunder of the firing could be heard as far away as London. The Germans fired 3.2 million rounds on 21 March alone.[1] Using their new infiltration tactics, the German infantry starting advancing at 0940 hours, following closely behind a creeping barrage. The heavy fog that lasted until late that morning screened the movements of the attackers and prolonged the effects of the gas. By 1400 hours the Germans had penetrated through the Fifth Army's forward zone, and at the end of the day the British III Corps and the right flank division of XVIII Corps were fighting in the rear of their own main battle zones.[2]

Haig received the first official report of the attack just after 1100 hours. He ordered five divisions from the First and Second Armies to the Fifth and Third Army sectors, but only one of those divisions went to the beleaguered Fifth Army.[3] There is no record of any direct telephone conversation between Haig and General Sir Herbert Gough that day.[4] At 2145 hours Gough ordered a limited withdrawal to a line behind the Crozat Canal. Haig approved the order.[5] Around midnight Haig requested reinforcements from Pétain, who even before receiving the request had ordered five divisions from the French Third Army to be ready to move by 1200 hours on 22 March. Those units were concentrated in the Noyon area, twelve to fifteen miles behind the right flank of the Fifth Army. Some 21,000 British troops surrendered on 21 March, the greatest number in history to that point.[6]

The attackers made the biggest single-day advance of the war so far. The kaiser was ecstatic, but Ludendorff and the other senior commanders were less sanguine. The three attacking armies had not advanced evenly. The Eighteenth Army made the greatest gains, advancing an unprecedented thirteen kilometers. The Seventeenth Army made the smallest gains and was stuck in front of the Third Army's battle zone, having advanced only four to five kilometers. It was still some seven kilometers short of its objectives for the day. The Second Army's right had not progressed well either. Its left wing made better progress, but the Cambrai salient had not been pinched out on the first day, and the basic operational concept was starting to unravel.[7]

Ludendorff had to make a decision. On the one hand, he could opt for consistency of purpose by reinforcing the overall German right wing to support the original operational scheme. On the other hand, he could shift his reserves to the left in an attempt to exploit General von Hutier's tactical success. At the tactical level, it is generally a sound practice to reinforce success rather than failure. At the operational level, it is not quite that simple. Such shifts are difficult to make because they require a rapid restructuring of the logistics system, and they usually produce unforeseen second- and third-order effects. Ludendorff decided for opportunism.[8]

On the morning of 22 March, British sappers blew the three rail bridges over the Crozat Canal, but one remained standing and was still capable of carrying infantry. Gough ordered his corps commanders to "fight rear-guard actions back to the forward line of the rear zone, and if necessary, to the rear line of the rear zone."[9] By the end of the day, the Eighteenth Army was on the Somme and the Crozat Canal.[10] The Fifth Army had lost its entire battle zone, and remnants of its forward corps were reeling back.

The German Second and Seventeenth Armies continued to make slow progress, especially on their adjacent right and left wings respectively, where the British troops in the Cambrai salient held out stubbornly. The Second Army's left wing, adjacent to the Eighteenth Army's right, made better progress and by the end of the day had broken into the British rear zone. According to the original plan, the Eighteenth Army upon reaching the Crozat Canal was supposed to shift its main effort to supporting the Second Army's pivot to the north. But the Cambrai salient inhibited that maneuver. Crown Prince Wilhelm's Army Group started arguing to OHL that the best way to support the Second Army was for the Eighteenth to continue its southwesterly thrust (keep in mind that the two armies were in different army groups). Late that night OHL ordered the Eighteenth Army to continue pushing forward on its current axis of advance.[11]

At 2000 hours Gough notified Haig that the Germans had broken through the Fifth Army's reserve line. Haig approved the fall back to the Somme but ordered Gough to hold the Péronne bridgehead. An hour and a half later GHQ ordered the Third Army to maintain contact with the left of the Fifth Army. A gap, however, was already starting to open up between the Third and Fifth Armies. Many historians today agree that Haig and GHQ were far too slow in recognizing the seriousness of the situation on the BEF's far right. Haig still was expecting the German main effort to hit the center of his line, just a little to the north of the German Seventeenth Army's right flank. Haig noted in his diary that day, "I expect a big attack to develop towards Arras."[12] Pétain, meanwhile, had seven divisions starting to move north, up to the line of the Somme and Crozat Canal.

The Germans so far had made a breach almost forty miles wide in the Allied line, but the friction of war was starting to take its toll. Early on 23 March the British V Corps abandoned the Cambrai salient, and as a result a gap between the Third and Fifth Armies started to grow wider.[13] That afternoon Ludendorff huddled in Avesnes with Generals von Kuhl and von der Schulenberg and told the two army group chiefs of staff that "a considerable part of the British force has been defeated." Ludendorff also estimated the remaining British strength to be about fifty divisions, and he thought it no longer probable that the French would be in a position to launch a relief counteroffensive. With only about forty divisions available for redeployment, Ludendorff assumed the French would be forced to concentrate south of the MICHAEL sector.

Based on his wildly optimistic and generally unsupported estimate of the situation, Ludendorff changed the overall objective of MICHAEL to separating the British and the French. North of the Somme, the Seventeenth Army, supported by the heretofore-uncommitted Sixth Army on its right, would combine to push the British forces in the sector into the sea. The Eighteenth Army now would attack southward across the Oise River between Noyon and Chauny and push the French back across the Aisne.[14]

Yet, the conditions that Ludendorff had prescribed for exploitation during his 20 March phone conversation with Kuhl did not exist. What Ludendorff was now ordering was a complete departure from the established operational scheme. Originally the main effort was the Second and Seventeenth Army attacks against the British. But now the entire objective of the operation was to separate the British from the French and to attack both simultaneously. That required a significant shift in combat power to the left, with the result that the Germans would be making diverging attacks.

On 23 March Haig met with Gough and General Sir Julian Byng for the first time during the battle. Later that afternoon Pétain and Haig met at Dury. With the gap between the Fifth and Third Armies growing wider by the hour, Haig now faced the hard decision of sacrificing the Fifth Army as the price of holding the rest of the BEF together. Haig asked for a large concentration of twenty French divisions in the vicinity of Amiens. Pétain demurred, saying that he still expected a major German attack in the Champagne sector. Pétain did, however, recommend that General Marie Émile Fayolle, the commander of Army Group Reserve, assume direct command of all Allied forces between the Oise and Péronne, which included Gough's Fifth Army. Haig concurred. Late that afternoon GHQ ordered the Fifth Army to hold the line of the Somme River at all costs: "There will be no withdrawal from this line."[15] But the Germans were already across the river. Early that evening Haig ordered General Sir Herbert Plumer's Second Army in Flanders to release three divisions and send them south. As J. P. Harris has noted, Haig arguably should have done such days or even weeks earlier. Considering the wet and soft ground still in Flanders at that time, there was little risk of a major German attack in that sector.[16]

On 24 March the British III and XVIII Corps fell back in disarray as the Eighteenth Army continued advancing to the southwest. Concluding quite incorrectly that the BEF had been broken completely, OHL started planning a grandiose series of maneuvers. Although OHL continued to receive reports of large French forces advancing from the south toward Noyon, Ludendorff ordered the reinforced left wing of the Eighteenth Army to seize the high ground overlooking Noyon and then prepare to cross the Oise. In his memoirs, Hindenburg wrote that the unprecedented advance the Germans had made during the last three days now made an advance on Amiens feasible: "Amiens was the nodal point of the most important railway connections between the two war zones of central and northern France."[17] Hindenburg in that statement essentially admitted that Amiens was an after-the-fact objective.

Haig, meanwhile, was still faced with the gut-wrenching question of whether to abandon the Fifth Army and pull the Third Army back to the north or to try to hold the line between his two southern armies. Haig's quartermaster general staff, meanwhile, started developing contingency plans to abandon the Fifth Army.[18] The British Third Army continued pulling back its own right flank as it attempted to maintain contact with the Fifth Army. All throughout 24 March, French infantry arrived piecemeal, and as soon as they detrained they were thrown into the battle, frequently without their communications equipment or supporting weapons.[19]

Earlier that morning Pétain had issued a new order to his army commanders, specifying that the primary objective of the battle was keep the French armies together, preventing Army Group Reserve from being cut off. The secondary objective was to maintain, if possible, contact with the BEF.[20] Pétain still anticipated a major German attack in the Champagne sector, and he was worried about any possible threat to Paris. Thus, Pétain seemed to be making it clear that he would continue to support the British only so long as he could hold his own forces together.[21] Foch, meanwhile, concluded that the mutual support agreement between Haig and Pétain was no longer working. Earlier that day he met with Prime Minister Clemenceau to argue for the establishment of unified command.[22]

That evening Haig essentially made the decision to abandon the Fifth Army. He ordered Third Army commander Byng "to cling to the First Army near Arras, to his north, rather than to Fifth Army or to the French to the south."[23] Later that night Haig and his chief of staff, Lieutenant General Sir

Herbert Lawrence, met with Pétain at BEF headquarters. The French army commander told Haig that if the Germans continued moving in the direction of Paris, he would be forced to pull the French reserves back to cover the capital.[24]

By the evening of 25 March the Eighteenth Army had severed the contact between the British Fifth and French Third Armies and was threatening the French flank northeast of Roye. The Fifth Army was almost completely cut off on both flanks. But the Eighteenth Army was now fifty-six kilometers ahead of its nearest standard-gage railhead.[25] Nor was Ludendorff satisfied, as he wrote in his postwar memoirs: "Strategically we had not achieved what the events of the 23rd, 24th, and 25th had encouraged us to hope for. That we had also failed to take Amiens, which would have rendered communications between the enemy's forces astride the Somme exceedingly difficult, was especially disappointing."[26] This is another ex post facto rationalization. All the German plans and orders through 25 March identified Amiens only as a direction of advance, never as a key operational objective.

French forces, meanwhile, continued moving up from the south. Haig ordered Byng to withdraw the Third Army to the Ancre River. He also told Byng that he should conduct any further withdrawals to the northwest and that he could no longer rely on any mutual support from either the Fifth Army or the French. The Third Army's mission now was to secure the BEF's open and vulnerable southern flank.[27] Haig's quartermaster general staff prepared to shut down the BEF's southern lines of communications and increase the supply flow through the northern ports.[28] As Foch saw the situation, "Two distinct battles were being fought by the Allies: a British battle for the ports, and a French battle for Paris. They were carried on separately and farther and farther away from one another. The Allied commanders thus tended to emphasize the separation of their armies, the primary objective of the German operations."[29]

Haig wrote in his diary that in the very early morning hours of 25 March he reported Pétain's presumed unreliability to London via telegram. He requested that Sir Henry Wilson, the new chief of the Imperial General Staff, and Lord Alfred Milner, a key member of Prime Minister Lloyd George's War Cabinet, "come to France at once in order to arrange that General Foch or some other determined general who would fight, should be given supreme command of the operations in France."[30] But as historian Elizabeth Greenhalgh has pointed out, there are many discrepancies in Haig's account of his role in Foch's appointment.[31] There is no surviving copy or record of the telegram Haig said he had his chief of staff send to London. And Wilson was already in France at that point. He and Haig met at Montreuil, at 1130 hours that very morning. Wilson wrote in his own diary that it was he who told Haig that Foch should be the one to assume the unified command and that Haig agreed only after some time.[32]

Greenhalgh postulates that Haig and Lawrence did not understand Pétain properly during the 24 March meeting, which was conducted in French. It was actually Pétain who by 23 March was concerned that Haig was withdrawing north too far, too fast, and that the BEF would not stand on the Somme.[33] Historian Tim Travers also has argued that it was Pétain who was afraid that the BEF would cause the break between the British and the French, rather than the other way around. "In fact, the whole situation was the reverse of what Haig actually believed or afterwards stated. Instead of Haig facing a crisis because of Pétain's proposed actions, in reality it was Haig who created a crisis for Pétain in the suggestion of a break with the French," Travers noted.[34] An order issued to Fayolle by Pétain on 26 March supports the conclusion that it was Haig who misunderstood the intention of the French commander in chief. Pétain wrote that the first mission of Army Group Reserve—which now included the British Fifth Army—was to close the road to Paris and to cover Amiens: "This present order which aims at the same time at the keeping of Amiens and the continuity of the Allied Front between the Somme and the Oise cancels all former instructions."[35]

On 26 March the German Second Army took Albert. Some German officers lost control of their troops advancing through the town, as the *Landser* stopped to loot the unimaginable foodstuffs and clothing items they found in the British supply depots.[36] By taking Albert the Germans cut the double-track Amiens–Albert–Arras line. Although the loss of that line did not reduce severely the Allies' capacity to shift forces from north to south, the lateral rail communications were reduced to a single track.

As the Eighteenth Army continued advancing, OHL believed that the BEF's entire right wing had been caved in. But German intelligence also reported large bodies of French troops moving north to Compiègne and beyond toward Noyon. With elements of six French divisions redeployed by 26 March, the French First Army was now starting to form an Anglo-French blocking force between the Germans and Amiens. Two more French divisions were in the process of moving up.[37]

Late that night OHL issued new orders for 27 March.[38] Although the Seventeenth and Eighteenth Armies on either flank of the Second Army were attacking in diverging directions, the main effort now shifted back to the Second, which was ordered to push south of the Somme and capture Amiens ("nimmt Amiens"). The war diary of Rupprecht's Army Group noted, "Everything depends on the breakthrough in the direction Doullens–Amiens." But as Kuhl later wrote, the new scheme of maneuver was "a renewed widening of the already widely stretched frame of operations," and "the offensive power of the armies soon proved insufficient for all these tasks."[39]

Some French writers have suggested that Ludendorff intended to drive on Paris, but as Major General Sir James Edmonds, editor of the British official history of the war, correctly pointed out, nothing in the German orders suggested such.[40] In his own memoirs, Ludendorff tried to justify his decisions by writing, "The original idea of the battle had to be modified and the main weight of the attack vigorously aimed in this direction [Amiens]. I still hoped we should get through to open warfare and followed this perspective in my instructions to the armies."[41] But by this stage of the battle the Germans were increasingly facing the harsh realities of "the tyranny of logistics." Their infantry units were too far ahead of their own artillery, and the artillery was outrunning its ammunition trains.

Despite the perceptions of both Haig and Foch, Pétain at that point had seventeen infantry and four cavalry divisions reinforcing the British.[42] But when the Allied leaders met at Doullens on 26 March, there was still panic in the air. Although it was difficult to see it at the time, the MICHAEL Offensive had already reached culmination. The conference, however, was still one of the pivotal events of the last year of the war, one that had a far greater impact on the final seven months than it did on the immediate situation. After years of debating about it, the Allies finally establish a unified command—of sorts.

French president Raymond Poincaré, Prime Minister Clemenceau, Armaments Minister Louis Loucheur, Foch, Pétain, Milner, Wilson, and Haig convened shortly before 1300 hours. Pershing was not there; it was a British and French conference only.[43] Just before the start Pétain nodded toward Haig and told Clemenceau, "There is a man who will be obliged to capitulate in the open field within a fortnight, and very lucky if we are not obliged to do the same." Pétain's pessimism shook the prime minister, who relayed the comment to President Poincaré. That comment probably cost Pétain any chance of becoming the Allied commander in chief.[44] Foch, meanwhile, exuded his characteristic confidence. When Pétain recommended the evacuation of Paris, Foch retorted, "Paris has nothing to do with it! Paris is a long way off! It is where we now stand that the enemy will be stopped!"[45]

Without consulting the Americans, Belgians, or Italians, Clemenceau and Milner agreed to give Foch the authority for "coordinating the action of the Allies' armies on the Western Front."[46] In earlier private meetings Haig had told Milner that he would support the appointment of Foch, and Pétain told Clemenceau the same thing.[47] Initially the idea was to give Foch the authority only to coordinate the operations of Allied forces in the vicinity of Amiens. Haig then recommended that Foch's authority extend to all British and French forces operating in France and Belgium.[48] The final protocol issued by the conference, which applied only to the French and British, read, "General Foch is charged by the British and French governments with coordinating the action of the Allied armies on the western front. To this end, he will come to an understanding with the commanders-in-chief, who are requested to furnish him with all necessary information."[49]

The conference lasted a little more than an hour and a half. Lloyd George, through his emissaries, had supported giving Foch coordinating control of the battle as a way of imposing greater operational restrictions on Haig. The true effect, however, was to reduce London's control over Haig, who actually had greater operational freedom of action once Foch finally was appointed Allied supreme commander.[50] As the conference broke up, Clemenceau said to Foch, "Well, you've got the place you so much wanted." Foch shot back, "To assume the direction of a battle which during the seven [sic] successive days had been largely lost could hardly be the object of any great desire on my part."[51] Foch also had the unenviable task of managing and synchronizing Pétain, Haig, and later Pershing, none of whom could be described as team players.

Foch, however, lost no time grasping the reins. Within a matter of hours, he bypassed both Haig and Pétain and started issuing orders to their subordinate commanders. After meeting with Gough, Foch sent a written order to the French Army Group Reserve ordering Fayolle to hold Amiens "at all costs."[52] He also sent direct orders to General Marie-Eugène Debeney's First Army not to halt at Montdidier and wait for the Germans but rather to move forward in support of the British on Gough's right flank. As Foch later wrote in his memoirs, "Instead of a British battle to cover the Channel ports and a French battle to cover Paris, we would fight an Anglo-French battle to cover Amiens, the connecting link between the two armies."[53] Ironically, Foch saw clearly what Ludendorff from the start had not seen and still did not see at this point.

Despite Foch's bypassing of the standard chain of command procedures, Pétain issued a strong supporting order to the French armies, stressing that the Germans had to be stopped from separating the British from the French: "He must be stopped! Your comrades are coming! United you will throw yourselves upon the invader. It is a great battle. Soldiers of the Marne, of the Yser, and Verdun, I appeal to you! The fate of France is in your hands."[54] Coming from Pétain it was an emotional statement.

Backing down somewhat from his staunch resistance to putting American units under foreign command, Pershing drove to Pétain's headquarters late on the night of 25 March to offer four American divisions to relieve French divisions currently deployed in the Champagne sector.[55] But although it did not yet affect him directly, when Foch the following day was appointed overall commander of the French and British forces, Pershing believed that the whole thing was an "accident." Pershing thought Foch to be cold and austere, "narrow, haughty, Napoleonic, and moderately conceited."[56]

By the end of the day on 26 March, all the rail lines east of the Amiens–Arras main line had been evacuated.[57] The British that night destroyed all the remaining Somme bridges. OHL ordered the Eighteenth Army to cross the Arve River on 27 March. Around dawn that morning Ludendorff issued supplemental orders directing the Eighteenth Army to pivot to the southwest, reach the line Montdidier–Lassigny, and form a blocking position there to hold the French. Ludendorff insisted that all had to be accomplished that day but that the Eighteenth Army was not to go beyond the objective line for any reason. Ludendorff then made a most uncharacteristic comment for a man who once said that he could not "abide the word operations." He said that the present situation was no longer the time for battles but for operations ("nicht mehr gekämpft, sondern operiert warden").[58]

Making good progress, the Eighteenth Army closed in on Montdidier about noon. The Germans overwhelmed the newly arriving French troops in that sector and started entering Montdidier that evening. In the process, they cut one of the major rail lines over which the French reserves were moving, and a temporary gap opened up between the French First and Third Armies. Immediately south of the Somme, the Second Army's left wing proved too weak to reach Amiens. Between 25 and 27 March alone, the frontage of the Second

Army had fanned out from twenty-five to almost forty kilometers, weakening its forward combat power proportionally.[59]

The Seventeenth Army made only minor progress on 27 March, advancing only one and a half kilometers after two days of fighting.[60] The Seventeenth Army's right wing, meanwhile, was making final preparations to launch the MARS attack the following day. On the afternoon of the twenty-seventh, Crown Prince Rupprecht asked OHL for three of its reserve divisions to support the MARS attack. OHL refused, and when Rupprecht learned that the three divisions he asked for had already been diverted to the sector south of the Somme, he blurted out in exasperation, "Now we have lost the war."[61]

Despite Foch's orders of the previous day, Pétain ordered Fayolle to give first priority to covering Noyon (and thus Paris) and second priority to covering Amiens.[62] Fayolle responded that Foch told him Amiens was the first priority and Noyon the second. But a gap of more than five miles had opened up between the French Third and First Armies while the gap between the French Third and British Fifth Armies continued to grow. Foch sent Pétain an order: "Not one more foot of French soil must be lost."[63]

Although Pershing the previous day had agreed to put American divisions into the line to relieve the French, the AEF commander still refused steadfastly to put individual American battalions into British divisions. In response, the British War Cabinet decided to send a strongly worded note from Lloyd George to President Wilson.[64] The Supreme War Council that day issued its Joint Note 18 recommending that the U.S. government should permit "temporary service of American units in Allied army corps and divisions" and that combat troops only should be sent across the Atlantic during the emergency.[65] Pershing objected to Joint Note 18. General Tasker Bliss, however, supported it, and Secretary of War Baker for once overruled Pershing and recommended that President Wilson approve the note.[66]

The Eighteenth Army accomplished the final rupture of the French and the British on 28 March. Although the Second Army was stalled to the east of Amiens, the Eighteenth Army had a clear path to it from the south. Only twelve miles to the west of Amiens lay the main rail line from Paris to Calais over which the French reserves were moving. But the Eighteenth Army was exhausted and its mobility all but expended. Later that day Wilhelm's Army Group reported to OHL, "The Eighteenth Army is not in a position to advance to Amiens."[67] Rupprecht and many other German generals considered 27–28 March the turning point of the offensive.[68] Seeing very clearly that the attack had reached culmination, Ludendorff's chief operations officer, Lieutenant Colonel Georg Wetzell, recommended that MICHAEL be broken off and the forces shifted north for a strong GEORG attack, not merely the reduced KLEIN-GEORG. Ludendorff refused, hoping that a successful MARS attack would breathe new life into MICHAEL.[69]

MARS, however, no longer made any operational sense. The operation's original purpose was to secure the Seventeenth Army's pivot to the northwest. But the Seventeenth Army's direction of advance already had been changed to the west. So just what was MARS supposed to accomplish? Ludendorff seemed to be trying to reach back to the original operational concept he abandoned late on 21 March. And with the major action now largely south of the Somme, any additional attack to the north would only further dissipate the force.

In this case, MARS was launched without sufficient forces for even a chance of success. The attack jumped off at 0730 hours. General Otto von Below attacked with inadequate artillery support, and his troops moved forward en masse, almost shoulder-to-shoulder. Even the German official history noted that the MARS attack was made with no hint of the infiltration tactics that had been so successful in the early stages of MICHAEL.[70] The British Third Army's well-prepared defenses stopped the Germans cold, and the British retained complete control of all the key terrain, including Vimy Ridge. When OHL canceled MARS that evening, Ludendorff started looking to the north. The originally planned Operation GEORG, or even the reduced KLEIN-GEORG, was no longer possible. Too many resources had been squandered on MICHAEL. The planners, therefore, were forced to improvise an even more reduced version, renamed GEORGETTE. The warning order went out for the right wing of the Sixth Army to be ready to launch GEORGETTE I in eight to ten days, depending on the weather. The Fourth Army on the Sixth Army's right would conduct with its left wing a supporting attack designated GEORGETTE II.[71]

That day Foch also issued his General Directive Number 1, stressing the necessity of maintaining the connection between the French and British armies.[72] Despite the failure of MARS, the danger to the British in the south was far from past. The BEF had already cleared its ordnance depot at Amiens and was developing plans to blow up the ammunition dumps on its southern line of communications.[73] Late that day Pershing visited Foch and offered to commit all the trained American divisions to the battle.[74] But what

Foch wanted was U.S. troops sent to France to be piecemealed out, while Pershing was still thinking in terms of complete divisions, with American commanders.

On the morning of 29 March, Ludendorff ordered the Seventeenth Army to go over to the defensive.[75] The Eighteenth Army was still making limited progress in the south, and Ludendorff kept shifting more forces to it. The Germans now held Bapaume, Albert, Péronne, Nesle, Ham, Chauny, Noyon, Roye, and Montdidier. All the British Fifth and Third Army's forward railheads had been overrun. British GHQ reacted by reducing tonnage at the southern ports of Le Havre and Rouen by 60 percent and increasing Calais by the same amount.[76]

Foch and Haig met at Abbeville late that morning. Foch assured Haig that everything was being done to expedite the arrival of French divisions to link with the British to cover Amiens.[77] Five more fresh divisions had reached the French First Army, which already had relieved in place the entire British XVIII Corps.[78] That allowed Haig to reconstitute his reserves and reorganize the Fifth Army without pulling it completely out of the line. Later that evening Haig informed Gough that he would be relieved as commander of the Fifth Army. His replacement was General Sir Henry Rawlinson, who himself would be replaced as British permanent military representative to the Supreme War Council by Major General Charles Sackville-West, a close ally of Henry Wilson. Never having commanded above the brigade level, Sackville-West's appointment was just another indicator of the declining influence of the PMRs. Tasker Bliss was now the only PMR with any real gravitas. Sackville-West is not even mentioned in Haig's published diary or in the five 1918 volumes of the British official history.

Gough always believed that the Fifth Army had been in an impossible position at the start of the battle and that he was made the after-the-fact scapegoat. Haig offered to resign in support of Gough, but the resignation was not accepted. When Gough returned to London, he requested a formal inquiry to clear his name but never got one.[79] Many at the time and even to this day believe the British government's treatment of Gough was shabby at best. Even Lieutenant General Hunter Liggett, who at the end of the war was the commander of the U.S. First Army, said, "Why the gallant and able Gough was ever blamed, I do not yet understand. He was not so blamed by his chief, but by the civil authorities, who kept an army in England to repel a mythical invasion."[80]

The German attacks resumed on 30 March, but they generally stalled all along the line. That evening OHL sent Rupprecht's Army Group a warning order for the execution of GEORGETTE. OHL also started shifting the necessary heavy artillery northward.[81] Nonetheless, late that night Ludendorff ordered the Second Army to continue attacking along its whole front on the thirty-first. The Second Army protested vigorously that it no longer had the combat power and required adequate preparation time and additional resources to keep attacking. Ludendorff relented and postponed the attack.[82]

Haig met with Clemenceau that day in Dury. According to Haig, Clemenceau told him that he had no doubts that he (Haig) would cooperate loyally with Foch. Rather, the French prime minister was more worried about Pétain and Foch squabbling. As Haig recorded in his diary, Clemenceau said, "Pétain is a very nervous man and may not carry out all he has promised."[83] On the other side of the Atlantic, meanwhile, Secretary of War Baker agreed that Pershing should act under the operational direction of Foch, just as Pétain and Haig were doing. Baker also recommended to President Wilson that the United States should support the appointment of a "Commander-in-Chief of the Allied Armies."[84]

Ludendorff was running out of viable options for continuing offensive pressure on the Allies. He could terminate MICHAEL immediately and start the preparations for another major attack somewhere else. An expanded version of the reworked GEORGETTE plan was the best possibility. His only other option was to resume MICHAEL after committing fresh reinforcements and giving the troops already in the line a couple days of rest. On the morning of 31 March, OHL ordered all units to transition temporarily to the defensive and be prepared to resume MICHAEL on 4 April.[85] As OHL assessed the situation, "The English Army at the moment has no operational capability. The French can mount a 20 to 30 division attack against the southern wing of the Eighteenth Army."[86]

Ludendorff met in St. Quentin on 1 April with the chiefs of staff of the Eighteenth and Second Armies and both army groups. He was still convinced that the British and French had been split, the British had been all but defeated, and Operation GEORGETTE would finish the BEF off.[87] Later that day OHL issued the orders for MICHAEL to resume south of the Somme toward Amiens on 4 April. On 7 or 8 April the Sixth Army would then launch GEORGETTE against the BEF in Flanders.[88]

The Allies, however, had almost completely contained the Eighteenth Army's penetration. The French had thirty-three divisions in front of Hutier, and they had effected a solid linkup with the British Fourth Army—as the Fifth Army had been redesignated. The Germans resumed attacking on 4 April but accomplished almost nothing. That day elements of the Second Army reached the outskirts of the village of Villers-Bretonneux, only ten miles east of Amiens. They were stopped and driven slightly back by a combined British-Australian counterattack. On the evening of 5 April Ludendorff sent out a message: "The supply situation does not allow the continuation of the attack by the Second and Eighteenth Armies. The attack is henceforth temporarily discontinued."[89]

Although neither the Eighteenth nor the Second Army managed to reach Amiens, the Second Army did get close enough to shell the rail center with 150mm guns.[90] The fire did not halt the Allied rail operations through that vital node, but it did cause significant disruption. The BEF's major forward marshaling and switching yards remained under artillery and air interdiction until the summer, and most rail traffic had to be routed through the much lower capacity station at Beauvais.[91] But the Germans never fully exploited that advantage. On 7 April the Second Army sent OHL a telegram requesting the assignment of a super-heavy 280mm battery specifically to hammer the rail facilities around Amiens.[92] The following day OHL responded with a telegram signed by Ludendorff, curtly denying the request, stating those guns were needed elsewhere.[93] Ludendorff still had not fully grasped the significance of Amiens as an operational objective.

On 1 April Foch issued his "Instructions with the Object of Assuring Cooperation Between the British and French Air Services." Particularly emphasizing coordinated attacks on key German rail targets, the man who once said that the military value of aviation was "zero" now wrote, "The essential condition of success is the concentration of every resource of the British and French bombing formations on such few of the most important of the enemy's railway junctions as it may be possible to put out action with certainty, and to keep out of action." The instruction included specific target lists. As the British official history noted, the lists showed "a strategic mind surveying the whole battlefield, irrespective of boundaries."[94]

That same day Foch also wrote to Clemenceau, complaining that he still did not have sufficient operational authority to fight the battle. He proposed that his mandate be expanded from *coordinating* the actions of the Allied armies

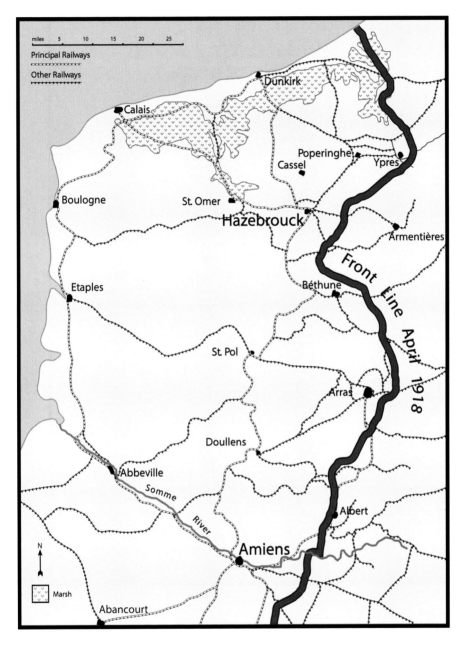

MAP 1 British Rail Network (March–April 1918)

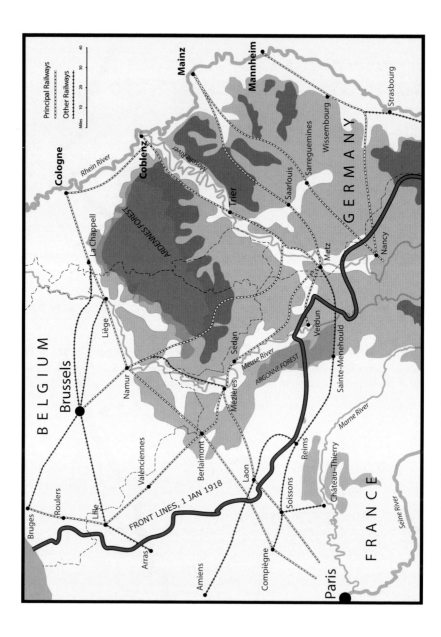

MAP 2 German Rail Network (1918)

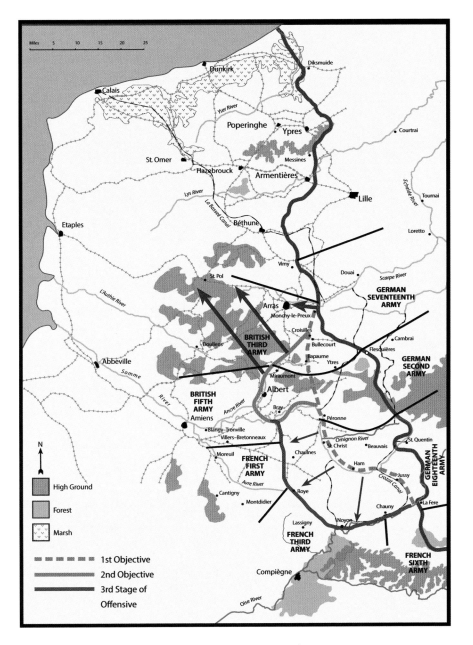

MAP 3 Operation MICHAEL Plan (10 March 1918)

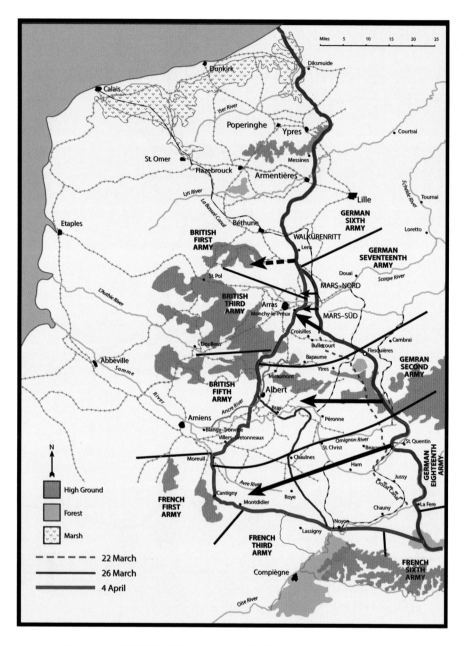

MAP 4 Operation MICHAEL Execution (21 March–5 April 1918)

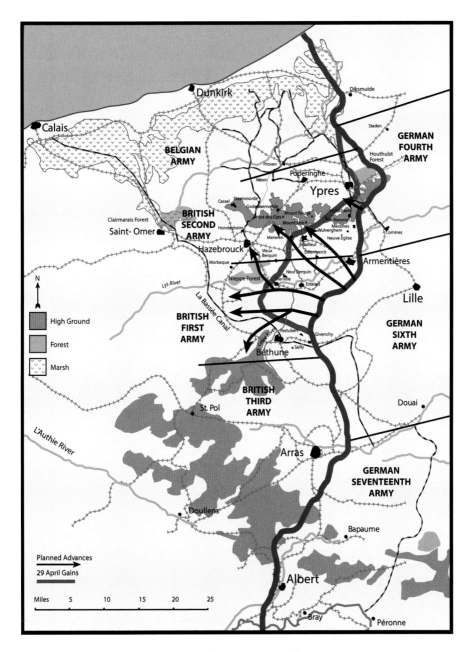

MAP 5 Operation GEORGETTE (9–29 April 1918)

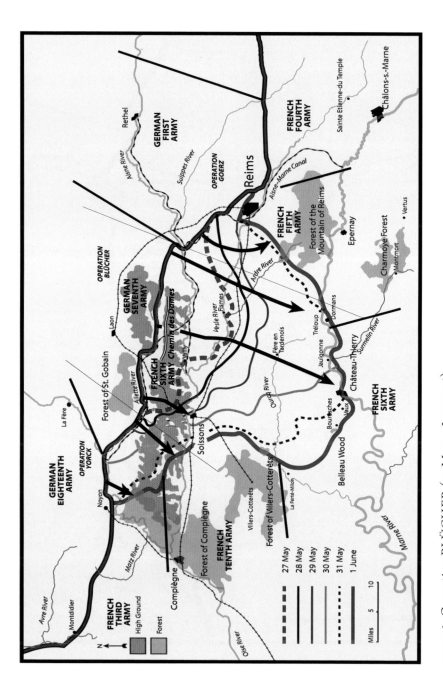

MAP 6 Operation BLÜCHER (27 May–5 June 1918)

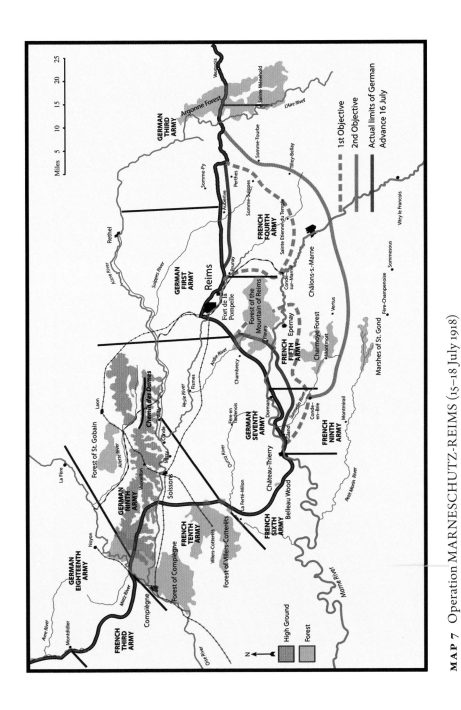

MAP 7 Operation MARNESCHUTZ-REIMS (15–18 July 1918)

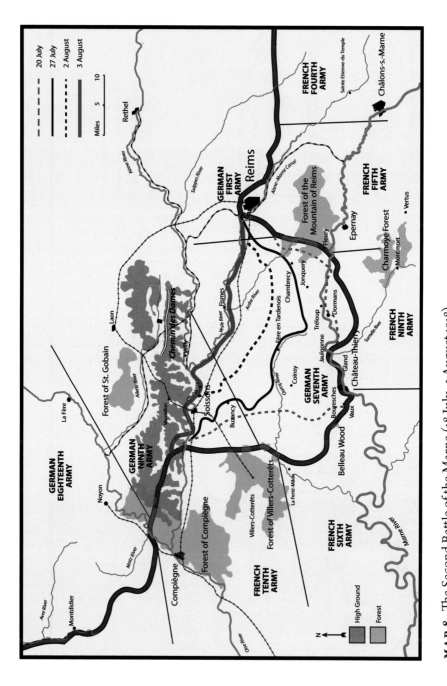

MAP 8 The Second Battle of the Marne (18 July–5 August 1918)

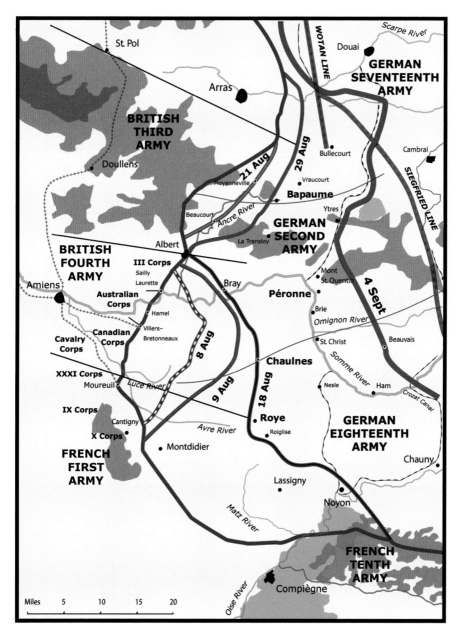

MAP 9 Battle of Amiens (8–14 August 1918)

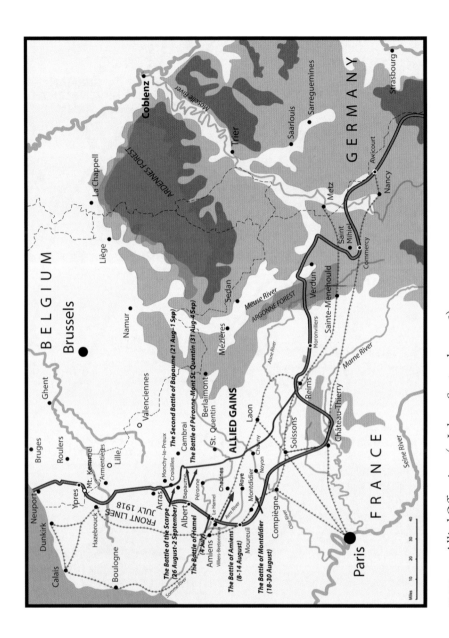

MAP 10 Allied Offensives (4 July–9 September 1918)

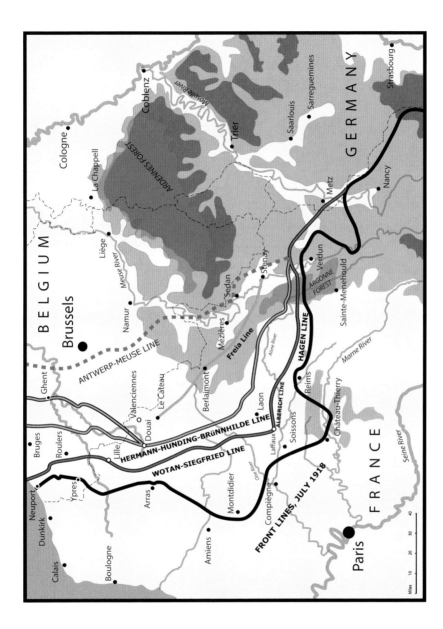

MAP 11 German Defensive Lines (1918)

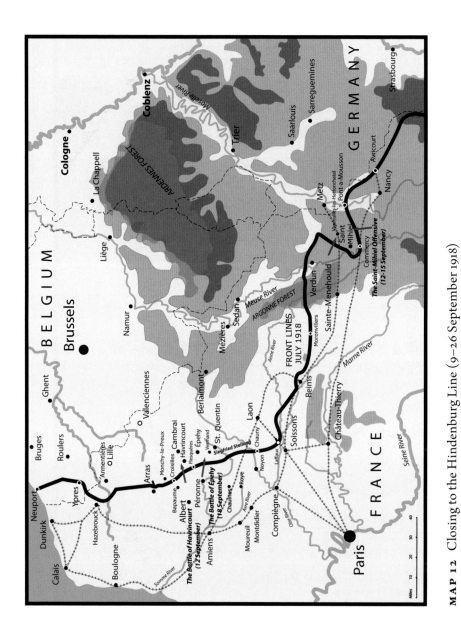

MAP 12 Closing to the Hindenburg Line (9–26 September 1918)

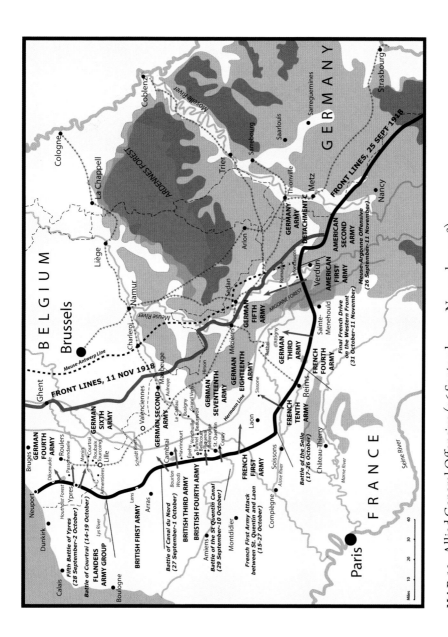

MAP 13 Allied General Offensive (26 September–11 November 1918)

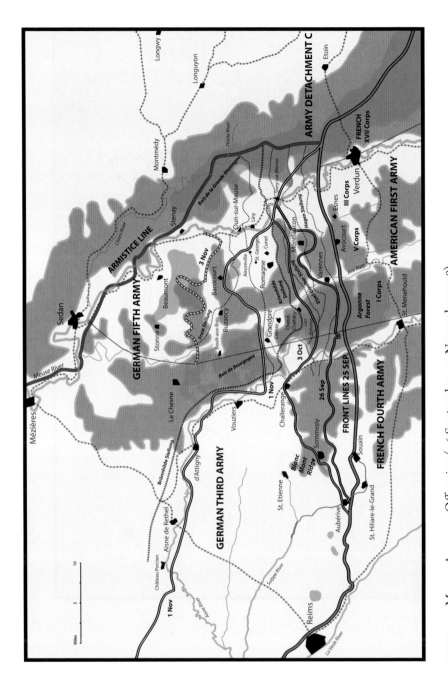

MAP 14 Meuse-Argonne Offensive (26 September–11 November 1918)

Field Marshal Paul von Hindenburg, chief of the Prussian
General Staff and commander of the German Field Army.

Photograph by Nicola Perscheid, 1914.

6165

General of Infantry Erich Ludendorff, first quartermaster general of the German army.

Photograph via George Grantham Bain Collection, Library of Congress Prints and Photographs Division [LC-B2- 5240-7].

Marshal of France Ferdinand Foch, Allied supreme commander.
Photograph by Melcy, 1921.

Marshal of France Philippe Pétain, commander in chief of the
French Armies of the North and Northeast.

Portrait by Marcel Baschet, 1926.

Field Marshal Sir Douglas Haig, commander in chief
of the British Expeditionary Force.

Photograph by Elliot and Fry, 1917.

General of the Armies John J. Pershing, commander in chief
of the American Expeditionary Force.

Photograph via Library of Congress Prints and Photographs Division [LC-USZ62-13554].

Major General Fritz von Lossberg, chief of staff of four different field armies and two army groups during the war. Like General Hermann von Kuhl, he was one of Ludendorff's critics and one of his closest advisers.

By Wkloot (own work) [CC BY-SA 4.0 via Wikimedia Commons].

General of Infantry Hermann von Kuhl *(third from the left)*, pictured here earlier in the war with the First Army staff of Colonel General Alexander von Kluck *(fifth from the left)*.

Photograph via hr.wikipedia.org.

General of Division Charles Mangin, arguably France's best fighting general.

Photograph via Agence de presse Meurisse, 1923.

General Sir William Robertson, chief of the Imperial General Staff and Haig's closest military ally in London.

Photograph by Elliot and Fry, 1917.

Field Marshal Sir Henry Wilson, Robertson's successor as chief of the Imperial General Staff and one of Haig's most severe critics.

Photograph via George Grantham Bain Collection, Library of Congress Prints and Photographs Division [LC-B2- 4426-3].

General Peyton C. March, chief of staff of the U.S. Army,
who clashed frequently with Pershing.

Photograph by Harris & Ewing, via the Harris & Ewing Collection, Library of Congress Prints and Photographs Division [LC-H25- 2874-DK].

General Tasker H. Bliss, former chief of staff of the U.S. Army and American permanent military representative to the Allied Supreme War Council. Bliss generally supported Pershing, although at times reluctantly.

Photograph by Harris & Ewing, via the Harris & Ewing Collection, Library of Congress Prints and Photographs Division [LC-USZ62-36188].

Lieutenant General Hunter Liggett, who succeeded Pershing as commanding general of the U.S. First Army. Liggett arguably was America's best senior
battlefield commander.

Photograph via Library of Congress Prints and Photographs Division [LC-F81- 1884].

Facing, Foch's tomb, Hôtel National des Invalides, Paris.

Photograph by Marlies Schweigler.

Pétain's tomb, Ile d'Yeu, France.

Photograph by Mathardy via Wikimedia Commons.

to *directing* them.[95] Two days later Clemenceau, Foch, Pétain, Bliss, Pershing, Lloyd George, Wilson, and Haig met at Beauvais to consider the matter. Haig and Pétain were less than enthusiastic. Pershing, apparently changing his attitude toward Foch, supported the expansion of his operational authority.[96] The conference participants finally agreed: "General Foch is charged by the British, French, and American governments with the coordination of the action of the Allied armies on the Western Front. To this end all powers necessary to secure effective realization are conferred on him. The British, French, and American governments for this purpose entrust to General Foch the strategic direction of military operations." The final communiqué also stated that each national commander in chief retained full tactical control of his forces and had the right of appeal to his respective government in case he thought the safety of his army was being put at risk by any of Foch's orders.[97] Belgian king Albert I, however, flatly refused to recognize Foch's authority over Belgian forces. Foch was still not fully and officially the Allied supreme commander, but he was the closest thing to it.

Immediately after the conference broke up, Foch issued his General Directive Number 2 on the strategic direction of Allied military operations.[98] Regardless of what the Germans did, Foch wanted to counterattack south of the Somme as soon as possible "in order to drive the enemy away from the Paris–Amiens railway and the Amiens rail center, both essential for our communications supply."[99] Foch directed Pétain to prepare to attack in the Montdidier sector, and he wanted Haig to counterattack in the Somme sector while simultaneously defending north to Arras. Those plans came to nothing six days later when Ludendorff launched Operation GEORGETTE.

The MICHAEL Offensive was over. Tactically, the results were spectacular—far beyond anything that had been achieved to date in World War I. On the first day of the attack alone, the Germans had taken as much territory as the British and French combined had needed 140 days to wrest from the Germans in 1916. But operationally, MICHAEL was a failure, and even worse, it was a strategic failure. The Germans lost 239,800 troops that were almost impossible to replace. Allied casualties totaled 254,739, but the Americans put 329,005 soldiers into France in March 1918 alone. Germany no longer had any possibility of achieving a battlefield victory. The best the Germans could accomplish was a battlefield stalemate, from which some sort of political compromise might have been worked. As General Max Hoffmann, who had been Ludendorff's brilliant operations officer on the Eastern Front, summed up the operational-strategic situation: "At the moment when OHL saw that they could not get Amiens, that they had not been able to break through the enemy's front, they ought to have realized that a decisive victory on the Western Front was no longer to be expected." And: "On the very day which OHL gave the order to cease the attack on Amiens, it was their duty to apprise the government that there was no longer any prospect of finishing the war with a decisive victory on the Western Front."[100]

Within the first couple of days of the offensive, Hindenburg, Ludendorff, and many other senior German commanders knew it was failing. That, however, did not stop the kaiser from declaring a magnificent victory early on and lavishly handing out awards and decorations. On 24 March, the kaiser personally decorated Ludendorff with the Grand Cross of the Iron Cross, awarded only five times between 1914 and 1918. The following day Hindenburg received the special Blücher Star of the Iron Cross. The only other recipient ever had been the legendary Prussian field marshal Gebhard von Blücher, who had helped defeat Napoleon at Waterloo. On 26 March the artillery expert Bruchmüller received from the kaiser the Pour le Mérite with Oak Leaves (Pour le Mérite mit Eichenlaub), awarded only 122 times during the Great War.[101] Ironically, none of these officers seemed to hesitate accepting decorations for winning a battle they knew they were in the process of losing.

It is impossible to undervalue the importance of the French reinforcements in securing and stabilizing the entire British southern flank. Despite what many British commanders at the time considered as a far too slow and far too disordered response, it was an essential factor in the BEF's survival. By the end of Operation MICHAEL, the BEF had committed forty-six divisions. The French, meanwhile, had redeployed thirty-eight infantry and six cavalry divisions north of the Oise, leaving them with only sixty divisions between the Oise and Alsace.[102] The French reinforcements included 1,344 guns and seven hundred aircraft.[103] Some critics and historians have argued that the French response would have been quicker and more effective if the Allies had managed to form a general reserve prior to the start of the battle. But as Robert Doughty has noted, "Petain's personal control over French Reserves and his ability to employ them quickly provided the Allies the edge they needed during the first German attack. In fact, there is no evidence to suggest that an allied general reserve under Foch's control would have arrived more quickly or been more effective."[104]

The appointment of Foch had a decisive impact on the remaining seven months of the war but somewhat less of an influence on the outcome of the immediate March battle. The British official history does state, "The appointment of General Foch to co-ordinate and control the Allied efforts prevented the disaster of the separation of the two Armies."[105] By the time the Allied leaders met at Doullens on 26 March, however, MICHAEL had culminated. Ludendorff lost that battle almost single-handedly.[106]

- He focused exclusively on tactics with almost no operational concept behind MICHAEL.
- He failed to weigh the main effort by allocating too many divisions and too much artillery to the Eighteenth Army's tertiary attack.
- He violated the principle of unity of command by putting two army groups over three field armies.
- Without having a sufficiently superior force ratio, he tried to conduct a force-on-force battle.
- He ignored the critical vulnerability of the BEF's fragile logistics network, designating the Amiens rail center as an objective only as an afterthought.
- He more than once tried to change the scheme of maneuver during the course of the action, when such shifts are difficult if not impossible with very large-scale operations.
- As the battle progressed, his forces diverged rather than converged.

Ludendorff would make many of the same mistakes again during the four subsequent German offensives during the spring of 1918, but from here on he would be dealing with Foch, who would miss no opportunities to exploit those mistakes.

GEORGETTE: 9–29 APRIL 1918

The final plan for Operation GEORGETTE was based on far fewer forces than the original GEORG plan, or even the reduced KLEIN-GEORG. Operation MICHAEL had depleted too many German divisions. The March offensive also extended the German front line by thirty-three miles, which required additional forces to man and defend. Originally the concept of the GEORG plan was a frontal attack to fix the British First Army, followed by converging attacks against the northernmost British Second Army. The line of the Flanders

Hills from Kemmel to Godewaersvelde was the key terrain in an otherwise flat plain. By taking that high ground, the Germans would force the British to evacuate the Ypres salient. The line of hills ran from the low Passchendaele Ridge south-southwest to the Messines Ridge and then swung almost straight west through a line of relatively high peaks. Mont Kemmel (156 meters) was the eastern anchor of the line, and Mont des Cats (158 meters) near Godewaersvelde was the western end. Farther to the west and separated from the Cats–Kemmel ridge by a stretch of flat ground, Mont Cassel (158 meters) was the last piece of high ground before the coast. Dunkirk could be observed directly from Mont Cassel, which was the ultimate objective of the original GEORG plan.[107] But the Germans no longer had the necessary forces for an operation on that scale.

On 3 April, Ludendorff met in Tournai with Kuhl and the chiefs of staff of the Fourth and Sixth Armies to finalize the GEORGETTE plan. The main effort would now be made by the Sixth Army against the sector from Givenchy to Fromelles, thrusting northwest toward Hazebrouck. On the first day, the attackers had to reach and cross the Lys River between Estaires and Armentières, forcing the British back behind the river. The Fourth Army would launch a supporting attack on the Sixth Army's right wing. Both arms of the pincers had to be deeply echeloned; "objectives for follow-on attack [would] depend on the situation."[108]

Ludendorff intended for the right wing of the Sixth Army and the left wing of the Fourth Army to attack on 9 April simultaneously, but Sixth Army chief of staff Colonel Fritz von Lossberg pointed out that the Germans had only enough heavy artillery to support one attack at a time. The Sixth Army would have to attack on 9 April and the Fourth Army the next day, after the guns were shifted north. The Sixth Army deployed eighteen divisions in three echelons, along a twenty-seven-kilometer front, and the Fourth Army had eight divisions on a seventeen-kilometer front. The original GEORG plan had been based on fifty-five divisions and the reduced KLEIN-GEORG on thirty-five, but now GEORGETTE had only twenty-six. The attackers would have a force superiority ratio of only 2.2:1 over the defenders.

Nonetheless, Ludendorff ensured that he would get the most out of the artillery by seconding Bruchmüller and his entire Eighteenth Army artillery staff to the Sixth Army to take charge of the fire planning. Bruchmüller was ordered to report directly to Ludendorff at OHL, effectively bypassing the army and army group commanders.[109] This was yet another example of Ludendorff's tendency to micromanage.

The British chief of the Imperial General Staff, General Sir Henry Wilson, recognized the most dangerous German course of action for the British. In a telegram to Foch he wrote that his estimate of the German course of action would be to "mass an attack of 40 to 50 divisions against the British between Albert and the La Bassée Canal. If the enemy does this and at the same time is prepared to give up ground in front of a French attack, I am quite certain the British line will not be able to sustain such an attack without the direct assistance of French divisions, or unless the French take over much more of the British line to enable Field-Marshal Haig to have many more troops than he now has in reserve."[110]

Haig, for once, agreed with Wilson, thinking specifically that the German attack would come against the Vimy Ridge sector. Haig asked Foch to relieve four British divisions south of the Somme, but the French declined to take over any more of the British line.[111] French reserves were west of Amiens, but Haig wanted them moved farther north, to the vicinity of St. Pol. Foch agreed with the British assessment that the next major German attack would come between the Somme and La Bassée. To counter that threat, however, he ordered the preparation of an attack by the French First and British Fourth Armies between the Avre and the Somme to drive the Germans back from the Paris–Amiens rail line. His two primary objectives at this point were to strengthen the connection between the British and the French and to "cover Amiens."[112]

Haig reorganized his GHQ reserve into two groups: one consisting of eight divisions (five fresh) between the Ancre and Doullens, and one of seven divisions (two fresh) northwest of Arras. The British Second Army, under Plumer, had five divisions on line and one in reserve. The First Army on its right had four divisions on line and two in reserve. One of those divisions in the line, however, was the very weak and unreliable Portuguese Division. Pétain, meanwhile, started shifting his Tenth Army from the south to the west of Amiens.[113]

Haig visited the First Army's headquarters on 8 April. General Sir Henry Horne told him that all the intelligence indicators pointed to the First Army being attacked the next day. Haig then asked Foch for French forces to relieve the six British divisions in the Ypres sector, where the British Second Army linked in with the Belgian army, so that Haig could establish an adequate reserve behind his left flank.[114] Foch's chief of staff, Maxime Weygand, later told Haig's staff that it could not be done. Foch still insisted on launching his own attack on 12 April.[115] The Germans struck first.

On 9 April, the Sixth Army attacked from Givenchy to Fromelles. The German artillery opened up at 0415 hours, firing a total of 1.4 million artillery rounds that first day.[116] At 0845 hours the German infantry moved forward, once again screened by heavy fog. In the center of the British line the weak Portuguese Division collapsed almost immediately. By the end of the day the Germans had crossed the Lys, pushing to a penetration depth of six miles. As on 21 March, the initial results looked spectacular, but once again the Germans failed to achieve all their first-day objectives. It proved very difficult to move the supporting artillery forward, and on the German left wing the stubborn resistance of the British 55th Division held the Germans fast in front of Festubert and Givenchy.[117]

As soon as the attack started, Haig ordered the last divisions he dared to withdraw from Picardy to move north. Haig also sent Foch a demand for French support. Believing that the German attack in the British sector was a preliminary for an attack between Arras and the Somme, Foch told Haig that he would have to deal with the attack in Flanders on his own. Foch did, however, order Pétain to start shifting the French Tenth and Fifth Armies farther north, but at that point he did not anticipate committing French reserves to the fighting in Flanders.[118]

The Fourth Army started its one-and-a-half-hour artillery preparation at 0245 hours on 10 April, followed directly by the infantry assault. The Sixth Army resumed the attack at 0600 hours. That afternoon British troops started to evacuate Armentières. By end of the second day the Sixth Army had fought its way over almost the entire line of the Lys. The British, however, continued to hold out stubbornly at Festubert and Givenchy.[119]

That morning in Paris, Henry Wilson warned Clemenceau of the serious threat to the Channel ports and the consequences of their loss. Although Foch at that point still thought the attack in Flanders was a diversion, he nonetheless ordered the French Tenth and Fifth Armies to continue shifting toward the north. He also ordered Pétain to move a French division to Dunkirk by rail. In his memoirs Foch did note, "Our available railway lines had been reduced by the attack of March 21st, and the difficulty of moving troops was considerably increased."[120]

That same day Foch sent Haig instructions on the further conduct of the battle: "Moreover, it remains understood that the absolute preservation of the present front in Flanders is as compulsory as in the Arras region: that any voluntary evacuation, such as that of the Passchendaele Ridge, can only be interpreted by the enemy as a sign of weakness as an incentive for an offensive, and is therefore not to be carried out without being compelled to such action by a direct enemy attack."[121] The Passchendaele Ridge, of course, was ground that the British had shed untold gallons of blood to take the previous autumn.

Haig's chief of staff, Lieutenant General Sir Herbert Lawrence, reported back to Foch that the British First and Second Armies had been ordered to hold their present lines at all costs and that the BEF was preparing to shift to the north forces from the Fourth Army's reserve.[122] Late that night Foch and Weygand met with Haig at BEF headquarters. Foch now concurred that the attack against the BEF was the German main effort, and he agreed to move more French reinforcements to the north.[123]

On the third day of the attack the Germans committed seven more divisions to GEORGETTE, as the Sixth Army ordered two of its corps to capture the high ground at Bailleul, Méteren, and Strazeele. The correlation of forces was now thirty-one divisions to thirteen in Germany's favor, but ten of the German divisions had fought in MICHAEL. The British continued to hold fast on the German left wing. As Ludendorff laconically noted in his memoirs, "On the left, at Givenchy and Festubert, we were held up. The result was not satisfactory."[124]

By the end of the third day the Germans were close to the edge of the Nieppe Forest, less than ten miles from the crucial British rail junction of Hazebrouck. They had advanced almost nine miles since the start of the operation, and they were close to splitting the British First and Second Armies. Haig sent Foch a message reporting the criticality of the situation and stressing that he had to have at least four French divisions between St. Omer and Dunkirk. Foch remained resolute in his refusal to take over any of the British front or to provide the divisions to establish and man a defensive line in front of Hazebrouck.[125] Contrary to the "noria" method that Pétain had used so effectively at Verdun to rotate divisions in and out of the battle quickly, Foch believed that relieving units in contact while the battle was in progress would "immobilize both the relieving troops and those relieved during the time required for the operation."[126] But in 1916 Pétain had proved such a system to be quite feasible. Nonetheless, the British official history grudgingly noted, "It will probably be accepted by readers of the story of the battle as it proceeds that General Foch was right in assuming that the British would manage somehow or other to hold on and bring the Germans to a halt in their fierce assault against the sector covering the Channel ports, which meant so little to the French but were vital to the British."[127]

By 11 April the Germans had committed an additional seven divisions to GEORGETTE, and the correlation of forces now stood at thirty-one German to thirteen Allied. That day Haig issued his famous "Backs to the Wall" message to the BEF: "There is no other course open to us but to fight it out. Every position must be held to the last man: there must be no retirement. With our backs to the wall and believing in the justice of our cause, each one of us must fight on to the end."[128] After Haig's reputation went into eclipse in the early 1930s, that message often became an object of ridicule as unnecessarily melodramatic and a prime example of Haig's incompetent generalship. Ironically, it bears a remarkable resemblance to another commander's message that is iconic in British history. During the crisis at Waterloo, at approximately 1730 hours on 18 June 1815, the Duke of Wellington sent a reply to one of his generals who requested reinforcements: "Tell him what he wishes is impossible. He and I and every Englishman in the field must die on the spot which we now occupy."[129] Haig's message that day is also very similar to the emotional appeal issued to the French troops by Pétain on 27 March.

By 12 April the Germans were less than five miles from Hazebrouck and on the verge of capturing that vital rail center. On the flanks, however, the Sixth Army still had not taken all of its assigned objectives from 11 April. To correct that situation, Ludendorff at midday ordered a maximum push against Bailleul by the combined inner wings of the Fourth and Sixth Armies.[130] That, however, shifted the main effort more to the north, away from Hazebrouck and toward Mont Kemmel. That was the turning point of the battle, as once again Ludendorff's tactical opportunism caused him to lose the focus on the true operational objective.

At noon on 12 April, Haig shifted to the south the boundary between Plumer's Second Army and Horne's First Army. That simplified the command lines by giving the very competent Plumer tactical control of almost the entire battle sector. Foch, meanwhile, moved to establish a Franco-Belgian reserve groupment behind the British First Army but under the operational control of Plumer. Foch sent a telegram to the Belgians saying that a unified command in the north was essential to stopping the Germans and requesting that all available Belgian units be put under Plumer.[131] Foch also issued a directive for the further conduct of the defensive battle, which called for establishing two converging lines: one in the south from Béthune to St. Omer, facing the northeast, and one in the north from Mont Kemmel to Cassel, facing the south. Between these two solid converging lines Foch ordered a series of successive lines facing east to slow down and eventually stop the German advance.[132]

The most agonizing decision that Haig and Plumer made on 12 April was to pull back the Second Army's line north of Ypres in order to free up forces for the fight in the Lys valley. That meant the BEF would have to give up almost all the territory won at the cost of almost a quarter of a million casualties during the previous year's Passchendaele Offensive.[133] But the withdrawal also forestalled an attack by the German Fourth Army. As historian Basil Liddell Hart later wrote, "[Haig's] timely withdrawal of his line in the Ypres salient largely nullified the German blow planned at this point, and he would have made other elastic withdrawals but for Foch's opposition."[134]

The four-division German attack against the Nieppe Forest on 13 April made little progress. The Sixth Army also failed to take Bailleul on its right and Festubert and Givenchy on its left. Foch, meanwhile, ordered the defense of Hazebrouck to be conducted "as near as possible to the eastern edge of the Nieppe Forest."[135] The Australian 1st Division arrived in front of Hazebrouck and joined with the British 4th Guards Brigade to form a solid barrier in front of the vital rail center. Nonetheless, the German main effort had already shifted to the Mont Kemmel–Mont des Cats ridge.

By 14 April the German offensive was becoming one of diminishing returns. Ludendorff, however, ordered all committed units to keep pushing forward. The Germans still failed to take Festubert and Givenchy. Later that day the Sixth Army reported to OHL that its attack was stalling and the troops were exhausted. The British, meanwhile, remained highly anxious about the threat to the Channel ports. The Admiralty was especially concerned about the possibility of losing Calais and Boulogne. Because the potential substitute ports of Dieppe, Le Havre, Rouen, and Cherbourg were farther away from the British coast, they were out of range for smaller ships. Using larger ships would slow down the flow of supplies.[136]

Haig and Foch met at Abbeville, where the BEF commander demanded that the French Tenth Army be deployed to Flanders to support the British forces under attack and the French Fifth Army also be deployed northward to reinforce the British between the Somme and Arras. Foch refused point-blank to order a relief in place in the middle of a battle, but he did agree to shift the Tenth Army to Flanders and remove it from Pétain's operational control.[137] Once again, the British official history endorsed Foch's decision: "Though General Foch's decision cost the British Army many lives, and its leaders many anxious hours, in the circumstances one cannot but admire his judgment of the situation and his resistance to the very heavy pressure put upon him."[138]

Earlier that day Foch sent a memo to Clemenceau, requesting that based on the agreement at the Beauvais Conference he officially be given the title "Commander-in-Chief of the Allied Armies."[139] Clemenceau sent Lloyd George a telegram recommending support for Foch. At the end of the day Lloyd George responded that the British government had no objections to Foch formally assuming the title. After Tasker Bliss concurred for the Americans, the announcement was made that evening.[140] After almost four years at war, the Allies finally had an undisputed single commander to make all the operational decisions on the Western Front.

On 15 April Kuhl complained in his diary that Ludendorff was bypassing the army group headquarters and issuing orders directly to the army commanders. In order to keep abreast of the tactical situation, the army group continually had to ask the armies what specific orders they had been issued by OHL.[141] That same day the French Tenth Army's four divisions, including the artillery and aviation units, were now north of the Somme. By the following day, Foch finally came to the conclusion that the situation in Flanders was more dangerous than he had estimated.[142] That morning he ordered Pétain to alert another division to move north to Flanders and ordered the Tenth Army to send its lead division to Flanders by trucks. Later that afternoon Foch visited the Second Army's sector and promised Plumer a French division. Chief of the Imperial General Staff Wilson later criticized Foch's hands-on approach to command, complaining to Weygand that Foch should not talk directly to the British commanders without clearing it with Haig first. Haig, however, had given Foch permission to do so on 26 March.[143]

On the morning of 17 April, the German Fourth Army attacked the Belgians north of Ypres. Not only did the Belgians stand firm, but they also launched a series of unexpectedly fierce counterattacks.[144] That night Ludendorff, Kuhl, and Lossberg discussed the situation in a running series of phone conversations between 1930 hours and midnight. Lossberg reported that the Fourth Army's situation was very bad and that its left wing was in an especially poor tactical position. He recommended the immediate termination of all efforts to take Mont Kemmel and Mont Noir by direct attack on a broad front.[145]

Even though the German attack had every appearance of stalling, Foch was annoyed that the British were still making contingency plans to destroy and evacuate the port of Dunkirk.[146] When Foch and Wilson met that day, the Allied supreme commander told the British chief of the Imperial General Staff that he refused to authorize a pullback in Flanders that would cover Calais but abandon Dunkirk.[147] Foch did, however, finally order the six French divisions of the newly formed Army Detachment of the North to move into the line along a seven-mile sector south of the Flanders Hills.[148] At end of that day, Foch left Flanders and did not return until the twenty-seventh. Wilson, meanwhile, told Haig that the BEF would most likely lose Dunkirk.[149]

Morale steadily declined as the German troops continued attacking. On 18 April, Lieutenant Colonel Albrecht von Thaer, a General Staff officer at OHL, noted in his diary, "The moral influence on the troops has passed to the company commanders and the troop leaders."[150] What he meant was that the junior officers on the line were all that was holding the German army together. The German attack again failed to make any progress that day. Both Mont Kemmel on the right and Festubert and Givenchy on the left held out.

As additional French forces continued to move toward Flanders, the French Army Detachment of the North and Tenth Army now had a combined total of nine infantry and three cavalry divisions north of the Somme. Four of the Army Detachment of the North's divisions assumed control of the sector around Mont Kemmel. Foch sent Haig a message stating his intention of maintaining a reserve of fifteen French divisions behind the British, but he could do so only if Haig would agree to rotate tired British divisions to quiet sectors in the south to relieve French divisions in the line. Haig agreed on the condition that any such reassignments would not be permanent.[151] On 23 April, five bloodied British divisions were withdrawn from the line and sent south to the quiet sector along the Chemin des Dames, where they formed the British IX Corps under the operational control of General Denis Duchêne's Sixth Army.

On 19 April, Rupprecht's Army Group sent OHL a message saying that GEORGETTE had turned into a battle of attrition and requesting permission to halt the attack and pass to the defensive.[152] That same day, Foch issued a memorandum outlining his concept for the continuation of the battle: "We cannot afford to lose any ground on the Franco-British front. . . . Therefore, the territory must be defended step by step."[153] Despite his broad operational vision, Foch still had trouble abandoning the old tactical principles of rigid forward defense. That 19 April memo would later cause problems for Pétain with some of his subordinate army commanders.

OHL finally ordered the Sixth Army to halt its offensive on 20 April. But before passing entirely to the defensive, OHL insisted that Festubert and Givenchy be taken.[154] The Sixth Army continued to make some half-hearted efforts, but it never did take the two British bastions. OHL also ordered the Fourth Army to halt, but then it ordered a renewed push to take Mont Kemmel, scheduled for 25 April. Thus, although the general attack was halted, the flank attacks to take Festubert and Givenchy on the left and Mont Kemmel on the right would continue.[155] It was a bad decision. Those were widely divergent and non-mutually supporting efforts. Even less directly linked to the main effort, the Second Army on 24 April launched a ten-division attack at Villers-Bretonneux. As at the first Battle of Villers-Bretonneux three weeks earlier, a combined British-Australian force drove the attackers back. This Second Battle of Villers-Bretonneux is best remembered today for history's first tank-on-tank fight, during which three British Mark IV tanks drove back three of the huge and ponderous German A7V tanks.

The Germans assaulted Mont Kemmel on the morning of 25 April and reached the summit in a little more than two hours. That thrust opened up a gap of four miles in the Allied line. Between Vierstraat and just to the west of Mont Kemmel, the Allies had only three battalions in the gap. The German main force swept over the summit at midday and continued down the north-facing reverse slope but then halted behind a defensive artillery barrage and established a defensive line at the base of the hill along the Kemmelbeek. Failing to exploit the situation to their front, the Germans paused until their supporting artillery could move forward. During that pause the British 25th Division moved into the threatened sector with orders to retake Mont Kemmel. That effort failed, but it did close the gap in the Allied lines.

Perhaps the Germans might have been able to take Mont des Cats and then roll up the entire ridgeline from the rear. Many German officers writing after the war said so, but others doubted that the forces available and their mobility were adequate. Curiously, Hindenburg wrote in his memoirs that it was the British who lost Mont Kemmel and that the French were upset with them about it. It was, in fact, exactly the opposite.[156] Writing in 1935, Hermann

Balck, who was a young company commander in the Alpenkorps and would later be an army group commander in World War II, essentially blamed Ludendorff for the failure: "Ludendorff had not intended to make a decisive attack. He was playing a less risky game. He wanted to play it safe and postpone the decisive break-through for later. These were, perhaps, the first indicators of an impending crisis. One only wins through boldness, especially if everything is on the razor's edge."[157]

Fearing that the loss of Mont Kemmel might trigger a general withdrawal to the Mont Noir–Mont Rouge–Poperinghe line, Foch telephoned Haig, insisting that there must be no withdrawal by British forces.[158] Plumer, nonetheless, pulled back another three kilometers north of Ypres, freeing up more reserves for the battle to the south. Foch was irritated that any ground had been given up, but Plumer had made the right move.[159]

The Germans launched their final GEORGETTE push on 29 April. At noon Lossberg reported to Ludendorff that the Allied artillery deployed in great depth made any advance almost impossible. The Germans accomplished very little that day, failing to take Mont Rouge, much less Mont Noir and the Scherpenberg. Ludendorff halted the attack at 2300.[160] Although Operation GEORGETTE came to an end on 29 April the Germans made half-hearted attempts periodically throughout May to take Mont Rouge and Mont Noir.

The German official history optimistically called Operation GEORGETTE "a skillful and effective operational chess move" (*operativer Schachzug*).[161] But although GEORGETTE was another stunning tactical success, it also was another operational failure. Ludendorff repeated some of the same operational-level mistakes he had committed during MICHAEL, most importantly not going for a key vulnerability and shifting the main effort in mid-operation. The British successfully held Hazebrouck and all three of their northern Channel ports. The Allies suffered 112,000 casualties to 86,000, but the German losses were irreplaceable. And in the end, the Germans once again were left with an even greater length of front line that required more troops to man. As historian Gary Sheffield has written, the new German infiltration (storm-troop tactics essentially shifted the inherent advantage of the defense from the initial break-*in* phase of the battle to the subsequent break-*through* phase. "When the BEF went on to the offensive later in the year they did not make the same mistakes," he noted.[162]

While the Allied soldiers on the front lines in Flanders battled the Germans head-to-head during April, the infighting between their senior generals and the generals and the politicians continued unabated. The BEF had lost almost 260,000 men in MICHAEL and GEORGETTE, and the replacements were still not immediately forthcoming from Britain. Haig was forced to disband five divisions in order to bring the rest up to strength by cross-leveling. The French army now held 580 kilometers of front, the British 92, and the Belgians 35.[163] Foch was faced with Pétain's resentment at having to use up his reserves to support the BEF. On 24 April Pétain sent Foch a long memo complaining about the lack of British cooperation and especially about Haig disbanding five divisions. "Such procedure is inadmissible," he groused.[164] Nor was Pétain any too happy with Pershing's continued intransigence on any form of amalgamation.[165] He was not alone in that sense of frustration about the American commander in chief. In his diary entry for that day, Henry Wilson wrote that he considered Pershing "so stupid, so narrow, so pigheaded."[166]

Pershing was wrestling with his own problems with the U.S. War Department and the general staff back in Washington. In his memoirs, he complained that the general staff was sending divisions to France with too many untrained men. He also wrote that the general staff "failed to provide men for special [support] services and relied upon taking them from combat divisions instead of anticipating such requirements and segregating these specialists from the start and training them as such."[167]

Meanwhile, there was still the shipping problem. Pershing and his chief of staff, General James Harbord, met in London on 24 April with Henry Wilson and the new secretary of state for war, Lord Alfred Milner. In what became known as the London Agreement, British and American shipping would, during the month of May, transport six divisions of U.S. combat troops, without their heavy equipment or artillery. Those divisions would then be attached temporarily to the BEF for training.[168] Pershing was now bending slightly on the amalgamation question in exchange for increased sealift. But rather than entire divisions, the British would much rather have had battalions or even companies with which to level out the BEF divisions. Back on the Continent, Pershing and Bliss met with Foch and informed him about the London Agreement, to which the French had not been a party.[169] Foch was not at all pleased.

Haig was having his own internal problems. Major General Sir Frederick Maurice, the Imperial General Staff's director of military operations, was a close ally of the recently deposed chief, General Robertson. On 6 May Maurice published in the British press a letter that was a scathing accusation that Lloyd George had misled the Parliament about the strength of the BEF in early 1918, and consequently the prime minister and the government were responsible for the weakness of the BEF when the Germans attacked in March. After the war U.S. general Hunter Ligget said much same thing: "Had Haig been given the reinforcements he pleaded for, Gough would have parried the German blow as Byng parried it."[170] It was one thing for an American general to make such a comment after the fact but quite another for a serving British general to criticize his own government so openly. Maurice had stepped far over the political-military boundary in a democracy, and in doing so he knowingly ended his own military career. The resulting uproar forced Lloyd George to face a vote of confidence in the House of Commons on 9 May. He survived that vote. Haig had been firmly opposed to Maurice's actions, but the result was even more bad blood between the BEF commander and the prime minister.[171]

Meanwhile, Hindenburg, Ludendorff, and other senior offices at OHL were losing their grips on reality and exhibiting many of the symptoms of "Château generalship." When Colonel von Thaer was transferred from the field to OHL in April 1918, he bluntly told Hindenburg, Ludendorff, and Wetzell about how bad the real conditions were in the front lines. Hindenburg patronizingly told Thaer that he could not possibly understand the bigger picture based on his own limited experience in a sector of only twelve miles. Since OHL got reports from across the entire front every day, the General Staff obviously had a better grip on the overall situation. Hindenburg assured Thaer that his attitude would soon improve in the more optimistic atmosphere at OHL. Ludendorff told Thaer, "If the troops are getting worse, if discipline is slipping, then it is your fault and the fault of all the commanders at the front for not being tough enough." Thaer also noted that right until the very end, the operational planners at OHL continued to regard all divisions posted on the map as equal. Wetzell refused to believe that a division that recently had conducted an attack in Thaer's former sector had been down to an average strength of thirty riflemen per company.[172]

NINE

BLÜCHER AND GNEISENAU: LUDENDORFF VERSUS FOCH AND PÉTAIN

The actions of the Eighteenth Army had not altered the strategic situation created by the attack of the Seventh Army, nor had it produced any tactical results.

General of Infantry Erich Ludendorff, My War Memories

General Ludendorff shares my view that in all probability a crushing defeat of the enemy is out of the question; he is now resting his hopes upon the success of a deus ex machina in the hope of an internal collapse in the Western Powers.

Bavarian crown prince Rupprecht to Chancellor Georg Graf von Hertling, quoted in John W. Wheeler-Bennett, Hindenburg: The Wooden Titan

LUDENDORFF GROPES FOR PLAN B

Both MICHAEL and GEORGETTE had failed, and the Germans were running out of time and manpower. They no longer had any hope of winning the war on the battlefield, but if they could manage to defeat the British, they still might achieve a strategic stalemate. As Hindenburg hedged the true situation in his memoirs, "The attack against the British northern wing remained the focal point of our operations. I believed that the war would be decided if this attack was successful."[1] Did he really believe that, or was it something for postwar consumption at home? Something President von Hindenburg said to Chancellor Heinrich Brüning on 11 November 1931 indicates the latter: "I knew already in February 1918 that the war was lost, but I was willing to let Ludendorff have his fling."[2]

On 13 April, more than two weeks before GEORGETTE ended, Rupprecht's Army Group issued the planning guidance to develop courses of action for follow-on operations. The two primary options were resumptions of either MICHAEL or GEORGETTE, initially designated NEU-MICHAEL and NEU-GEORG. They later were redesignated WILHELM and HAGEN, respectively.[3] The main operational problem for the Germans at that point was that in responding to the German attacks against the British, the French had weakened their other sectors to support their allies. The combined British and French forces north of the Somme were now too strong to attack with any possibility of success. The Germans, therefore, would have to draw off a large portion of the French reserves by conducting a large-scale diversionary attack at some vital point in the French sector. As Ludendorff wrote in his memoirs, "I hoped that it would lead to such a heavy drain on the reserves of the enemy as would enable us to resume the attack in Flanders."[4] In essence, Ludendorff was now acting on the recommendation that his own chief of operations, Georg Wetzell, had proposed the previous December.

On 17 April, OHL issued a warning order to Crown Prince Wilhelm's Army Group to start planning and preparing to launch an attack in the sector of General Hans von Boehn's Seventh Army. In its basic concept, the original objective of the new attack in the south was to be the line of the Aisne River, which as an initial step required the capture of the Chemin des Dames ridge between the Ailette and the Aisne. This third major German offensive was designated Operation BLÜCHER. The Germans at that point were deployed along the far bank of the Ailette River, which ran along the northern base of the ridge. They had been in that position since the French had taken the Chemin des Dames in October 1917, during one of Pétain's limited objective attacks to seize key terrain for future operations.

The ground favored the defenders. The Chemin des Dames was a twenty-four-mile-long "hog's-back" ridge, running east and west. It rose steeply from the Ailette River and then dropped only somewhat less sharply to the south and the Aisne River. The top of the ridge is relatively flat and several hundred meters wide. South of the Chemin des Dames ran a series of relatively parallel rivers with elevated ground in between—the Vesle, then the Ourcq, and finally the Marne. The prevailing road network also ran east and west, all perpendicular to the German axis of advance. Even worse, there was only one major rail line south of the Aisne, which ran roughly east to west from Reims to Soissons and then to Compiègne. As a Seventh Army operations order noted, "Of course, the very few roads running east-west prove difficult for this attack."[5] And even Hindenburg later wrote, "The ground was extremely unfavorable for attack."[6]

The key to the BLÜCHER thrust in the general direction of the Marne was to make the French believe that their capital was once again under direct attack, as it had been in August and September 1914. And, of course, the French had experienced a great deal of anxiety about just that two months earlier during Operation MICHAEL. But BLÜCHER was purely a feint. Despite widespread belief during the hundred years following the end of the war, the Germans never actually intended to try to reach Paris. Nothing in any of the surviving operations orders, war diaries, or operational message traffic indicates that the French capital was even a deep objective. And if the Germans really had intended to reach Paris, they could not have done it with an attack originating north of the Chemin des Dames. The roads, rivers, and railroads all ran the wrong way, and the Germans simply did not have the mobility, logistics, or operational range to reach Paris before the Allies could block them. During both world wars, logistics was the Achilles' heel of the German army.

At a meeting with the army group chiefs of staff on 29 and 30 April, Ludendorff made the final decision to proceed with the Chemin des Dames attack. The purpose of the operation was stated clearly: "To disrupt the unity of the Allied front opposite Army Group Crown Prince Rupprecht, and create the possibility of renewing the offensive against the British." The main BLÜCHER attack would be made by five corps of General von Boehn's Seventh Army, with two supporting attacks on either flank. Operation YORCK on the right would be made by Boehn's remaining corps, plus one corps of General Oskar von Hutier's Eighteenth Army. Operation GOERZ on the left would be made by two corps of General Fritz von Below's First Army. The attack was scheduled tentatively for 20 May, with the HAGEN attack against the British scheduled for mid-June.[7]

As the plans and preparations progressed, the start date slipped to 27 May and the operation underwent a significant amount of "mission creep." The original objective was the north bank of the Aisne, which Ludendorff estimated would frighten the French enough to force them to pull in all their reserves to cover Paris. But then the attack objective was extended to the south bank of the Aisne, then to the next ridgeline between the Aisne and the Vesle, and then to the north bank of the Vesle itself. On 23 May, four days before the start of the attack, Ludendorff again extended the objective line to the far bank of the Vesle and the dominating high ground to the south.[8]

At the start of MICHAEL, the Germans had 191 divisions on the Western Front. By mid-May, they had 207. The extra divisions were all late arrivals from the Eastern Front, but they were of low quality. For BLÜCHER, the Germans managed to assemble 29 attack divisions and 10 trench divisions on a forty-eight-kilometer front. Some 26 of the attack divisions had participated in MICHAEL or MARS, but none had been in GEORGETTE; 11 of the attack divisions were already in position at the start of the buildup while the remainder had to be shifted from other sectors.[9] Of course, much of that force—especially the heavy artillery, aviation units, and support troops—would have to be reshifted rapidly to the north for HAGEN.[10] OHL massed 5,263 guns and 1,233 trench mortars for BLÜCHER,[11] and Ludendorff seconded Colonel Georg Bruchmüller to the Seventh Army to take charge of the fire planning.

THE ALLIES BRACE FOR ROUND THREE

The Allies now had a unified command structure, but inter-Allied relations remained anything but harmonious. Following a preliminary meeting of Allied leaders on 27 April, the Supreme War Council met in Abbeville on 1–2 May, with Lord Alfred Milner, General Sir Henry Wilson, Haig, Foch, Pershing, Pétain, and Prime Minister Georges Clemenceau in attendance. Clemenceau complained bitterly that the French had not been consulted on the London Agreement. Foch worried that all new arriving American units would go to the British. Clemenceau finally accepted the situation, but he insisted that in the future all such agreements should involve all three governments.[12]

When the inevitable topic of amalgamation came up, Pershing continued to resist all pressures to break up American units. In exasperation, Foch told Pershing, "I am commander-in-chief of the Allied Armies in France, and my appointment has been sanctioned not only by the British and French governments, but also by the President of the United States. Hence, I believe it my duty to insist on my point of view." Pershing didn't budge. As he later wrote, "We all knew that no authority to dictate regarding such matters had been conferred upon General Foch."[13]

Foch continued to press the attack. "Are you willing to risk our being driven back to the Loire?" Pershing shocked all those present when he shot back, "Yes, I am willing to take the risk. Moreover, the time may come when the

American army will have to stand the brunt of this war, and it is not wise to fritter away our resources in this manner."[14] Pershing continued that the morale of the Allied armies was low and that of his own troops was very high. He did not want his Doughboys being contaminated by French and British pessimism.

Lloyd George, Clemenceau, Italian prime minister Vittorio Orlando, Foch, and Milner all tried to argue with Pershing. After another forty minutes of wrangling, Pershing banged the table and said, "Gentlemen, I have thought this program over very deliberately, and I will not be coerced." Then he walked out of the meeting.[15] As Haig recorded in his diary, "I thought Pershing very obstinate and stupid. He did not seem to realize the urgency of the situation." And a little further on: "He hankers after a 'great self-contained American Army' [original emphasis] but seeing that he has neither Commanders of Divisions, of Corps, nor of Armies, nor Staffs for same, it is ridiculous to think such an Army could function alone in less than 2 years' time."[16] At that point, there were 429,375 Americans in France but only four divisions deployed in quiet sectors of the front lines.

On the second day of the conference, the participants did reach a general consensus on the strategic objectives of the Allied armies in France. The two priorities were the maintenance of contact between the British and the French and the security of the Channel ports. If events made the accomplishment of both impossible, however, the British forces would retire toward the Somme, essentially abandoning their three northern ports. Foch, true to character, exuded confidence that such an action would never be necessary.[17] The final action of the conference was to dissolve the Executive War Board, which had become superfluous since Foch's appointment.[18] Following the conference, Clemenceau sent a memo strongly criticizing Pershing to the French ambassador in Washington, asking him to forward it to President Wilson.[19]

After the Abbeville Conference, Pershing justified his position on amalgamation by writing, "The fact that neither the British nor the French had trained their armies for open warfare, either offensive or defensive, was at least in part one cause of the tremendous success of the German drives with divisions trained expressly for that kind of warfare."[20] Pershing, however, failed to understand the crucial differences between the old, infantry-centric open warfare tactics he advocated and the new German infiltration tactics grounded in combined arms warfare. As late as September 1918 Pershing wrote that "the essential difference between open and trench warfare . . . is characterized by the presence or absence of the rolling barrage ahead of the infantry."[21] In fact, the meticulously planned, well-organized, and massive creeping barrage of the type organized by Bruchmüller was one of the key elements of the German offensive tactics. American units that tried to attack without adequate artillery support between July and November 1918 would pay very heavy prices in casualties.

On 5 May Foch issued an order for Allied forces to hold their current frontline positions at all costs and fight for every foot of ground. That order effectively countermanded Pétain's defense-in-depth Directive Number 4, issued the previous December. In the Chemin des Dames sector, Sixth Army commander Denis Duchêne complied with Foch. He placed his main line of defense along the crest of the Chemin des Dames ridge, which put his rear dangerously astride the Aisne River. Based on the experience of GEORGETTE, the commander of the newly redeployed British IX Corps, Lieutenant General Sir Alexander Hamelton-Gordon, pleaded in vain with Duchêne to be allowed to establish a flexible defense-in-depth in his own sector at least. Duchêne refused even to consider it with a curt "*J'ai dit*" ("I have spoken").[22] When Pétain tried to force compliance with his defense-in-depth orders, Foch backed Duchêne, who had been his chief of staff when Foch commanded XX Corps in 1914.[23] Several days later Foch sent a note to Pétain, attempting to dictate the tactics of the French army. Foch was clearly overstepping his role as Allied commander in chief. He could not have gotten away with sending such a note to a non-French national commander.[24]

On 20 May Foch issued his General Directive Number 3. Noting that the Germans had been inactive for the last three weeks but could be expected to resume the offensive at any time, Foch concluded that the time was right to beat the Germans to the punch. "Between the Oise and the North Sea important results can be sought so important that they of themselves alone impose the offensive." Foch ordered the Allied armies to start immediate preparations for two possible offensives, one between the Oise and the Somme and the other in the Lys sector. But as Elizabeth Greenhalgh has pointed out, Foch's scheme had little basis in reality at that point. Against the eighty divisions the Germans then had in reserve, Foch could count on only a quarter of that number.[25]

German operational security for BLÜCHER was masterful. Until just before the attack, neither British GHQ nor French Grand Quartier Général (GQG) could forecast with any accuracy where the German blow would fall next. GHQ initially predicted the Germans would resume the offensive between Albert and Arras. By 7 May the German deception measures seemed to indicate the resumption of the attack on both sides of the Scarpe. A week later conspicuous radio silence in the area of the La Bassée Canal convinced the British the attack would resume in that sector. A couple days later everything seemed to point to the area between Albert and Arras. On 25 May, GQG reported that the attack would come between the Oise and the sea. Finally, just one day before the Germans launched BLÜCHER, Haig noted in his diary that an attack against the Chemin des Dames was the most likely.[26] Ironically, as early as 25 April the AEF's G-2 (intelligence) section had predicted accurately where the next blow would fall. The American assessment was based on German capabilities derived from an analysis of the enemy's order of battle and logistical realities. The French and British, however, virtually ignored the assessment of the inexperienced Americans.[27]

On the eve of the battle the French had forty-seven divisions north of the Oise, with twenty-three in the line and twenty-four in reserve. They had fifty-five divisions between the Oise and the Swiss border, with forty-three in the line and only twelve in reserve. Pétain complained to Foch about the vulnerability of the French line south of the Oise and his very limited ability to respond to a German attack.[28] Duchêne's Sixth Army had only eleven divisions in the front lines of its seventy-five-kilometer-long sector and five divisions in reserve. His artillery force totaled some 1,400 guns, only about a quarter of the number of tubes Bruchmüller massed for BLÜCHER.

BLÜCHER: 27 MAY–5 JUNE 1918

When the German artillery started shooting at 0200 hours on 27 May 1918, the Allies were caught almost completely by surprise. This fire preparation was Bruchmüller's masterpiece. Although the shelling lasted just two hours and forty minutes, the German artillery fired 3 million rounds on the first day of the battle, 50 percent of which was gas rounds.[29] The bloodbath was even worse than it otherwise might have been because of Duchêne's refusal to yield an inch of French soil to "the Boche." The Sixth Army commander had packed all of his troops into the most forward positions of his line, where they were just so many targets for the German guns.

The Germans considered the key terrain in the initial attack to be the ground around Craonne and the California Plateau, the eastern end of the Chemin des Dames ridge. That was also the boundary between the British IX Corps on the right and the French XI Corps under General Louis de Maud'huy on the left. The three French divisions in the first line were attacked by ten German divisions, and the three British divisions in the first line were hit by seven German divisions. The German infantry crossed the Ailette at 0440 hours. It took the troops only about an hour to reach the top of the ridge. They kept advancing rapidly, and by about 0900 hours the German lead elements reached the Aisne near Gemicourt. The main body closed in strength along the river's length within the next hour. As the attackers surged forward, a gap opened up between XI and IX Corps, with the French being pushed to the southwest and the British to the southeast.

The Germans moved so fast that the Allies were unable to evacuate all their artillery to the south side of the Aisne. The Germans captured some 650 French guns as they pushed forward. Two of the attacking divisions reached the Vesle that evening, and their lead elements crossed the river near Fismes. By the end of 27 May, the German infantry had penetrated twenty-two kilometers into the French lines, the largest single-day advance of any attack in World War I. About midnight OHL ordered the lead forces to continue attacking throughout the night, with the objective of taking the high ground south of the Vesle.[30]

Duchêne attempted to mount a defense by ordering his troops to halt the German attack on 28 May at the Sixth Army's second defensive position behind the Vesle. Duchêne, however, had unwittingly helped the Germans by waiting too long to order the destruction of the bridges over the Aisne between Vailly and Pontavert. He also squandered his reserves needlessly by committing them piecemeal and too early. That afternoon on the first day, 27 May, Pétain ordered the headquarters of the Fifth Army, with six divisions and heavy artillery, to reinforce the Sixth Army.

On the twenty-eighth the Germans crossed the Vesle on a wide front just before noon. As the gap between the Allies' IX and XI Corps continued to widen to as much as ten miles, the German advance made good progress in the center, but the attacking units on the flanks were starting to lag behind.[31] Early that morning Ludendorff conducted an operational assessment meeting at Seventh Army headquarters. He was faced with another decision point. So far, the final objective of the operation had been to cross the Vesle and take the high ground to the south. The German forces were already past that line, and Ludendorff once again had two basic options. He could follow the original plan by slowing the pace of the BLÜCHER attack—which was starting to draw in a limited number of the French reserves—and then shift rapidly as planned to the northern attack against the British. Or, he could continue to exploit the stunning and unexpected tactical success of BLÜCHER—but to what operational objective? No definite orders came out of that meeting, but at 1300 hours OHL signaled the second course option by issuing an order that effectively extended BLÜCHER's objectives.[32] By that point the Germans had captured more than 20,000 prisoners. Twenty-one German divisions were advancing against sixteen reeling and badly shaken Allied divisions.

Within twenty-four hours of the German penetration, Pétain started moving sixteen divisions to the threatened sector, including all four divisions of the Fifth Army, which had been placed in reserve behind Amiens to support the British. He did so without requesting approval from Foch. Most of the French were moved by truck and then deployed into position by regiments, usually without their supporting artillery. GQG also ordered the insertion of the Fifth Army headquarters into the line between the Fourth and Sixth Armies, on the east side of the salient, with an effective date of 2 June. About 1000 hours, GQG ordered that the line of the Vesle had to be held, but that order had been overcome by events before it was ever issued. Some thirteen hours later Pétain recognized the impossibility of counterattacking from the line of the Vesle. He therefore directed that the German advance be limited by putting heavy pressure on its flanks, with particular emphasis on holding Montagne de Reims, the key high ground south of Reims.[33]

Foch did not panic over the BLÜCHER attack. He saw almost right away that it could not lead to any decisive operational results, attacking as it did into the Allied depth. He correctly concluded it was a feint designed to draw off the Allied reserves, preparatory to a main attack in a more decisive direction. He therefore told Clemenceau that he did not intend to move any more of the French forces that were then deployed in Flanders and the Somme sector.[34] The French at that point still had thirteen divisions from the Oise north to the Channel, where the Germans had forty-one divisions in reserve behind Rupprecht's Army Group.

On that same day, the AEF conducted its first divisional-size attack of the war. The objective was the village of Cantigny, on the western face of the BLÜCHER salient. The attack was supposed to be a test case of the ability of the American command and staff structure to plan and execute an offensive, albeit a minor one. Success would support Pershing's arguments for an independent army; failure would support the Allies' argument for amalgamation.[35] The U.S. 1st Division had the mission of reducing the small, three-mile-deep salient. The operation also would be a test case for Pershing's theories of open warfare and the power of the infantry rifle.

It was anything but. The primary planners were two future chiefs of staff of the U.S. Army: the 1st Division's operations officer, Lieutenant Colonel George C. Marshall, and the commander of the divisional artillery brigade, Brigadier General Charles P. Summerall. It was a classic trench warfare operation, based on limited objectives, overwhelming firepower, and detailed planning. It essentially was a regimental-size action conducted by an entire division. The initial attack was supported by 234 pieces of American and French artillery and 10 French tanks, and the Doughboys used trench mortars, machine guns, and flamethrowers. The Americans attacked just before 0700 hours on 28 May and took the town in a little more than half an hour. Then the Germans counterattacked, as they always did. The fight to hold Cantigny continued until 31 May. What had cost the 1st Division 50 men to take cost 1,603 killed, wounded, missing, or captured to hold. The village itself was of only minor tactical significance, but the AEF passed its first test of fire. Nonetheless, as Mark Grotelueschen points out, it was "no attack of 'self-reliant infantry.'"[36]

On the third day of BLÜCHER the Germans pushed the French south of the Ourcq River. By that point nine Allied divisions, including four British, had been almost completely destroyed. The British committed their last reserve division, and by the following day the 19th Division managed to absorb the remnants of the four decimated British divisions. Ludendorff, meanwhile, continued to expand the mission creep by adding the objectives of Reims on the eastern shoulder and of Dormans on the Marne River at the apex of the advance. But the two wings of the attack still trailed far behind the center, and the heavy hand of "the tyranny of logistics" was once again making itself felt. Later that day the Germans did take Soissons. But that did not help their rail situation. From Soissons the only operable railway line through the salient continued running west to Compiègne, which was more than twenty miles from the German positions. The Allies still held the entry points at both ends of the rail line. The only other major rail line into the salient was a single-track line that ran from German-held Laon south to Soissons. That line, however, ran through a tunnel at Vauxaillon that the Germans themselves had blown up during their 1917 withdrawal to the Siegfried Position. The German engineers estimated that it would take at least six weeks to reopen the tunnel.[37] At the end of the third day the apex of the German salient was near Fère-en-Tardenois, some twenty-five miles south of the German army's line of departure on the Ailette. But its perimeter also had increased from thirty-six miles to almost sixty.[38]

That evening Pétain concluded that the pressure on German flanks was not slowing down the center adequately. He again considered launching a counterattack, this time scheduled for 31 May. Pétain requested from Foch authority to move the Tenth Army and also to redeploy the Army Detachment of the North from Flanders. Foch refused, saying that there was too much of a possibility for another major offensive in the British sector. French intelligence that day estimated that Rupprecht's Army Group still had thirty fresh divisions in reserve.[39] Nonetheless, Foch later warned Haig that he might have to withdraw the Tenth Army and even require Haig to commit British reserves in support of the battle in the south. Haig responded that he would give consideration to forming a corps of three divisions to support the French if necessary.[40]

On 30 May, the French XI Corps continued to be pushed to the southwest and was now south of Soissons. What was left of the British IX Corps, essentially the 19th Division, had been pushed back to the Andre River, southeast of Fismes. Midmorning on 30 May, Ludendorff again enlarged the objective of BLÜCHER, hoping to capture Reims through a double envelopment conducted by the left wing of the Seventh Army and the right wing of the First Army.[41] Later that day Ludendorff sent out a message reminding the subordinate commanders that the objective of BLÜCHER was to "threaten Paris" for the primary purpose of forcing the French to pull their reserve forces away from Flanders to cover their capital.[42] In all the surviving primary records, the various mentions of *threatening* Paris, or *advancing toward* Paris, are not indicators that Paris was at any point an actual objective. Ludendorff understood only too well that after advancing more than twenty-five miles from the initial line of departure, the German army simply did not have the necessary ammunition, rations, or transport capability to go the additional forty miles—especially with no useful rail lines behind it. As early as 2 May, General Friedrich von der Schulenburg, the chief of staff of Army Group German Crown Prince, had suggested to Ludendorff that Paris should be an objective. Ludendorff rejected the recommendations, citing insufficient forces, especially artillery.[43] By the end of 30 May the German forces were closing in on the Marne along a twenty-kilometer stretch from Château-Thierry to Tréloup. The Germans were just about as far as they could go.

When Foch and Pershing met that day the American commander recommended counterattacking as soon as possible against a flank of the salient.[44] But the French XXX Corps opposite the western shoulder was starting to fall back. Pétain, meanwhile, continued to demand more reinforcements from Foch. Pétain wanted operational control of the divisions of the Army Detachment of the North, as well as of the American divisions training in the British sector. Starting to lose confidence in his original estimate of the situation, Foch ordered the Tenth Army with its four divisions to redeploy from the British sector between the Somme and the Lys to the Marne. Even writing after the war, Foch remained convinced that there was "no doubt that the [German] Supreme Command intended to open the road to Paris at all costs."[45] Once the Tenth Army redeployed, that still left the BEF in Flanders supported by the French Army Detachment of the North with nine divisions. Petain asked for those forces too, but Foch refused to release them.[46] Foch had other problems as well. The French government certainly believed that the Germans were coming to Paris, and some members of the Chamber of Deputies started calling for Foch to be replaced with Pétain.

On 31 May the Germans reached and crossed the Marne at Dormans and established a small bridgehead on the south bank at Jaulgonne, but they made little significant progress on the flanks. Their left wing failed to take Reims, and their right wing failed to take the Forest of Villers-Cotterêts. Both failures would later cost them dearly.[47] The logistics situation was getting worse. A Seventh Army order issued to LXV Corps stated it was of the highest importance "for the advance *toward* Paris" that the rail line through Reims be opened as soon as possible.[48] Three corps were now attacking Reims from two directions. Some historians have identified this as the point at which the Germans shifted the main objective of BLÜCHER to Paris, but the disposition of forces and reserves on 31 May did not support such a decision. The closest point to Paris on the German perimeter was just to the north of Château-Thierry, at the extreme southern tip on the BLÜCHER salient. The designated main effort on 31 May, however, was on the right wing. Of the twenty-seven German divisions in the front line, there were eight each in the German center and on the left wing but eleven on the right wing pushing west and southwest, out from the vicinity of Soissons toward Compiègne. That critical rail junction was some forty miles north-northeast of the French capital.[49]

That morning General Franchet d'Espérey, the commander of Army Group North, gave the commander of the Fifth Army permission to evacuate Reims to shorten the French front and reconstitute a reserve. Fortunately for the Allies, General Alfred Micheler held Reims, thus maintaining the stranglehold on the key German rail line.[50] Later that afternoon the French Sixth Army counterattacked north toward Soissons and northeast toward Fismes.[51] All the French counterattacks failed that day, but the continual pressure on the flanks of the German salient prevented the Germans from gaining much more ground, except in the center, between Château-Thierry and La Ferté Milon.

Foch, now coming back to his original assessment, agreed with Haig that the Germans were waiting for the right moment to launch a full-scale attack in Flanders. Pétain, meanwhile, remained convinced that the German main objective was Paris.[52] Pétain advised Clemenceau to evacuate the government from Paris, but Foch refused to advise the government to move, insisting the German offensive was a feint. Pétain again requested from Foch control of the Army Detachment of the North. Foch refused, telling Pétain that he had enough forces to deal with the situation.[53]

Still fearing the worst, the chief of the Imperial General Staff, General Sir Henry Wilson, on 29 May had ordered the general staff in London to start making the necessary preparations to evacuate the BEF from the Continent. Now on the evening of 31 May, Haig and Lloyd George met in Paris with Sir Eric Geddes, the First Lord of the Admiralty, and Admiral Sir Rosslyn Wemyss, the First Sea Lord, to consider the possibility of an evacuation of Dunkirk. The correlation of forces looked grim at that point. Of the thirty-two French and five British divisions already committed to the battle, seventeen were completely expended. During the period of the next ten days, the Allies would have only fourteen more fresh divisions available for commitment.[54]

The Americans, meanwhile, were preparing for their second major battle of the war. With most of the Allied leaders still believing that the German objective was Paris, the Allies concluded that they had to stop the Germans from crossing the Marne and establishing a bridgehead from which to continue the drive. Fears of such led the government to begin preparations to abandon the French capital for Bordeaux in the south. On the night of 30 May the U.S. 2nd and 3rd Divisions started moving toward Château-Thierry to reinforce the

French. The 2nd Division deployed northwest of Château-Thierry, and the 3rd Division occupied positions on the south bank of the Marne directly opposite Château-Thierry. The lead elements of both divisions reached their initial positions late on the thirty-first.

The Germans kept pushing forward but apparently without a clearly defined objective. OHL continued to reinforce the battle by drawing more divisions away from Rupprecht's Army Group. The number redeployed now totaled five highly trained attack divisions that had been husbanded carefully for Operation HAGEN. On the afternoon of 1 June, OHL informed Rupprecht that HAGEN would have to be pushed back to the middle of July. The initial objective of drawing the French reserves away from Flanders was now secondary to reinforcing the attack of the Seventh Army, turning it into an attempt at a decisive operation. But to what end? What was the objective?

Later that afternoon OHL issued a message with a note of panic to it: "It appears that the attack of the First Army is coming to a standstill."[55] It was critical for the First Army, to the left of the Seventh Army, to take Reims, which would open up the rail line into the BLÜCHER salient. Ludendorff telephoned Army Group German Crown Prince with the information that the Seventh Army had to cross the Marne near Jaulgonne and Dormans and attack east toward Épernay in order to reenergize the First Army's arm of the pincers.[56] That meant the Seventh Army would be moving away from Paris, not toward it.

By the morning of 1 June, the left wing of the 19th Division had been forced to the south side of the Andre River, but the British still held both banks below Bligny. Defending tenaciously, the 19th Division that day blocked the German advance up the Andre valley, the main approach route to the Montagne de Reims. Had the Germans taken that key piece of high ground only six miles directly south of the city, Reims very likely would have fallen.

OHL's orders for 2 June specified that the operational objective was to break the Allied defensive resistance between Soissons and Villers-Cotterêts, taking the latter town.[57] That evening, the Seventh Army's orders for 3 June designated VII Corps on the right shoulder of the salient as the main effort. Control of that ground would facilitate a supporting operation by the Eighteenth Army to the west, which was being scheduled for 7 June. The objective of Operation GNEISENAU would be the capture of Compiègne.[58]

On 1 June Foch issued a very pointed memorandum directed at the United States: "[The Americans] must now consider a greater effort in order to pursue a war, which will last for a long time. For this object, they must contemplate a progressive increase of their army, up to 100 divisions, and achieve this result by using their available shipping. The training of these troops will be intensified in France as well as in the United States."[59]

That same day, in response to the crisis, the Allies convened their sixth meeting of the Supreme War Council at Versailles.[60] The French requested Lloyd George to release all American divisions training in the British sector under the London Agreement for redeployment to the French sector to relieve French divisions in other sectors, which then could be committed to the battle.[61] Lloyd George countered by proposing that Pershing relinquish the complete operational control of those divisions to Haig.[62]

Pershing initially rejected both proposals. Clemenceau remarked that the Germans would not postpone their attacks until the Americans were ready. Pershing shot back, "Neither would we rely on untrained men in battle."[63] Insisting that nothing else mattered but *"La bataille, la bataille,"* Foch demanded that America send 250,000 infantrymen to France in both June and July, trained or untrained. Pershing responded that he was 205,000 troops short for his Services of Supply system, which would be necessary to support an independent American army in the field. Contrary to most of the Allied representatives present, the British transportation expert Graeme Thompson supported Pershing on the need for more support troops.

In his postwar memoirs, Pershing stated that he clearly recognized the German operational rail problem in the BLÜCHER salient, especially because of the destruction of the rail tunnel at Vauxaillon. He also identified the critical rail nodes of Reims and Soissons, without which the Germans would have to rely on sixteen mostly cross-country roads for their logistics system.[64] The key question, however, is whether he recognized that in early June 1918 or only after the war when he was writing his memoirs.

In the end, Foch and Pershing agreed, despite Haig's strong objections, that the five American divisions currently training with the British would be committed to quiet French sectors to free up French divisions.[65] Foch, Pershing, and Milner also agreed that 250,000 men would be transported in June and July, with priority for 170,000 combat troops in June and 140,000 in July, for a total of 310,000. The remaining 190,000 would be supply troops. Any excess shipping capacity above 250,000 a month would be combat troops.[66]

Pershing's critics were still not placated. On 2 June, Haig wrote in his diary, "Really, the ignorance of the Americans in all things connected with an Army is appalling."[67] Several days after the SWC conference, South African general Jan Christian Smuts, who was a member of the British War Cabinet's War Policy Committee, recommended that the American army in France should be taken away from Pershing and put under the command of someone better capable of using to best advantage its first-class manpower material. Smuts had himself in mind. It was a completely outlandish suggestion, one that the American government would never accept and almost no Allied leaders would consider supporting. But, it was a telling indicator of how low the Allied opinion of Pershing had sunk.[68]

On 3 June, Army Group German Crown Prince recommended suspending BLÜCHER until the Eighteenth Army launched GNEISENAU. Ludendorff, however, ordered operations to continue by conducting well-prepared, limited-objective attacks to minimize casualties.[69] On the Allied side, the French completed the withdrawal of their forces to the south bank of the Marne, and the U.S. 3rd Division deployed in force into defensive positions on the south bank around Château-Thierry.

The Germans on 4 June made no significant gains on either flank. Reims was almost completely surrounded, but it still held out. That day Foch asked Haig to shift three divisions from his general reserve to the west of Amiens, "where they can act either to the profit of the British or to the profit of the French Army."[70] Haig complied grudgingly, but he also wanted his heavily battered IX Corps back from the Marne sector. Meanwhile, French Army Group Reserve commander General Émile Fayolle finally managed to pull together a cohesive defense-in-depth facing BLÜCHER. At that point, the Allies had committed to the battle forty-one French divisions (including six cavalry divisions) and five British, two Italian, and two American divisions. Seven more divisions were still moving up.[71]

The military crisis may have passed but not so the political crisis. In a state of near-panic, French legislators demand the relief and court-martial of both Pétain and Foch. Clemenceau blocked that initiative by defending vigorously the two generals in the Chamber of Deputies: "We must have confidence in Foch and Pétain, those two great chiefs who are so happily complementary to each other."[72] Nonetheless, Clemenceau had come to develop a greater respect for Foch than for Pétain, although relations between the French prime minister and the Allied commander in chief remained somewhat prickly. As Clemenceau told President Raymond Poincaré, "Pétain, who has his faults, belongs more in the second rank than in the first."[73]

On 5 June, the German Seventh Army halted Operation BLÜCHER and ordered all of its corps to go on the defensive.[74] Trying hard to put the best face possible on things, OHL's official assessment of the operation read, "One must resist the notion that the offensive did not result in a major breakthrough success, but stalled in the end. On the contrary, it advanced much farther than its original objective. The Allies suffered one of their heaviest defeats. For us it is the foundation for future successes."[75] No one, least of all Ludendorff, had any real notion of what those "future successes" were supposed to be. The stark strategic reality was that like MICHAEL and GEORGETTE before it, Operation BLÜCHER had been an operational failure, although simultaneously a virtuoso performance on the tactical level. General Hermann von Kuhl ominously noted in his personal war diary that Ludendorff was lurching from one tactical success to another, without the slightest idea of how "to end the war or to bring about a decision."[76]

That was not the end of the fighting in the BLÜCHER salient, however. A brutal and bloody tactical action that started the following day resulted in one of the most cherished but distorted myths of World War I. At the start of June, the U.S. 2nd Division had moved into the line a few miles to the northwest of Château-Thierry and astride the Paris–Metz highway. The 2nd Division was a mixed organization, consisting of an army brigade and the U.S. 4th Marine Brigade. The division came under the operational control of the French XXI Corps, commanded by General Jean-Marie Degoutte. Just as BLÜCHER came to an end, Degoutte ordered American forces to take the Bois de Belleau, a small patch of forest near the southwestern extremity of the German salient. The woods, about a mile in length and half that at its widest point, were defended primarily by the 237th Infantry Division, a *Stellungsdivision* (trench division), trained and organized specifically to hold ground. Throughout most of the BLÜCHER advance the 237th Division had followed behind the leading attack divisions, but as the advance was slowing to a halt, it moved forward to establish a defensive line.

The 4th Marine Brigade was commanded by U.S. Army brigadier general James G. Harbord, who until recently had been Pershing's chief of staff. Harbord was a staunch advocate of his boss's theories of open warfare and self-reliant infantry. With woefully inadequate artillery support, the Marines attacked into the woods on 6 June. As military historian Richard Holmes put it, "The Marines attacked in long, straight lines, with the sort of tactical innocence that European armies had long since lost."[77] The leading ranks were cut down in droves by German machine-gun fire. But the Marines kept at it. The fighting in the woods raged back and forth for almost three weeks. As the Marines continued attacking, they adopted tactics based on massive fire support and limited-objective, set-piece advances. They finally cleared the Belleau Wood on 26 June. Including the army troops who supported the Marines, the attackers lost 1,811 killed, including 1,087 total casualties on 6 June alone.[78]

The merits of the Marine victory at Belleau Wood have been much debated. Many French believed at the time that the Marines had "saved Paris" by halting the Germans. At only thirty-nine miles from Paris, Belleau Wood was as close as the Germans got to the French capital in 1918. As noted above, however, the Germans never intended to attack Paris. As all their operations orders make clear, the purpose of Operation BLÜCHER was solely a diversion. Furthermore, the Germans themselves halted the offensive the day before the start of the attack, and the Americans were attacking against a relatively immobile German trench division. The Germans were not going anywhere at that point. Finally, it is impossible to conclude that one single American brigade could have halted the forty-two-division German attack across a sixty-mile front. But even writing well after the war, Pershing continued to contribute to the myth. He actually was writing about the deployment of both the U.S. 2nd and 3rd Divisions on either side of Château-Thierry, but the theme was still one of the Americans saving Paris: "Although in battle for the first time, our men maintained their positions and by their timely arrival stopped the German advance on Paris."[79]

The real significance of the Battle of Belleau Wood was the impression it made on the enemy. German commanders and staff officers were shocked by how tenaciously, albeit unskillfully, the Americans had fought. They were forced to face the reality that their assumption that it would be at least another year before the Americans would be combat effective was wishful thinking at best. As the commander of the German Seventh Army, General Hans von Boehn, put it, "It is not a question of the possession or non-possession of this or that village or woods, insignificant in itself; it is a question of whether the American claim that the American Army is equal to or even the superior of the German Army is to be made good?"[80] Ludendorff thought he knew the answer to that question. On 8 June, he issued a general directive to all German forces to "cause as much damage as possible, within the limits of the general situation, to the American units inserted in the front line, as they are to form the nucleus for the new [Allied] organizations."[81]

GNEISENAU: 9–15 JUNE 1918

The failure of Operation BLÜCHER left the Germans in an operational predicament of their own making, with almost no way out. By June 1918 the German army was nearly completely spent. From a total population of 67 million, Germany during the Great War mobilized 11 million men and suffered 7.2 million casualties (dead, wounded, missing, and prisoners.) On 17 December 1917, OHL estimated the monthly replacement requirements at 150,000, of which returning convalescents contributed only 60,000 per month.[82] During Operations MICHAEL, GEORGETTE, and BLÜCHER, the Germans had sustained a total of 431,000 casualties.[83] In that same period, the Americans alone put 568,000 troops into Europe. The last possible manpower draw, 637,000 men born 1899–1900, was probably insufficient to continue the war, and they would not be ready to enter service until late in 1918.[84] Even horses were becoming impossible to replace. During MICHAEL alone the Germans lost almost 29,000 horses, which were desperately needed for transport.[85]

The German equipment also was worn out; morale was reaching an all-time low; and there was widespread political and social unrest in the homeland. The worldwide flu pandemic of 1918 made things even worse. Although all sides were hard hit, the German troops suffered more because of their inadequate diets and the overstrained military medical system. The tactical gains made by BLÜCHER only created another huge salient that required more troops to man and was almost impossible to supply without that critical rail line, which required control of either Reims or Compiègne. The large wooded areas on the western flank of the BLÜCHER salient, especially the Forests of Villers-Cotterêts and Compiègne, provided ideal cover for an Allied counterattack force.

Refusing to face the strategic realities, Ludendorff still believed that Operation HAGEN could defeat the BEF in the field if only the remainder of the French reserves could be drawn away from Flanders. Nevertheless, simply standing on the defensive was not an option either. The Germans' overextended tactical and logistical situation between the Chemin des Dames and the Marne forced them to renew the attack in that sector in an attempt to improve their position. Although Crown Prince Wilhelm later wrote in his memoirs about "our jumping off point for an attack on Paris,"[86] the German focus was certainly more limited in the early days of June. As Ludendorff himself noted, "We wanted to gain more ground to the west, on account of the rail line that leads from the Aisne valley east of Soissons into that of the Vesle."[87]

As early as the end of April, Ludendorff had ordered the Eighteenth Army to develop contingency plans for an attack between Montdidier and Noyon. After the failure of GEORGETTE, the Eighteenth Army's attack, now designated GNEISENAU, became a supporting follow-on attack for BLÜCHER. It had to start several days after BLÜCHER because of the time required to shift the necessary supporting heavy artillery. The objective for GNEISENAU was the line Montdidier–Compiègne. OHL also estimated that once BLÜCHER was well under way, the French would have shifted most of their reserves from in front of the Eighteenth Army to the newly threatened sector.[88] But all that was based on the assumption that BLÜCHER would be a limited attack, advancing no farther that the Vesle.

On 30 May, as BLÜCHER was in progress, OHL designated 7 June as the start day for GNEISENAU. By 3 June BLÜCHER had clearly reached culmination, and Army Group German Crown Prince recommended halting the attack until the Eighteenth Army could launch GNEISENAU.[89] The following day Hutier complained in his diary that Ludendorff had been troubling him continually over the smallest tactical details of GNEISENAU. Hutier also noted the now-widespread concern among General Staff officers that Ludendorff's obsession with the small picture completely overshadowed his focus on the larger operational picture.[90]

Delays in the preparations for the attack forced OHL had to reschedule GNEISENAU for 9 June. That additional two days, however, gave the Allies—who anticipated the attack—extra time to move up their own reserves. By the time the Germans on 5 June went over to the defensive in the BLÜCHER sector, the original supporting nature of GNEISENAU had changed and any operational connection between BLÜCHER and GNEISENAU no longer existed.[91] Just before the start of the attack the plan changed again, and GNEISENAU was extended eastward, over the Oise. During the first phase of the attack, the Eighteenth Army was supposed to advance five miles to the Matz River, pivoting on Montdidier. There was no final objective designated for the second phase, but OHL hoped the Eighteenth Army would be able to reach the line Montdidier–Compiègne. That would give the Germans control of the critical rail line, which connected at that point to the rail junction at German-held Noyon. It also would put the Eighteenth Army's left wing six miles south of the Matz.[92]

On 4 June Foch warned Haig that if "the enemy pursued his maneuver without pause in the direction of Paris between the Marne and the Oise, or if he developed it on a wider front—between Château-Thierry and Montdidier, for example—all the Allied forces in France would have to give their aid to a battle which, in all probability, would decide the fate of the war."[93] Haig, naturally, was still concerned primarily with another German offensive in Flanders. Despite all the divisions that Ludendorff had diverted from Rupprecht's Army Group to BLÜCHER, French intelligence estimated that Rupprecht still had forty-nine divisions, twenty-six of which were fresh.

Although Foch too was worried about a German attack in the north, he ordered Haig to put three divisions in reserve west of Amiens, from where Foch could commit them to reinforce either the French or the British sectors.[94] Haig complied, but he protested to London under the provisions of the Beauvais Agreement. Shocked by the way Foch and the French had been taken by surprise by the BLÜCHER attacks, London was sympathetic to Haig.[95]

On 7 June Haig attended a meeting at the French War Ministry. Foch insisted that as Allied generalissimo he had the authority, on short notice, to move divisions of any nationality wherever he saw fit. Clemenceau, however, agreed in principle that French GQG could not withdraw any French divisions from the BEF sector without going through Haig first. Milner and Wilson, who had come to Paris for the meeting, expressed concern over the redeployment of French and American reserve divisions from behind the British front.[96] Wilson, who had been a long-standing personal friend of Foch's, was now becoming a severe critic of the Allied generalissimo's handling of the war. In the end, however, the conference supported Foch, which effectively confirmed his control over Allied reserves. Foch, on the other hand, came to accept the limits on his practical authority as Allied commander in chief and henceforth conducted himself more or less accordingly.[97]

This time the Germans were in a rush, and their hasty preparations cost them greatly in operational security. German ammunition and gasoline supplies were very low. Their supply lines ran long distances to the railheads, and the roads were in bad shape.[98] The Germans committed four corps of Hutier's Eighteenth Army and the right-wing corps of Boehn's Seventh Army to GNEISENAU. The five corps had sixteen low-mobility trench divisions and only eight attack divisions available on the first day. Getting the 2,276 guns into position and supplied with ammunition proved a major problem. Bruchmüller was sick, but Ludendorff still pressed him back into service to plan and manage the fire support.

Any commander or intelligence officer with a map could have forecast the area of the next German attack. If nothing else, the rail network pointed directly to the spot. French aerial observers reported major German troop movements right at the start of June. French intelligence, however, somewhat overestimated the German strength, reporting that the Germans had sixty divisions in reserve and could attack with forty-five divisions between the Oise and the Somme. But unlike the first three German offensives, the preparations for GNEISENAU were so obvious that Allied intelligence thought it all might be a huge deception.[99] Then on 3 June, French cryptologist Lieutenant Georges Panvin broke the German ADFGVX signals code and decrypted a German radio transmission that detailed the attack originally scheduled for 7 June. And then on the night of 8 June, a German deserter revealed the exact date and time of the attack.[100]

Pétain on 3 June sent a warning order to the French Third Army to prepare for a defensive battle west of the Oise. Pétain also reminded Third Army commander General Georges Louis Humbert of Directive Number 4. He ordered Humbert to thin out drastically his frontline infantry positions and to pull his artillery back. Humbert's corps commanders, however, still believed in Foch's ideas about holding every inch of ground. Thus, when the Germans did attack, the French still had nearly half their infantry within 2,000 meters of the front line.[101] Overall, Humbert had nine divisions in his front lines and six in reserve. They were supported by four tank groups and 1,058 guns.

On the evening of 4 June, Foch sent Haig a message warning him of "the probability of an immediate attack extending from Noyon to Montdidier."[102] On 6 June, the same day the U.S. Marines attacked into Belleau Wood, Foch sent Pétain a directive designating the Allied strategic objectives as the denial of the road to Paris and the covering of the northern ports while at the same time maintaining control of the Allies' rail lines.

The German artillery started their preparation fires at 0050 hours on 9 June. The infantry moved out at 0420 hours. Along the line the start times were not synchronized well because French counter-preparation fires disrupted the German formations. Despite the ragged start, the German lead units reached Ressons-sur-Matz at about 1100 hours. An hour later the Germans were into the French second lines on a front of more than 7 miles. The Eighteenth Army's left-wing corps reached the Oise River at 1600 hours. Two hours later they reached the north bank of the Matz, having penetrated to a depth of 6.5 miles in a little more than fourteen hours. That same day the German First Army launched a small supporting attack directly against Reims, which failed.[103]

Although the Third Army had too much of its infantry too far forward, the French were not routed on the first day of the attack. They fell back under pressure in an orderly manner and then even launched a spoiling counterattack against the Seventh Army's VII Corps. The commander of Army Group Reserve, General Émile Fayolle, started shifting divisions from other sectors to the Third Army. That evening, Pétain asked Foch to let him have the British XXII Corps, which Haig had placed on-call to Foch. The Allied commander in chief refused because Rupprecht's Army Group still had too many divisions opposite the BEF. Foch, however, did ask Haig to give Pétain one division from that corps.[104] The French at that point had five field armies in the line from Amiens to Reims, with twenty-five divisions in the front lines and twelve in reserve in the Oise valley directly southwest of Compiègne.

Foch was concerned about the threat to Compiègne, the capture of which would relieve the Germans of their most pressing logistics problem.[105] Pershing also recognized that the objective of GNEISENAU was to widen the base of the BLÜCHER salient and to open the rail lines, but he still believed that was all preparatory to "open the way to Paris."[106]

On 10 June, the Eighteenth Army advanced another three miles, completely routing the French 53rd Infantry Division and exposing Humbert's right flank. The French had been planning a pincer counterattack into both flanks of GNEISENAU, but now the attack in the east was impossible.[107] Late that afternoon, General Charles Mangin assumed command of a five-division counterattack force on the French far left. Nicknamed "The Butcher" by his own troops, Mangin was one of the most aggressive commanders on either side of the war who once said, "Whatever you do, you lose a lot of men."

The German center was well across the Matz by the end of the second day of the offensive. The Eighteenth Army's right wing, however, was lagging far behind. The French now had eleven divisions facing thirteen German, far too small a force ratio to continue a sustained offense. For the following day the Eighteenth Army intended to reach the Montdidier–Estrees-St.-Denis–Compiègne rail line. Many of the Allied leaders still continued to fear that Paris was Ludendorff's ultimate objective. Pershing wrote to Secretary of

War Baker warning of the possibility that Paris might fall but also conveying French assurances that they would continue fighting even if their capital was overrun.[108] Writing after the war, however, Pershing could not resist pointing to GNEISENAU as further proof of his own tactical theories: "This defeat of the French furnished the second striking confirmation of the wisdom of training troops for open warfare."[109]

Early on the morning of 11 June the Germans detected that the French to their front were pulling back. Two divisions started to move cautiously into the abandoned French positions, but the German main effort still continued to be Compiègne.[110] Shortly after noon, Mangin's force of five divisions attacked into GNEISENAU's west flank on both sides of Mery. Fayolle originally had planned to attack on 14 June, giving the French artillery an additional forty-eight hours to plan and fire a preparation to neutralize the German artillery. Mangin, with the full support of Foch, insisted on attacking as soon as possible. Not all his divisions were ready, but Mangin attacked anyway. The French infantry went straight into the assault without an artillery preparation but preceded by a creeping barrage. Mangin's forces also were supported by ground-attack aircraft and ten groups of tanks. They operated in a coordinated manner similar to the British counterattack at Cambrai the preceding November. Mangin's force cleared the Aronde valley within a few hours, but German artillery finally brought the counterattack to a halt. The French did manage to disrupt the Eighteenth Army's advance and force the Germans to assume temporary defensive positions.[111] Despite the limited results of the French counterattack, it was the model and served as something of a dress rehearsal for the decisive counterattack that Mangin would launch on 18 July.

By 12 June the actions on both sides were grinding to a halt. Early that morning the French resumed counterattacking against the right wing of the Eighteenth Army. During the night, the advance lines and the rear areas of all the German corps committed to GNEISENAU had suffered from heavy French artillery fire. The French counterattack stalled by midmorning after achieving only modest success, but it again completely disrupted the Eighteenth Army's plans for that day.[112]

Both Foch and Pétain agreed to suspend Mangin's operation. On 13 June, the Germans conducted only local attacks to improve their positions. The following day OHL ordered the end of GNEISENAU, while elements of the Seventh Army continued to fight their defensive battle against the U.S. Marines in Belleau Wood.[113] The fourth of Ludendorff's 1918 offensives was over. Like the first three offensives, GNEISENAU too was an operational failure. But for the first time in 1918, the Germans had failed tactically. Compiègne still remained firmly in Allied hands, and the vital rail lines in the German sector were still effectively frozen.

The threat to Paris now seemed effectively blocked, but the Allies were still worried about a resumed attack on the BEF. Foch sent a message to Pétain and Haig, noting that all available reserves of Army Group German Crown Prince had been committed but relatively few from Army Group Crown Prince Rupprecht. Foch projected that the next major assault would be in the British sector, and he directed both Pétain and Haig to have plans ready to shift all their reserves to the other's sector, if necessary.[114] Foch also told Pétain to send extra artillery to the Army Detachment of the North. Pétain objected, telling Foch, "I continue to refuse Ypres the same value as Paris." But on a somewhat unsarcastically optimistic note, Pétain also wrote, "If we can hold until the end of June, our situation will be excellent. In July, we can resume the offensive. After that, victory is ours."[115]

The British, however, now believed that their French Allies were close to breaking. On 5 June, General Wilson and British secretary of state for war Lord Milner attended a meeting with Lloyd George in London to discuss the possibility of evacuating the BEF from the Continent, should France collapse. Milner followed up by sending a group to France on 13 June to evaluate the evacuation plans.[116] Pershing, meanwhile, stated unequivocally that he did not intend to attach any more American divisions to either the French or the British for training.[117] Lloyd George was incensed. General Wilson responded with a note to Foch complaining about Pershing's decision, insisting that six American divisions should always be training behind the British lines.

Forced into an operational box of his own making, Ludendorff now was faced with the same problem he had after each of his previous offensives had failed—what to do next? He believed that if the Germans abandoned any of the gains they recently had achieved at such high prices, the psychological and morale repercussions would be disastrous. Ludendorff concluded that he had no choice but to continue attacking—somewhere, anywhere. But when some General Staff officers at OHL suggested that Germany could not continue launching large-scale offensives indefinitely, Ludendorff snapped at Lieutenant Colonel Thaer, "What do you expect me to do? Make peace at any price?"[118]

TEN

OPERATION MARNESCHUTZ-REIMS AND THE SECOND BATTLE OF THE MARNE: FOCH WRESTS THE INITIATIVE

A real improvement to our supply system as well as our tactical situation was only possible if we captured Reims. In the battles of May and June we had not managed to get possession of that town. The capture of Reims must now be the object of a special operation, but the operation thus required fitted into the general framework of our plans.

Field Marshal Paul von Hindenburg, Out of My Life

It is commonly believed, I find, that Ludendorff struck straight for Paris in July 1918. He did not.

Lieutenant General Hunter Liggett, A.E.F. Ten Years Ago in France

LUDENDORFF ATTACKS AGAIN: MARNESCHUTZ-REIMS (15–17 JULY 1918)

By the end of the first half of 1918, the German strategic imperative of defeating the British remained unchanged, but Operation BLÜCHER had made the Germans' operational situation much worse. Eight corps of Crown Prince Wilhelm's Seventh and First Armies now held a salient with a perimeter length of more than a hundred kilometers and a chord at the base of some sixty kilometers. The position was vulnerable to attack from all sides and almost impossible to supply as the rail situation then stood.

With Reims and Compiègne still in Allied hands, the double-track line into the salient running from Laon to Soissons was still blocked at the Vauxaillon tunnel. German engineers thought they could have the tunnel opened by 7

July, but only with a single line running initially. Several weeks earlier they had managed to put into service a new low-capacity single-track line that ran through the Aisne valley, branching off the main line between Laon and Reims. A new three-kilometer-long connection to that line was finished on 16 June, running between Guignicourt and Bahnwald. It tied into the local lines in the Vesle valley, establishing a through-route to Laon from Crouy (three kilometers northeast of Soissons), as well as via Bahnwald–Vailly–Missy to Braisne, and farther through Fère-en-Tardenois or through Fismes toward the front. A connection from Vailly directly to Braisne also was under construction but would not be completed until at least 30 July.[1]

On the western side of the salient, the Germans did have a single-track line running from Soissons south to Château-Thierry. But the meager supplies that trickled into the forward-most railheads had to be moved onward overland. All the rivers and the majority of the roads ran east and west, but even then the Germans were woefully short of motorized transport, and they were starting to run out of horses as well. During Operation MICHAEL alone they lost almost 29,000 hard-to-replace horses, and by the end of Operation GNEISENAU the average trench division was 400 to 500 horses short.[2] Thus, the Germans were forced to give transport priority to ammunition over food, forcing their frontline troops to forage off the already depleted countryside.

Ludendorff had only two feasible alternatives—he could order a withdrawal from the Marne salient, or he could try to open it up by enlarging it. For political and psychological reasons, he refused to consider a withdrawal. Thus, the Germans had to resume the attack, but not for the purpose of simply opening an additional rail line; rather, it was for gaining full control over the network in the salient. To do so, they had to seize not only Reims but also Épernay to the south and eventually Châlons to the southeast, both on the Marne River. Châlons was the key to the entire eastern sector of the network. The lines from Châlons to Épernay and from Épernay to Reims formed the two sides of a rough right triangle, with the hypotenuse being the line from Châlons northwest to Reims. The triangle enclosed the heavily wooded and hilly Foret de la Montagne de Reims, directly south of Reims, which dominated the rail lines running along its three sides. The Germans, thus, had to take that high ground as well.[3]

The rail lines, then, were the entire purpose of the fifth 1918 offensive. The main thrust would have to be to the southeast, away from Paris. Despite what Hindenburg later wrote in his memoirs, such an operation was anything but one that "fitted into the general framework of our plans."[4] Aside from the possibility of drawing off a few more French reserves from Flanders, the fifth offensive would be a purely tactical affair with no direct operational link to future operations. As Crown Prince Wilhelm later wrote, "There [was] no strategic objective south of the Marne."[5] He also noted, "This new offensive also had no great strategic purpose in view of a kind to decide a campaign."[6]

Once the situation was stabilized in the Marne sector, Ludendorff had every intention of turning his attention back to the British with Operation HAGEN. He still believed this late in the game that if he could crush the BEF, the French would collapse politically and the steadily arriving American forces would become irrelevant. Many of Ludendorff's subordinate commanders, however, believed his optimism to be little more than wishful thinking. Writing after the war, Wilhelm confessed, "In our eyes the contemplated Marne-Reims blow, under the compulsion of the dynamic law, was probably the last great offensive effort of which we were capable. And it was not intended to produce, and could not produce, a strategic decision, even in the case of complete success."[7]

On 14 June, the day before the official termination of GNEISENAU, Ludendorff convened a conference in Roubaix to plan further operations. Rather than attacking Reims directly, he intended to envelop it with a giant pincer attack from the west and the east. Designated Operation MARNESCHUTZ ("Marne Defense"), the Seventh Army would cross the Marne east of Château-Thierry and then attack east toward Épernay by advancing along both banks of the river. Operation REIMS, conducted by the First Army, would attack east of Reims, south toward Châlons. Once past the Reims hills, the First Army would then swing to the west, and the two arms of the pincers would link up just east of Épernay. The jump-off date was set for 10 July. Rupprecht's Army Group would follow up with Operation HAGEN approximately ten days later. It was a very complex plan. The MARNESCHUTZ-REIMS attack frontage was almost ninety kilometers, and it required almost all the heavy artillery and aviation assets the German army could muster. Then those forces would have to shift rapidly back to Flanders to support HAGEN.[8]

As the planning continued, MARNESCHUTZ-REIMS, like BLÜCHER before it, succumbed to "mission creep." With BLÜCHER, it was an extension in depth. With MARNESCHUTZ-REIMS, the extension was lateral. Under the original plan, the Third Army had the mission of guarding the First Army's left flank. But then the Third Army's leadership started to lobby for a greater role in the offensive. During an 18 June meeting in Rethel with Ludendorff and the staff chiefs of Army Group German Crown Prince and the Seventh, First, and Third Armies, the Third Army's chief of staff, General Wilhelm von Klewitz, pushed hard for a greater role in the operation. He argued that his army could best cover the First Army's flank by making a parallel advance on as broad a front as possible, all to way to the Marne.[9]

Ludendorff agreed, despite the strong objections of his operations chief, Georg Wetzell, who argued that the preparations necessary to accommodate the extension would delay the start of the attack, and even then, the necessary forces were not immediately available.[10] OHL nonetheless issued the order expanding Operation REIMS to the east into Champagne, "as far as the Wetterecke." The following day Ludendorff postponed the start of MARNE-SCHUTZ-REIMS until 14 July.[11]

The lateral extension was a bad decision. West of Reims, most of the line of departure ran along the Marne River, which meant that the Seventh Army would have to start its attack with a deliberate river crossing. But about ten miles east of Épernay the Marne cut sharply to the southeast, placing the river some ten to twenty miles from the lines of departure of the First and Third Armies. The attacking forces of the left arm of the pincers would be advancing over relatively flat and open ground long before they reached the river. The defending French would have good fields of observation in-depth, and the heavily cratered ground from battles earlier in the war would reduce the mobility of the attacking infantry and make it especially difficult for their supplies and artillery to displace forward in support.

An important factor about the 18 June meeting was that, like the 11 November 1917 meeting, no commanders were present. It was a chiefs-of-staff-only affair. And although this was fairly typical of the German army of the Great War, one can only wonder where the commanders of the three echelons—army, army group, and OHL—were. How much of the details did Hindenburg know, and did he not see the inherent flaws in the plan? Why were three field armies now committed to what was supposed to be a limited-objective operation in Champagne when the strategic center of gravity was supposed to be in Flanders? Hindenburg tried to justify the decision in his memoirs:

> After we had originally decided to limit our operation practically to the capture of Reims, our plan was extended in the course of various conferences by adding an attack eastward and right into Champagne. On the one hand our motive was an intention to cut off the Reims salient from the southeast also. On the

other, we believed that in view of our recent experiences, we might perhaps reach Châlons-sur-Marne, attracted as we were by the prospect of great captures of prisoners and war material, if an operation on such a scale succeeded. We therefore *decided to risk the weakening of our forces at decisive points* [emphasis added] for the sake of securing a broad front of attack.[12]

It is very difficult to understand that a trained and experienced General Staff officer, much less one who had passed out of the Kriegsakademie with honors, would try to justify weakening his forces at any decisive points for the nebulous advantage of "securing a broad front of attack." And even then, for what purpose?

After the culmination of BLÜCHER and GNEISENAU, both Foch and Pétain recognized that the Germans south of the Vesle were off-balance and vulnerable. Intent on giving their enemy no breathing space, the French between 6 June and 13 July launched some forty local attacks against the west side of the salient between Soissons and Château-Thierry. Foch, meanwhile, continued to stress that the Allies' most vulnerable point continued to be the junction of the French and British armies in the vicinity of Amiens. But based on their current situation, the two most likely places for the Germans to make their next attack were in Champagne toward the south or in Artois and Flanders toward the west. Those two courses of action were divergent and too widely separated to be mutually supporting, which made it almost impossible to conduct them simultaneously. Besides, the Germans no longer had the forces to try something on such a scale. The Allies, therefore, had to prepare for the most likely possibility while also preparing to deal with the other, either as a follow-up or as the primary attack.[13]

The more he assessed the situation, the more Foch thought it likely that next blow would fall in the south, and he also identified the most vulnerable point for the Germans: "It was easy to see that in the deep but comparatively narrow pocket where the enemy was operating, the railways constituted the only suitable lines of supply for his troops, and these all passed through Soissons. Therefore, the day this vital center of communications came under the fire of our artillery, any German offensive in the direction of Château-Thierry would be deprived of its life blood."[14] Thus, while Ludendorff was planning to put his main effort on the east side of the salient, Foch was planning to counterattack the west side. Foch was slightly off in thinking that Ludendorff's main effort would be directed toward Château-Thierry, but he still accurately identified the most vulnerable point.

On 14 June Foch ordered Pétain to start developing an attack "to capture the high ground commanding Soissons on the west."[15] Six days later General Charles Mangin submitted to Pétain the plan for his Tenth Army to make that attack with forces massed in the Forests of Compiègne and Villers-Cotterêts, east and southeast of Soissons respectively.[16] Shortly thereafter, the French Deuxième Bureau (intelligence) very accurately forecast that the Germans would not be able to attack in the Marne sector before 15 July. On 22 June French intelligence also issued a special study identifying the vulnerable points in the German rail system, which then became the basis for Allied aerial targeting plans.[17]

Meanwhile, although the Allies finally had a single supreme commander, they still had far from a unified command structure. Unlike General Dwight D. Eisenhower's large, multinational, and completely integrated headquarters of World War II, which numbered in the thousands, Foch's tiny group of about twenty general staff officers were all French, with only liaison officers from the British and American armies.[18] As Elizabeth Greenhalgh has pointed out, Foch commanded through personal intervention, but his staff did little detailed planning. Foch also conducted very few conferences with all the national commanders in chief together, preferring one-on-one meetings. In the midst of the fighting in March and April, the supreme headquarters had to be cobbled together on the fly. Once there was a lull in the fighting, difficulties quickly emerged with both the British and French and later the American headquarters. And the major problem was between Foch and Pétain, the two senior-most officers of the French army.[19]

Pétain and Foch had already clashed over Foch's 13 June message to Haig and Pétain telling them to be prepared to support each other, with Pétain categorically refusing to give "Ypres the same value as Paris." Three days later Pétain again exploded when Foch sent another message to Haig and Pétain saying that defenses-in-depth were vulnerable to German infiltration tactics and directing the strengthening of the forward defenses.[20] Such a directive would undermine all the tactical principles that Pétain had been working on implementing for more than a year, and he quite correctly thought Foch was meddling in purely tactical matters that were beyond the scope of his authority. On 17 June Pétain sent an appeal directly to Prime Minister Clemenceau and also shot an angry note back to Foch: "I am informing you that I have no intention of communicating your note of 16 June to the armies under my orders."[21]

On 22 June Prime Minister Lloyd George sent Clemenceau a letter detailing problems that were arising from Foch's inadequate headquarters staff. The letter, drafted by Chief of the Imperial General Staff General Sir Henry Wilson and Secretary for War Lord Alfred Milner, complained especially that Haig's BEF GHQ had to coordinate with Pétain's equal-level GQG for transportation, when Foch's supreme headquarters should be managing all such matters across the theater. Two possible solutions were to give Foch a truly integrated Allied general staff. Wilson, however, opposed that option. Another was to give Foch Pétain's GQG staff and form a new one for Pétain. Nobody in the French government, least of all Pétain, thought much of that option. It was a recipe for chaos. The compromise solution, which still irritated Pétain, was to transfer to Foch's staff Pétain's Direction de l'Arriere department, which was responsible for all rear area transport and supply. Along with that function went the department's more than one hundred general staff officers.[22]

The gulf between Foch and Pétain continued to widen, with each one complaining to Clemenceau about the other. Finally, on 26 June, Clemenceau brought the matter to a head during a meeting of the French War Committee. The committee unanimously endorsed Clemenceau's recommendation that the clause of the Beauvais Agreement that gave the national commanders in chief the right of appeal to their governments would no longer apply to Pétain. It was the final step in the consolidation of Foch's authority over Pétain.[23] To cement the point, however, Foch followed up with the completely unnecessary cheap shot of convincing Clemenceau to order the relief of Pétain's chief of staff, General François Anthoine, without even consulting Pétain.[24]

While all this French infighting was going on, Pershing continued his running series of clashes with the Allies over the issue of American reinforcements. On 17 June Foch and Weygand went to AEF headquarters at Chaumont to try to convince Pershing to release more American units, which they wanted to integrate into the French and British divisions by regiment. Pershing refused to budge. Pétain, however, was furious with Foch for usurping his lead role in dealing with Pershing.[25] Since the AEF was not yet a functioning command and control headquarters and the Americans were deploying into the French sector with French units on either side, the AEF at that point was under Pétain's operational control, although not under his direct command.

In a letter the following day to Secretary of War Newton Baker, the AEF commander commented, "The morale of both the French and British troops is not what it should be. The presence of our troops has braced them up very much, but their staying powers are doubtful. Our 2nd and 3rd Divisions actually stopped the Germans. The French were not equal to it."[26] It was a disingenuous comment that vastly overstated the role of the two American divisions in stopping fifty-four German divisions during Operation BLÜCHER. Operationally, the Germans had reached culmination well before the American divisions went into the line, although heavy fighting continued at the tactical level, during which the Americans acquitted themselves far better than expected.

On 23 June Clemenceau and Foch (again without Pétain) met with Pershing to discuss the flow of American forces into France. The French leaders pressed Pershing to have one hundred American divisions in France by July 1919—keeping in mind the almost double size of the American divisions. Pershing agreed to have forty-six divisions in France by October 1918, sixty-four by January 1919, eighty by April 1919, and one hundred by July.[27] But Pershing made that commitment without coordinating with the U.S. War Department, which subsequently refused to support the AEF commander. The War Department finally committed to having eighty divisions and 3.2 million troops in France by July 1919.[28] Significantly, less than five months before Germany sued for peace, almost all the Allied political and military leaders expected the war to continue well into 1919.

On 1 July Foch issued his General Directive Number 4 concerning future operations. He continued to emphasize Amiens as the most critical point of Allied vulnerability. He noted that the Germans were sixty kilometers from Abbeville, which itself was only forty kilometers west of Amiens. If the Germans managed to advance two-thirds of the way to Abbeville, they would split the British and French armies. He also said that if the Germans tried to thrust more to the southwest toward Paris, an even smaller advance would produce panic and political disruption, although such a move would not have great operational significance. Such an attack could be expected to come from the Château-Thierry corner of the Marne salient. He concluded by reemphasizing the necessity for both the French and the British armies to be prepared to commit their general reserves in support of each other.[29]

The British were now having second thoughts about the unified command. On 4 July the Supreme War Council held its seventh session at Versailles. It would not meet again until October. Lloyd George submitted a motion to reinstate the Executive War Board and its direct control over military operations. Such would completely undercut Foch as Allied supreme commander, making him little more than a conduit for orders. Clemenceau initially seemed to be inclined to concur, but Foch protested and threatened to resign. After a great deal of discussion between Lloyd George and Clemenceau, the SWC finally agreed to leave operational control in Foch's hands, answerable only to the heads of governments. Foch's authority, however, was more tightly delineated to the Western Front only, rather than to the entire Allied war effort.[30] Nonetheless, it was the last significant challenge to Foch's position.

On 5 July Mangin recommended a larger-scale attack on Soissons with his Tenth Army. Pétain approved the basic plan, but he intended to launch the counterattack only after halting the Germans on both sides of Reims. Although Foch was still reluctant to shift reserve divisions from the north, Pétain managed to convince him that the next major blow would fall again in the south, and he finally ordered the movement of the Army Detachment of the North and its six divisions from Flanders to the south, where it was redesignated the Ninth Army and inserted onto the lines between the Sixth and Fifth Armies.[31] That same day Pétain sent a directive to Army Group Center commander General Paul Maistre and the subordinate army commanders that very accurately forecast the objectives of the anticipated German offensive:

> To draw the mass of our reserves from the region of Paris and the zone of the France-British junction.
>
> To effect the fall of Reims and gain a foothold on the Montagne de Reims.
>
> To bring the Épernay–Châlons–Revigny Railroad within range of its artillery.
>
> To enlarge the salient formed by the front of the Second Army by means of an advance west of the Argonne.[32]

On 8 July General Jean-Marie Degoutte's Sixth Army submitted to Pétain a plan to support the Tenth Army's right flank with an attack along the line from Villers-Cotterêts to Château-Thierry. At a meeting in Provins the following day, Foch ordered Pétain to extend the attack of the Tenth and Sixth Armies with supporting attacks by the newly inserted Ninth Army from Château-Thierry west to Fleury and with the Fifth Army west to Châlons. Farther to the east of Reims, the Fourth Army would screen the right flank of the Fifth and deal with the southward attack of the German Third Army. The French were now prepared to counterattack around the entire perimeter of the BLÜCHER salient. While the Tenth and Sixth Armies in the west would thrust toward Soissons, the Ninth Army in the south and the Fifth Army in the southwest would drive toward the high ground north of Fère-en-Tardenois.[33] The objective was not merely to push the Germans back across the Vesle and the Chemin des Dames but to cut off and then eliminate all the German forces south of the Ourcq River.

Foch was convinced that any German attack along the Marne would be more than just a simple feint, and he knew he would need additional American and British forces to contain it before the Allies could counterattack.[34] In addition to the U.S. 2nd and 3rd Divisions already in the front line on either side of Château-Thierry, Foch wanted more American units committed, sooner than later. When he and Pershing met in Bombon on 10 July, the Allied supreme commander told Pershing that he expected more American divisions to participate in the counterattack scheduled for 18 July. Pershing tentatively agreed, and Foch then asked the AEF commander to expedite the formation of American corps in the French sector, offering to provide the necessary artillery.[35]

On 11 July Foch authorized Pétain to withdraw French reserves from the Amiens area. The following day he ordered Haig to shift two British divisions to the French sector south of the Somme. He also warned Haig that based on the coming German attack, he might have to ask for three more British divisions. Although Haig was convinced that Ludendorff intended to follow-up any attack along the Marne with a major blow in Flanders, he nonetheless complied with Foch's request, albeit reluctantly. But Foch was convinced, and correctly so as events played out, that the massive Allied counterattack would tie down so many German forces that they would not be able to attack in force in Flanders, or at least not immediately. Foch wanted to exploit the situation by having the BEF launch its own major attack "from the front Festubert–Robecq, in order to regain control of the mines at Bruay and the communications hub at Estaires."[36] That essentially was an attack that Foch had outlined previously in his General Directive Number 3 of 20 May.

Meanwhile, the tug-of-war over tactics between Foch and Pétain continued unabated. Meeting with Pershing at Provins on 13 July, Pétain complained that he could not get specific guidance from Foch on how to respond to the impending German offensive. Pershing, in turn, grumbled that his divisions were strung out along the entire Western Front, from the Channel to Belfort. The AEF currently had twenty-six divisions in France. The 1st and 2nd Divisions were already in combat, and thirteen more were in currently nonactive British and French sectors of the line for training and orientation. The 30th Division was on the British far left, north of Ypres, and the 32nd Division was on the French far right, south of Mulhouse. Pointing out that six American divisions were now concentrated near Château-Thierry—including the engaged 1st and 2nd—Pershing suggested that he take direct command of that sector for the coming battle. Pétain demurred.[37]

A rigid, forward defense versus a flexible defense-in-depth continued to be a major sticking point. Although as Allied supreme commander Foch had no authority to dictate tactics to the British or Americans, the French government's decision of 26 June gave him just that authority over the French army. Pétain refused to give up on the efficacy of defense-in-depth. The Tenth and Sixth Armies were not in the projected sector of the German attack. The American divisions were under Degoutte's Sixth Army. General Antoine de Mitry, whose Ninth Army faced the southern nose of the salient, generally ignored Pétain's defense-in-depth directives and instead complied with Foch. In Mitry's case, however, he had a far stronger starting position, because his forward line fronted the Marne and his mission was to defeat the German crossing.

Pétain had better luck on the eastern end of the line with the commanders of the Fifth and Fourth Armies, Generals Henri Berthelot and Henri Gouraud. In those sectors the German front line ran from ten to fifteen miles north of the Marne, and the ground east of Reims was relatively flat and open with good observation. When in early July Pétain first approached Gouraud about establishing a defense-in-depth, the Fourth Army commander refused and threatened to appeal to Foch if necessary. Pétain final convinced Gouraud of the logic of positioning the main body of his infantry beyond German artillery range. Thus, when the blow finally fell, the French forces east of Reims were deployed skillfully in great depth. The outpost line was very thinly manned. The main line of defense was 2,000 meters or more from the German lines, containing some two-thirds of the French infantry and three-quarters of the artillery. Farther to the rear was the second line of defense, and the reserves were behind that.[38]

The Germans deployed forty-eight divisions along the 119-kilometer attack front. Bruchmüller, who once again was in charge of the fire planning, massed 6,353 guns and 2,200 trench mortars. The French Sixth, Fifth, and Fourth Armies had only thirty-six divisions and 3,080 guns.[39] The Allies, however, were well prepared. Unlike the first three offensives, German security measures for MARNESCHUTZ-REIMS were poor at best. This time the enemy would not have the advantage of surprise. Nor were the German divisions of the same quality as those that had fought in operations MICHAEL, GEORGETTE, or even BLÜCHER. Of the twenty-seven divisions in the first line, Allied intelligence rated only ten of them as fully combat effective. Sixteen had fought in one of the previous offensives, and five had fought in two.[40]

Mangin's Tenth Army started to deploy into its counterattack positions on 14 July. Late that night Crown Prince Wilhelm went to a forward observation post to witness the artillery preparation, scheduled to start at 0110 hours on the fifteenth. When he got there, the sector artillery commander reported that the German lines were receiving only the normal harassing fire. Wilhelm thought differently: "I had, on the contrary, a decided impression that the French were keeping up a very lively fire on our rear areas. Many explosions were heard, and we could see several of our ammunition dumps on fire. My doubts increased."[41] Those doubts were well placed.

On the first day of the attack, 15 July, the German artillery fired 4.5 million rounds, including their first large-scale use of smoke projectiles to obscure Allied observation during the river crossing. Gas, however, made up only one-eighth of the total rounds fired, down significantly from the one-third average of the earlier attacks.[42] But French intelligence had determined from prisoner interrogations the exact starting time of the German attack. Crown Prince Wilhelm's suspicions were right. One hour before the German artillery preparation started, the French artillery started an increased program of harassing and interdicting fire. Then ten minutes after the German preparation started, the Allies opened up with a full-scale counterpreparation. Heavily outnumbered in total number of guns, the French decided to forgo counterbattery fire and concentrate totally on the enemy infantry.[43] The German infantry jumped off at 0450 hours. On either side of Reims the attackers encountered completely different tactical situations.

East of Reims, the Third Army's attack met very little resistance on the ground, as the defenders' outposts withdrew on first contact. French artillery fire, however, was far heavier than anticipated, inflicting heavy casualties. At about 0730 hours the German artillery reached its maximum range, and the creeping barrage lifted. To the attackers' front the Germans found themselves facing a fully manned zonal defense that their artillery had hardly touched.[44]

And just when the attackers needed their artillery, most of the German batteries had displaced and were attempting to move forward. By noon the Third Army was completely bogged down.[45] Closer to Reims, the Seventh Army pushed five miles up the Andre River valley and reached the southern slope of the Montagne de Reims. But it was stopped there by reserves that Pétain had positioned in the woods.

West of Reims the French counterpreparation played havoc with the Seventh Army's river-crossing operation. The Germans managed to get a few bridges up, but they could not get any guns across. Small groups of infantry crossed in small boats.[46] By noon, elements of four corps were on the south bank. Another corps on the north bank started advancing east along the river. Progress was slow, too slow. By nightfall the Germans had some six divisions on the south bank but almost no artillery. All the while, French artillery and aviation continually hit the bridges and pounded the German forces on both banks.[47] As Hindenburg later understated the situation, "The results certainly did not correspond to our high hopes."[48]

During a phone conversation that evening, General Hermann von Kuhl and Ludendorff discussed the dismal first day's results. Kuhl, of course, was not the chief of staff of Army Group German Crown Prince Wilhelm, but Kuhl was habitually one of the first ones Ludendorff turned to when things were not going right. Kuhl recommended continuing the attacks of the First and Third Armies. Ludendorff was reluctant to risk taking the additional casualties for what he now recognized as nebulous gains in the east.[49]

Late that night OHL ordered the continuation of a somewhat scaled-back version of the operation. Shutting down the Third Army attack in the east, the main effort would now concentrate entirely on cutting off the Reims salient—which had been Wetzell's original recommendation.[50] But OHL also ordered the start of the planned massive transfer of supporting forces north for Operation HAGEN. In the face of stark reality, Ludendorff still believed that by continuing MARNESCHUTZ-REIMS, he could scare the Allies into shifting more of their reserves from Flanders.[51] But at the same time, Ludendorff was withdrawing from the Seventh and First Armies the very artillery, aviation, and engineer support they would need to have any chance of accomplishing anything. As an entry that day in the war diary of Army Group German Crown Prince noted pessimistically, "It is now clear that the objective of the operation—to cut off the enemy in the Reims valley through a junction of the Seventh and First Armies in the vicinity of Épernay—cannot be attained. We have to be satisfied with minor success."[52]

Pétain's general reserve in the south of the Marne was thirty-eight divisions, of which four were British and five American. Behind his entire front, from the Argonne to Switzerland, he had only one division in reserve and only a single British division covering the approaches to Paris from the north.[53] Early in the attack Pétain was forced to commit more reserves that he had planned to reinforce the Fifth Army. That left him short of the forces necessary for his counterattack on both sides of the salient.[54] By midmorning Pétain ordered a postponement of the counterattack. He also ordered Mangin and Degoutte to release some of their reserves for redeployment to the eastern side of the salient. On his way to a meeting with Haig at Mouchy-le-Châtel, Foch stopped on his way at General Émile Fayolle's headquarters, where he learned of Pétain's postponement order. Foch immediately canceled Pétain's order and ordered Mangin to attack on schedule: "It must be understood that until there are new developments that you will communicate to me, there can be no question at all of slowing up and less so of stopping the [counteroffensive]."[55]

Foch and Haig met at Mouchy-le-Châtel that afternoon. Under protest, Haig complied with Foch's order to transfer four more of the BEF's divisions to the French sector. Foch assured the BEF commander that he would get those divisions back immediately if the Germans did attack in Flanders.[56] BLÜCHER followed by MARNESCHUTZ-REIMS badly shook the British government and again raised questions about Haig following Foch's orders. Worried about the large reserves that Crown Prince Rupprecht still had facing the British sector, the War Cabinet told Haig, "If you consider the British Army is endangered, or if you think that General Foch is not acting solely on military considerations, . . . rely on your judgment under the Beauvais Agreement as to the security of the British front."[57]

Just after midnight on the morning of 16 July, Army Group German Crown Prince ordered the Seventh Army to resume the advance on both sides of the Marne in the direction of Épernay. About the same time, General Karl von Einem ordered the right wing of his Third Army to continue pushing forward to cover the First Army's left flank, as it tried to envelop the east side of Reims. He ordered the left wing of his army to go over to the defensive.[58]

On the second day of the battle the Germans made some progress north of the Marne, but they were unable to expand their bridgeheads on the south bank. By the end of the day, Einem was forced to halt the attack by his right wing.[59] That made it virtually impossible for the Germans to complete a deep envelopment from south of the Montagne de Reims. The best the Germans could do now was to cut Reims off with a shallow envelopment just south of the town. But even that would prove impossible.

All that day the French continued pounding the German bridges and bridgeheads with air attacks and heavy artillery and also started attacking deeper against the rear lines of communications. Three French divisions along with elements of the newly committed U.S. 28th Division counterattacked against the German western end of the bridgehead and drove the attackers back one mile.[60] As Foch mused, "I wonder if Ludendorff knows his craft?"[61]

By the end of 16 July, the First and Third Armies ceased all offensive operations. That evening Army Group German Crown Prince ordered the Seventh Army to halt its operations south of the Marne but to continue attacking the next day toward the Reims hills with their two corps north of the Marne.[62] But even that attack made little sense, because the right arm of the pincers no longer had a left arm to link up with. Meanwhile, the supporting forces for HAGEN started moving north that day, continually draining the German combat power along the Marne.

At that point, it was obvious to all that the German offensive was dead in its tracks. Pétain now regained his confidence that Mangin's counterattack could proceed as planned. Late that day the U.S. 1st and 2nd Divisions withdrew from the line around Château-Thierry and moved north into counterattack assembly areas in the Compiègne and Retz Forests, just to the west of Soissons. The deployment went anything but smoothly for the inexperienced Americans. As General Hunter Liggett described the deployment in the pouring rain, "Transport moves hub-to-hub in the black, wet night, driving the infantry off the roads to feel its way in columns of files along bypaths and over fallen timber. Little tanks and big tanks, crazily camouflaged, lumber by. Tractors labor past, towing 155 howitzers and 155 longs, and horses pull the wicked 75s."[63]

On the morning of 17 July, OHL decided to terminate MARNESCHUTZ-REIMS. But the rail network problem still existed, and the Germans had to take Reims. Later that day OHL ordered the Seventh and First Armies to prepare a limited objective to cut off Reims from both directions. The start date for the resumption of the attacks was set for 21 July, with the First Army's leadership protesting vigorously that they did not have enough time to get ready.[64] Meanwhile, all units were ordered to go on the defensive, and the heavy support units continued to roll north, away from the battle. Ludendorff left OHL for Rupprecht's headquarters at Tournai for a final coordination meeting on HAGEN. That same day, Lieutenant Colonel Hermann Mertz von Quirnheim, a General Staff officer in the OHL operations section, wrote in his diary,

"I am convinced at this moment that neither Ludendorff nor Wetzell knows what further action they must take."[65]

By the end of the day a state of chaos reigned along the German front lines. Most of the bridges over the Marne were down, and the Seventh Army's units on the south bank were cut off and subject to relentless attack by French artillery and aircraft. About midnight, OHL finally ordered a withdrawal from the bridgehead by echelon. All forces were supposed to be back on the north bank by the night of 20 July.[66]

With the immediate crisis now past, Haig sent Foch a message to try to get his four divisions back for the attack against his sector that he believed was coming next and that Ludendorff at that point still had every intention of launching. After Foch responded that the Allies would launch a major counterattack the following day, Haig finally told the Allied supreme commander that he could use the four BEF divisions for exploitation, but that would leave him dangerously short of forces in Flanders.[67]

Pershing, meanwhile, was having a change of heart about the piecemeal use of the American forces, or perhaps he wanted to get more of his divisions in on the big show. The 3rd, 28th, and 42nd Divisions were already engaged along the Marne battle line, and the 1st and 2nd Divisions had redeployed as part of Mangin's counterattack force. Pershing now offered Foch the U.S. 32nd and 29th Divisions.[68] That night Pétain issued the final orders for the counteroffensive, as a heavy thunderstorm helped to mask the assembly of the Allied forces.

FOCH HITS BACK HARD: THE SECOND BATTLE OF THE MARNE (18 JULY–7 AUGUST 1918)

The German failure to detect the massive buildup for Mangin's counterattack was an intelligence fiasco equal to the Allies' failure to detect the buildup for BLÜCHER until it was too late. Supported by 346 tanks, 1,545 guns, and 581 aircraft, the Tenth Army had ten divisions in the first line and six infantry divisions and a cavalry corps in the second line. Degoutte's Sixth Army on the right flank had seven divisions, supported by 147 tanks, 588 guns, and 562 aircraft. Degoutte also had on-call priority for three more of the double-sized American divisions. Farther back, the Allies had ten divisions, 918 guns, and approximately 800 aircraft in army or army group reserve. Along the forty-kilometer attack sector, the Germans had ten divisions in the first line and six in the second line, but only two of the sixteen were rated as fully combat capable. Making the situation even worse, OHL had already stripped much of the heavy artillery out of that sector, giving the Allies a tube superiority ratio of 2.3:1.[69]

At 0535 hours on 18 July the French Tenth Army achieved total surprise by attacking behind a creeping barrage from out of the wooded area of Villers-Cotterêts, but without an artillery preparation. The Sixth Army attacked an hour later following a short preparation. By midmorning the Tenth Army captured Chaudun, Vierzy, and Villers-Helon, north of the Ourcq. It also had the Soissons rail center under heavy artillery fire.

That day in Tournai, Ludendorff convened the final planning and coordination meeting for HAGEN. Right at the start he intended to quash the many rumors about a major Allied counterattack in the south: "Before we start our discussions on Operation HAGEN, I want to quell any rumors that the French have major reserves in the Villers-Cotterêts Forest. OHL has a reliable intelligence system. The enemy cannot possibly have combat-ready reserves available. We know the casualty rates and decreases in strength in the French and British units. OHL can state categorically that any such rumors are unfounded."[70]

Almost as soon as Ludendorff made those comments, the reports of an Allied counterattack in force started coming into Rupprecht's headquarters. Ludendorff immediately ordered an infantry division from the OHL reserve to move to the threatened sector. He then ended the conference and left for OHL at Avenues "in the greatest state of nervous tension."[71] A few hours earlier OHL had ordered the Seventh Army to establish a main a line of resistance running from Soissons to the high ground north of Château-Thierry and to hold that line until ordered otherwise. OHL also ordered the Seventh Army to evacuate the Marne bridgehead.[72] Soon after Ludendorff's return, OHL ordered a halt to the HAGEN transport movements and also ordered Rupprecht's Army Group to transfer two of its HAGEN attack divisions to the Soissons sector.[73]

By midday on 18 July the French XX Corps, consisting of the U.S. 1st and 2nd Divisions with the French 1st Moroccan Division between them, carried the plateau just west of Buzancy, which gave Allied artillery command of the main road between Soissons and Château-Thierry. By the end of the day, however, the attack was starting to run out of steam, although the Allies had advanced seven kilometers, taking some 12,000 prisoners and 250 guns from eleven German divisions. As good as those results were, the planned schedule was for an advance of twelve to fourteen kilometers. The French also lost more than 80 percent of their tanks to a combination of German artillery fire and mechanical breakdown. Nonetheless, the Germans were facing a critical situation. With the Soissons rail center under Allied fire, the entire Seventh Army line of communications system on the right flank of the salient was seriously threatened. The heavy Allied fire made it impossible for the German reinforcements to detrain directly at Soissons. As Hindenburg described the situation in his memoirs, "We were compelled to detrain the arriving reinforcements and reliefs in the neighborhood of Laon and far away from the salient. They then proceeded to the battlefield by forced marches, which took days. Often they reached their destination only just in time to take over the line from their exhausted comrades and save a complete collapse."[74]

When Pétain, Fayolle, and Mangin met to review the day's actions, Mangin asked Pétain for more forces to continue the attack. Pétain said he had none to give, but Foch gave the Tenth Army four divisions from the general reserve. Foch also issued a special directive on reinforcing the Tenth and Sixth Armies' attacks. He stressed that forces were not to be withdrawn from the Ninth, Fifth, or Fourth Armies. Foch wanted to attack the east side of the German salient as soon as possible.[75] At the end of 18 July an anonymous but somewhat prophetic General Staff officer, who saw clearly what Ludendorff could not, wrote in the Seventh Army's war diary, "The effort to recover ourselves and support the front between the Aisne and Marne cost us so heavily that Army Group German Crown Prince was forced to give up all intentions of continuing our offensive for some time to come. And here, we at once see an undoubtedly great strategic success for General Foch and, based on this viewpoint, July 18, 1918 marks a turning point in the history of the World War."[76]

As the Allies resumed the attack on 19 July, OHL was trying desperately to stabilize the situation in an attempt to salvage HAGEN. But it was slipping away from the Germans, fast. The Germans already had been forced to redeploy four of Rupprecht's twenty-six carefully husbanded attack divisions. OHL, meanwhile, continued to pour more forces into the Marne salient, but the Seventh Army's situation continued to deteriorate. Around midday Hindenburg uncharacteristically intervened in the operations process. He opined that all the German reserves should be pulled out of Flanders immediately and redeployed to shore up the Seventh Army's right wing. Ludendorff brushed off the idea as "utterly unfeasible," because it would mean the end of HAGEN. When Hindenburg brought it up again later that evening, the agitated Ludendorff blurted out in the presence of other staff officers that the idea was "nonsense." The first quartermaster general of the German army was deeply offended that the commander in chief would presume to interfere in the operational planning. Hindenburg responded by calling Ludendorff into his office for a private discussion.[77]

Ludendorff had crossed all the red lines. Although a German chief of staff was permitted and even expected to argue with his commander, such discussions were not supposed to take place in the presence of others. That was the first major open eruption between the two. As long as everything had been running smoothly, from their initial collaboration at Tannenberg in 1914 through the at least impressive tactical success of BLÜCHER, there had been no open fissures in what Hindenburg once called a "happy marriage" between commander and chief of staff. In their memoirs neither Hindenburg nor Ludendorff mentioned the blowup between the two, although Hindenburg did note what he thought the correct course of action should have been. It would not be their last clash. Over the course of the next three months, as Germany's battlefield position deteriorated steadily, the rift between the unflappable Hindenburg and the irascible Ludendorff only grew.

Just after noon Foch sent Pétain an instruction, reemphasizing that the Allied objective was to destroy the German forces south of the Aisne and the Vesle. To accomplish this, the Tenth Army would continue advancing eastward to take the high ground to the north and east of Fère-en-Tardenois. The Sixth Army would continue covering the Tenth Army's right flank. The Ninth and Fifth Armies were to assume the offensive as soon as possible, with the Ninth Army pushing the Germans back to the north of the Marne and the Fifth Army pushing in on the salient from the east.[78]

The Germans had started out attempting a giant pincer movement, and now they were caught in the jaws of one themselves. The Seventh Army continued to withdraw its forces back across the Marne while simultaneously trying to hold back the Allied attacks against its right flank. Momentum was not on its side. The Seventh Army's war diary entry for 19 July once again summarized the situation quite clearly:

> Even if the initial push of the attack has been stopped, resistance to continued attacks will have to be maintained until such time as the troops, equipment, and supplies have been withdrawn over the Vesle. This means in terms of the artillery

of the approximately 40 divisions a total length of march of about 600 kilometers. If the defense, already weak and undermined, does not hold off the enemy during the withdrawal, a catastrophe could still occur.[79]

The French Ninth and Fifth Armies attacked on 20 July. All three sides of the BLÜCHER salient were now under siege. OHL withdrew another three attack divisions from Flanders, leaving only nineteen available for HAGEN.[80] But by the time the two French armies attacked from the east, the two attacking from the west were losing momentum rapidly. The Allies did clear Château-Thierry that day. As the Germans reinforced the shoulders of the salient, they also started withdrawing methodically to the north. That meant that they were being pushed back, but not cut off as Pétain initially intended. By insisting on frontal attacks around the entire perimeter of the salient, Foch most likely helped the Germans withdraw somewhat intact.[81] Much the same thing happened during the Battle of the Bulge, December 1944–January 1945.

It is doubtful, however, that Mangin had sufficient force and momentum left to complete a thrust across the salient. That afternoon Pétain shifted the main effort to the Sixth Army, which had just brought into the line the fresh American 3rd, 26th, and 28th Divisions. The Tenth Army was to continue to push toward Soissons. The Ninth Army was to attempt to cut off any further German retreat across the Marne. The Fifth Army was ordered to move northwest along the Andre valley, to maintain pressure on the eastern side of the salient.

Ludendorff, whose nerves were all but shattered, summoned to OHL Major General Fritz von Lossberg, the chief of staff of the Fourth Army that was supposed to make the main effort of Operation HAGEN. "Der Abwehrlöwe" was the German army's undisputed master of defensive operations. Whenever the Allies had attacked on the Western Front during the second half of 1916 and throughout 1917, Ludendorff habitually sent Lossberg to take over as chief of staff at the threatened sector. So far, he always had managed to save the situation.

Lossberg was not quite prepared for what he found when he reached OHL. Ludendorff was on the verge of panic. As Lossberg recalled in his memoirs, "To my regret, he unjustifiably made accusations against the chief of the Operations Section, Colonel Georg Wetzell, and his staff. Ludendorff believed that they had 'failed' to evaluate the combat power of the Seventh Army correctly. It was a rather embarrassing scene. Wetzell remained silent, as a good soldier, but it was obvious that he took the reproach very hard."[82] A few weeks later

Ludendorff completed making Wetzell his scapegoat by firing him. Many of the senior officers in the German army knew better. Wetzell eventually retired in 1927 as a general of infantry and chief of the Truppenamt (Troop Office), as the clandestine General Staff of the Weimar Republic was called.

After Wetzell's operations section briefed the overall situation, Lossberg recommended that the Seventh Army withdraw immediately behind the Aisne and the Vesle. Newly arriving replacements should be redirected to the old Siegfried Position of 1916, to begin preparing it for a general withdrawal from the Somme sector starting in three weeks' time. That, of course, would mean returning to the German starting positions of March, giving up all the ground that had been won since then at such a terrible price. Lossberg also recommended that HAGEN still be launched, but later and in a reduced form, which would achieve only limited tactical and not major operational results. The purpose would be to buy time to establish an even more cohesive defense along the entire line. If in the event the limited HAGEN attack did not achieve any tactical results, then Lossberg recommended that the Fourth and Sixth Armies should withdraw to their original starting line for GEORGETTE and the entire Western Front go on the defensive immediately.

After thinking about it, Ludendorff told Lossberg that his recommendations were sound, but he could not accept them for political reasons. Asked what those political reasons were, Ludendorff indicated the conclusions that would be drawn by the enemy, by the German troops, and by the civilians and political leaders in the homeland. Despite the recommendations of the best defensive tactician in the German army, Ludendorff intended to continue the fight from the current forward battle lines. As a fallback course of action, he did agree to the reconnoitering of a new defensive position along the Combles–Péronne–Noyon line, which was still well forward of the old Siegfried Position. Lossberg countered that the preparation from scratch of such a position would take far longer than putting the already existing Siegfried Line back in shape for rapid occupation. Ludendorff refused to dedicate any resources to the Siegfried Line, and in the end, the Allied attacks throughout August overran the Combles–Péronne–Noyon line before it was even ready.

Not one to be intimidated in the face of superior rank, Lossberg in the best tradition of a German General Staff officer continued to push for what he considered to be the correct course of action. As Ludendorff became increasingly despondent, he finally said that if Lossberg was right, then he (Ludendorff) should immediately offer his resignation to Hindenburg. Lossberg talked Ludendorff out of resigning, but he later admitted to regretting doing so. Ludendorff then ordered his defensive expert to visit the Seventh Army to assess the situation on the ground and report back to him. Lossberg left for the front under the mistaken belief that he had convinced Ludendorff to act on his recommendations. Both Wetzell and the chiefs of staff of both army groups concurred with Lossberg's recommendations.[83] Rupprecht himself came to the conclusion that Germany had culminated strategically and operationally and the German army had no choice but to go on the defensive.[84]

By the end of 20 July, seven HAGEN attack divisions had been withdrawn from Rupprecht's Army Group. That night Ludendorff issued an order postponing HAGEN indefinitely.[85] The Seventh Army's last troops reached the north bank of the Marne around dawn on 21 July. After a heavy artillery barrage, the Allies attacked with tanks, but that push stalled in the face of heavy German fire. Later that day Kuhl arrived in Avesnes to argue for launching a reduced form of HAGEN to be called KLEIN-HAGEN.[86] Despite his continued reluctance to adopt Lossberg's recommendation to withdraw from the Marne salient, Ludendorff understood full well the precariousness of the German position. Much to Kuhl's chagrin, Ludendorff outlined the plans for a major counterattack from both flanks of the salient, which would require Army Group Crown Prince Rupprecht to give up five more fresh divisions.[87] Ludendorff was starting to build castles in the air.

By the end of 21 July, the Allies had recaptured Château-Thierry, but OHL believed that the French attack finally had been halted. Nonetheless, with Soissons under heavy artillery fire, it became almost impossible to reinforce or resupply the Seventh Army in its current positions. The Seventh Army therefore, recommended a general withdrawal back from the Marne. Army Group German Crown Prince concurred and forwarded the recommendation to OHL.[88]

The influx of American troops into France by that point gave the Allies a 200,000-man superiority over the Germans on the Western Front.[89] On 22 July, Foch sent Pershing a message confirming the results of a discussion that the two had with Pétain the day before. The Allied commander in chief approved the formation of an American field army under Pershing's command. The new U.S. First Army would consist of those American divisions that were trained and combat ready. At that point, eight American divisions were already in the fight, under the operational control of the four French armies. As those divisions rotated out of the line, they would revert to Pershing's direct control. Once the First Army was established, it would come under the overall operational control of Pétain, as commanding general of the French Armies of the North and Northeast.[90]

The Allied counterattack was losing momentum, but Ludendorff finally faced the reality that he had to order a withdrawal from the Marne. He still, however, did not accept Lossberg's recommendation to pull back all the way to the Vesle. Instead, he approved only a withdrawal to the line of the Ourcq. That afternoon Hindenburg informed the kaiser that the retrograde movement was necessary to avoid further casualties and to establish a stronger defensive position.[91] As the Germans withdrew north, their artillery lost the range to interdict the Paris–Châlons rail line. Once the full length of that line was open, Americans had a direct rail network from their Atlantic ports to their operational bases centered around Saint Mihiel.[92]

On 23 July Foch sent Pétain a message complaining about the slackening of momentum in the Allied advance. Despite the fact that Pétain had shifted the main effort to the Sixth Army, Foch insisted that the Tenth Army continue as the main effort.[93] By that point, however, the Germans had managed to organize their trademark tenacious defense, and the Allied attack made little headway that day. Ludendorff began to vacillate on the necessity of a withdrawal, regaining some confidence that aggressive offensive action might restore the situation. OHL postponed the retrograde movement and ordered the First Army to be ready to attack Reims from the west on the twenty-fifth.[94] Wetzell objected, still supporting Lossberg's recommendation to withdraw to the north of the Aisne. Mertz von Quirnheim noted in his diary that day Ludendorff's steadily declining psychological state: "The real impression is that His Excellency has lost all confidence. The army commanders suffer terribly from this."[95] Army Group German Crown Prince also objected to the plan to remain fighting in place, reporting to OHL that eighteen of the Seventh Army's divisions were no longer combat effective and had to be withdrawn from the line immediately.[96]

The following day Army Group German Crown Prince, apparently on its own initiative, ordered a general pullback to the Aisne. Ludendorff canceled the order and in turn ordered an attack toward Soissons by the Ninth Army, which recently had been inserted into the line on the Seventh Army's right flank. But General Fritz von Below, the Ninth Army's commander, demanded five fresh attack and ten fresh trench divisions, and even then, he insisted that his army could not be ready to attack for at least fourteen days.[97]

The First Army attacked Reims on 25 July but ended up losing ground rather than taking it. That day Lossberg returned to OHL from the Seventh Army and resumed his argument for major withdrawals. Ludendorff gave in, but only partially. At midnight, OHL ordered the Seventh Army to prepare for the retrograde movement starting the night of the twenty-seventh. Rather than all the way to the Aisne, however, the pullback objective was only to Fère-en-Tardenois and the line of the Ourcq—an intermediate position designated the "Great Bridgehead Position."[98] Lossberg returned to his Fourth Army headquarters in a state of complete exasperation.[99]

Since 18 July, Mangin's Tenth Army had been reinforced with six fresh divisions, and two more were moving up. The Germans were falling back slowly but in good order. Pétain's original intention of cutting off large German forces in the salient was no longer possible. On 26 July, the French War Ministry gave Foch's headquarters authority over all the French railways, thereby expanding his strategic authority.[100]

The Seventh Army started withdrawing to the Great Bridgehead Position on the night of 27 July. Before that move was even completed, however, Ludendorff finally caved in to reality and approved the planning and preparations for the withdrawal to the north of the Vesle, with all forces closing on the night of 1–2 August.[101] The Allies were still a mile short of Soissons, and the French Ninth Army north of the Marne was stalled after taking heavily casualties. The following day Hindenburg went through the formalities of requesting official permission from the kaiser for the withdrawal. The kaiser had no real say in the matter. OHL had already issued the order before Hindenburg sent his message.[102] Summarizing his assessment of the overall situation that Ludendorff up to that point had refused to accept, Rupprecht wrote in his diary, "We can exercise resistance successfully for a long time. Our last hope is to hold out long enough until the enemy concludes that the sacrifice in blood and material are out of proportion to the results, especially since every one of our retreats means the complete destruction of the land between the lines."[103]

Ludendorff, however, had no intention of pursuing a strategy of delay and defend. The first quartermaster general insisted that Germany had to achieve what he called a "Hindenburg Peace." That meant permanent German control over Belgium and France's Briey-Longwy iron ore basin, plus control of the southern Baltic coast and much of the conquered territory in the east. The Allies would never agree to such a settlement. Britain in particular would never permit the loss of the neutrality of the Belgian coast. But Ludendorff still believed that he could accomplish those objectives, not simply by holding out and grinding the Allies down, as Rupprecht suggested, but by resuming the offensive as soon as possible.

Not only was Ludendorff still clinging to the hope of launching HAGEN or KLEIN-HAGEN, but as early as 26 June he had issued the warning order to start planning and preparing an attack to follow up HAGEN. Still believing that he could push the BEF off the Continent, Operation KURFÜRST would then drive directly for Paris.[104] Both army groups went through the motions of drawing up the plans, but everyone knew that the required forces existed on paper only. The state of mind surrounding Ludendorff at OHL in July 1918 was something of an eerie foreshadowing of the mindset in Hitler's bunker in April 1945, with the Führer moving nonexistent divisions around on the map.

On 28 July Foch sent a memo to Pershing commenting on issues that the AEF commander had raised with Pétain over the deployment of the American First Army and the subsequent raising of a U.S. Second Army. Reminding Pershing of who ultimately held the Allied supreme command, Foch wrote, "Finally, once the two American armies formed, situations may arise which demand that the American divisions newly arrived either hold a quiet sector in the French zone in order to free necessary units for the battle, or that American divisions ready for combat go and support a part of the attacked but inadequately supported front. I will therefore if need be call to the help which you always generously offered to the Allied armies."[105]

Relations between Foch and Pershing were not getting any better. Still completely discounting the Allies' four years of experience in the war, the AEF commander sent a complaining cable to Secretary of War Baker:

> I have had to insist very strongly, in the face of determined opposition, to get our troops out of leading strings. You know the French and British have always advanced the idea that we should not form divisions until our men had three or four months with them. We have found, however, that only a short time was necessary to learn all they know, as it is confined to trench warfare almost entirely, and I have insisted on open warfare training. To get this training, it has been necessary to unite our men under our own commanders, which is now being done rapidly.[106]

By 29 July the Germans had twenty-three divisions in the front line between Soissons and Reims and only eight divisions in reserve. Thirteen of the divisions on the front line were completely spent.[107] That day Pétain sent a telegram to Fayolle and Pershing, saying that the objective now was "to throw back the enemy on the Vesle gradually by successive efforts." Despite Foch's continued emphasis on the Tenth Army, Pétain once again shifted the main effort to the Sixth, which now had four American divisions under its command.[108] Pétain, however, was growing increasingly pessimistic. The French armies in the Marne sector were short 120,000 men and Pétain had only one fresh division left. "We are at the limit of our effort," he told Foch on 31 July.[109]

On the afternoon of 2 August, the last German forces pulled out of Soissons. The French Tenth, Sixth, and Fifth Armies linked up south of the Vesle, forcing the Germans to withdraw another eight miles north of the river.[110] Three days later the Allies pushed the Germans back to the Chemin des Dames ridge, their starting line for Operation BLÜCHER. Continuing to waffle on HAGEN, Ludendorff that day issued a muddled order directing that while the German forces continued to consolidate their defenses, they still had to be prepared to launch KLEIN-HAGEN, or possibly KURFÜRST, or possibly an attack farther to the east in the Champagne region.[111]

By 5 August the French and Americans had inflicted some 110,000 casualties on the Germans, capturing in the process 612 irreplaceable artillery pieces, 3,330 machine guns, and 1 million rounds of artillery ammunition.[112] The Allies actually suffered higher casualties, at 160,000 dead, wounded, missing, and captured. But in the bloody calculus of war, the Allied losses were being made up rapidly by American replacements. And very importantly, the Paris–Châlons rail line immediately south of the Marne was now cleared, opening the major line of communications for the AEF.[113]

Trying to put the best spin on the disaster, Hindenburg after the war wrote, "It was not the power of the enemy's arms which forced us out of the Marne salient, but the hopelessness of our situation as the result of the communications in the rear of our troops fighting on three sides. General Foch had thoroughly realized those difficulties. He had a great goal in sight. The magnificent behavior of our men prevented him from reaching it."[114] What Hindenburg conveniently glossed over was the fact that he and Ludendorff were the ones responsible for their army being in that untenable position in the first place.

LUDENDORFF VERSUS FOCH

Although all of the Ludendorff Offensives were operational failures, MICHAEL, GEORGETTE, and BLÜCHER produced impressive tactical results. Why then was MARNESCHUTZ-REIMS such a dismal tactical failure? In his postwar analysis conducted for a Reichstag committee investigating the German collapse of 1918, Kuhl wrote, "The principal reason for our reverse must therefore be ascribed to the failure to achieve surprise."[115] That answer is correct as far as it goes, but there was more to it—much more.

Many of the German senior leaders, including Hindenburg and Ludendorff, continued to insist that "treason" was the reason for the loss of surprise, meaning that German deserters revealed the attack plans to the Allies. That argument is too simplistic and deflects the blame from the failures of the German senior leadership. As already noted, anyone on the Allied side who could read a map could come close to pinpointing where the Germans had to attack next. And even so, the German preparations and attack deployments were slipshod and rushed compared to the earlier attacks. The very stringent security measures of the earlier attacks were just not there. The Allies had plenty of time to prepare their defenses and the subsequent counterattack.

Another factor was the predictability of the German tactics. After surviving the first four offensives, the Allies finally knew what to expect and how to deal with it. Throughout the 1920s, the failure of MARNESCHUTZ-REIMS was the subject of a long-running debate in the German professional military journals. In the June 1921 issue of *Militär-Wochenblatt*, retired Major General Hans Waechter laid the blame for the failure of the entire attack on Bruchmüller, because he had used the same fire support tactics for the fifth time in a row. Waechter blasted Bruchmüller for being too "rigid and dogmatic."[116] Several other German officers agreed with Waechter, but Bruchmüller's many supporters quickly pointed out that the critics were unable to suggest any viable fire support alternatives. Seemingly, there was a great reluctance to criticize either Hindenburg or Ludendorff about anything. As noted earlier, even the German official history called the failed Operation GEORGETTE "a skillful and effective operational chess move" (*operativer Schachzug*).[117]

It is not that the Germans failed to anticipate or detect the Allied counterattack; rather, they worked hard on rationalizing away the intelligence indicators. Far too many of the German leaders, especially those at OHL, believed that the Allies were on the edge of the breaking point after four months of being on the receiving end of the German attacks. Yet as early as 29 June an order from Army Group German Crown Prince to the Seventh Army stated, "We must count on the French continuing their attacks against the west front of the Seventh Army prior to and during MARNESCHUTZ."[118] The following day a Seventh Army intelligence assessment indicated Soissons as the key point of vulnerability in the salient but also forecast that the French were unlikely to strip their other sectors to muster the force for a large-scale attack.[119] Few at OHL, least of all Ludendorff, took issue with that estimate. There were, however, some lower-echelon General Staff officers who recognized the dangers of a French counterattack from the Villers-Cotterêts Forest. Among them at Army Group German Crown Prince was Major Ludwig Beck, who in the 1930s would become the chief of the German General Staff and one of the key leaders of the opposition to Hitler during World War II.[120]

Another key difference in MARNESCHUTZ-REIMS was the condition of the German units. As well as they did tactically during the first four offensives, by July 1918 the German army, as noted previously, was all but burned out. Short of calling up sixteen-year-olds, there were no replacements left in Germany. The direct combat losses of the previous four months, combined with the influenza epidemic, had gutted the infantry divisions. In early July every division in the Seventh Army had between three hundred and two thousand troops in the hospital with the flu.[121] The trench strengths of some companies were down to sixty-five, and in some cases even down to forty and thirty. In most cases, the effective trench strengths were even lower than indicated in the daily reports to the higher headquarters. OHL and the subordinate level commanders could not know from one day to the next what the unit strengths would be on the day of the attack.

Despite the high expectations Ludendorff had for HAGEN, thorough analysis of the surviving complete operational plans in the Bavarian War Archives in Munich leads to the conclusion that it had almost no chance of succeeding.[122] Wetzell on 12 June accurately assessed that none of the conditions of the previous tactical successes were present: surprise was unlikely; for the last three months the British had been able to reconstitute their units and strengthen their defenses; and the Allies had their reserves concentrated and well positioned. Even tactically, HAGEN was far too ambitious and expected better first-day results than even BLÜCHER had produced. The main effort, to be made by the III Bavarian Corps with only two divisions in the first line, two in the second line, and two in the third, was expected to take Cassel in a single rush, independent of the actions of the flanking corps. On the first day, the Bavarians would have had to advance ten miles on foot, five miles beyond Hazebrouck, through the high Flanders hills in the July summer heat wearing wool uniforms and under enemy fire all the way.[123] It is difficult to understand how German General Staff officers could have come up with such an utterly unrealistic plan.

Summarizing the German operational failure of 1918, Bundeswehr official historian Colonel Gerhard Gross recently wrote,

> There was no clear operational line connecting the offensives at all. Depending on their success, OHL allowed successful attacks to continue instead of focusing on clear operational objectives. Consequently, Operation MICHAEL and all the follow-on offensives got lost in an eccentric operational void. In the end, the German forces won engagements, but no battles that were decisive for the outcome of the war. One cannot help thinking that the General Staff in the person of Ludendorff focused exclusively on the tactical challenges of trench warfare, while completely forgetting the operational skills.[124]

FOCH VERSUS LUDENDORFF

As historian Tim Travers has noted, the Allies certainly did not win the battles of the German spring offensives campaign, but neither did they lose. By the morning of 18 July they had not lost sufficient ground, men, or matériel to bring them to the point of collapse, as Ludendorff believed. According to Travers, "By not losing, and by staying in existence, rather like the RAF in the Battle of Britain, the BEF and the French Army essentially took the initiative away from the German Army."[125]

Despite his tendency to meddle in tactical details and his reluctance to abandon the old prewar tactical principles, almost all the operational decisions Foch made throughout the campaign were the correct ones. Without Foch's direct intervention, Pétain's innate pessimism and inclination to delay or possibly even cancel Mangin's counterattack almost certainly would have led to different results in the Marne salient. Strategically, the Germans no longer had any hope of achieving a military victory, but if they had emerged from the July fighting in a somewhat better position, the war could have drug on much longer than it did.

Haig, too, when he insisted on the return of his four divisions just as the French were getting ready to launch the counterattack, failed to recognize the changed strategic situation. The strategic opportunity that was there for the Allies to grasp was far clearer to Foch than it was to either Haig or Pétain.[126] As historian Robert Doughty wrote, "At a time when the situation called for decisive measures, Foch and Pétain bet everything on the outcome of this battle. With all their chips on the table, Foch would demonstrate stronger nerves and steadier composure than Pétain when the Germans revealed a surprisingly strong hand on the eve of Mangin's counteroffensive."[127]

Nonetheless, Pétain's contribution to the victory was not insignificant. Despite Foch's blindness to the efficacy of defense-in-depth, Pétain's skillful deployment against the initial 15 July attack allowed him to hold off forty-eight German divisions with only thirty-six. That economy of force made it possible to assemble between the Tenth and Sixth Armies a counterattack force of twenty-four divisions against only ten divisions on the German right flank. The Germans in that sector were outnumbered approximately two-to-one in infantry and more than that in artillery. The Allies also mustered air superiority and a large tank force against no German armor. The timing of the counterattack struck the Germans precisely at the culminating point of their attack. The forward momentum on the Germans' right flank had been exhausted, but they had not yet had time to consolidate and set their defense. The Germans thus were caught off balance and forced into a retrograde movement that took them several days to gain control of.

By the start of August, then, the Germans were stymied, strategically and operationally. No amount of tactical virtuosity could rescue their situation. And now that the balance had tipped in the Allies' failure, Foch intended to exploit it. As historians William Astore and Dennis Showalter have written, "It was now Foch's turn to play the role of Ulysses S. Grant to Hindenburg and Ludendorff's Robert E. Lee. Foch recognized that by shifting assaults along an attenuated German front, Hindenburg and Ludendorff would be forced to commit whatever reserves remained."[128]

ELEVEN

HAMEL TO MONT ST. QUENTIN: HAIG ASSUMES THE OFFENSIVE

Who would have believed this possible even 2 months ago? How much easier it is to attack, than to stand and await an enemy's attack!

> *Field Marshal Sir Douglas Haig to Lady Haig,*
> *8 August 1918, in Gary Sheffield and John Bourne, eds.,*
> Douglas Haig: War Diaries and Letters, 1914–1918

By the early hours of the forenoon of August 8th I had already gained a complete impression of the situation. It was a very gloomy one.

> *General of Infantry Erich Ludendorff,* My War Memories, 1914–1918

THE BATTLE OF HAMEL (4 JULY 1918)

The BEF had not been sitting idly on the defensive while the Germans attacked in the French sector during May, June, and July. The British and Dominion troops conducted local and limited-objective attacks to improve their defensive positions and secure key jump-off positions for when the BEF would be able to shift to the overall offensive. The most significant of these preparatory attacks was conducted at Hamel on 4 July by the Fourth Army's Australian Corps, augmented by four companies of U.S. infantry. It proved so successful and innovative that it became the tactical model for all BEF offensive actions for the remainder of the war and was an example of a combined arms operation in every modern sense of the term.

Few historians would give Haig much direct credit for the success of that battle. He approved the attack, of course, but it was General Sir Henry Rawlinson,

Fourth Army commander, who developed the operation and Lieutenant General Sir John Monash, the corps commander, who devised and executed the tactical plan. Earlier in the war Haig would not have given subordinate commanders so much freedom of action. But by the middle of 1918, the command and control structure in the BEF had become much more decentralized. The point of disagreement among historians is why this had finally come to pass. The two opposing schools on this argument have come to be known as "Command Paralysis" versus "The Learning Curve."

Historian Tim Travers has argued that Haig was largely irrelevant to the final victory in 1918. By the time the Allies went on the offensive in mid-July, Haig had been marginalized to a great degree by the appointments of Foch as Allied supreme commander and Henry Wilson as the chief of the Imperial General Staff, along with the forced replacements of Haig's longtime chief of staff and chief intelligence officer. The catastrophic bloodletting at Third Ypres was the tipping point in the reliefs of Lieutenant General Sir Launcelot Kiggell and Brigadier General John Charteris. Kiggell was replaced as chief of staff by the far more competent Lieutenant General Sir Herbert Lawrence. Travers has further maintained that following the shock of the MICHAEL and GEORGETTE Offensives, Haig's subordinate army commanders filled the "command vacuum" by taking a more direct control of their own formations. The resulting successes of the "Hundred Days" period was, therefore, the product of "creative anarchy."[1] According to Travers, "It is significant that this Hamel attack was organized by Rawlinson, and not by GHQ, since Rawlinson was an advocate of both limited objective offensives and of mechanical warfare."[2]

Gary Sheffield and Dan Todman pursue a different line of argument. Rather than the British successes during the last phase of the war being in spite of Haig, the actual reason was the achievement of a remarkable level of operational and tactical flexibility that the senior commanders had tried to reach since the first days of the war. Right from the start, Haig's general theory of command was one of "hands off," but in the rapidly expanded British army there were far too few experienced command or staff officers to make it work.[3] Peter Simpkins reinforces this argument by noting that the senior British commanders gained the confidence from the spring 1918 crises: "Even when major elements in the formal command and control system temporarily broke down, improvisation at the local level could still retrieve the situation."[4] Thus, with greater assurance in the resilience of the BEF's command and control system, both Haig and his army commanders were prepared to adopt a more tractable approach during the final battles of the war. By the middle of 1918, the BEF had finally climbed its long learning curve.

As early as 3 May Foch wrote to Haig urging a series of BEF attacks to clear the Paris–Amiens rail line.[5] There were several potential advantages to attacking the village of Hamel, which sat on a low ridge about four miles northeast of Villers-Bretonneux. Taking that position would increase the depth of the British Fourth Army's defenses east of Amiens and improve observation over the Somme valley. On 18 June Rawlinson tasked Monash and Brigadier General Anthony Courage, commander of the British 5th Tank Brigade, to prepare a combined attack. Although Monash had only recently assumed command of the five-division Australian Corps, he already had a reputation for thorough and meticulous planning. The final plan was based on infantry, artillery, tanks, and aircraft working together as a combined arms team. The ground around Hamel was good tank country.

The main body of the assault force was the 4th Australian Division, augmented with two brigades from other divisions. Deployed across a four-mile attack front, they were supported with 608 guns, massed machine-gun fire, sixty of the new Mark V heavy tanks, and strong air cover. At the time, the U.S. 33rd Division was training with the Australian Corps. The original plan had been for one company of Americans to be attached to each of the ten Australian battalions committed to the attack. Rawlinson purposely set the attack date for 4 July, America's Independence Day. Pershing, however, objected on 2 July to the use of the American companies. Rawlinson reluctantly agreed to withdraw six of the companies, but the other four were so deeply integrated into the plan of attack that they could not be withdrawn without postponing the operation. Pershing and Haig met in Paris the following day. Pershing still objected to the four companies being committed, but Haig refused to postpone the attack.[6]

The night before the attack the Royal Air Force dropped some 350 bombs on the German positions. Following a very short ten-minute artillery preparation, the first attack wave moved out at 0310 hours. Low-flying aircraft masked the engine sounds of the accompanying tanks. As the infantry advanced, aircraft dropped ammunition and medical supplies by parachute, in what was probably history's first combat airlift mission. Tanks also were used to transport supplies forward. Admittedly, the German positions were weakly held, but the defenders were nonetheless caught completely by surprise. It took the attackers only ninety-three minutes to secure all their objectives. At that point, they stopped and dug in rather than pushing beyond to their culminating point. The Australians suffered 1,400 total casualties, while the Americans sustained 176. German losses were estimated at some 2,000 killed, with 1,600 captured.

The Battle of Hamel was the most effective combination of infantry, armor, artillery, and air power so far. It was also a perfect example of a limited-objective "bite and hold" operation. Rawlinson followed up with similar tactics on 19 July, taking Méteren, only seven miles to the east of the key rail junction at Hazebrouck. Most important, the tactics used at Hamel became the model for the much larger BEF attack east of Amiens a little more than one month later.

THE BATTLE OF AMIENS (8–14 AUGUST)

On 12 July, three days before the Germans launched MARNESCHUTZ-REIMS, Foch sent Haig a memo suggesting that the BEF should preempt the anticipated German offensive in Flanders by launching a spoiling attack from the southern edge of the Lys battlefield, where Operation GEORGETTE had ground to a halt.[7] Five days later Haig replied that a better option would be an offensive more to the south that would relieve the pressure on Amiens by attacking farther east of Villers-Brettoneaux. Haig proposed a combined Franco-British operation on both sides of the Amiens salient, with the British attacking north of the Luce River and the French south of Moureuil. Rawlinson also had recommended much the same thing to Haig.[8] Foch responded on 20 July, agreeing to Haig's concept and specifically noting the success of the Australian Corps' tactics at Hamel.[9]

On 23 July, a German POW disclosed that HAGEN had been postponed indefinitely. Now fairly confident that Crown Prince Rupprecht would not attack, Haig gave Rawlinson the go-ahead to begin preparations for the Amiens attack, set tentatively for 10 August.[10] Amiens and Hazebrouck had been under German shellfire for the last several months, but Amiens was still capable of handling up to 150 trains per day.[11]

The following day Pétain, Haig, and Pershing met with Foch at his headquarters in Bombon. It was one of the pivotal Allied leadership meetings of 1918. With the Germans steadily falling back in the Marne salient and the Americans landing 250,000 men in France every month, Foch noted that the balance had now tipped irrevocably against the Germans: "The moment has come to abandon the general defensive posture, which until now had been imposed upon us by inferior numbers, and to take the offensive."[12] The Allies, however, were still in no position to attempt a decisive operation. The first necessary step would be to improve operational mobility by clearing the Allies' key rail lines:

1. The Paris–Avricourt line in the Marne sector, which was being cleared by the Allied counteroffensive currently in progress.
2. The Paris–Amiens line, to be cleared by the planned combined operation of the British Fourth and French First Armies.
3. The Paris–Avricourt line in the region of Commercy, to be cleared by the reduction of the Saint Mihiel salient that would be executed as soon as the Americans were prepared to mount the attack.[13]

Foch also projected a supporting operation with the objective of freeing the coal-mining region in the north and pushing the Germans away from Dunkirk and Calais, thereby eliminating the threat to the British ports. "These movements should be executed with such rapidity as to inflict upon the enemy a succession of blows," he indicated. "This condition necessarily limits their extent. Their extent will likewise be limited by the small number of units now at the disposal of the Allies for these offensives after four months of battle." The projected operations could be conducted separately or any two in combination, as resources permitted. He continued, "As noted, those actions must be executed in short intervals in order to disrupt the enemy's use of his reserves and give him no time to regroup his units."[14] Thus, Foch's thinking at that point centered on a synchronized series of limited-objective attacks designed to keep the Germans off balance and improve the Allies' positions in preparation for future, more decisive attacks. Such was the essence of operational art that completely eluded Ludendorff during his own series of "go for broke" offensives.

During the conference, Foch also stressed the importance of tanks and mechanical transport over horses. He asked commanders in chief to request increases of such resources from their respective governments. Haig estimated that by the end of summer, the BEF would have seven hundred to eight hundred tanks in operation. Pétain, on the other hand, said the French army was very short of tanks. Foch specifically asked Pershing to look into an American supply of tanks.[15] In the end, however, virtually every tank, as well as every piece of artillery used by the AEF, was French-built.

The reception to Foch's plan was less than enthusiastic. Although Haig was committed to the Amiens Offensive, he also said that the BEF was still completely disorganized from the March and April battles and needed more time to reconstitute before it could mount more extensive operations. Pétain said that after four years of war the French army had been bled white, and his troops needed time to rest. Pershing said that the American army asked nothing better than to fight, but it had not yet been formed—meaning a separate force completely under American command. (Earlier that day AEF headquarters issued the formal order to stand-up the U.S. First Army effective 10 August.) Foch told the Allied generals to study the plan carefully for forty-eight hours and let him know what they thought. Haig and Pershing concurred well before the designated time. Pétain took some more convincing. On 26 July, he sent Foch a memo recommending that the French army's main operations should be an attack on the Saint Mihiel salient in conjunction with a push to clear the Armentières pocket.[16]

At the strategic level neither Foch nor Pétain nor Pershing nor any of the Allied political leaders believed that the war would end in 1918. Almost all believed that it would take a massive campaign in 1919 based on the fresh American divisions and thousands of tanks, trucks, and aircraft. British prime minister David Lloyd George believed the war would drag on into 1920, and even Foch advised French prime minister Georges Clemenceau to call up the 1920-year group effective October 1919. Only Haig was beginning to see that the war could end before the turn of the year. In opposition to Lloyd George and the other British "Easterners," which included Winston Churchill, Haig understood that the Western Front was the war's center of gravity, not some peripheral theater like the Balkans or the Middle East. On 25 July, the general staff at the British War Office issued a memo projecting a stalemate in France well into 1919 and recommending major operations elsewhere. Haig wrote on the cover of his copy of the memo, "Words! Words! Words! Lots of words! And Little else."[17]

In his 1928 memoirs, U.S. lieutenant general Hunter Liggett gave his own assessment of the Easterners' strategy: "A plausible case might be made out for the Lloyd George theory, but anyone who believes that Germany would have quit had her armies not been smashed back and back by an irresistible foe in October and November has only to read the history of those two months and examine the German attitude after the Armistice."[18] Liggett commanded the U.S. I Corps until 16 October, when he assumed command of the U.S. First

Army from Pershing, who then remained the American army group commander as commander of the AEF.

Foch, Haig, Rawlinson, and French First Army commander General Marie-Eugène Debeney met at Sarcus on 26 July to develop the overall plan for the Amiens attack.[19] The final plan, however, was far more open-ended than what Rawlinson originally envisioned. Two days later Foch issued a special directive for the operation. The objective was to free the Paris–Amiens rail line and push the Germans back between the Somme and the Avre.[20] In the process the Allies would interdict the German lateral lines of communications running east of Amiens, which supplied most of the German units in Picardy and Artois. In a separate message to Haig, Foch put the French First Army under his operational control for the purpose of unity of command. He also asked Haig to move the start date up to 8 August.[21]

Monash played a key role in developing the Fourth Army plan, which was based on consolidating a line of villages seven miles from the existing front along the line running from Albert to Villers-Bretonneux. After reaching that objective, Haig planned to drive against the Germans from the direction of Chaulnes, while the French attacked in the direction of Roye. Surprise was a key element. Massed tanks would substitute for an artillery preparation. The extensive security measures were similar to those employed with such effect by the Germans during March through May. The purpose of the deception plan was to make the Germans think that the attack could come in Flanders rather than in the Amiens sector.

The strength of Rawlinson's Fourth Army was virtually doubled to fourteen infantry and three cavalry divisions of British, Canadian, and Australian troops, as well as two regiments of the U.S. 33rd Division, all deployed on a ten-mile front. They were supported by 532 tanks, 800 aircraft, and 700 of the BEF's 1,236 available artillery pieces. The French First Army had seven divisions, 1,066 guns, and 1,104 aircraft but only 90 tanks. With so little armor, Debeney refused to attack without an artillery preparation, but to maintain surprise he agreed to attack forty-five minutes after the British assault started.

On the other side of the line, General Georg von der Marwitz's Second Army had fourteen divisions, 749 guns, and 365 aircraft. On 3 August, Marwitz reported to OHL that only two of his divisions were fully combat ready, and five were functional only as trench divisions. The weak German divisions had a rifle strength of only about 4,000 each. Nor were their defensive positions anywhere close to the usual German high standards. Writing after the war, Hindenburg conceded that the German troops had done relatively little to improve their positions in the ground they had captured since 21 March, on the assumption that they would be moving forward again soon.[22]

German intelligence completely misread the situation. On 2 August, OHL sent an assessment to the four army groups on the Western Front: "The situation requires, first, that we stand on the defensive and, secondly, resume the offensive as soon as possible." Failing completely to identify Amiens, OHL projected potential full-scale attacks in any of the following sectors:

1. Mount Kemmel and the Sixth Army salient
2. Between the Somme and the Oise, as far east as Soissons
3. The Moronvillers sector, twelve miles east of Reims
4. The southern face of the Saint Mihiel salient
5. The Lorraine sector and the Sundgau, west of Mulhouse

Meanwhile, in preparing to repel any major Allied attack, contingency plans would be developed for the following offensive options:

1. KLEIN-HAGEN in Flanders
2. KURFÜRST on both sides of the Oise
3. Smaller attacks east of Reims and in the Army Detachment C sector
4. An attack in Alsace by Army Group Duke Albrecht of Württemberg

"In these attacks, especially west of the Moselle, it is of less importance to conquer much ground than to inflict loss on the enemy and gain better positions," recorded James Edmonds in his multivolume *Military Operations*.[23]

Ludendorff and his immediate circle at OHL had far greater confidence in resuming the offensive than did his army group and field army commanders. Nonetheless, OHL staff officers did start drawing up the contingency plans for a gradual withdrawal from the Lys plain and the evacuation of the bridgeheads on the Ancre and Avre.[24] As he continued lurching back and forth between despondency and bellicosity, Ludendorff several days later made it clear to the OHL staff what he expected of them:

> At home and in the army, all eyes are turned upon the OHL. Whether rightly or wrongly, each member of the Supreme Headquarters is looked upon as being well informed and corresponding value is put upon all he says. . . . The OHL is free from despondency. Sustained by what has previously been achieved on the front and at home, it prepares stout-heartedly to meet the challenges that are to come. No member of OHL may think and act in a manner other than this.[25]

Rawlinson wanted the Amiens attack to be a tightly controlled and limited bite-and-hold operation. Foch, contrary to his memo of the 24 July commanders' conference, envisioned a more ambitious attack. As late as 5 August he made a significant enlargement to the Amiens plan by extending the attack to the south with General Georges Louis Humbert's Third Army, which would attack after Debeney's First Army pinched out Montdidier. Foch also insisted on extending the objective of the British Fourth and French First Army attacks to Roye, twenty-five miles southeast of Amiens.[26] Haig concurred, telling Rawlinson, "The cavalry must keep in touch with the battle and be prepared to pass through *anywhere* [original emphasis] between the River Somme and the Roye–Amiens road."[27]

The day before the start of the Amiens attack, Foch was promoted to marshal of France, solidifying his position over Pétain and giving him the five-star rank equal to Haig. There was no moon that night. At 0420 hours on 8 August the Fourth Army started moving forward, preceded by a creeping barrage. Monash's Australian Corps was in the center, Lieutenant General Richard Butler's British III Corps was on the left, and Lieutenant General Sir Arthur Currie's Canadian Corps was on the right.

The attackers reached their initial objectives by 0730 hours, taking some 6,000 prisoners in the first two hours. By 1100 hours the Canadians took their second objectives. Attempting to advance rapidly from the second objectives, the Cavalry Corps moved forward against the third objectives just after noon, but they were held down by heavy German fire. By the end of the day the cavalry and the infantry reached the third objectives about the same time. After four years of war the BEF's cavalry finally had the long-awaited opportunity for a decisive exploitation that Haig had been hoping for, but it came to nothing. Meanwhile, the French First Army also made good progress, advancing five miles. By the end of the day the French left wing was a little more than one mile behind the Canadian Corps' right wing.[28]

As the battle progressed, OHL moved three divisions up to reinforce the Second Army's rear defenses, and three more moved up later that night. The Second Army's losses for the day came to some 650 officers, 26,000 enlisted soldiers, and 400 guns. More than two-thirds of the total losses had surrendered. A stunned Ludendorff later wrote in his memoirs, "August 8th was the Black Day of the German Army in the history of the war. This was the worst experience I had to go through. . . . August 8th made things clear for both army commands, both for the German and for that of the enemy."[29] But despite

Marwitz's readiness report of three days earlier citing only two fully combat-ready divisions, Ludendorff also wrote, "Six or seven divisions which could certainly be described as battle-worthy had been completely broken. Three or four others, together with the remnants of the battered divisions, were available for closing the broad gap between Bray and Roye."[30]

Ludendorff ordered the Second Army to hang on along the Somme and the Eighteenth Army to pull its own right wing back to Roye while anchoring its left wing on the high ground along the Matz.[31] Ludendorff also made Marwitz's chief of staff, Colonel Erich von Tschischwitz, the scapegoat for the debacle. Lossberg had much different thoughts on the matter: "In the final analysis, however, this catastrophe fell back on General Ludendorff, who greatly overestimated the ability of the German fighting front to resist in the great battle of France, and who did not accept my recommendation on 19 July to pull the front lines back to the Siegfried Position."[32]

On the second day of the attack the Allies did not have a plan as carefully worked out as they had for the first day. The Allies started 9 August with only 145 tanks still operational.[33] The British III Corps, which included the two regiments of the U.S. 33rd Division, captured Morlancourt on the Ancre River and the ridge behind it. But the attackers were now at the edge of the old Somme battlefield, where the ground was completely torn up with shell holes and trenches and laced with wire entanglements. It was slow-go terrain for both tanks and infantry. That afternoon three more fresh German divisions moved up, for a total of nine. Meanwhile, the Allied attacking force was still the same as it had been on the first day.[34]

Despite the forces that OHL fed into the battle, the reinforcing divisions arrived piecemeal and were committed piecemeal. The Allied attack was slowing down, but the German situation was deteriorating as well. Ludendorff, nonetheless, steadfastly opposed any withdrawal, even to shorten the line north of the Somme. General Hermann von Kuhl argued with Ludendorff that by trying to hold all places at all costs, they were burning up their resources and exposing themselves to danger everywhere. Kuhl recommended that the Second Army hold long enough to cover the Eighteenth Army's right flank as it withdrew from the Montdidier salient, after which Marwitz could pull his forces behind the Somme. For a long time Ludendorff refused to consider it, but he finally caved in that evening.[35] Instead of the planned and orderly withdrawal Lossberg had recommended on 19 July, however, the disorganized and demoralized German troops were now falling back under heavy pressure from the attackers.

The Allies had only sixty-seven tanks still operational on 10 August. Rather than operating in groups as they had during the first two days of the attack, they were now fighting isolated engagements.[36] The Fourth Army's lead elements managed to push ahead another three miles. Humbert's Third Army, on Debeney's right, joined the attack that day, and the French made their largest gain of the battle, advancing almost five miles on a frontage of fifteen miles.[37]

Foch and Haig met just before noon.[38] Foch was worried that the Germans would fall back behind the Meuse to the Antwerp–Namur–Strasbourg line, which was only about half the length of their current line. Once they consolidated, they could launch a concentrated counterattack from there. That type of maneuver was essentially what Joseph Joffre had done in 1914.[39] Foch wanted the British Fourth Army to keep pushing forward, "to reach the Somme below Ham, in order to make preparations for a crossing."[40]

Haig objected to the Fourth Army continuing to attack frontally against the stiffening resistance. Instead, he recommended that General Sir Julian Byng's Third Army and the right wing of General Sir Henry Horne's First Army attack to the north of Rawlinson's Fourth Army. After some back-and-forth debate, Foch finally agreed. Later that day he issued a general directive: "The attention of the Field Marshal is drawn to the importance of making preparations as soon as possible for operations of the British Third Army in the general direction of Bapaume and Péronne, in order to break the enemy front and exploit any withdrawal without delay."[41] Debeney's First Army was ordered to continue advancing toward Ham and Humbert's Third Army toward Noyon.

The Germans evacuated Montdidier that night, as the Eighteenth Army pulled its right wing back. But four more fresh German divisions reached the front and formed a new and almost complete line from the Amiens–Roye road to Chaulnes. OHL also regrouped the Second, Eighteenth, and Ninth Armies into Army Group Boehn, between the army groups of the two crown princes. Lossberg was assigned as Boehn's chief of staff.[42] Complaining in his diary again about Ludendorff's constant interference in the smallest tactical details, Kuhl wrote in frustration, "There is no dealing with Ludendorff."[43]

The German defense firmed up by 11 August, as the fierce fighting continued south of Albert and between the Somme and the Avre. The French First Army was running short of artillery ammunition. That morning Rawlinson convinced Haig that his Fourth Army had reached culmination. Total German casualties so far were some 57,800, while the Allied casualties—French, British, Canadian, Australian, and American—came to about 51,000. Foch and Haig met at Haig's headquarters late that night, and Foch agreed to reducing the British frontage but not to halting the attack.[44]

Ludendorff that day met with several of the frontline divisional commanders. He was shocked by reports of German troops surrendering en masse and of reserves moving up being taunted as "Blacklegs" and prolongers of the war. As he later wrote, "There was no hope of materially improving our position by a counterattack. Our only course, therefore, was to hold on."[45] Later he and Hindenburg met with the kaiser and Crown Prince Wilhelm at Avesnes, where Ludendorff offered his resignation.[46] Although the kaiser despised Ludendorff and feared Hindenburg, he declined to accept, if for no other reason than he had no idea himself what to do next.

When Haig and Pershing met on 12 August, the AEF commander told the BEF commander that he intended to withdraw the five U.S. divisions then in the British sector. Haig was furious. He had planned to use those divisions for an attack against Kemmel at the end of September.[47] In the end, Foch issued an order to both Haig and Pershing to have the 33rd, 78th, and 80th Divisions redeploy to the American sector but to leave, to Pershing's chagrin, the U.S. 27th and 30th Divisions with the BEF.[48] Those two units remained under Haig's operational control until the end of the war.

Foch on 12 August issued new instructions to Pétain and Haig: "In view of the resistance offered by the enemy, there is no question of obtaining results by pressing all along the front; this would only lead to being weak everywhere. On the contrary, it is a matter of using concentrated and powerful action at the most important points of the area, that is to say those whose possession would increase the enemy's disorganization, in particular would disturb his communications." Foch stressed the need for rapid action with coordinated tanks, artillery, and infantry. He wanted two attacks launched immediately: a continuation of the push to take Roye and the capture of the Amiens–Brie road. Supporting lateral attacks would be conducted by the British Third Army in the direction of Bapaume–Péronne to outflank the Germans and farther south and east of the Oise by the French Tenth Army in the direction of Chauny to force the Germans back from Noyon.[49] Haig agreed to renew the offensive on 15 August, with the objective being the general line of Roiglise (two miles southeast of Roye)–Chaulnes.[50]

Boehn and Lossberg, meanwhile, failed to convince Ludendorff that the best possible course of action was an immediate withdrawal to the Siegfried Position, reinforcing the line with the reserves currently moving up. By 12 August all Army Group Boehn's reserve divisions had been committed, and additional divisions withdrawn from the other army groups by OHL were starting to move up. As soon as they reached their initial deployment positions they were committed directly into the front lines. Lossberg later complained that throughout the entire period of its short existence, Army Group Boehn never was able to assemble a dedicated and ready reserve force.[51]

While the Allied armies were regrouping, Hindenburg and Ludendorff on 13 September met at Spa, Belgium, with the kaiser, the weak Chancellor Georg Graf von Hertling, and the equally ineffectual Secretary of Foreign Affairs Rear Admiral Paul von Hintze. A badly shaken Ludendorff informed the kaiser, "We have reached the limit of our endurance." Trying to deflect the responsibility, Ludendorff blamed the mood of the population back home and their failure to support to the fullest the army in the field. He argued, however, that by remaining entrenched on French soil they could force the Allies to accept a negotiated peace on Germany's terms.[52] To Ludendorff that meant keeping the Ukraine in the east and Belgium in the west.

Hindenburg and Hertling tried to argue that peace feelers would be premature until Germany could improve the military situation on the Western Front.[53] Ludendorff was bordering on the delusional, and even the usually implacable Hindenburg did not seem to be far behind him. Many other senior German commanders at that point, however, believed that a protracted defense-in-depth, which had been so effective in 1916–17, was impossible in 1918 because Germany no longer had the necessary numbers of soldiers. Grasping at the straw offered by Ludendorff, the kaiser instructed Hintze to open peace negotiations, if possible through the queen of the Netherlands.

The Paris–Amiens rail line was now cleared but still threatened.[54] By 14 August intelligence reported that the German positions in front of the British Fourth Army were now too strong to attack with the forces available. Rawlinson told Haig that he was no longer capable of attacking. The BEF commander then informed Foch that he was calling an operational pause. During a tense meeting between the two marshals in Sarcus the next day, Foch pushed Haig to renew the attack toward Roye–Chaulnes on schedule. Haig refused, citing the heavy casualties that would result. Foch kept insisting, but Haig made it clear that he would exercise his right to appeal to London, in which case all actions would come to a halt while the final decision was thrashed out by the British and French governments. Haig instead recommended launching Byng's Third Army toward Albert and Bapaume, with the attack to start five days after the French Fourth Army renewed its attack.[55]

Foch finally agreed to Haig's plan, but he withdrew the French First Army from Haig's operational control and put it back under Fayolle's army group.[56] On 15 August, Foch's chief of staff, General Maxime Weygand, issued an operations priority order in Foch's name directly to the French First, Third, and Tenth Armies to start preparing for attacks "to clear the region Lassigny–Noyon–Foret de Carlepont, also to prepare the later clearing of the region Roye–Chauny–Soissons and to let me know the dates when it can be accomplished. These operations, as well as those of the British armies, have the goal of forcing the pullback of the German troops west of the Somme. Energetic pressure should be applied on those forces."[57] Pétain's headquarters was not an addressee on that order.

THE BATTLE OF MONTDIDIER (18–30 AUGUST)

The French attacked on 18 August, pushing the German Second and Eighteenth Armies back with heavy losses to a line running from Albert to just south of Noyon. Within two days Mangin's Tenth Army managed to take the high ground between the Aisne and the Oise, capturing in the process some 8,000 prisoners and 200 guns. The German position along the north bank of the Vesle was now threatened.[58] The following day the German Ninth Army, between the Eighteenth and Seventh Armies, was pushed back to a line running from Noyon to Soissons.[59] Between 27 and 29 August, the French First and Third Armies exploited the advance made by the Tenth Army to push forward seven miles and seize Noyon.

THE SECOND BATTLE OF BAPAUME (21 AUGUST–1 SEPTEMBER)

As Haig in his final dispatch to the British government explained the situation immediately after Amiens, "A successful attack between Albert and Arras in a southeasterly direction would turn the line of the Somme south of Péronne, and gave every promise of producing far-reaching results. It would be a step forward towards the strategic objective St. Quentin–Cambrai."[60] More than any other Allied senior military or political leader at that point, Haig began to see the true strategic situation. During a meeting on 21 August, Minister of

Munitions Winston Churchill told Haig that the general staff in London currently estimated that the decisive point in the war would not come until July 1919. Haig told the skeptical Churchill, "We ought to do our utmost to get a decision this autumn."[61] It is, however, not surprising that almost no one was taking Haig seriously at that point. Too often in the past he had claimed that the Germans were on the verge of breaking. In June 1917, during the discussions leading up to the BEF's Third Ypres Offensive, Haig had written to the War Cabinet assuring Britain's political leadership that the final Allied victory could be achieved that year. That skepticism continued to hang over Haig until the final months of 1918. Nonetheless, U.S. general Hunter Liggett later wrote,

> The war could not have been won in 1918, in all likelihood, had not Sir Douglas Haig been willing to take on his own individual shoulders a responsibility which his own government refused to accept. The great Allied drive to end the war was to have come in the spring of 1919, but every day of the late summer of 1918 so improved the Allied prospects that by the end of August Marshal Foch was convinced of the strong advisability of an early converging attack with the whole force of the Allied armies, with the possibility of driving the enemy out of France before winter. There was, as I have said, no suggestion from the French or the British governments or high commands that the war could be ended in 1918.[62]

On 21 August, Byng's Third Army attacked across the old Somme battlefields between Moyenneville and Beaucourt and pushed the Germans back beyond the Arras–Albert railway.[63] Byng's forces broke through the lines of the German Seventeenth and Second Armies and reached Croisilles and Bapaume on 25 August.[64] Bapaume had been one of the major objectives when the BEF attacked on the Somme on 1 July 1916, but the British were still two miles short of the town when that campaign had ended on 15 November 1916.

Haig increasingly was leaving the conduct of the battles to his army commanders. But sensing that they were now in a position to fight a different sort of war, he sent the army commanders a message late that night: "Risks which a month ago would have been criminal to incur, ought now to be incurred as a duty. It is no longer necessary to advance in regular lines and step by step. On the contrary, each division should be given a distant objective which must be reached independently of its neighbor, and even if one's flank is thereby exposed for the time being. Reinforcements must be directed on the points where our troops are gaining ground, not where they are checked."[65] Earlier in the war such an order would have been impossible owing to the BEF's level of leadership, experience, and training at that time. Now Haig was starting to adopt an almost classic German approach to command and control—what the Germans later would call *Auftragstaktik*, or mission command.

Crown Prince Wilhelm that day sent a message to Ludendorff recommending the immediate withdrawal of the entire German army to strong defensive positions with shorter front lines in order to free up much-needed reserves. Ludendorff rejected the recommendation, pointing out that the Germans had inadequate labor forces even to prepare properly the former German defensive positions in the rear.[66] Such labor forces, however, would have been available and already working had Ludendorff accepted Lossberg's 19 July recommendation.

The left wing of Rawlinson's Fourth Army moved up between the Somme and the Ancre on 22 August. Byng's forces took Albert that day. The Germans brought up a counterattack force, which quickly was beaten back. The British Third and Fourth Armies then pushed forward toward Bapaume, taking 8,000 German prisoners on a twenty-two-mile front and forcing the German Second Army back. The German line, however, did not break. By 24 August the original eight German divisions facing the British Third Army had been reinforced by nine more divisions.[67]

Nonetheless, the Germans were still being pushed back, slowly but steadily. OHL ordered the Second and Seventeenth Armies to start withdrawing on the night of 27–28 August to the line from Noyon, along the east bank of the canal to Nesle, and then along the Somme to the northwest of Péronne. The left wing of the Seventeenth Army was to conform by swinging back to La Transloy–Vraucourt, leaving Bapaume exposed.[68] Later on the twenty-seventh Byng's forces closed to the left bank of the Somme.[69] By the twenty-ninth the Third Army enveloped Bapaume from both north and south, and the Germans evacuated the town that night. Monash's Australian Corps reached the Somme south of Péronne and captured the town on 1 September.

The Germans established themselves on the high ground east of Bapaume, behind the Somme above Péronne and behind the Canal du Nord.[70] With their left flank increasingly exposed by the Allied advance to their south, the Sixth and Fourth Armies of Crown Prince Rupprecht's Army Group started on 30 August withdrawing from the Lys sector of the old GEORGETTE battleground.[71] Every step they took toward the east reduced that much more the pressure on the BEF's vital ports.

THE BATTLE OF THE SCARPE (26 AUGUST–2 SEPTEMBER 1918)

Five days after Byng attacked, the right wing of Horne's First Army attacked east of Arras on a seven-mile front. Currie's Canadian Corps advanced five miles and took the high ground at Monchy-le-Preux. The following day the Canadians seized a crossing over the Sensee River south of Croisilles. On 28 August they captured that town and pushed to the Wotan Position, the northern hinge of the Siegfried Position. The following day the Germans launched violent but ultimately unsuccessful counterattacks. Late that day Currie's lead forces reached the Scarpe River.[72]

Once the Canadians penetrated the Wotan Position, British units with tanks swung south to cut the Queant–Cambrai rail line. On 2 September the BEF, heavily supported by tanks, overran the Wotan Position, as the Canadian Corps and the British XVII Corps broke through the Drocourt–Queant line south east of Arras.[73] The Siegfried Position was now vulnerable to being turned from the north. OHL ordered the withdrawal to the Siegfried Position of the largest part of the Seventeenth Army, the entire Second and Eighteenth Armies, and the right wing of Ninth Army, from the Scarpe to the Vesle. The German forces were ordered to destroy all roads, railroads, and coal mines in the process.[74] As Lossberg later lamented, "Unfortunately, the Siegfried Position still had not been rebuilt."[75] To that point in the fighting, the Seventeenth, Second, Eighteenth, and Ninth Armies had lost much more than 100,000 men.

THE BATTLE OF PÉRONNE–MONT ST. QUENTIN (31 AUGUST–4 SEPTEMBER)

On 30 August, the Allies continued attacking relentlessly on a front of ninety miles, from Arras to Soissons. Foch that day issued an order for continuing operations to the three Allied commanders in chief. Stressing the importance of exploiting the current favorable situation by "bringing into it all the Allied forces in one great convergent attack," the Allied supreme commander ordered the continuation of the two ongoing operations. The BEF, supported on its right by French forces, would continue attacking in the general direction of St. Quentin–Cambrai. Haig, in fact, had the day before ordered his First, Third, and Fourth Armies to "continue the pursuit."[76] The French armies in the center, meanwhile, would continue to push the Germans beyond the Aisne. Foch also alerted the AEF and the French forces on its left to prepare to attack in the general direction of Mézières, the critical German rail junction.[77]

Later that morning Haig met with his army commanders, briefing them on Foch's plan to engage the Germans continuously on a very wide front and reminding them of his guidance on risk-taking in his 22 August message.[78] In the British Fourth Army's sector the key terrain was Mont St. Quentin, approximately a mile north of Péronne. Sitting in a bend on the north side of the Somme, the three-hundred-foot-high hill dominated the crossing sites. The final German fortified position overlooking the river, it was an observation point that controlled the northern and western approaches to the old turreted and moated town. The town and the hill would be the objective of the attack launched the next day by Monash's Australian Corps.

During the night of 30 August, Monash infiltrated units of his 2nd Australian Division across to the north bank of the Somme. At 0500 hours the next morning, the Australians attacked with heavy artillery support from the far side of the river. Two understrength battalions stormed up Mont St. Quentin in a frontal attack. They caught the Germans completely by surprise, many of whom, including troops of the elite 2nd Guards Division, surrendered en masse. Once the attackers gained control of the summit, two Australian brigades crossed the Somme over the partially destroyed Feuilleres bridge, which had been made serviceable by Australian engineers. Once across, the engineers established new bridgeheads, and Australian units advanced to cut the German rail lines south of Péronne.

True to form, the Germans counterattacked just two hours after they lost the summit and pushed the vastly outnumbered Australians off. By nightfall the Germans held the high ground, but the Australians managed to hold on just below the top. They counterattacked on the morning of 2 September, retook the summit, and this time held it. Later that day the Australians pushed the Germans out of Péronne. By 3 September the battle effectively was over, although some mopping up continued the following day. At a cost of 3,000 casualties, the Australians had defeated elements of five German divisions, taking some 2,600 prisoners.[79]

Clearly, the German resistance was crumbling but not yet breaking. Haig, however, had not given up his hopes of creating a decisive breakthrough followed by a deep exploitation. On 1 September he vetoed a recommendation to commit a cavalry division to mopping-up operations around St. Quentin. As he wrote in his diary, "I hoped to have an efficient Cavalry Corps ready to act vigorously when the decisive moment comes."[80]

THE WITHDRAWAL TO THE HINDENBURG
LINE (2–9 SEPTEMBER)

The combined battles of Montdidier, Bapaume, the Scarpe, and Mont St. Quentin shattered the German forward lines. The widely separated but coordinated Allied attacks that followed Amiens caused a great deal of uncertainty at OHL, forcing the Germans to commit their reserves as they moved up piecemeal to any sector under threat. Once the Allies overran the Arras–Cambrai Road, OHL on 2 September ordered the entire German line to withdraw to the Siegfried Position.[81] In doing so, the Germans relinquished all the territorial gains they made earlier in the year from the five Ludendorff Offensives. The withdrawal started that night. The Allies pursued.

The Hindenburg Line was a name used by the Allies, never by the Germans. But what the Allies called the Hindenburg Line was not quite the same thing that the Germans called the Siegfriedstellung, which was the original and center sector of three deeply echeloned defensive belts. The various sectors of the belts were named after Wagnerian gods or heroes. The first and second belts had for the most part three zones of up to three or more deeply echeloned trench lines each.

The Siegfried Position was the strongest. It ran from Arras to Laffaux, near Soissons on the Aisne. It was built during the winter of 1916–17, when the Germans pulled their positions back during Operation ALBERICH. Later, the Siegfried Position was extended by the Wotan Position, running from Arras north to the coast. The Alberich Position extended the Siegfried to the Aisne River, south of Laon, and the Hagen Position extended to the east and then the south to Metz and Strasbourg.

Directly behind that first belt ran the Hunding Position. It was not as strong as the Siegfried, but it made excellent use of the terrain, especially between the Aisne and Oise Rivers. The Hermann Position then extended the second belt north to Douai on the Scarpe River, and from there the Ghent Extension ran toward the coast north of Ghent. The Brünnhilde Position extended the Hermann south and east to Grandpré on the northern end of the Argonne Forest, and then the Kriemhilde Position ran east behind the Hagen.

The third belt was the Freia Position, which ran behind the Hunding, from the vicinity of Le Cateau southeast to the Meuse, just south of Stenay. The Freia, however, had not been completed by the time of the Armistice. Beyond that third belt was the notional Antwerp–Meuse Position, which was planned to run from the Scheldt estuary to the Meuse, at about the end of the Freia Position. The Antwerp–Meuse was a much shorter line that, had it been built, would have allowed the Germans to mass their forces into a much stronger defense. Foch was constantly preoccupied with preventing the Germans from conducting an orderly retirement to that position. Fortunately for the Allies, by the time the Germans started falling back to the Siegfried Position, they were woefully short of the necessary labor manpower required to establish their final fallback line.[82]

On 3 September, British and Canadian units cleared the entire Arras front, breaking nine understrength German divisions in the process. They then started advancing toward the Canal du Nord, which would put them within striking distance of Cambrai. That night the right wing of the Seventh Army in the south withdrew behind the Aisne at Maizy.[83]

Throughout 6 and 7 September, aggressive and continuous British raids and patrols in Flanders kept up the pressure as the Germans completely abandoned the Lys salient. As the Germans pulled back, the Allies increasingly threatened the German rail lines running north to the sea. If the British could take the higher ground to the east of Ypres, they would have a good line of departure from which to attack and cut the German trunk line that ran through Roulers.[84]

On the night of 6 September, Ludendorff met at Avesnes with the three army group chiefs of staff. The first quartermaster general was a nervous wreck, blaming everyone but himself for the situation. As Lossberg later recorded, "He blamed the soldiers and their leaders for the recent events, without acknowledging that his own misguided leadership was in large part the reason for the failures."[85]

Lossberg told Ludendorff that based on his visits to the field with General von Boehn, they both agreed that the Siegfried Position was in poor shape, with very little wire. They did not think it would be possible to conduct a prolonged resistance from there. Lossberg recommended that after they were pushed back from the Siegfried Position, the entire German front from Verdun to the sea should withdraw in a single bound to the Antwerp–Meuse Position, jumping over the Hermann–Hunding–Brünnhilde Position and the Freia Position. Such a maneuver continued to be one of Foch's greatest fears. But although the Antwerp–Meuse Position had been reconnoitered and laid out on the ground, it still had to be built, and that construction should start immediately.

Ludendorff rejected Lossberg's recommendation. He instead opted to devote all the labor resources available to reinforcing the Hermann–Hunding–Brünnhilde Position. Lossberg later wrote, "This was a grave mistake, because when the Siegfried Position was overrun on 8 October, the northern wing of the German Army then collapsed during the retirement to the Meuse through the continuous pursuit of the enemy."[86]

All the Allied commanders except Haig still saw the war going well into 1919. On 7 September Pétain started planning a major offensive that would thrust into Lorraine. As the planning continued, Foch on 20 October gave the final go-ahead for the operation, which was set to jump off on 14 November. The basic concept was to exploit the results of the Franco-American attack toward Mézières that Foch had specified in his 30 August order to the national commanders in chief. Pétain envisioned using General Noël de Castelnau's heretofore underused Eastern Army Group, with thirty divisions on a thirty-six-mile front, heavily supported with tanks, artillery, and aircraft. As Pétain noted at the time, "The battle of 1919 will be a battle of aviation and tanks."[87]

By 9 September all German forces on the Western Front were back in the Siegfried Position and its extensions to the north and south.[88] The German effective reserves were down to just nine divisions. The Allies were deployed along the line Arleux–Marquion–Vermand–Tergnier–Vailly and preparing to close up to the Siegfried along its entire length.[89] Ludendorff justified the withdrawal by saying, "Our task is not for the purpose of gaining terrain nor to hold it at any cost, but to reduce the fighting power of the enemy."[90]

Wetzell finally had enough. That day he requested to be relieved as Ludendorff's chief of operations at OHL. Wetzell was replaced by Carl-Heinrich von Stülpnagel, who in the 1930s became a key operational planner for the Wehrmacht. On 30 August 1944 Stülpnagel was executed as a member of the 20 July Plot against Hitler.[91]

TWELVE

CLOSING TO THE HINDENBURG LINE: FOCH TIGHTENS THE VISE

I had been appointed to OHL, not to make peace, but to win the war, and had thought of nothing else.

General of Infantry Erich Ludendorff, My War Memories

To sum up, in six weeks the enemy had lost all the gains he had made in the spring. He lost heavily in men and matériel. Most important of all, he had lost the initiative of operations—he had lost his moral ascendancy.

Marshal Ferdinand Foch, Memoirs of Marshall Foch

THE GERMANS HAD WITHDRAWN TO the Siegfried Position in the center of their line, but on the northern and southern wings they still held forward positions and outposts.[1] By 9 September the Germans in the British sector held a general line from Vermand to Épehy to Havrincourt and then along the east bank of the Canal du Nord. Just south of the British, the French had reached the line of the Crozat Canal.[2] On the southern end of the German sector, German lines from Reims east to Verdun ran some three to five miles in front of the Alberich–Hagen extensions of the Siegfried Position. Immediately east of Verdun the German line turned sharply south to just west and south of Saint Mihiel, forming a large salient that at its maximum point was some twenty miles from the Hagen Position. The German frontline trace then cut sharply to the east, to join the Hagen in the vicinity of Pont-a-Mousson. The Allies spent the middle two weeks of September closing up to the Hindenburg Line all along the front.

By September 1918 the Americans had well over one million troops in Europe, roughly twice the number of casualties the Allies had suffered since the start of Operation MICHAEL. But of the thirty-nine American divisions in France at that point, many were not yet combat capable, and only thirteen had any combat experience. The American divisions did, however, have almost double the trench strength of the European divisions. The Germans, meanwhile, in a desperate effort to maintain the number of divisions in their front lines, had in August started reducing their infantry battalions from four to three companies but retaining the number of machine guns.[3] The Germans in Flanders had twelve divisions in their first lines facing eighteen Allied divisions. In the central sector of the Siegfried Position they had fifty-seven divisions facing the British Third and Fourth Armies of forty British and two American divisions. On the German left they had twenty frontline divisions facing thirty-one French and fifteen large American divisions.[4]

The Allies finally had seized the initiative, but like the Germans during the first half of 1918, the tempo of their operations was limited to the tactical realities of the pace of marching infantrymen and horse-drawn field guns. The Allies, however, and particularly the BEF, came to recognize those limitations and tailored their operations accordingly. Thus, the Allied offensives from mid-July through the end of the war increasingly were conducted across a broad front with a sequenced series of shallow and logistically sustainable thrusts. Rather than attempting to make deep penetrations to encircle and destroy major German forces, the limited objective attacks all along the line were designed to force the Germans slowly but steadily back, giving them no respite or opportunity to regroup, all the while inflicting losses that could not be replaced.[5] Undoubtedly, this was attritional warfare, but it was skillfully conducted attritional warfare and the only viable strategy then available with the 1918 military technologies.

Even before the British attacked at Amiens on 8 August, Foch and the other Allied commanders in chief were discussing the course of future operations against the Germans: What to do? Where to do it? When to do it? The ensuing debates were contentious at times, although they generally agreed that the immediate task was to close to the Hindenburg Line along its entire length. One of the key operations in that process was the American attack to reduce the Saint Mihiel salient. The deliberations over that attack continued into the start of September, and the final decisions greatly influenced the planning for the course of operations after the Germans were all behind the Hindenburg Line.

THE SAINT MIHIEL OFFENSIVE (12–15 SEPTEMBER)

Saint Mihiel was the U.S. First Army's first major offensive operation. Hailed as a great American feat of arms at the time, the Germans were already planning to evacuate the salient when the Americans attacked. There still remains some debate among historians regarding whether or not the offensive was even necessary. After initially approving the operation, Foch had second thoughts and wanted to cancel it. Pershing, though, argued furiously for the continuation of the attack. Foch finally gave in to Pershing, but the Saint Mihiel operation had the net effect of causing significant logistical and operational problems for the American Meuse-Argonne Offensive that started less than two weeks later.

As early as June 1917, Pershing's staff had identified the Saint Mihiel sector as the logical location to deploy the AEF when fully formed. The assessment was based on the availability of western French ports centering on St. Nazaire and the existing rail network between the two points. Pershing also saw the salient as a tempting and vulnerable target, a perfect objective to prove his beliefs in open warfare and the inherent superiority of American rifle marksmanship and the bayonet. He recommended the basic plan to Pétain, who agreed tentatively. For the next fourteen months, the Saint Mihiel Offensive was the focal point for all of the AEF's planning, organization, and training.[6]

It was a logical objective at the time. The salient was approximately twenty-five miles wide and sixteen miles deep. Across the base of the salient ran a defensive line called the Michael Position, which was in front of and parallel to the main Hagen Position. The salient's frontline trace was the result of the failed German offensive into Lorraine during the summer of 1914. In April 1915 the French attempted but failed to cut the salient off with an attack by three corps.[7] Rather than draw back to a shorter and more defensible line, as much of the rest of the German army did during Operation ALBERICH in the spring of 1917, the Germans continued to hold the Saint Mihiel salient because it provided some defensive depth to several vital points. Metz, the eastern terminus of the Antwerp–Metz rail system, was only fifteen miles behind the eastern shoulder of the salient. If the Allies could seize Metz, they would be in a position to turn from the south all of the German defensive lines. The salient also covered the entrance to the Briey Basin, from which Germany drew much of its iron ore.[8] Holding onto the basin was one of the key elements of Ludendorff's "Hindenburg Peace." Nonetheless, the field marshal himself recognized only too well the problems involved in holding the salient, calling it "a tactical abortion, which invited the enemy to attempt a great blow. It is not easy to understand why the French left us alone for years in this great triangle that projected into their front."[9]

During a meeting at Bombon on 10 July 1918, Pershing asked Foch for approval of the plan for the reduction of the Saint Mihiel salient that Pétain and Pershing previously had agreed upon.[10] Foch did not approve the attack immediately, but twelve days later he sent Pershing an order approving the establishment of the U.S. First Army on the Marne and later the U.S. Second Army on the Meuse.[11] Pershing agreed to place the First Army under the operational control of Pétain's Armies of the North and Northeast. But Foch also told Pershing that he would not immediately return to Pershing's control the U.S. 32nd Division, which was already committed to a pending operation under the French Tenth Army. Pershing protested vehemently. Foch wrote back that if the 32nd Division did not remain with the Tenth Army, he then would have to rethink the activation of the U.S. First Army.[12] Pershing backed down, and the 32nd Division remained with the French until 2 September.

The Saint Mihiel Offensive was approved formally when Foch, Pétain, Haig, and Pershing met at Bombon on 24 July.[13] That same day AEF headquarters issued the order to stand up the First Army effective 10 August.[14] But only a week later Pétain wrote to Foch, citing the condition of the French forces and the threats to his sector and requesting that none of his units be committed to either the British Amiens attack or the American Saint Mihiel Offensive.[15] AEF headquarters, meanwhile, started assembling American forces on the southern face of the salient and developing the final attack plan. The Americans originally intended not limiting their operation to the geographic confines of the salient. They envisioned, rather, an advance beyond the Michael Position to reach the Longuyon–Metz rail line, some ten miles to the northeast. Many of the American planners at that point were entertaining grand visions of taking Metz at a single bound and thereby collapsing the entire German rail system. But when Pershing recommended a follow-up attack on Metz to Pétain, the French commander in chief pointed out that the German forces in the Meuse-Argonne sector would threaten the left flank of any attack toward Metz, and such an attack would be possible only after the Meuse-Argonne had been cleared.

Pershing and Pétain on 9 August reached agreement on the basic plan. The attack would be made by fourteen divisions supported by four French divisions, despite Pétain's reluctance only a few days earlier.[16] An addendum note to the 9 August basic agreement estimated that the Americans would have to be augmented with eighty 75mm batteries, forty 155mm batteries, and 150 Renault tanks.[17] Some historians have suggested that the fact that Pétain entrusted four French divisions to the Americans for the operation was proof of the French commander in chief's confidence in Pershing and his corps commanders. Elizabeth Greenhalgh, on the other hand, has noted, "One might equally argue that Pétain wanted to place some tested and reliable French troops into the equation, given that Pershing was insisting on independence."[18]

There was sufficient cause for concern that any experienced battlefield commander would recognize. Despite strong recommendations to the contrary by the AEF's chief of operations, Brigadier General Fox Conner, Pershing decided that he personally would assume direct command of the U.S. First Army while simultaneously retaining command of the American Expeditionary Force. That meant that Pershing would have to divide himself between two separate headquarters, the one fighting the battle and the one supporting and sustaining it. After losing the argument, Conner helped Pershing all he could by reassigning his own highly capable deputy, Colonel George C. Marshall, to the First Army's operations section, where he later became chief of the section. The "dual-hating" of Pershing worked after a fashion during the short Saint Mihiel battle, but it later caused serious problems during the subsequent long and drawn-out Meuse-Argonne Offensive.

On 23 August, Foch sent Pershing a note confirming that the U.S. 27th and 30th Divisions would remain under Haig's operational control for the BEF's upcoming offensives and the 28th, 32nd, and 77th Divisions would remain under French operational control. Foch closed by asking Pershing to brief him as soon as possible on his planned dispositions for the Saint Mihiel attack. When they met the following day, Foch gave the final go-ahead for the attack to start on 8 September.[19]

Haig had serious doubts about the whole thing. On 27 August, he wrote to Foch suggesting that Pershing deploy his divisions so that the British and Americans could conduct converging attacks, with the British driving toward Cambrai and the Americans toward the key German rail center at Mézières. The idea made a great deal of operational sense. The capture of Mézières would disrupt three major rail lines from Germany to France: (1) from Cologne to Liège and then following the Meuse and Sambre Rivers to Aulnoye, Mézières, Montmédy, and Longuyon; (2) from Coblenz to Luxembourg to Longuyon; and (3) the critical four-track line from Mainz and Mannheim to Strasbourg,

Sarrebourg, Metz, and Longuyon. Cutting the line between Montmédy and Mézières would seriously reduce German logistics throughput between Mézières and the English Channel coast. And in addition to losing control of the Mézières–Montmédy rail line, if the Germans could be driven up against the hilly Ardennes Forest, which had no trunk lines, their position in France would be untenable.[20]

In a letter to Chief of the Imperial General Staff Henry Wilson that same day, Haig commented, "The attack on St. Mihiel will lead to nothing (a) because it is eccentric, and (b) Germans have already taken steps to make a new line across the salient." But then he also allowed, "A small attack in this salient would educate the American higher command and might be allowed for the purposes of camouflage."[21] Haig's recommendation apparently had a significant influence on Foch's entire concept of the Allied General Offensive. Foch wrote back to Haig the following day, saying that he seriously was considering canceling the American Saint Mihiel Offensive and instead have the Americans attack north along the west bank of the Meuse toward Mézières.[22]

Foch and Pershing met at the First Army's headquarters on 30 August. It was a stormy confrontation, during which the two generals almost came to blows. Arguing that the fate of the 1918 campaign would be decided in the Aisne region, Foch said that he now wanted to limit the Saint Mihiel attack so that the Americans could then participate in the Meuse Offensive, which would produce greater results. Foch said he therefore wanted to limit the Saint Mihiel attack to the southern face of the salient only. Following that, an attack north toward Mézières would be made by two field armies: an American army under Pershing and a Franco-American army under French command.[23]

Pershing responded hotly by accusing Foch of wanting to reduce the Saint Mihiel operation so that he could take away several American divisions, assign some to the French Second Army, and use others to form an American army to operate on the Aisne in conjunction with the French Fourth Army. The result would be that Pershing would have little to do except hold what would become a quiet sector after the Saint Mihiel Offensive. "Marshal Foch," Pershing said, "you have no authority as Allied Commander-in-Chief to call upon me to yield up my command of the American Army and have it scattered among the Allied forces where it will not be an American army at all."[24]

Pershing continued to insist that the Saint Mihiel attack be made on both sides of the salient. Foch argued that there was too much of a risk that the Americans would become too deeply committed in that sector, which would detract from their ability to execute the follow-on attack toward Mézières. Events would prove the validity of Foch's concerns. Pershing at one point offered to take over the entire sector of the French Second Army west of the Meuse, but Foch convinced him that his then-available sixteen divisions were not enough. Pershing finally dug in his heels: "Marshal Foch, you may insist all you please, but I will decline absolutely to agree to your plan. While our army will fight wherever you may decide, it will not fight except as an independent American army."[25]

The meeting ended with the two generals still at loggerheads. As he left, Foch handed Pershing a memo detailing his concept of the continuing operations and the role of the American forces in those operations. Foch asked Pershing to study it carefully and then let him know what he thought. The memo's key passages bear repeating here as an example of clarity in operational thought. It is significant, of course, that it evolved from an original recommendation by Haig.[26]

I.
The operations which, on the 24th July, it was decided to undertake in the course of the summer and autumn of 1918 were suitable to the situation at that time.

Today, the favorable development of the first two of these operations has thrown the enemy well beyond the first objectives which were selected; the battle extends from Reims to the Scarpe on a front of 120 miles, and the enemy is retiring, giving manifest proof of his disorganization.

It is of the greatest importance to exploit this favorable situation to the utmost, continuing and extending the battle to the Meuse and bringing into it all the Allied forces in one great convergent attack.
For this purpose:

1. The British armies, supported by the left of the French armies, will continue attacking in general direction of St. Quentin–Cambrai.
2. The center of the French armies will continue vigorous action to throw the enemy beyond the Aisne.
3. The American Army and the right of the French armies, operating on the Meuse and westward, will attack in the general direction of Mézières.

And:

III.
To carry [these attacks] out it is necessary first of all to make the necessary reduction in the original plan for the Saint Mihiel operation, to settle on a new plan and carry it out, also to work out the resources which will be left available for other operations.

When Pershing and Pétain met on 31 August, Pétain agreed that Foch had overstepped his authority in telling the AEF commander to attack the southern face of the Saint Mihiel salient only. Foch's authority was strategic, not tactical. Pétain encouraged Pershing to stick to his original plan for the larger attack. Pétain and Pershing then discussed Foch's concept for deploying a large portion of the AEF astride the Aisne River, which the marshal considered the decisive sector. Pershing had strong objections to that plan. As he pointed out to Pétain, the heights on the west bank of that river dominated those of the east, while the valley's deep ravines and projecting ridges would be serious obstacles. Pershing's main objection, however, was that the plan would split the AEF, with the French in between the two segments. Pétain supported Pershing's assessment, recommending that Americans take over the entire sector from Saint Mihiel west to the Argonne Forest. Unfortunately, that terrain east of the Aisne was even worse and the German defenses stronger.[27]

Later that day Pershing sent his formal reply to Foch: "I can no longer agree to any plan which involves the dispersion of our units." The AEF commander also complained that the currently experienced American divisions had had such great difficulties while under the operational control of the Allies that he also could not support the return of any of those units to French or British control—although at that point two American divisions were still operating under British control and three under the French. Pershing then addressed the standard Allied complaint that the American army was little more than a fiction because it did not have sufficient artillery or support units. Pershing reminded Foch that it was his own arguments that had led to the decision to give trans-Atlantic shipping priority to infantry rather than to support units, and on that basis the Allies would provide any shortfalls in artillery or services.

Pershing continued to push for the Saint Mihiel attack, but at the same time he said, "If you decide to utilize the American forces in attacking in the direction of Mézières, I accept that decision, even though it complicates my supply system and the care of my sick and wounded; but I do insist that this American army be employed as a whole, either east of the Argonne or west of the Argonne, and not in four or five divisions here and six or seven there." He concluded by saying that even if the AEF executed only a reduced Saint Mihiel Offensive, it would be impossible to redeploy by 15 or 20 September the twelve to sixteen American divisions that Foch wanted for the Mézières operation.[28]

The next day Foch fired a memo back to Pershing: "If you think—as you let me know in your letter of 31 August—that you cannot make the Saint Mihiel operation before [the Mézières attack] or simultaneously—even if reduced—I think we need to renounce it."[29] On 2 September Foch, Pétain, and Pershing met, and Pétain mediated a compromise. Foch still wanted to scrub the Saint Mihiel Offensive and concentrate all efforts on the attack toward Mézières. Pershing said that if that was the final decision, he would abide by it, but he continued to argue the importance of reducing the Saint Mihiel salient first to eliminate any threat to the American rear. Pétain supported Pershing, and they both believed that the capture of Saint Mihiel "by the Americans would immensely stimulate Allied morale."[30]

The final agreement was for a more limited Saint Mihiel attack scheduled for 10 September, with only eight to ten American divisions and no more than four French. Foch then let Pershing choose whether to attack toward Mézières into the difficult terrain and strong German defenses between the Argonne Forest and the Meuse or into the somewhat easier terrain and defenses west of the Argonne and along the Aisne.[31] Still determined to keep all his forces unified on the ground, Pershing chose the far more difficult sector. Foch later wrote that he had preferred that the Americans take up the sector west of the Argonne in the Champagne, but he ultimately gave in to Pershing's insistence upon taking the eastern sector.[32] As historian Richard Holmes has suggested, Pershing chose the Argonne because he thought "no troops but his own would have the fighting spirit for such an attack."[33] Thus, Pershing would have the responsibility for a ninety-mile-long S-shaped line running from the Argonne to the Meuse just south of Saint Mihiel and then to the Moselle north of Pont-a-Mousson.

Yielding to Pershing's arguments about the time needed to redeploy his forces after Saint Mihiel, Foch agreed to a projected start date of 20 to 25 September for the Meuse-Argonne Offensive, with a force of twelve to fourteen divisions. Simultaneously, the French Fourth Army would attack on the American left. The overall senior commander of the operation would be Pétain as commander in chief of the French Armies of the North and Northeast.[34]

But in agreeing to conduct sequential attacks in two widely separated sectors, Pershing committed the AEF far beyond its capabilities. Because he was planning to use most of his available experienced divisions at Saint Mihiel, that meant that most of the divisions initially deployed for the first line of the Meuse-Argonne attack would be the inexperienced ones. Even with the ten to twelve days of separation between the start of the two offensives, Pershing did not have sufficient time to redeploy his experienced divisions from the one sector to the other. The transportation assets were not equal to the task, and the newly formed U.S. First Army staff had no experience in planning such a complex sequence of operations that would require the deployment of 600,000 men and 2,700 guns. More than half of that force would have to move some sixty miles from the Saint Mihiel sector over poor roads and almost entirely during the hours of darkness. On the very day the commanders in chief were meeting, in fact, the First Army staff had no real inkling that they would have to plan the Meuse-Argonne Offensive on such short notice. It was an immense undertaking that even the most experienced operational staff would find daunting in the short time available.

On 3 September Foch issued the directive for a concentric attack across the entire front designed to push the Germans completely back behind the Hindenburg Line.[35] It essentially was a recapitulation in the form of an official directive of Foch's concept memorandum of 30 August, modified to allow for the American Saint Mihiel Offensive, as agreed upon during the 2 September meeting. Foch later complained to Haig that he had a difficult time getting Pershing to agree to the Meuse-Argonne attack, but he finally managed to bring Pétain and Pershing together to approve the details of a combined attack under Pétain's overall command.[36] Pershing, meanwhile, proceeded in full confidence that both of the coming offensives would prove once and for all the combat effectiveness of his fresh and spirited Americans, and especially his own tactical theories. On 5 September Pershing issued *Open Warfare Instructions* to the AEF: "The infantry commander must oppose machine guns by fire from his rifles, his automatics, and his rifle grenades and must close with their crews under cover of this fire and of ground beyond their flanks."[37]

The American and French divisions completed deploying to their respective lines of departure on 11 September. The remaining divisions under AEF control started moving east of Verdun to their assembly areas for the Meuse-Argonne Offensive. The main attack at Saint Mihiel would be made against the southern face of the salient with seven American divisions. The supporting attack would be made against the western face with one and a half American divisions and one French. Three French divisions would conduct a tertiary attack against the nose of the salient, and three American divisions would be held in reserve. In total, there were 550,000 American and 110,000 French troops. They were supported by 3,010 guns (1,329 manned by French) and 267 light tanks (113 manned by French). The Americans also would have operational control of more than 1,400 aircraft from three different air forces.

Of the 609 aircraft flown during the battle by American airmen, all were of either French or British manufacture.[38] Contrary to the AEF's doctrine of self-reliant infantry and open warfare, Saint Mihiel was, as Mark Grotelueschen has noted, a set-piece attack based on massive firepower and overwhelming numerical superiority.[39]

By the start of the battle, German Army Detachment C under the command of General Georg Fuchs had nine divisions in the front line and one in reserve, totaling about 55,000 troops. AEF intelligence estimated that the Germans could reinforce the sector with two divisions within two days, two more divisions by the third day, and four more by the fourth day. The Germans had plenty of indicators that the Saint Mihiel attack was coming. On 8 September, Fuchs recommended to Army Group Gallwitz a spoiling attack against the Allied buildup. OHL instead ordered Army Group Gallwitz to start the preparations to evacuate the salient and then fall back when attacked.[40] Army Detachment C then developed two courses of action: a deliberate withdrawal requiring eight days and a two-day hasty withdrawal under pressure with very little destruction of the abandoned defensive positions. On 11 September, the Germans started withdrawing their stocks of war materials from the salient.[41]

Following a four-hour artillery preparation, the main attack against the southern face started at 0500 hours on 12 September—two days later than the original target date. Three hours later the secondary attack against the western face jumped off, preceded by a seven-hour preparation. The attackers achieved tactical surprise, which forced the Germans to initiate their hasty withdrawal option. The Allies made rapid progress, and by that evening there was a gap of only ten miles between the lead elements of the U.S. 1st Division in the main attack and the U.S. 26th Division converging on Vigenulles-les-Hattonchatel from the secondary attack. One of the units defending the western face was one of the four Austro-Hungarian divisions serving on the Western Front in 1918. As Ludendorff later laconically commented, it "might have fought better."[42]

Aware that the Germans were starting to withdraw, Pershing ordered the offensive speeded up, to include a nighttime pursuit. The two leading divisions linked up about 0600 hours on the morning of 13 September, and by that evening the attackers had captured all their assigned objectives in the salient. Mopping-up operations continued for two more days, as the withdrawing German forces took up positions in the Michael Position and prepared for further attacks. Pershing stopped any further advances on the predetermined halt line so that American units committed to the Meuse-Argonne attack could be withdrawn and prepared for redeployment.

The Allies had recovered more than two hundred square miles of French territory, and the attack cleared the Paris–Nancy rail line and the roads that ran parallel to the Meuse from Saint Mihiel to just north of Verdun, thereby eliminating finally the threat to that fortress city.[43] German and Allied casualties, killed and wounded, were roughly the same, about 7,500 each. The Germans also lost some 14,500 prisoners and 450 guns. The operation, however, was not the sweeping success it has been portrayed as in much of the American literature. Among other problems, poor movement planning and road discipline resulted in traffic jams backed up for miles. The tanks consumed three times their estimated fuel and ran out of gas on the afternoon of the first day.[44] Identical problems, but on a much larger scale, would continue to plague the AEF during the Meuse-Argonne Offensive. Ludendorff also commented later that considering the American overwhelming force superiority ratio of more than 10 to 1, the ultimate results of the Saint Mihiel operation were a "foregone conclusion."[45]

Telegrams of congratulations poured into AEF headquarters from all directions, especially from President Wilson, Foch, and Haig. Writing in his postwar memoirs, Pershing said, "This striking victory completely demonstrated the wisdom of building up a distinct American Army."[46] He felt totally vindicated in everything he had been saying about the efficacy of open warfare and the innate superiority of his American troops vis-à-vis the "tired Europeans." Notwithstanding, on 15 September he again sent a note to the general staff in Washington complaining about the inadequate rifle marksmanship training of the American replacements arriving in France.[47]

Pershing also wrote that the American victory at Saint Mihiel "probably did more than any single operation of the war to encourage the Allies. After the years of doubt and despair, of suffering and loss, it brought them assurance of the final defeat of an enemy whose armies had seemed well-nigh invincible."[48] It was a vast overstatement and a myopic one. Very few British, French, or German senior leaders at the time would have agreed with it, nor would many British, French, or German historians today. For the British, 8 August 1918, during the Battle of Amiens, was "The Day We Won the War." For the French, that day, during the Second Battle of the Marne, was 18 July. The Germans themselves were rather split on the matter. Ludendorff said that 8 August was the "Black Day of the German Army." Lossberg said Germany lost the war on 18 July. And General Max Hoffmann said it was 26 March, the day Operation MICHAEL failed to take Amiens. In much of the American literature, however, Pershing's claim had for many years a great deal of resonance.

Pershing also believed that if he had not had to halt to reconsolidate for the Meuse-Argonne, American forces could have pushed beyond the Hindenburg Line and possibly into Metz.[49] Marshall, the First Army operations chief, believed that the AEF could have captured Metz by 14 September, and Brigadier General Douglas MacArthur also believed that fortress city could have been taken easily. General Hunter Liggett, the commander of the U.S. I Corps at Saint Mihiel, did not agree with that optimism. After the war, he wrote that taking Metz was possible "only on the supposition that our army was a well-oiled fully-coordinated machine, which it was not yet." Had the First Army attempted to advance, it "had an excellent chance of spending the greater part of the winter mired in the mud of the Woëvre [Plain], flanked both to the east and the west."[50] In other words, it could have turned into an American Passchendaele.

Despite the operational success of the Saint Mihiel operation, the Germans were fairly critical of American tactical performance. An after-action report from Army Detachment C noted,

> In their behavior, the American infantry displayed insufficient military training. They advanced mechanically, demonstrating great awkwardness in the management of their consecutive skirmish formations in open country.
>
> Officers, as well as privates, did not understand how to utilize the advantages of the country.[51]

That was precisely how they had been trained to fight, in accordance with Pershing's "open warfare" theories. And although the Germans at the time anticipated that the Americans would continue advancing,[52] General Max von Gallwitz in 1928 said that the defenses of Metz, which were based to the south and the city's flanks, would have been a formidable obstacle to overrun.[53] Writing after the war, Hindenburg attempted to put a positive spin on the situation at that point: "Although as a result of the enemy irruptions our Western Front had to be repeatedly withdrawn, it had not been broken through. It was shaking, but it did not fall."[54] OHL General Staff officer Lieutenant Colonel Albrecht von Thaer saw things more realistically. On 15 September he wrote in his personal war diary that the German army was now fighting for its very existence.[55]

THE BATTLE OF HAVRINCOURT (12 SEPTEMBER 1918)

During a meeting at the War Office in London on 10 September, Haig told Milner, "The character of the war has changed." He recommended that all the reserves currently being held in the UK should be committed to France immediately to exploit the BEF's successes since 8 August.[56] Despite Foch's directive of 3 September, however, Haig was reluctant to continue pushing with the forces he then had on hand, troops that had been fighting constantly for more than a month. He wanted to give his units time to regroup and reconstitute before launching the main attack to break the Hindenburg Line. While Haig was still in London, Third Army commander Byng took advantage of a target of opportunity to launch an attack at Havrincourt, which was on the shoulder of the old Flesquières salient that had caused the Germans so much trouble the previous March during Operation MICHAEL. Byng's intent was to establish a line of departure for a direct assault on the Canal du Nord sector of the Hindenburg Line.[57]

Four divisions of the Seventeenth Army defended Havrincourt. At dawn on 12 September the Third Army attacked with three divisions, including the redoubtable New Zealand Division. By 0730 hours Byng's forces had control of the western end of village. The Germans launched repeated counterattacks from a fortified château south of the village, which the British finally took on the morning of the thirteenth. It was a relatively small-scale action as World War I battles went, but there were two things significant about it. In the first place, it showed that the esprit and combat effectiveness of the German army were continuing to deteriorate. In the second, the attackers for the first time in the war actually managed to break into the leading edge of the Siegfried Position.

On 12 September OHL made a change to the German defensive doctrine. Partially abandoning the elastic defense concept, units were now ordered to fight in and hold at all costs the main line of resistance (*Hauptkampflinie*). Ground down by the steady Allied pressure and having to rely ever increasingly on inexperienced and hastily trained young troops, the Germans were forced to fall back on the old, more rigid but easier to manage tactics.[58]

THE BATTLE OF ÉPEHY (18 SEPTEMBER)

Since the end of the first week in September, Haig had been keeping a tight rein on his Fourth Army. But after Byng's success at Havrincourt, Haig gave

Rawlinson the go-ahead for a similar limited objective attack against the German line around Épehy, with the objective of establishing a line of departure for a subsequent main attack against the St. Quentin Canal sector of the Siegfried Position. This, however, would be a larger-scale attack than Havrincourt, and Épehy was a good three miles in front of the Siegfried Position's leading edge. Rawlinson intended to attack with all three of his corps, supported on the left by one corps of Byng's Third Army and on the right by elements of Debeney's French First Army. The attack was conducted on a 7,000-meter front, with the fire support provided by 1,500 guns and 300 machine guns. The British also deployed dummy tanks to deceive the Germans into believing that the BEF fielded more tanks than they actually had. The Allies attacked with twelve divisions against six divisions of Marwitz's Second Army.

When the attack started on the morning of 18 September, Rawlinson's left wing bogged down. On the right, the French support failed to materialize, which held up Rawlinson's right-wing corps. The Fourth Army did make significant progress in the center, with two divisions of Monash's Australian Corps advancing three miles to seize the high ground overlooking the Siegfried Position east of St. Quentin. The battle ended that day with the BEF capturing more than 4,000 Germans and eighty-seven artillery pieces. It was less of a success than anticipated. Although the Fourth Army had secured a good line of departure in the Australian Corps' center sector, the failure of the left-wing British III Corps to seize all of its objectives would have consequences for the British when they attacked against the line of the St. Quentin Canal eleven days later.[59]

THIRTEEN

THE ALLIED GENERAL OFFENSIVE: FOCH MOVES IN FOR THE KILL

Indecision was no longer justified if one compared the paucity of the results obtained by the enemy with the magnitude of his effort and the mighty forces which his initiative had unchained.

Marshal Ferdinand Foch, Memoirs of Marshall Foch

Unlike the enemy, we had no fresh reserves to throw in. Instead of an inexhaustible America, we had only weary Allies who were themselves on the point of collapse.

Field Marshal Paul von Hindenburg, Out of My Life

BY THE SECOND HALF OF September 1918, all the objectives Foch had identified in his 24 July Bombon memorandum had been achieved. The Germans were pushed back to and in some places beyond their starting lines for the Ludendorff Offensives. The Paris–Amiens, Paris–Nancy, and Lerouville–Verdun rail lines had been cleared and were now available to support the next phase of Allied operations.[1] Meanwhile, the Germans themselves had grown ever more dependent on their own rail network to shift their reserve divisions back and forth to deal with the Allied threats. Between November 1917 and July 1918, the German army had averaged 48 divisional moves per month by rail, which included all the troop deployments required for the five spring offensives. But in August the Germans were forced to move 104 divisions by rail, 130 in September, and 105 in October. It took forty-five trains totaling 2,250 cars to move a single division and all its equipment and horses.[2] According to General Fritz von Lossberg, a typical divisional move by rail took eight to ten days.[3]

Based on Haig's recommendations at the end of August, Foch was now fairly confident that the Germans could be defeated by the end of 1918, and he was ready to launch a more far-reaching general offensive than he heretofore had envisioned. The key to the plan that emerged was to cut the lateral rail lines that ran almost parallel behind the German front. As demonstrated by their five great offensives earlier in the year, German military thinking was still fixed solidly on force-on-force battles. Despite understanding the importance of their own logistical lines, they nonetheless had something of a blind spot for the opportunities of their enemy's logistical vulnerabilities. Foch, on the other hand, recognized that at the operational level, a wide range of factors could contribute to the outcome of a campaign, logistics sustainment especially.

Up to this point, Belgian king Albert had refused to put any of his troops under the Allied unified command. On 9 September Foch met with the king to propose a drive into Belgium north of the Lys River with nine Belgian and two British divisions. The initial effort would be to secure the Houthulst Forest, the Passchendaele Ridge, the heights at Gheluvelt and Zandvorde, and the Comines Canal. The exploitation phase to Bruges and the Meuse River (called the Maas in Flanders) would then be executed by the entire Belgian army, the British Second Army, and three divisions and the cavalry corps of the French Sixth Army. The projected start date for the operation was between 20 and 25 September.[4]

Albert agreed, and he also agreed to accept French general Jean-Marie Degoutte as his chief of staff and principal operational planner—and the de facto tactical commander. Combined with the other Allied forces, Degoutte's Sixth Army was redesignated the Flanders Army Group. Later that day Foch met with Haig at Cassel. Haig agreed to put General Sir Herbert Plumer's Second Army under the operational control of the Belgian king, but Haig also declined to provide three cavalry divisions Foch asked for.[5]

During a meeting at the War Office in London on 10 September, Haig told Lord Alfred Milner, "The character of the war has changed." He urged that all the reserves currently being held in the United Kingdom should be committed to France immediately to exploit the recent Allied successes. The BEF commander also told Milner that the current plan to have all the British units in France up to full strength by 1 April 1919 was "thoroughly unsound." Milner warned Haig that if the BEF got "used up" in 1918, there would not be sufficient replacements for 1919.[6]

Milner left the decision with Haig whether or not to attack in accordance with Foch's plan. In a meeting later that day, however, the secretary of state for war told Chief of the Imperial General Staff Sir Henry Wilson that he thought Haig was being ridiculously optimistic, and he feared that the BEF commander was about to launch off on another Passchendaele. Many of the other generals that Milner had talked to in France also expressed optimism, but "manpower is the trouble, and Douglas Haig and Foch and Du Cane can't understand it."[7] (Lieutenant General Sir John Du Cane was Haig's representative at Foch's headquarters.)

From this point on, Foch's rallying cry was *"Tout le monde à la bataille!"* (Everybody into the battle!) On 23 September, he met at Mouchy with Haig and Pétain to make the final decisions about the General Offensive. Only General Sir William Birdwood's British Fifth Army in the north, General Henri Barthelot's French Fifth Army, and General Charles Mangin's French Tenth Army were not committed to the initial phase. The Allied generals agreed upon the following sequencing for the four converging operations:[8]

- 26 September: The U.S. First Army and French Fourth Army between the Suippe in the direction of Mézières.
- 27 September: The British First and Third Armies in the general direction of Cambrai.
- 28 September: The Flanders Army Group between the sea and the Lys River.
- 29 September: The British Fourth Army supported by the French First Army in the direction of Busigny.

Ludendorff's greatest vulnerability was on his left. The four-track rail line just south of Mézières was a major choke point in the German transportation network. If the Germans lost that line, their entire position in northern and northeastern France would be threatened. That would leave the lines in the north running through Liège as the sole remaining withdrawal route for the German army, with Army Group Flanders aiming ultimately at that city. The AEF would be starting from a line only about forty miles from its ultimate objective. Army Group Flanders had three times that distance to reach Liège.[9]

The primary threat to Foch's operational concept was the German general reserve divisions. With the advantage of operating on interior lines, the Germans could move those units to threatened points fairly quickly, before the Allies could penetrate deeply enough to cut the rail lines. Foch's challenge was either to destroy those divisions or force their early commitment and pin them down. For that reason, Haig particularly wanted the Americans to be the first to jump off, because that would start drawing German reserves to their front and away from the British fronts. Haig even thought that if the timing was right, the bulk of the German reserves might be caught completely out of position by the Franco-American attack on one end of the line and the British attack on the other.[10]

OHL, meanwhile, had projected that the most likely Allied action would be a Franco-American attack into Lorraine, to exploit the success at Saint Mihiel.[11] On 26 September the Germans had 197 divisions on the Western Front. From north to south, Crown Prince Rupprecht's Army Group, consisting of the Fourth, Sixth, and Seventeenth Armies, had 54 divisions; Boehn's Army Group, consisting of the Second and Eighteenth Armies, had 41 divisions; the German Crown Prince's Army Group, consisting of the Ninth, Seventh, First, and Third Armies, had 60 divisions; Gallwitz's Army Group, consisting of the Fifth Army and Army Detachment C, had 19 divisions; and Duke Albrecht's Army Group, consisting of the Nineteenth Army and Army Detachments A and B, had 23 divisions.[12]

The correlation of forces aside, Germany's strategic position by the autumn of 1918 put it on the brink of defeat. The Royal Navy's maritime blockade was an important factor, if not the most important factor, in weakening Germany's capacity for resistance and that made it so vulnerable to Foch's General Offensive.[13] The German food situation was critical. The military in the field had priority for sustenance, but the people in the homeland suffered wretchedly, especially during the "Turnip Winter" (Steckrübenwinter) of 1917. An estimated 700,000 Germans died directly or indirectly as a result of the blockade.[14]

THE MEUSE-ARGONNE OFFENSIVE, PHASE I (26 SEPTEMBER–3 OCTOBER)

Following Saint Mihiel, the U.S. First Army had only two weeks to shift positions by moving to the west and relieving in place the 220,000 troops of the French Second Army. The Americans had to transport 500,000 troops, 900,000 tons of supplies and ammunition, and 2,000 pieces of artillery. The

AEF had only nine hundred trucks, and many of the infantrymen had to walk the sixty miles, leaving them exhausted when they arrived. The trucks could make the move in a single night, but the horse-drawn vehicles took three to six days. According to Colonel George Marshall, the principal planner of the movement, shifting the guns was the hardest task to coordinate. Just the seventy-two guns of a single division took up nine miles of road space. Large numbers of critically needed horses died during the move.[15]

The Meuse-Argonne today is thought by many to be synonymous with the Argonne Forest. The forest, however, was only a relatively small area in the southwest corner of the AEF's area of operations. Nonetheless, the entire Meuse-Argonne sector was classic defender's ground. It was bordered on the east by the Meuse River, and the heights on the eastern bank dominated that valley. In the west, the hills of the Argonne Forest commanded the valley of the Aire River. In the center, a hog's-back ridge consisting of the heights of Montfaucon, Cunel, Romagne, and the Bois de Barricourt were natural strong points that gave the Germans dominating observation over the entire sector. The ground over which the Americans had to attack was one big channelized corridor twenty miles wide and thirteen miles long, with the high ground in the center dividing it into two large defiles. The Germans had most of their heavy artillery on the eastern heights of the Meuse, enfilading almost the entire American sector. Their lighter field batteries were interspersed throughout the corridor.[16] As for the Argonne Forest itself, it was known in French geography books as the "Thermopylae of France" because of its near impassability for military operations.[17]

The German defenses in the American sector consisted of four belts in depth. The leading Hagen Stellung ran through Varennes on the eastern edge of the Argonne Forest to the far side of the Meuse. It was only two to three miles from the American line of departure. Two to three miles behind that, the double Etzel–Gieslher Stellung was anchored in its center by Montfaucon, with the Etzel line running just south of the heights and the Gieslher line running roughly parallel two miles to the north. Four miles north of Montfaucon the third belt was the Kriemhilde Stellung, which was the southern extension of the Hermann–Hunding–Brünnhilde Stellung. The strong Kriemhilde Stellung included the heights of Cunel and Romagne and the village of Grandpré. Finally, some nine miles north of Montfaucon, the relatively weak Freia Stellung was the final defensive line. It ran through Buzancy and Barricourt Heights.[18] The German defensive positions converged as they approached the

Meuse. Thus, in the AEF's sector the distance from no-man's-land to the third position averaged only about ten miles, while farther to the northwest around Laon the average distance was thirty-six miles. The closeness of the defensive belts made the American tactical problem more difficult, because they could support each other more easily.

Running north from the American line of departure were only three key roads, which became the main supply routes for each of the first-line U.S. corps: through Esnes in the east, through Avocourt in the center, and through Varennes in the west.[19] All of them were in bad shape and required continuous maintenance. Each dirt road had to carry a corps headquarters and the support tail for three of the double-sized American divisions. Each of those divisions averaged one thousand vehicles in a ten-mile-long column of horses and wagons.[20] Complicating the deployment, the two corps of the French Second Army had to use those same roads to move out of the sector while the Americans were moving in. The AEF had only a single engineer regiment trained and equipped for road repair. It reached the Meuse-Argonne sector the night before the start of the attack, and even then without most of its equipment.[21]

Oddly enough, German intelligence failed to detect the significance and scope of the clumsy American buildup, although the German scouts continuously reported motor vehicle noises in the sector.[22] At the start of the campaign, General Georg von der Marwitz's Fifth Army had only five divisions in the line between the Meuse and the Argonne. American intelligence estimated that the Germans were capable of reinforcing the sector with four divisions on the first day of the battle, two more by the second day, and nine more by the third day. By the time it was over, Army Group Gallwitz had fed some 450,000 troops into the battle.[23]

On 22 September Pershing assumed command of all Allied forces in the American sector, with General Henri Gouraud's Fourth Army under his operational control. Pétain was the overall operational commander.[24] The following day, Foch issued his operations note for the Meuse-Argonne Offensive.[25] The Americans were to make the main effort by pushing toward Buzancy as rapidly as possible. The Fourth Army had the mission of advancing toward Aisne de Rethel, covering the American left flank and without slowing the U.S. First Army down. The order stressed especially that the sectors of the two armies were fixed; the boundaries were not to be crossed. Before the campaign was over, the violation of that order would result in a major crisis.

The First Army issued its operations order for the offensive on 20 September. Unlike Foch's operations note issued three days later, Pershing did not designate a main effort. Nor did anything in the order of battle and the allocation of forces indicate any weighting of a main effort. Each of the three attacking American corps was allocated three first-line divisions and one as a corps reserve. The First Army reserve consisted of three divisions, with one deployed in the rear of each of the three corps sectors. The artillery was likewise evenly distributed, with each corps being allocated around 650 guns and some 100 to 130 trench mortars. The deployment of the forces resembled one massive frontal attack.

If there was a main effort by default, it was with U.S. V Corps in the center, where the high ground at Montfaucon gave the Germans observation dominance over much of the battlefield. But that key terrain was only a little more than one mile to the west of the boundary with III Corps, on V Corps' right. The coordination of fire and maneuver across unit boundaries is one of the most difficult and complex of all combat tasks, and the way the boundaries were established severely limited V Corps' ability to maneuver against Montfaucon from both flanks. And even within V Corps' sector, Montfaucon sat almost directly on the inner boundary between the 79th Division on the corps' right and 37th Division in its center. Thus, even on the divisional level the two attacking divisions could maneuver only against one of the objective's flanks. It was an extremely difficult tactical problem, one that neither the 37th nor the 79th Division was up to. Both were green units with less than two months of training as divisions. The 79th Division, with one of the most difficult missions of the first phase of the offensive, was the least experienced and most undertrained of all the attacking forces.[26]

The First Army's initial objective was the line Dun-sur-Meuse–Grandpré–Challerange–Sommepy; the follow-on objective was the line Stenay–Le Chesne–Attigny–Rethel. Pershing's scheme of maneuver required his forces to advance more than eight miles on the first day. In the process, the Americans were to link up with the French Fourth Army at Grandpré, at the northern tip of the Argonne Forest, thereby forcing the Germans out of the woods. But that required the Doughboys to take the key high ground at Montfaucon and then break through the German third belt of the Kriemhilde Stellung and capture the heights of Romagne. After taking Romagne the Americans were to advance another ten miles to the line of Stenay and Le Chesne, to outflank the Germans along the Aisne River to the front of the French Fourth Army and clear the way for the advance to Mézières or Sedan. The next task would be to clear the heights of the Meuse with the yet-to-be-established U.S. Second Army attacking northward along the east bank of the river between Beaumont and Sivry-sur-Meuse, to clear the crest south of the Bois de la Grande Montagne. From there the final thrust would be made against the Sedan–Mézières rail line.[27]

Pershing's plan had no basis in reality, especially with inexperienced troops trying to punch through the deeply echeloned German defenses. The tested and battle-hardened Germans had managed to advance only twelve miles on the first day (27 May) of the BLÜCHER Offensive, and even then the attackers had to break through only one very thin defensive belt instead of three deeply echeloned ones. Pershing and his operations planners had drawn the wrong lesson from their experience at Saint Mihiel. The Germans, instead of already withdrawing, would be defending and reinforcing in the Meuse-Argonne sector. And as already noted, Pershing had committed almost all of his experienced divisions at Saint Mihiel, and most could not redeploy in time to lead the Meuse-Argonne attack. Three of the first echelon divisions were considered trained but had never been in combat, and another five had not even completed the AEF's most abbreviated training program. Three of the first echelon divisions were not even supported by their own organic artillery brigades, which were still strung out along the line of march from Saint Mihiel.[28] As Pershing later explained his reasoning at the time, "It was thought reasonable to count on the vigor and the aggressive spirit of our troops to make up in a measure for their inexperience."[29]

The ever-pessimistic Pétain doubted that the Americans would get any farther than Montfaucon before the onset of winter.[30] Things, however, did not turn out nearly as badly as Pétain had feared, but they likewise fell far short of Pershing's expectations. Following a three-hour artillery preparation, the Americans attacked at 0530 hours on 26 September. On the American left flank, the French Fourth Army moved out along a forty-kilometer front against the front of the German Third Army and the left wing of the First Army. The left flank of the American advance was met by devastating flanking fire from the German guns in the Argonne foothills, and the right flank took fire from the German artillery on the high ground east of the Meuse. Predictably, massive traffic jams along the main supply routes prevented food and ammunition from moving up and the wounded from moving back.

Although impressive by World War I standards, and especially so for inexperienced troops, the Americans advanced only three miles the first day instead of the intended eight. In the center, the V Corps' 37th and 79th Divisions failed to coordinate their attacks, as they approached Montfaucon. To their immediate right, in the III Corps sector, the veteran 4th Division made good progress penetrating the German defenses, and managed to advance to the northeast of Montfaucon, where it was in position to attack the hill from the rear. The 4th Division's leadership, however, hesitated to attack across the boundary into the V Corps' sector without coordination and approval, and thus lost the opportunity to envelop the key German position. At the end of the first day the Germans still held Montfaucon. Pershing insisted that the 79th Division press forward another three miles to take the key high ground. Still certain at this point that the attack was a diversion to mask the true main attack from Saint Mihiel, General Max von Gallwitz nonetheless moved up five divisions that night. Frustrated, Pershing sent a blistering message to his V Corps divisional commanders: "There should be no delay or hesitation in going forward. . . . All officers will push their units forward with all possible energy. . . . Commanders will not hesitate to relieve on the spot any officer of whatever rank who fails to show in his energy those qualities of leadership required to accomplish the task that confronts us."[31]

Although no food or water was getting forward, the 79th Division managed to take Montfaucon on the twenty-seventh, but both the American and the French advances were starting to bog down. The Germans were nonetheless alarmed by this point. On the evening of 28 September, Hindenburg and Ludendorff conferred at OHL in preparation for a meeting the following day with Foreign Minister Paul von Hintze to consider calling for an armistice. The Duo at this point still optimistically believed that in the end the Entente would be forced to come to terms with Germany to halt the rise of Bolshevism in the east.[32] But on 29 September, Bulgaria became the first of the Central Powers to capitulate, resulting in the collapse of the Macedonian front. At that point even the most optimistic of the German leaders realized that they no longer had any chance of winning on the battlefield.

Pershing continued to blame the failures and delays on inexperienced and timid officers.[33] During a visit to V Corps headquarters on the evening of 28 September he issued another order to the division commanders to "push on regardless of men or guns, night and day."[34] The following morning Pershing relieved the commander of the 28th Division's 55th Brigade. Throughout the remainder of the campaign he relieved senior commanders ruthlessly. By the end of October, the AEF commander had sacked four brigade commanders, three division commanders, and one corps commander.[35] Nonetheless, the Kriemhilde Stellung, which was supposed to have been broken into on the first day, remained intact, and the Germans committed six more divisions to the fight.

French premier Georges Clemenceau made a visit to the American sector on the twenty-ninth. He was shocked by the chaos and disorganization he saw, with transportation in both directions in a state of gridlock. Clemenceau tried to get forward to Montfaucon, but his car got jammed up in traffic five miles short. During a visit to French Fourth Army headquarters later that day, Gouraud told Clemenceau that his own lack of progress was caused by the slowness of the Americans on his right.[36]

Constant Allied air attacks forced Gallwitz on 29 September to displace his army group headquarters from Montmédy twenty miles west to Longwy. The following day, however, the AEF was able to continue attacking with only a single division. Pétain told Foch that the American failure was largely the result of the inexperienced American general staff.[37] Angry with the lack of American progress, Foch sent Pétain a message proposing to insert the headquarters and command group of the French Second Army between the French Fourth Army and the U.S. First Army.[38] The Second Army would then assume command of one corps from the right wing of the French Fourth Army and one corps from the left wing of the U.S. First Army. Foch's sound idea was to place all Allied forces operating on both sides of the Meuse under Pershing and all forces on both sides of the Argonne Forest under the French Second Army commander. Pershing refused. Believing that Foch had insulted the AEF, he resolved to drive his troops even harder.[39]

That night OHL finally gave the orders to start reconnoitering the defensive positions on the Meuse–Antwerp line, more than three weeks after Lossberg had first urged Ludendorff to initiate the action. Hindenburg also told the army group commanders that OHL could no longer provide reserves. From that point on, the units in the line had to make do with the troops they had.[40] Nonetheless, Ludendorff as late as 2 October still believed that the German army was strong enough to hold off the Allies "for months."[41]

By 30 September the French Fourth Army was held fast in its sector by stubborn German resistance at the Blanc Mont Ridge, which outflanked the

Argonne Forest and was the last natural defensive line south of the Aisne. Foch asked the AEF to loan the Fourth Army two divisions. Pershing detached temporarily the veteran U.S. 2nd Division and the untried 36th Division. Under the command of Marine major general John A. Lejeune, the 2nd Division's capture of Blanc Mont Ridge on 3 October was one of the most innovative attacks ever conducted by an American division during the Great War. Rather than blindly following the AEF's "open warfare" tactical dogma, Lejeune devised a methodical, set-piece plan of attack based on limited objectives and deeply echeloned assault forces supported by massed artillery fire. After taking the ridge, the 2nd Division spent the next six days repelling German counterattacks and systematically advancing the Allies' line north to St. Etienne. On the morning of 10 October, the German forces on the front of the French Fourth Army began a general withdrawal to the Aisne. The American attack had been an unprecedented success, but Lejeune's 2nd Division was nonetheless criticized by the AEF's inspector general, Major General Andre W. Brewster, for failure to follow the official American tactical doctrine—regardless of any actual battlefield success.[42]

Despite the success at Blanc Mont, however, the American offensive in the Meuse-Argonne sector had all but ground to a halt in front of the Kriemhilde Stellung. That line remained anchored on three strongpoints: from east to west, the heights of Cunel, the heights of Romagne, and the northern apex of the Argonne Forest, which included strong positions at Cornay and Chatel-Chéhéry. The strongpoints were mutually supporting. Gallwitz then had twenty-six divisions in line, with seventeen in reserve. After receiving reports of the gridlock along the American lines of communications, which had forced the AEF to stop for several days and regroup, Haig on 1 October wrote in his diary, "What very valuable days are being lost! All this is the result of inexperience and ignorance of the needs of a modern attacking force."[43] The criticism, of course, was a not very veiled jab at Pershing.

The American artillery was delivering its heaviest fires on the inner flanks of the German Third and Fifth Armies. On 2 October, OHL transferred the command of the left-wing corps of the Third Army to the Fifth Army, putting the entire fight against the Americans under Gallwitz's Army Group.[44] That same day a small task group of six companies from the 77th Division's 308th Infantry and one from the 307th Infantry was cut off in one of the Argonne Forest's deeply wooded ravines. After being encircled for six days, constantly beating off German attacks, the legendary "Lost Battalion" was rescued when American units broke through to its relief. The original force of 550 suffered 111 killed in action and 199 wounded, captured, or missing.

THE BATTLE OF CANAL DU NORD (27 SEPTEMBER–1 OCTOBER)

The Canal du Nord sector was one of the strongest segments of the Siegfried Stellung. It was a formidable obstacle for both infantry and tanks. The Germans had flooded some sections, but most of the canal was dry. It was more than one hundred feet wide, with a ten- to twelve-foot-high western bank and a four- to five-foot-high eastern bank. Behind the canal the Germans had their usual deeply echeloned positions, interlaced with barbed wire and machine guns. Thirteen divisions of General Adolph von Carlowitz's Second Army held the line, with eleven in reserve. They occupied the high ground and thus could easily observe the Allies' movements.

The attack was planned as a continuation of the advances made during the Battles of Havrincourt and Épehy. The main axis of advance was along the inner-army boundary of General Sir Henry Horne's First Army and General Sir Julian Byng's Third Army. The task of the First Army, spearheaded by Lieutenant General Sir Arthur Currie's Canadian Corps, was to cross the canal and occupy Bourlon Woods, the high ground on the left of the battlefield overlooking the village of Cambrai. The remainder of the First Army and three corps of the Third Army would then advance toward Cambrai to capture the key German rail and supply center. The Third Army also had the task of securing the Scheldt River to establish a position from which to support the British Fourth Army during the Battle of St. Quentin Canal, scheduled for 29 September.

The attack jumped off at 0520 hours on 27 September. Supported by tank fire, the First Army's 1st and 4th Canadian Divisions crossed the canal behind a creeping barrage fired by thirty-one artillery battalions. With the Canadians on the far bank, the British 11th Division on their left then crossed almost unopposed. The British forces then started fanning out in both directions. On the First Army's right, the three corps of the Third Army made significant gains, but not as great as those of the First Army. By that evening, the Canadians were in possession of Bourlon Woods.

On 27 September, Foch sent a message to all the major Allied commands. He noted that surprise and the scope of the attacks would disrupt the ability of the Germans to respond effectively. If they were given no time to recover or consolidate, they would be able to mount only disorganized and piecemeal

responses. "Under those conditions, the attack must immediately aim to produce effects of rupture by organizing groups of attack (infantry, artillery) des-
tined to march to objectives whose possession guarantee[s] the shaking of the
enemy front," Foch noted.[45]

The First Army on 28 September pushed beyond Bourlon Woods while
the Third Army reached the outskirts of Cambrai, effectively interdicting the
town's rail center. On the twenty-ninth the British established more bridges
over the canal. Later that day the Fourth Army on the Third Army's right attacked, starting the Battle of St. Quentin Canal. Having broken through the
German main defenses, the BEF on 1 October called an operational pause in
the Canal du Nord sector. The First and Third Armies had driven a salient
twelve miles wide and six miles deep into the German lines, capturing more
than 10,000 prisoners. On the night of 1–2 October, the Germans fell back on a
seventeen-mile front from Armentières to Lens.[46] As they withdrew, the Germans systematically destroyed and mined all the rail lines in the abandoned
sector, but the Allies successively repaired and reopened the rail lines as they
advanced and the Germans retreated.[47]

THE FIFTH BATTLE OF YPRES (28 SEPTEMBER–2 OCTOBER)

In accordance with the 9 September agreement between Foch and the Belgian
king Albert, General Jean-Marie Degoutte and his staff arrived at the king's
headquarters on 18 September. Degoutte was designated as the chief of staff
of Albert's Army Group Flanders, although it was understood tacitly that
the latter would actually direct the operations. In addition, Degoutte also retained command of his own French Sixth Army. The newly established army
group consisted of Degoutte's six divisions, ten divisions of General Sir Herbert Plumer's Second Army, and twelve Belgian divisions. For the first time in
the war, Belgian troops were now part of the Allied unified command. Army
Group Flanders had 2,550 guns in support. Its mission was to drive toward
the Belgian city of Liège as the left pincer arm of Foch's General Offensive.
Immediately opposing the Allies, Army Group Crown Prince Rupprecht had
sixteen divisions in the line and eight in reserve, under General Friedrich
Sixt von Armin's Fourth Army and the right wing of General Ferdinand von
Quast's Sixth Army.

Early in the evening of 27 September, the chief of staff of the German Fourth
Army reported to Rupprecht's Army Group that an attack on both sides of the
Houthulst Forest was imminent.[48] At 0530 hours the following morning the

attack opened on a twenty-three-mile front following a three-hour artillery preparation. In the British Second Army sector, Plumer's two northern corps to the east and southeast of Ypres attacked without an artillery preparation.[49]

The British recaptured the Passchendaele Ridge on the first day. By evening the Allies had advanced seven kilometers, taking some 4,000 prisoners. The attackers were greatly aided by the fact that Ludendorff had shifted reserves from Flanders to defend Cambrai against the attack Haig had launched the day before. The Fourth Army reported to Rupprecht's headquarters, "The troops will no longer stand up to a serious attack."[50] That evening OHL put out a message to the army groups: "Given the shortage of combat-ready reserves and the stretched railway situation, the army groups cannot plan on receiving any additional reinforcements."[51]

The Allies occupied Diksmuide on 29 September, and the British Second Army retook Messines Ridge. During the following days the advance started to stall because of rain, mud, and bad roads, but by 1 October the Allies had cleared the entire left bank of the Lys. The following day the Germans withdrew from Lens and Armentières, but they also were starting to move up reserves.[52] The Allies, however, were forced to suspend the operation on 3 October. The drive had been so rapid that the logistics system could not keep up, especially given the muddy conditions and torn-up ground caused by the heavy shelling. The Allies suffered about 9,000 casualties. The number of German dead and wounded are unknown, but the Allies took some 10,000 prisoners, along with six hundred machine guns and three hundred artillery pieces. It was not until 14 October that the Allies were able to consolidate and get the required logistical support forward to resume the advance. (See Battle of Courtrai, below.)

THE BATTLES OF ST. QUENTIN CANAL AND THE BEAUREVOIR LINE (29 SEPTEMBER–6 OCTOBER)

The fourth arm of Foch's General Offensive started on 29 September. General Sir Henry Rawlinson's Fourth Army had the toughest job of the opening phase of the campaign. It had to break the Hindenburg Line at its strongest point, a twelve-mile sector between St. Quentin and Vendhuille, with up to six successive lines in some places. Rawlinson was supported on his right by elements of General Marie-Eugène Debeney's French First Army and on his left by one corps of Byng's Third Army. The canal itself was incorporated into the German defenses, forty feet wide and up to thirty feet deep. Its key weak point was a 3.5-mile-long tunnel north of Bellicourt. The German defensive line was a wide and natural bridge over the canal, but the Germans had turned the tunnel itself into a massive bunker that was impervious to artillery fire.

Rawlinson's Fourth Army had fourteen divisions, including Lieutenant General Sir John Monash's Australian Corps of five divisions and the untested American II Corps of two divisions. The Australians had been in almost constant combat since early August, and only the 3rd and 5th Divisions were combat effective. They were opposed by Carlowitz's Second Army, which was still battling the British Third Army on its right wing. Allied intelligence estimated that the Germans could reinforce the threatened sector with six divisions within seventy-two hours.

The plan of attack called for the two larger American divisions to spearhead the main effort, breaching the first German line and the second a little more than a half-mile back. The two effective Australian divisions would then exploit the opening, passing through the Americans and pushing forward another 2.5 miles to take the Beaurevoir Line. The Allies had 141 tanks in support. The attack plan was based in large part on a detailed map of the Hindenburg Line that the British had captured from a German corps headquarters on 8 August.[53]

The Allied artillery preparation started on 26 September. On the twenty-seventh, two days before the start of the attack, the American 27th Division attempted to clear its assigned axis of advance by eliminating three German outposts to its front. It did so, but the division failed to mop up behind it, which later cost the Americans dearly. The main attack jumped off at 0530 hours on 29 September, with five divisions attacking on a nine-mile front. In the main sector, the U.S. 30th Division was in the center, the U.S. 27th Division was on the left, and the British 46th Division was on the right.

The U.S. 27th Division opened a wide and deep gap, crossing over to the eastern side of the canal. But then German machine-gun positions that had not been mopped up two days earlier started firing on the Americans from their rear, pinning down the 27th Division. Attacking across the top of the tunnel, the U.S. 30th Division penetrated into the German main positions. However, instead of following the plan of holding in place and letting the Australians pass through, the Americans pushed forward. They were taken under fire from their rear by German machine gunners who emerged from the canal

246 The Generals' War

tunnel. At that point, the Americans were cut off and the Australian advance was blocked.

Farther south, Lieutenant General Sir Walter Braithwaite's British IX Corps had the most success. Using all sorts of watercraft, scaling ladders, and 3,000 life belts secured from Channel ferries, his 46th Division fought its way across the canal near Bellenglise. It captured the Riqueval Bridge intact and then moved against the Beaurevoir Line, which threatened to outflank the German positions along the tunnel line. That relieved the pressure on the U.S. 27th Division in the center. On the far right, the French First Army attacked south of St. Quentin and captured the German strongpoint at Cerizy. As historians Gary Sheffield and John Bourne have noted, the 46th Division's assault crossing of the St. Quentin Canal was "arguably the single most important action of [Foch's] Grand Offensive."[54]

On 30 September, the British cleared the southern entrance of the tunnel and captured a key piece of ground called "The Knoll." The Australian 5th Division then passed through the Americans and continued the attack, capturing the heavily fortified village of Bellicourt. The German defenses started to crumble, and that night the enemy began pulling back. Gallwitz, the army group commander, glumly recorded in his diary, "Telephone conversation with the gentlemen at OHL in these days was not encouraging."[55]

The French encircled St. Quentin on 1 October. By 3 October the British Fourth Army had opened a six-mile-wide breach in the Hindenburg Line. The last line of the Siegfried Stellung, the Beaurevoir Line, was only three miles away. The British Third Army, meanwhile, was still held up at the St. Quentin Canal, but the Fourth Army was starting to turn the defender's flank. Under continuous pressure, the Germans on 4 October started falling back to the Beaurevoir Line. The German withdrawal, in turn, reduced the resistance in front of the Third Army, which was then able to cross the canal on 5 October. By 4 October, however, the Allied drives in Flanders and the Meuse-Argonne had stalled, which meant that Haig's forces were now carrying the main weight of the General Offensive.

On 6 October the British captured Beaurevoir and the high ground dominating the Beaurevoir Line and then started mopping up the fortified villages immediately to the rear of the line. The vaunted Hindenburg Line was effectively broken. But the Allied forces were exhausted. Following more mopping-up actions, the offensive finally halted on 10 October.[56] A British intelligence

estimate of 1 October reported a roll-up of the German divisions engaged
since 26 September:

· twelve in Flanders, including five committed as reinforcements
· thirty-two opposite Cambrai, including thirteen reinforcing divisions
· twenty-three in Champagne and the Argonne, including thirteen reinforcing
  divisions in the Argonne alone

This supports Pershing's later assertion that the American operations in the
Argonne drew off key German reserves, but the largest German troop concen-
tration still faced the British Fourth and Third Armies and the French First
Army.[57]

The Allied leaders met on 7 October at Versailles. Present were Prime
Minister David Lloyd George, Chancellor of the Exchequer Andrew Bonner
Law, Chief of the Imperial General Staff Sir Henry Wilson, Lieutenant General John P. Du Cane (representing Haig), Deputy First Sea Lord Rear Admiral G. P. W. Pope, Foch, and his chief of staff, General Maxime Weygand.
Interestingly, the only two French representatives were military officers. No
French political leaders seem to have been present. The subject was British
manpower. Britain so far in 1918 had stripped manpower from industry to man
the BEF, but as a result the country now faced a coal shortage of 20 million
tons. The government was considering pulling back 50,000 coal miners from
the army, which would leave the BEF with a manpower shortage of 100,000 by
the end of 1918. Of the Allies, the British were the only ones putting eighteen-
year-olds into the line.

Although Foch was now convinced that the Allies could win the war in
1918, he still wanted guarantees that the BEF would be up to full strength by
April 1919 as a safety margin. Lloyd George reminded Foch of the manpower
requirements of the Royal Navy, which Foch never really did appreciate. Foch
countered that the Germans were no longer in a position to attack anywhere,
and it therefore made little sense to hold back troops for the defense of England against an attack that would never come. The generalissimo continued
to push the British hard to maintain their current number of divisions in the
field, even if the strength of those divisions had to be reduced. Lloyd George
concluded by thanking Foch for his views, but no decisions or commitments
were made.[58]

THE MEUSE-ARGONNE OFFENSIVE, PHASE II (4–28 OCTOBER)

Three of the four axes of the General Offensive had stalled temporarily. Only Haig's St. Quentin Canal Offensive was still moving forward, and it too was showing signs of running out of steam. Frustrated, Foch sent a very pointed note to Pétain on 4 October. Although there was widespread disappointment in the AEF's performance so far, Foch avoided mentioning the Americans directly. He instead focused his ire on the French Fourth Army on the AEF's left flank. Unloading on Pétain, Foch wrote, "Yesterday in particular shows a battle which was not *commanded*, a battle which was not *pushed*, a battle which *was not whole*, missing the drive and also the combinations realized in the action of the different army corps, and therefore a battle where there was *no exploitation* of the achieved results" (original emphasis). Foch went on to write that his comments about the Fourth Army applied to other armies as well, obviously a veiled jab at the U.S. First Army. He concluded by insisting that all senior commanders must understand that "to animate, pull, awaken, and supervise remain above all the first tasks."[59]

That same day Foch found himself the target of Clemenceau's frustration with the Americans. Following on his exasperating experience in the American sector on 29 September, the prime minister complained to the generalissimo, "If General Pershing continues along his current path he is risking a disaster." Clemenceau even went so far as to demand that Foch report Pershing's poor performance directly to President Woodrow Wilson.[60] This, of course, was a most curious demand. Normal protocol requires the political leaders of nations in an alliance to deal with each other directly rather than through their military subordinates. To his credit, Foch put off the demands of his political chief: "Having a more complete appreciation of the difficulties faced by the Americans, I could not support the radical solution envisaged by Mr. Clemenceau."[61] Pershing too was putting relentless pressure on his subordinate commanders. But the massive traffic jams that were plaguing the American sector were compounded by the fact that the AEF was short 106,263 horses, 43 percent of the requirement.[62] Making matters worse, influenza broke out among the American soldiers during the first week of October. Pershing calculated that he needed 90,000 replacements to bring his units back up to full strength. American rifle companies were now down to an average of 175 men from an authorized level of 250.[63] The Germans, however, were in far worse shape, with some companies down to as few as 65 men.

Foch, Pétain, and Clemenceau were not alone in their criticism of the AEF's operations. Based on a report from his liaison officer at Foch's headquarters, Haig on 5 October wrote in his diary that the complete breakdown in their logistics system prevented the Americans from advancing, even though "the enemy is in no strength in their front." Haig went on to note that the American units in the front line were starving and had to be relieved in order to be fed. He attributed the bad situation to "the incapacity of American HQ staff."[64] Haig may have had something of a point when comparing the number of German divisions facing his right wing to the number facing the AEF, but how well could the then relatively inexperienced BEF of 1915 have done in trying to execute such a large-scale and complex operation? Haig's comments on German strength at that point notwithstanding, Pershing recorded in his memoirs that the AEF alone was then facing twenty-seven divisions in line and seventeen in reserve.[65] The German official history, however, records that the Germans had only twenty-three total divisions facing the Americans.[66]

The renewed American attack jumped off at 0500 hours on 4 October. In the center, all of the V Corps' original frontline divisions had been replaced with veteran divisions that were rested. On 8 October, the Allies on the east bank of the Meuse started attacking to the north from Verdun. With two American divisions under the operational control of the French XVII Corps, the objective was to roll up the eastern Meuse heights, from which German artillery had been pouring such fierce enfilading fire into the Americans on the west bank. The following day the U.S. V Corps in the American center attacked the key high ground at Romagne.

Although Pershing generally had far better relations with Pétain than with Foch, the French army commander on 8 October opposed the establishment of the U.S. Second Army. He even told Foch that the U.S. First Army should be disbanded and that American divisions and corps should come under French operational control until the Americans got their logistics system organized enough to maintain a field army. Agreeing with Foch and Haig, Pétain said that the untrained and inexperienced American general staff was at the root of the problem.[67]

The Meuse-Argonne Offensive continued to make slow progress, but it was steady. By 9 October the U.S. I Corps on the left had advanced nine miles; the French Fourth Army on its left lagged almost two miles behind. On the east side of the Meuse the Germans also were under severe pressure. The German Fifth Army recorded in its war diary that day that it had been forced to commit its last reserves.[68] Gallwitz requested reinforcements from OHL, but Ludendorff responded only with vague promises.[69] All the remaining German forces in the Argonne were ordered to evacuate the forest, cross to the north side of the Aire River, and take up positions in the Brünnhilde Stellung.[70] The German Third Army was then forced to withdraw behind the line of the Aisne and Aire Rivers. That finally allowed the French and Americans to link up at Grandpré on 18 October.

Despite Pétain's reservations, Foch authorized the establishment of the U.S. Second Army on 12 October. But in doing so, Foch ordered Pershing to make a special effort to support the right wing of the French Fourth Army, which had reached the Aisne near d'Attigny.[71] Foch told Pershing that except for the AEF, the Allies were advancing on all fronts and he wanted results, not promises. Foch overstated the situation somewhat. Gouraud's Fourth Army really had not broken through either, and in the north the Flanders Army Group was bogged down with transportation problems similar to those of the Americans.[72]

Stepping down as commander of the U.S. First Army, Pershing became the commander of the American Army Group, the first American officer in history to command a formally established army group. The AEF was no longer under the operational control of Pétain. Like Haig and Pétain, Pershing now reported directly to Foch.[73] Pershing finally had his independent American army. General Robert Bullard assumed command of the Second Army, and General Hunter Liggett replaced Pershing as First Army commander. At that point, the First Army consisted of seventeen divisions. Although little remembered today, Liggett arguably was the best battlefield commander the AEF had.

The U.S. First Army west of the Meuse was now lined up against Marwitz's Fifth Army, and the Second Army east of the Meuse faced General Georg Fuch's Army Detachment C, the AEF's old opponent at Saint Mihiel. The French Fourth Army for the most part faced General Karl von Einem's Third Army, which was under Army Group German Crown Prince. By splitting the operational control of the defense between two different army groups, Ludendorff and OHL were violating the principle of unity of command, as they had during the Operation MICHAEL Offensive in March. Of course, the same could be said for the Allies once the Americans had their own army group and now that Pershing and Pétain each reported directly to Foch.

The AEF took Romagne with a double envelopment on 14 October, forcing the Germans to withdraw eight hundred meters to the north. The German Third Army along with the First Army on its right flank withdrew to the Hunding–Brünnhilde Stellung.[74] The AEF finally had taken the objectives that Pershing had originally set for the first day of the offensive. The French Fourth Army now held the south bank of the Aire and the west bank of the Aisne as far as Vouziers. Pétain ordered it to outflank the Germans on the American left. That same day Foch sent Pershing a message ordering him to send two AEF divisions to reinforce the resumption of the drive by the Flanders Army Group, which started that day. Foch also made it clear, "It is understood that this reduction of American forces does not modify the task assigned to the American Army, especially between Meuse and Aisne."[75] Pershing complied, hardly mentioning it in his memoirs.

On 16 October, OHL finally issued the preliminary plans for the withdrawal to the Antwerp–Meuse Stellung, ordering that the preparation work on the position be speeded up. For Gallwitz's Army Group, the left wing of the Fifth Army had to remain anchored on the Meuse, while the right wing had to wheel backward to the right. Thirteen divisions then had to cross to the east bank. Gallwitz noted at the time that the four existing bridges in the sector were not enough.[76]

Although Pershing had relinquished command of the First Army, he had a hard time letting go. His tendency to be a micromanager got the better of him. Lieutenant Colonel Pierpont Stackpole, Liggett's aide-de-camp, recorded in his diary on 16 October, "General Pershing is still around at his office on the train and butting into details, with numerous changes of mind." He also noted, "An extraordinary spectacle is presented by Pershing . . . hanging around and worrying everybody with endless talk, rather than giving his orders and leaving the 1st Army to carry them out."[77] The following day Stackpole wrote that Pershing was still trying to run the First Army. Under constant pressure from Foch to advance, he was passing that pressure down directly to the American commanders. Pershing admitted to Liggett, however, that the AEF had been pressured to the limit. Stackpole wrote, "General Liggett said he told Pershing to go away and forget it."[78]

Pershing relieved Major General George H. Cameron as the commander of V Corps on 11 October, and on 18 October he sacked two division commanders. Two days later Stackpole recorded in his diary, "Pershing turned up again, with his entourage and steam train." Liggett and his chief of staff, Brigadier General Hugh Drum, told Pershing that for the next several days the First Army would be capable only of mounting limited and local attacks. The constant broad-front attacks to that point had pretty well depleted the force, and any continuation would only result in more casualties. Liggett recommended that any push on a wide front should be delayed until at least six divisions could be rested and refitted.[79] Pershing agreed to a plan for the First Army to launch a general attack on 28 October that would drive through the German center, seize the Bois de Barricourt ridge, and then advance westward to Boult-aux-Bois, thereby outflanking the Bois de Bourgogne. That would eliminate the last cluster of wooded high ground to the American front.[80]

Foch had other ideas. In a 21 October order to Pétain and Pershing, he insisted on a renewed coordinated effort between the French Fourth and U.S. First Armies. The Americans were ordered to attack in force *"without any delay"* (original emphasis) in the direction of Buzancy, some eight miles north of the top of the Argonne Forest. The Fourth Army was ordered to attack through Vouziers toward Le Chesne, about ten miles northwest of Buzancy.[81] Liggett and Pershing agreed that their original plan was better, and they decide to stick with it. Pershing later wrote, "Of course, it was quite beyond the Marshal's province to give instructions regarding the tactical conduct of operations. I therefore disregarded his directions."[82] Pershing later postponed the start of the attack by four days, to 1 November, because the French Fourth Army could not be ready until then.

Foch wanted to eliminate fixed phase lines in the attack, which forced successful units to pause for less successful ones, thereby missing opportunities. On 25 October, he issued a note to both Pershing and Pétain reemphasizing that point: "The troops going into the attack need only to know *their direction of the attack*. They go in this direction as far as they can, attacking and maneuvering against the resisting enemy without any worry about alignment. The most advanced units work to the profit of the ones held up at the moment" (original emphasis).[83] Pétain, however, pushed back, reminding Foch that successive objectives, a main direction, and a designated zone of action were all operational control concepts that could be used either in a fortified zone or in open terrain.[84] As Historian Robert Doughty has pointed out, "The final battles fought by the French bore a stronger resemblance to Pétain's than Foch's operational concept."[85]

Foch on 27 October sent Pershing an order to resume the attack on 1 November, with the First Army seizing the Boult-aux-Bois–Buzancy road and moving east from there.[86] Foch more or less had acquiesced to Pershing's and Liggett's original plan. By the last day of October, however, the American supply situation remained terrible. The troops did not have winter clothing or pup tents. Rats and lice were everywhere, and the mess wagons carrying hot food were not able to get near the front lines because of the condition of the roads. Replacements and stragglers remained a constant problem. Untrained replacements being pushed into the line were little more than casualties waiting to happen. Of the 1,400 replacements received by the 78th Division on 14 October, 80 percent became casualties when the division went into the line two days later.[87]

Clemenceau, meanwhile, had not let up his fire against Pershing. On 21 October, the prime minister sent Foch a note renewing his demands that the generalissimo report Pershing's incompetence to President Wilson: "Indeed, neither you nor I have the right to conceal it from him." Hammering away at Foch, Clemenceau continued, "You have watched at close range the development of General Pershing's exactions. Unfortunately, thanks to his invincible obstinacy, he has won out against you as well as against your immediate subordinates." And although he conceded that the Americans were "unanimously acknowledged to be great soldiers," they nonetheless had failed to take their assigned objectives, despite suffering heavy losses. "Nobody can maintain that these fine troops are unusable; they are merely unused."[88]

Foch once more resisted the pressure from his political master: "For what is the good of giving orders, when for many moral and concrete reasons they cannot be executed? We have to treat men, and especially men of a different nation, according to what they are, and not according to what we should like them to be."[89] Pershing never really seemed to understand, or accept, that Foch backed him up more than Pétain did. Nonetheless, at a dinner in America after the war in Pétain's honor, Pershing put his hand on his French comrade's shoulder and said, "I want it understood that this man is the greatest general of the war."[90]

Rod Paschall has suggested that Clemenceau might have had ulterior political motives for his strong criticism of Pershing. By late 1918, peace negotiations with Germany were then underway based on President Wilson's proposals, particularly his Fourteen Points. With his insistence on the voice of the subject peoples being heard in the determination of all colonial issues, Clemenceau doubted that Wilson would act in France's overall interest. Undercutting Pershing would be a way of diminishing Wilson's influence in the peace process.[91]

THE SECOND BATTLE OF CAMBRAI (8–10 OCTOBER)

The Second Battle of Cambrai was a follow-on exploitation to the breaking of the Beaurevoir Line on 6 October. It was a set-piece attack on a twenty-mile front from Cambrai to St. Quentin, with Byng's Third Army on the left, Rawlinson's Fourth Army in the center, and two corps of Debeney's First Army on the right. As in the earlier battle, the U.S. II Corps of two divisions was part of Rawlinson's army. During a meeting on 6 October, Haig told Foch that if he could get three fresh American divisions, he could push farther to take the key rail junction at Valenciennes, seventeen miles northeast of Cambrai. Foch, however, refused to endorse Haig's request.[92] The British, then, had twenty-five divisions against Army Group Boehn, which had some twenty-two divisions in the line under Carlowitz's Second Army and General Oskar von Hutier's Eighteenth Army. No more than six of those divisions were fully combat effective.[93]

The Allied attack advanced more than three miles on 8 October. The Third Army's 2nd Canadian Division entered Cambrai but rapidly passed through to the northwest. The 3rd Canadian Division followed in close support, clearing the town on 10 October. The British now had control of the St. Quentin–Busigny–Cambrai double rail line.[94] They then regrouped for follow-on actions that would lead to the Battle of the Selle (17–27 October). Since 27 September, the BEF had captured nearly 50,000 German prisoners and 1,000 guns.

On the evening of 8 October, OHL ordered a general withdrawal to the Hermann Stellung.[95] OHL also disbanded Boehn's Army Group, reassigning the Second Army to Crown Prince Rupprecht's Army Group and the Eighteenth to Army Group German Crown Prince.[96] The British in the Allied center were now making the greatest progress. Foch knew that the BEF, supported by the Flanders Army Group on its left, should continue pushing forward. The French First Army should push to cross the Serre River.[97] During a 10 October conference with Haig and Pétain at Mouchy-le-Châtel, Foch issued a general directive changing the operational scheme of maneuver from four to three more concentrated converging attacks: (1) the Flanders Army

Group toward Ghent, (2) the BEF toward Maubeuge, and (3) the French and Americans toward Mézières. Foch noted that the BEF's center attack was the "most profitable to exploit."[98]

Haig later wrote in his diary, "I assured [Foch] that the enemy has not the means, nor the will-power to launch an attack strong enough to affect even our front-line troops. We have got the enemy down, in fact he is a beaten army, and my plan is to go on hitting him as hard as we possibly can, till he begs for mercy."[99] On the sidelines, however, Haig's chief of staff, Lieutenant General Sir Herbert Lawrence, commented bitterly to his boss that the British were doing all the fighting and that the French were doing nothing.

THE BATTLE OF COURTRAI AND CLOSING TO THE DUTCH BORDER (14–27 OCTOBER)

The Flanders Army Group was now poised to resume the offensive in the direction of Ghent. King Albert had a total of twenty-eight divisions from the British Second, French Sixth, and Belgian Armies. The three corps of the British Second Army north of the Lys River had the mission of securing the river line to beyond Courtrai, in order to establish bridgeheads on the southern bank. Opposing the Allies, Sixt von Armin's Fourth Army had seventeen divisions, only four of which were fully combat effective.[100]

The attack started on a fifty-mile front at 0530 hours on 14 October. The British Second Army in the center made the most progress, pushing the Fourth Army back. Rupprecht wanted permission from OHL to withdraw farther, but Ludendorff told him it was important to hold the triangle of towns Lille–Roubaix–Tourcoing, pending the answer on the peace proposal that the German government recently sent to President Wilson. Ludendorff had deluded himself into believing that Wilson would support Germany's claim to the Belgian coast. The following day, however, Germany received an unsatisfactory response, and Ludendorff told Rupprecht that there was no further sense in trying to hold onto Lille and the Flemish coast.[101] Rupprecht had little choice but to pull back. His logistics situation was worse than that of the Allies, and the morale of his troops was rock bottom. Rupprecht ordered the Fourth Army to withdraw to the line of Roulers and Menin, but by then both places were already in Allied hands. Late on the fifteenth OHL ordered a general withdrawal to the Hermann-Ghent Stellung.[102]

On 15 October, Birdwood's Fifth Army, on the right of the Second Army, attacked in support of the offensive. Although the Germans were pulling back, they put up strong resistance on 16 and 17 October, preventing several Allied attempts to establish bridgeheads over the Lys. The Belgians took Ostend on 17 October. Although the Germans had tried to destroy the port facilities, the Allies quickly repaired them, significantly improving the logistics situation of the Flanders Army Group. That same day the Fifth Army took Lille without opposition.

At a 17 October meeting of the cabinet in Berlin, Ludendorff, who for the last three months had been lurching between the poles of despair and optimism, was now in confidence mode: "It was a principle of elementary common sense: the stronger we were in the field, the better we could negotiate." Still believing that Germany could negotiate a peace settlement from a position of strength, he told the nominal political leaders of Germany, "We cannot, however, accept any conditions that do not provide for an orderly evacuation of the territory. This involves a time limit of not less than two or three months. Nor must we accept anything that makes it impossible for us to renew hostilities."[103]

Plumer's army crossed the Lys and took Courtrai on 19 October. The Belgians seized Bruges and Zeebrugge. Ludendorff ordered Rupprecht to hold the Hermann-Lys Stellung for at least eight days. Responding to a direct request for information from Germany's new chancellor, Prince Max von Baden, Rupprecht reported that his forces faced serious shortages of guns, ammunition, and supplies. The trench strength of most divisions numbered only about 3,000. The troops' morale was very low, their ability to resist was diminishing daily, and the men were surrendering in large groups when they came under attack. Rupprecht warned the chancellor, "Ludendorff does not realize the whole seriousness of the situation. Whatever happens, we must obtain peace before the enemy breaks through into Germany; if he does, woe on us!"[104] Ludendorff bitterly resented the government asking advice from any military commander other than himself.

The Allies secured the east bank of the Lys on 20 October. Two days later British forces closed to the Scheldt. Haig at that point requested the return of his Second Army to his control. Foch, however, refused, citing the political value of having the Belgian king in command of an Allied army when he reentered his capital.[105] The Germans continued withdrawing under deteriorating conditions. As Ludendorff later wrote, "The work of evacuation went on, in spite of the terrible condition of the railways."[106]

The northern flank of Allied attack reached the Dutch border on 27 October. Haig appealed to London for support for his demand for the return of the

Second Army, and the War Cabinet backed him up. Haig wrote in his diary, "It seems that Clemenceau and Foch are not on good terms. Foch is suffering from a swelled head, and thinks himself another Napoleon! So, Clemenceau has great difficulties with him now."[107]

THE FRENCH FIRST ARMY ATTACK ACROSS
THE SERRE RIVER (15–27 OCTOBER)

Mangin's Tenth Army took Laon on 13 October. In accordance with Foch's 10 October general directive, Debeney's First Army attacked between St. Quentin and Laon on 15 October and crossed the Serre River. Two days later the First Army attacked on a broad front roughly centered on the boundary between the German Eighteenth and Seventh Armies. Across their entire fronts the two German armies had some twenty-eight divisions in the line, but no more than six to eight of them were fully combat effective. On the night of the seventeenth, the Germans withdrew to the Hunding Stellung.

The following day a two-corps French attack failed to break through. Debeney consolidated his forces, renewing the attack on 24 October. The First Army broke through the Hunding Stellung on 26 October, the same day that the British to its north broke through the Hermann Stellung. That night the Germans pulled back five kilometers along the First Army's front. The only German defense remaining in front of them was the weak Freia Stellung.[108]

THE BATTLE OF THE SELLE (17–27 OCTOBER)

Pushed back during the Second Battle of Cambrai, the Germans took up new positions on the Selle River, close to Le Cateau. Haig's objective was to push across the Selle and secure a line from the Sambre River and Oise Canal to Valenciennes. That would bring within artillery range the German rail and supply center at Aulnoye, where the Mézières–Hirson rail line connected with the main line back to Germany via Maubeuge and Charleroi. The British First, Third, and Fourth Armies massed twenty-four divisions for the operation. Supported by the French First Army on the right, Rawlinson's Fourth Army would make the initial attack, with the Third and First Armies on the left jumping off a few days later. The German Seventeenth and Second Armies, and the right wing of the Eighteenth Army, had some thirty-one divisions, very few of which were fully combat effective. During the withdrawals between 3 and 10 October, the German rear guards had been mauled severely.[109]

Rawlinson's tactical problems included crossing the river itself, passing over the Le Cateau–Wassigny rail line embankment on the far side, and then taking the dominating ridge beyond. Because the Selle was quite narrow at that point, Rawlinson and his planners decided on a night assault along a ten-mile front south of Le Cateau, using long planks to put the infantry across single file. The artillery would follow as soon as pontoon bridges could be constructed.

Under cover of a heavy fog, Rawlinson's troops crossed the Selle with little resistance during the early morning hours of 17 October. Initially, the defenders were caught by surprise. Although German resistance stiffened as the attack progressed, the Fourth Army still took Le Cateau that day. The Fourth Army's right wing made the greatest progress, reaching the Sambre Canal. The Third and First Armies joined the attack on 20 October, with the troops of Byng's Third Army securing the high ground to the east of the Selle. By the end of the day Horne's First Army was in position to advance north of Le Cateau. The entire British offensive then paused for two days as the heavy artillery of all three armies moved up.

On 23 October, Haig resumed the offensive with a coordinated attack by all three armies. Rawlinson's and Byng's armies pushed the Germans back six miles toward the Sambre. The German Second Army commander recommended to OHL an immediate withdrawal to the Antwerp–Meuse Stellung. The following day, however, Carlowitz was ordered to continue holding his present positions. The Germans mounted a counterattack on 24 October but accomplished nothing. By 25 October the First and Third armies had advanced on a thirty-five-mile-wide front, reaching the Scheldt. The British were now some twenty miles beyond the rear of the Siegfried Stellung.

By the end of the day on 26 October, the British were on the left bank of the Scheldt, from Toutnai to Valenciennes. When the First Army cut the rail line south of Aulnoye on 27 October, the Germans lost the next to the last of their lateral rail lines near the front in the northern sector. The only one remaining was Brussels–Namur–Arlon–Thionville–Sarrebourg. As the Germans tried to pull back farther, the congestion on their rail network stretched to the Rhine.[110]

The day the Battle of the Selle ended, Foch sent Haig a message concerning follow-on operations. Debeney was preparing to attack to the east of the Sambre–Oise Canal, between Grand Verly and his First Army's left boundary. To support Debeney, Foch wanted the British Fourth Army to conduct a parallel attack east of the canal toward the La Grose–Bergues sur Sambre road.[111] Haig instructed his army commanders to prepare for what would be the final major British offensive of the war, the Battle of the Sambre.

FOCH MAPS OUT FUTURE ALLIED OPERATIONS (19 OCTOBER–14 NOVEMBER)

Although Foch knew the Germans were on the edge of the breaking point, and he fully intended to end the war in 1918, he continued to develop operational plans well out into the future, as would any competent commander. On 19 October he issued a general directive that modified his general directives of 3 September and 10 October. In what turned out to be his last general directive of the war, Foch established the final framework for the Allied drive to the Meuse River.[112]

1. The Flanders Army Group was ordered to attack toward Brussels, forcing in the process the lines of the Scheldt and Dendre Rivers. As much as possible this advance was to be coordinated with turning movements made by the BEF.
2. The British Fifth, First, Third, and Fourth Armies were ordered to attack beyond Maubeuge, pushing Germans back to the Ardennes at the point where their Sedan–Namur rail line entered the forest. The French First Army had the mission of supporting the British right flank by attacking toward Sissonne.
3. The French Fourth and American First Armies were to continue with their mission of reaching Mézières–Sedan, supported on the left by the French Fifth Army advancing in the direction of Château-Porcien.

The following day Foch sent Pétain a warning order to start planning and preparing a major offensive into Lorraine. As early as the end of 1917 Pétain had been thinking about such an offensive. With the large-scale influx of Americans, the French army commander was worried that the Western Front by the end of the war would be dominated by the Anglo-Americans. He intended to make sure that when the war ended, France would be in the dominant position in the peace negotiations, thereby justifying the huge manpower sacrifices made by the French army. In particular, Alsace and Lorraine had to return to France. Pétain's concept was to penetrate through Alsace to the Rhine at Mulhouse and then drive north down the Rhine through Strasbourg, into the Saarland and beyond, enveloping Lorraine in the process. As a supporting effort, the American army would conduct a holding attack against Lorraine.[113]

It was a bold and risky concept, especially for Pétain, and was very similar to what the French First Army's VII Corps had tried to do in August 1914 under Joseph Joffre's Plan XVII.

After 26 March, however, the strategic direction of the war was now in the hands of Foch, who thought more in terms of combined and coordinated Allied actions than in the only loosely connected actions of the French, British, and Belgians that had characterized the war so far. Foch was never convinced of the merits of Pétain's Alsace plan, but the generalissimo did agree with Pétain's counterproposal for a thrust directly into Lorraine.[114] Foch's warning order envisioned the Lorraine Offensive with thirty divisions under General Noël de Castelnau's Eastern Army Group, which had not been in any significant action for some time. Foch also wanted to include American divisions, which presumably would operate under the command of the U.S. Second Army.[115] The defenders would be Duke Albrecht of Württemberg's Army Group, with Army Detachments A and B, consisting of some seventeen divisions, no more than four of which were fully combat effective.[116] The attack would proceed from the east bank of the Moselle near Nancy, toward Saarbrücken and the German border.

Pétain responded immediately with a proposed command and control structure for the operation, and Foch approved the concept on 23 October. Urging an attack as soon as possible, Foch asked Pétain for the projected start date: "It will not be opportune to wait in order to start the operations west and east of the Moselle for the enemy to be pushed back at the Meuse and for the forces presumed necessary for the whole of the attack to deploy—which will take time and could reverse the situation to the advantage for the enemy."[117]

Pétain issued his planning guidance to Castelnau on 27 October.[118] With a projected start date of 14 November, the Allies would attack on a twenty-mile front with twenty infantry divisions—including five American—and a cavalry corps, supported by six hundred tanks. During the deployment phase, Mangin's Tenth Army would take up a position in the line between Bullard's Second Army and General Augustin Gérard's Eighth Army. The U.S. Second Army had the mission of screening the left flank of the attack against a German counterattack from the direction of Metz. Ever the fighter, Mangin made the somewhat prophetic comment, "We must go right into the heart of Germany . . . or the Germans will not admit that they had been beaten."[119] On multiple occasions after the end of the war, he would take ample opportunity to repeat that comment.

In a 5 November message, Foch now told Pétain that he intended to give him ten to twelve American divisions from the U.S. First and Second Armies for the Lorraine Offensive: "In any case I am putting at your disposition for the moment all the American divisions which I can take up from the American First and Second Armies and whose use I follow with attention."[120] Pershing, however, agreed to release only six, also insisting that they operate under the direct command of an American field army headquarters.[121] The main body of Mangin's Tenth Army closed south of Nancy on 6 November and began assembling for the attack. Five of six corps and eighteen of twenty divisions were in place by 11 November.

The Armistice, of course, took effect that day, and Pétain's Lorraine Offensive was never launched. Considering the significant numerical superiority of the Allied force and the poor state of the German divisions, the results almost certainly would have been catastrophic for Germany if the attack had gone in. Many generals at the time thought it was a serious mistake to grant Germany an armistice before the Lorraine Offensive. Liggett and Degoutte in particular believed that if the fighting had gone on for just one more month, the German army would have been forced to surrender unconditionally in the field.[122] Similar arguments about the failure to achieve complete victory were voiced after the United States and the Allies called a halt to military operations against Iraq after only one hundred hours during the First Gulf War in 1991. George Marshall, on the other hand, agreed that the German army would have collapsed completely, but then it would most likely have disintegrated into a chaotic mob, with fragmented groups pillaging and terrorizing the inhabitants of the still-occupied territories. Marshall was probably right.[123]

EXIT LUDENDORFF (26 OCTOBER)

Ludendorff threatened to resign many times during the war. Once he and Hindenburg became national icons after the Battles of Tannenberg and Masurian Lakes in 1914, threatened resignation became his favored tool of political leverage. The more popular and powerful they became, the more the kaiser and the entire German government was cowed by The Duo. Ludendorff knew that Hindenburg would be almost helpless without him, and the field marshal vaguely sensed as much too. More than once Ludendorff maneuvered the politically clueless Hindenburg into delivering a joint threat to resign. They did so to force the resumption of the unrestricted U-boat campaign and the resignations of Chancellor Theobald von Bethmann Hollweg and Foreign Minister

Richard von Kühlmann. On some occasions, Ludendorff simply threatened, "The Field Marshal and I will resign," without ever consulting the nominally senior partner of the team.[124]

Things changed in the wake of the Allied counterattack on 18 July. When Ludendorff talked to Lossberg about offering his resignation to Hindenburg, it was not a political maneuver; the first quartermaster general was shaken to his core. He either thought the situation was beyond his ability to save it, or he wanted to put as much distance as possible between himself and the blame for losing the war. Most of Ludendorff's postwar writing suggests the latter motivation. After the British attack of 8 August, Ludendorff actually did offer his resignation, but the kaiser refused to accept it. Once Foch launched his General Offensive in late October, the pressure mounting on Ludendorff became almost unbearable.

On 28 September, Hindenburg and Ludendorff arrived in Spa, Belgium, for a conference the following day with the kaiser and Foreign Minister von Hintze. Late that afternoon Ludendorff suffered a nervous breakdown and collapsed in his hotel room. That evening he told Hindenburg that Germany had to sue for peace. Ludendorff returned to OHL after the conference, but he was never the same after that. Right until the end he continued swinging from pole to pole, between demanding that Germany make peace immediately and insisting that the German army in the field could hold out well into 1919 and that Germany therefore could reach a peace settlement from a position of strength.

One of the outcomes of the 29 September conference was the resignation of Chancellor Georg von Hertling and his replacement on 3 October by Prince Max von Baden. Max had no intention of letting himself be bullied by Ludendorff, and friction between the two flared up almost immediately. Things built to a head throughout October, as U.S. president Wilson, much to the chagrin of France and Britain, started trading peace notes directly with the German government. Rather than paying full attention to military operations in the field, Ludendorff continued meddling with the government. Prince Max finally told the kaiser that there was no longer room at the head of the German government for both himself and Ludendorff.

On 23 October, a note from Wilson made it clear to Berlin that rather than starting peace negotiations, Germany had to surrender. Predictably, Hindenburg and Ludendorff were outraged. The following day OHL sent out a message titled "For the Information of All Troops," saying that Wilson's demands were a direct challenge to all German soldiers to continue the resistance. In his memoirs, Ludendorff rather disingenuously claimed he did not write the memo but that it went out over his signature on the assumption that it had been coordinated with government policy: "It appeared essential that OHL in its dealings with Berlin should take up a definite standpoint with regard to the note, in order to lessen its evil effects on the army."[125] In any other country, that would be akin to the tail wagging the dog.

The first quartermaster general had finally pushed it too far. Hindenburg and Ludendorff were recalled to Berlin on 25 October, where they walked into a firestorm. Hindenburg offered his resignation, but the kaiser refused to accept it.[126] The following day the kaiser summoned Ludendorff and, citing the OHL message of the twenty-fourth, curtly informed him that his resignation would be accepted. In his memoirs, however, Ludendorff says he offered his resignation.[127] Ludendorff recommended Kuhl as his replacement, but the government rejected that recommendation.[128] Lieutenant General Wilhelm Groener, who later served as minister of defense of the Weimar Republic, replaced Ludendorff as first quartermaster general, but he never established the relationship that Ludendorff had with Hindenburg.

Hindenburg owed virtually his entire military reputation to Ludendorff, but when it came to the final crunch, the field marshal did not lift a finger to save him. The "happy marriage" of The Duo was over. The two spoke to each other only a few times after that day. Ludendorff was finally out, but not quite everyone was happy to see him go. Crown Prince Wilhelm later wrote, "Ludendorff fell, and with his fall, the Homeland abandoned the struggle."[129] This is a rather odd comment, considering that more than any other individual, Ludendorff helped to bring about the fall of the House of Hohenzollern.

THE BATTLE OF VALENCIENNES (1–3 NOVEMBER)

The advance during the first part of October to the Selle River by the British First, Third, and Fourth Armies threatened to turn the left flank of the German Sixth Army, opposite the British Fifth Army. The key rail hub of Valenciennes, on the east side of the Scheldt Canal, was opposite the First Army's Canadian Corps. Seven German divisions defended the sector. Haig's headquarters decided not to shell the town prior to attacking to take it because of the high number of reported refugees. Horne then developed a plan to turn the town from the south, where his XXII Corps was already across the canal. Attacking on 1 November, the Canadians established a foothold on the far side of the canal, while XXII Corps moved up from the south. On their left, they were supported by the Third Army's XVII Corps. Later that day OHL issued the warning order for the withdrawal to the Antwerp–Meuse Stellung but did not yet project an execution date.[130] The Canadians entered Valenciennes on 2 November, and the Germans in that sector started pulling back from the Hermann Stellung that night. While the Canadians and British were mopping up on 3 November, the German navy that day mutinied at Kiel.[131]

THE SECOND BATTLE OF THE SAMBRE AND THE FINAL BRITISH DRIVE (4–11 NOVEMBER)

The British units were now far in front of their forward-most railheads, and the logistics lines were stretched to their limits. Nonetheless, the BEF resumed the offensive on 4 November. The British First, Third, and Fourth Armies, totaling seventeen divisions, and the French First Army with eleven divisions had the mission of advancing from south of the Condé Canal on a thirty-mile front toward Maubeuge and Mons, threatening Namur. In front of them the German Sixth, Seventeenth, Second, and Eighteenth Armies had forty-five depleted divisions in their forward lines.[132] On the northern end of the attack, the immediate obstacle was the sixty- to seventy-foot-wide Sambre–Oise Canal and the inundated ground around it.

The British Second Army reverted back to Haig's command on 4 November. On dawn that day, with heavy rain falling, the final British offensive of the war jumped off. Under fierce machine-gun and rifle fire, the attackers used footbridges to force the canal near the village of Ors. The New Zealand Division attacked the walled medieval town of Le Quesnoy, only five miles from the Belgian border. The British Third Army advanced slowly because of strong resistance from the German Seventeenth Army, poor roads, and limited room for maneuver. Canadian forces crossed the Aunelle and Honelle Rivers north of Valenciennes and entered Belgium. On the southern end of the attack, the French First Army captured the towns of Guise and Origny-en-Thiérache in what was called the Second Battle of Guise and the Battle of Thiérache, respectively. Along the line the Allies advanced two to three miles on that first day.

Shortly after midnight on 6 November, OHL issued the order for the general withdrawal to the Antwerp–Meuse Stellung, which still existed mostly on paper. Groener knew the Germans should have started pulling back much sooner. But Ludendorff's operational thinking had been clouded by his meddling in politics, and the Germans had stayed too long in the Hermann

Stellung for political rather than cogent operational reasons. The British Third Army reached Haumont on 7 November, and the Fourth Army captured Avesnes on the eighth. That day open revolution broke out in Germany. Insurgents occupied key rail stations and depots, but OHL's hands were tied. Any commitment of troops within Germany risked the cutoff of the army's entire food supply. The forces in the field at that point had only eight days of rations on hand.[133]

The Second Army, which had joined in the British offensive on the eighth, crossed the Scheldt River on 9 November. The lead elements of the Third Army occupied Maubeuge. The Canadian 3rd Division entered Mons on the tenth and cleared the town the next morning. By the time the Armistice went into effect at 1100 hours, the BEF held a line from Ghent through Hourain, Bauffe, and Havré to near Consoire and Sivry.[134]

THE FINAL FRENCH DRIVE ON THE
WESTERN FRONT (1–11 NOVEMBER)

Between 27 and 31 October the British Fourth, Third, and First Armies halted to regroup between the Selle River and the Sambre and Scheldt Rivers. On 28 October Wilhelm's Army Group joined the chorus recommending OHL to order the withdrawal to the Antwerp–Meuse Stellung. But Ludendorff was no longer there, and Groener would not be appointed as his replacement until the next day. OHL told Wilhelm to continue delaying while Germany held out for what it hoped would be better armistice terms from the Allies.[135]

Simultaneous with the renewal of the British and American attacks, Pétain ordered the resumption of the attacks by the French Fourth Army on the American left and the First Army on the British right. The First Army axis of advance was toward Guise; the Fourth Army's toward Mézières. Once the German positions along the Aisne were outflanked, Pétain then intended to exploit with his Third and Fifth Armies advancing toward the Meuse northwest of Laon. The First Army occupied Guise on 1 November, and the Fourth Army took Le Chesne the following day.[136]

In a memo that the generalissimo sent to the French and American commanders on 5 November, Foch stressed, "It remains, by the way, understood that the action of the American First Army is to follow in combination with the French Fourth Army on the road Le Chesne–Stonne, in order to advance through there in the direction of Sedan–Mézières."[137] But as the Allies continued to advance in the face of only marginal resistance, the French Fourth Army fell behind the American lead elements, setting the stage for one of the worst American operational blunders of the war.

THE MEUSE-ARGONNE OFFENSIVE, PHASE III (28 OCTOBER–11 NOVEMBER)

By the end of October, the AEF's objective of cutting off the key German rail line at Mézières had lost some of its operational importance. The British and French armies in the northwest had gone far beyond the key rail lines in their sector, in some areas as deep as fifteen miles beyond. The Americans would not be able to approach Sedan for another week.[138] By the start of November the Allies on the Western Front had a significant advantage in the correlation of forces. The Central Powers had a total force of 3,527,000; the Allies and the United States had 6,432,000.[139] As more American troops continued to land in Europe, the Germans during September and October alone had suffered 464,000 casualties, including 229,000 missing, a great number of which had surrendered.[140]

In the French Fourth Army's sector, the German Third Army of Crown Prince Wilhelm's Army Group had eighteen divisions. Facing the Americans, Army Group Gallwitz's Fifth Army and Army Detachment C had twenty-one divisions. The AEF had replaced its frontline divisions with fresh ones. The German divisions were weak and growing weaker. The only place where the Germans still had the advantage was in the air. The AEF's air commander, Brigadier General William Mitchell, placed a far greater priority on strategic and tactical bombing missions than on the close air support the infantry on the ground needed so critically.[141] The Germans, on the other hand, concentrated what air assets they had left on ground support.

The original plan for the resumption of the American attack on 28 October called for the U.S. I Corps to make the main effort on the left. But intelligence indicators suggested that the Germans were anticipating such a move and therefore had shifted more forces to that sector, weakening in the process the lines to their left—the American right. On 25 October, Liggett's First Army operations staff developed an alternate plan to make the main effort against the center of the German line between St. Georges and Aincreville with V and III Corps. Gouraud, meanwhile, reported that French Fourth Army could not be ready to attack before 2 November. Liggett actually welcomed the additional grace period. The final plan called for V and III Corps to attack on the morning of 1 November and for the Fourth Army and the U.S. I Corps to attack twenty-four hours later. Pershing, meanwhile, was still spending far more time at First Army headquarters than Liggett's staff liked. On 29 October, Stackpole recorded in his diary, "Pershing around again and worried (so General Liggett told me) by the form of an order which went out from [General Paul] Maistre as Commander of [the French Center Army] Group, giving impression that the 1st American Army was under him in these operations."[142]

The American attack resumed on 1 November, but this time it was a coordinated and unified action, with greatly improved artillery support. Liggett was not a great advocate of self-reliant infantry. The American guns fired high quantities of gas in the V Corps sector in particular. The attackers broke the positions in the German center and drove toward Barricourt Ridge. V Corps advanced some six miles and forced a ten-mile gap in the German lines. Gallwitz and Marwitz agreed to pull out of the remaining defensive positions and withdraw to the only partially finished Freia Stellung. Army Group German Crown Prince and Marwitz coordinated the withdrawal of the inner wings of their respective Third and Fifth Armies.[143] Early that evening Pershing telephoned Liggett and demanded to know why I Corps was not advancing. As Liggett later noted in his memoirs, "I replied that there would be no enemy in front of that corps the next day, as the advance in the center would force the Germans to go north, and go fast."[144] Liggett was right.

The period of relatively open, maneuver warfare finally started on 2 November. In his order issued that day, Foch directed the U.S. First Army to push forward without pause, capture Boult-aux-Bois and Buzancy, and move farther east.[145] As the U.S. First Army pivoted to the east, major elements of the German Fifth Army were pushed back across the Meuse. Elements of the U.S. First Army started crossing the Meuse opposite Liny. Near the end of the day OHL detached those Fifth Army units remaining on the west bank of the river and put them under the operational control of the Third Army.[146]

The Americans continued to press the attack. By the night of 3 November, they had advanced five more miles, clearing the Bourgogne Forest. That allowed long-range guns to move up into firing positions from where they could shell the rail centers at Longuyon and Montmédy, through which the Germans were attempting to withdraw troops, equipment, and wounded. Austria-Hungary capitulated that day, leaving the Germans alone to face the Allied and associated powers. Almost immediately Foch submitted a draft plan to the Supreme War Council for a concentric attack on Munich by three Allied field armies that would be assembled on the Austro-German border within five weeks.[147]

By 4 November the First Army had advanced thirteen miles since resuming the offensive. Major elements of III Corps were already on the east bank of the Meuse. The following day Pershing issued orders to his First and Second Armies to "push troops forward wherever resistance is broken, without regard for fixed objectives and without fear for their flanks." The First Army's objective was to push the Germans beyond the Thinte and Chiers Rivers; the Second Army had the mission to "prepare for an attack in the direction of Briey, along the axis Fresnes–Conflans–Briery."[148] On 6 November OHL finally issued the execution order to withdraw to the Antwerp–Meuse Stellung.[149]

The Americans continued to advance, but the French Fourth Army on the left started to fall behind. By 6 November the American lead elements were a little more than five miles south of Sedan, which itself was some ten miles southeast of the AEF's main objective of Mézières. Sedan was a place that loomed large in the French national psyche. It was there on 1 September 1870 that Emperor Napoleon III surrendered to Prussian king Wilhelm during the Franco-Prussian War. As a result of that war, Wilhelm became the first kaiser of the German Reich, and France lost the provinces of Alsace and Lorraine to Germany. France wanted revenge for 1870, and the boundary between the French and the AEF intentionally swung just to the south of Sedan, placing the town well within the French sector. Pershing, however, saw an opportunity to vindicate his open warfare theories and at the same time to enhance the role of the AEF in the final Allied victory. On 3 November Pershing met with Maistre, his fellow army group commander. Maistre reluctantly agreed that the rail connections between Mézières and Sedan were of such importance that the Americans should take Sedan if the Fourth Army continued to lag far behind. At that point, the U.S. 42nd Division on the American left flank was the closest to Sedan. The 77th Division was the next division to the right, with the two making up I Corps. On the 77th Division's immediate right was V Corps' 1st Division.[150]

Pershing now had the opening he was looking for. At 1630 hours on 5 November, General Fox Conner, the deputy chief of staff for operations of the AEF, showed up at the office of Colonel George C. Marshall, who now held the same position for the U.S. First Army. Conner handed Marshall a draft message for immediate release:

> Memorandum for Commanding generals, I Corps, V Corps.
> Subject: Message from Commander-in-Chief
> 1. General Pershing desires that the honor of entering Sedan should fall to the First American Army. He has every confidence that the troops of the I Corps, assisted on their right by the V Corps, will enable him to realize his desire.
> 2. In transmitting the foregoing message, your attention is invited to the favorable opportunity now existing for pressing our advantage throughout the night.[151]

Conner and Marshall were close friends, but Marshall was reluctant to issue the order immediately. Neither Liggett nor his chief of staff, Drum, were at the First Army headquarters at that time. Marshall finally agreed to release the order if neither returned by 1800 hours. Conner left for AEF headquarters at 1730 hours, and Drum returned shortly thereafter. Once he reviewed the message, Drum added a final sentence to the second paragraph: "Boundaries will not be considered binding." The message went out. Liggett did not even learn of the order until about noon on 7 November.[152]

It was a poorly crafted message. What the added last sentence was supposed to mean was that the boundary between the U.S. First and French Fourth Armies would not be binding. Some American commanders, however, assumed that inter-American divisional and corps boundaries would not be binding, either. Unit boundaries that define tactical areas of responsibility are among the most fundamental and important of all standard operational control measures. The order was a recipe for disaster, which is exactly what happened. Writing after the war, General James Harbord, Pershing's former AEF chief of staff, noted, "The test of an order is *not* can it be understood, but *can it be misunderstood*? By this test the Memorandum Order of November 5th is bound to be condemned. Yet it was drawn by experienced officers and issued to others equally experienced—all of them supposed to be familiar with at least the elementary principles of warfare" (original emphasis).[153]

When the V Corps commander, Major General Charles P. Summerall, got the directive, he either misread it or read more into it. He apparently concluded that rather than supporting I Corps on his right, as the first paragraph of the order specified, V Corps had carte blanche to lunge straight for Sedan.

Summerall passed the directive on to the commander of the 1st Division, Brigadier General Frank Parker, telling him that "I expected to see him in Sedan the next morning." Parker replied, "I understand, sir. I will now give my orders."[154] Summerall only days earlier had assumed command of V Corps after relinquishing command of the 1st Division, and that unit had long been Pershing's personal favorite. But the situation was even more confused. According to Marshall in his own World War I memoirs, even before the First Army directive went out, "it developed afterwards that General Pershing, in person, had given instructions to General [Joseph] Dickman of the I Corps about five o'clock that afternoon to advance directly on Sedan."[155] Pershing says nothing about this in his memoirs.

Still unaware of the 5 November order, Liggett was in the process of reorienting the First Army to wheel to the east to operate in coordination with the U.S. Second Army, which was preparing to start operations on the east side of the Meuse. But believing that he was following Pershing's directive and Summerall's orders, Parker on 6 November turned the 1st Division hard left to the west and sent his tired troops on a forced march directly across the front of the 77th Division and deep into the sector of the 42nd Division. Utter chaos ensued. The operations of the two I Corps divisions were completely disrupted. They were forced to stop moving and firing, virtually reducing their functional combat power to zero. As the 1st Division continued to drive forward throughout the night of the sixth, American troops shot at each other in the dark. But friendly fire from its left flank was only one of the 1st Division's problems. During the entire maneuver, the division's right flank was completely exposed to German fire from the far side of the Meuse. Meanwhile, the lead elements of the 77th Division reached the Meuse about three miles southeast of Sedan on the seventh, only to be cut off by the 1st Division advancing across their rear. The French Fourth Army also had started moving forward again. By that time, it had pretty well caught up with the Americans, but the 42nd Division had moved left into its sector, confounding the French operations.

The 1st and 42nd Divisions were now in a neck-and-neck race to reach Sedan before the French. In one of the more bizarre episodes of the entire fiasco, 1st Division soldiers reportedly took Brigadier General Douglas MacArthur prisoner temporarily. With his penchant for flamboyant uniforms and his insistence on wearing a peaked cap in the front lines instead of a helmet, the 1st Division troops thought that the commander of the 42nd Division's 84th Infantry Brigade was a German officer.[156] What was not so absurd but downright tragic was the number of casualties that the 1st Division sustained during just the two days of 6–7 November: 80 killed and 503 wounded, all for what Liggett later called a "tactical atrocity." For the better part of a day, three American frontline divisions remained stuck and powerless as their commanders tried to untangle them. It was the only time in the war that Liggett lost his temper completely. He had planned to hold the 1st Division back for later use as an exploitation force after the First Army crossed the Meuse in strength.[157] The whole debacle would have been an even greater disaster if the German army had any significant combat power left with which to mount a counterattack. Three American divisions would have been just so many sitting ducks.

There was no justification for such a reckless maneuver in the first place, especially one that violated the most fundamental principles of tactics. By the start of November 1918, the Germans were beaten. Everyone knew it, especially the Germans. The new German government under Prince Max had been exchanging peace feelers with the Allies since the middle of October. On the left and in the center of the Allied line the Germans were reeling back under the relentless hammering of the British and French offensives. Certainly, there was a need to maintain steady military pressure on the Germans all along the line until they finally threw in the towel, but there was no strategic or operational advantage to marching Allied, much less American, troops through the streets of Sedan. It was a glory grab, pure and simple. As soon as Foch knew what was happening, he quickly put a halt to the "Race to Sedan." The town remained within the French sector, but when the Armistice went into effect on 11 November, Sedan was still in German hands.

Many American generals at the time thought that Summerall should have been court-martialed. Pershing downplayed the whole affair as a misunderstanding. In the first place, there was the question of his own responsibility for the mess. Second, although Pershing was notorious for firing National Guard generals at the drop of a hat, he also had a reputation for going easy on the regular army generals, especially fellow West Pointers like Summerall. As Pershing's biographer Donald Smythe wrote, "If the shoe had been on the other foot, that is, if a National Guard division had marched across the front of a Regular Army one and not vice versa, Pershing would have blown up, all his prejudices confirmed about the 'goddamn militiamen' and their lack of professionalism."[158]

Stackpole, Liggett's aide-de-camp, was even more blunt in his criticism. As he recorded in his diary on 8 November, "It appears that Pershing had talked to General Liggett excitedly about taking Sedan, and General Liggett had not approved of the idea and said the French would not stand for it. . . . All this was in direct opposition to General Liggett's plan and notion of how the operation should be conducted. Another instance of ignorant meddling, in which Drum, who knew General Liggett's views, was involved."[159]

In his memoirs published in 1931, Pershing praised the soldiers of the Big Red One while also admitting that the Race for Sedan never should have happened: "The troops of the 1st Division carried out this unnecessary forced march in fine spirit despite their tired condition." He did not, however, note the terrible casualty count. Pershing also tacitly laid the blame at Summerall's feet: "Under normal conditions the action of the officer or officers responsible for this movement of the 1st Division directly across the zones of action of two other divisions could not have been overlooked; but the splendid record of that unit and the approach of the end of hostilities suggested leniency."[160]

In his own memoirs, Summerall wrote that when he told Parker he "expected to see him in Sedan the next morning," he assumed that Parker would do so by first crossing the Meuse from his present position seven miles southwest of Sedan and then move on the town from the far bank. Summerall went on to write that he was amazed when he learned that Parker had started moving laterally through the sectors of the adjacent American divisions rather than crossing the river first.[161] Pershing's comments in his memoirs infuriated Summerall, who had just retired as chief of staff of the army when the memoirs were published in 1931. He prepared a rebuttal accusing Pershing of disloyalty, but mutual friends talked him out of releasing it to the press.[162]

The animosities resulting from the Race to Sedan continued to ripple through the senior ranks of the U.S. Army during the interwar years. Four of the six chiefs of staff of the U.S. Army during that period—Pershing, Summerall, MacArthur, and Marshall—had been involved in the incident to one degree or another. The ultimate price, however, was paid by those 583 soldiers whose names are listed on a bronze plaque attached to the 1st Division's monument on the west bank of the Meuse that overlooks Sedan to this day.

Even if the Germans had been able to exploit the American fiasco south of Sedan, their overall situation was far beyond recovery. On 6 November Groener told Prince Max that the German army must retreat "behind the Rhine."[163] Bullard's U.S. Second Army commenced combat operations on 9 November by advancing north along the east bank of the Meuse. V Corps crossed the river in force the following day, seizing the Meuse bend between

Villemontry and Mouzon and then turning north along the east bank. At 0630 hours on 11 November the U.S. First and Second Armies were told that the Armistice would take effect at 1100 hours, but until then operations would continue without a halt.[164] When the guns finally fell silent, it did not come a moment too soon. Harbord later stated that if the Armistice had not come when it did, the AEF would have had to stop fighting because its logistics system would have totally collapsed.[165]

Between 18 July and 11 November 1918, the Germans suffered some 760,000 casualties (dead and wounded) and lost 386,000 captured. Total British casualties for the period came to 298,000; French, 279,000; and American, 130,000. Foch's General Offensive campaign had started on 26 September with the American attack into the Meuse-Argonne, which became the largest and deadliest battle in American history. During the forty-seven days of fighting, the AEF committed twenty-two of its double-strength divisions, which along with support troops totaled some 1.2 million men. American casualties came to 122,000, including 26,277 dead. The Germans suffered approximately 126,000 casualties, including 28,000 dead and 26,000 captured by the Americans. But the Meuse-Argonne campaign was in every sense a Franco-American victory. In addition to supplying the AEF with countless artillery pieces, tanks, and aircraft, the French Fourth Army also sustained 70,000 casualties and captured 30,000 German soldiers.

The overall significance of the campaign, however, remains something of a point of contention among historians. By the mid-1920s many British and French historians were arguing that Gallwitz essentially fought a delaying action and managed to prevent an American breakthrough for thirty-seven days. By the time that the AEF did break though, the British and the French had turned the German right flank and cut its key rail lines in the north, and the French Fifth Army was closing in on Mézières from the west. Thus, the Americans on the battlefield merely played an auxiliary role in the final defeat of the kaiser's army. Variations of that argument can still be heard to this day.

In his dispatch to the British government of 21 December 1918, Haig claimed the decisive role of the war for the BEF. Writing about the period from the end of April 1918 to the end of the war, he said, "In the decisive contests of this period, the strongest and most vital parts of the enemy's front were attacked by the British, his lateral communications were cut, and his best divisions fought to a standstill." He went on to report that the BEF during that period captured 187,000 prisoners and 2,850 guns. During the final three months of the war, starting with the 8 August attack at Amiens, fifty-nine British divisions engaged and defeated ninety-nine separate German divisions. "It is proof also of the overwhelmingly decisive part played by the British Armies on the Western Front in bringing the enemy to his final defeat," Haig noted.[166] Rather ungenerously, Haig made no mention of the four double-strength American divisions that fought under British operational control. Haig, however, did have a point. From 8 August until the Armistice, the BEF captured twice as many prisoners and almost twice as many guns as the French, Americans, and Belgians combined.[167]

And there can be little doubt that if the BEF had broken in March or April 1918, the final course of the war would have run much differently. Just how differently, of course, depended on too many variables to be able to say for sure. If the Germans had managed to push the BEF off the Continent, the Allies still might not have won in the end. Foch, for one, was determined to keep on fighting. And the British, too, most probably would have kept fighting so long as the Germans controlled the Belgian coast—and the British still had the overwhelming power of the Royal Navy. The American forces that were pouring across the Atlantic could have been diverted to Britain, which would then become a huge invasion base. That essentially is what happened between 1940 and 1945.

Pershing's exaggerated claims for the AEF's battlefield virtuosity certainly did not help the American cause, especially his comments about the significance of Saint Mihiel and the inherent superiority of American troops over the "tired Europeans." In his own memoirs, *A.E.F. Ten Years Ago in France*, Hunter Liggett made it clear that he saw things much more realistically than did his wartime boss. He pointed out that the German army of March to July 1918 was not the juggernaut it had been in 1914. By the time the Americans got into the fight, the kaiser's army was worn and scarred, although it was still a remarkable and disciplined fighting machine. Liggett went on to write, "As one who is proud of what the American Army did, I wonder what we might have done against the German Army of 1914? Not so well."[168] And departing significantly from Pershing's claims of innate American superiority, Liggett wrote bluntly, "I am under no patriotic illusion that one good American can whip any ten foreigners. I know, on the contrary, that a well-led foreigner is much more likely to whip ten good but untrained Americans."[169]

Liggett, however, was very critical about what he saw as the tendency in Europe to discount the American contribution to the final victory. With somewhat more than a little sense of vexation, he opened his book in this way:

> There is bound to be so much anger, disillusion, chagrin and self-pity in the backlash of such a war as a result; and Germany, whipped and disarmed, has ceased to be an adequate scapegoat. The Allies have about made up their minds that it is we who are to blame because we arrived too late. Perhaps if we could be made to believe that we paid money while our Allies paid in men, we might be so overcome with chagrin that we should never be able to speak of money again. A necessary step in this direction has been to minimize the contribution of the American Army in winning the war.[170]

Liggett had a point. As historian Edward Lengel has pointed out, Gallwitz fought a brilliant defensive battle in the Meuse-Argonne, one that was much more than a simple rearguard action. Gallwitz and Marwitz had orders to defend their sector at all costs. While the Germans could afford to trade space for time in Flanders and Picardy, they had little room for maneuver astride the Meuse. As the last viable defensive position between Verdun and the north-south railway that supplied most of the kaiser's western armies, the Kriemhilde Stellung had to be held.[171]

It is true that by the time the American First and French Fourth Armies were finally within range of Mézières, the Germans were in a complete state of collapse because their right flank had been caved in. But the fight in the Meuse-Argonne had drawn in forty-seven divisions and the last of Germany's reserves, accounting for 25 percent of the German divisions on the Western Front. And as the Germans tried to contain the Americans and French on their left, they were forced to weaken their right wing correspondingly, which undoubtedly facilitated the French and British attacks in the center and in the north. Haig had planned on as much when he scheduled the start of the Battle of Canal du Nord and the Fifth Battle of Ypres for one and two days respectively after the AEF first attacked on 26 September.

Major General Sir Frederick Maurice, who until May 1918 had been the director of military operations of the British Imperial General Staff, noted that British and French armies, after almost four years of hard experience, could not have attacked with anywhere near the confidence of the Americans, untrained and unprepared as they were: "There are times and occasions in war when the valor of ignorance has its advantages." Maurice went on to say that if the AEF had waited to gain more experience before launching major combat operations, the war most probably would have been prolonged by at least six months, resulting in far more casualties on both sides. If the AEF had not attacked in force into the Meuse-Argonne in September 1918, "it is almost certain that the Germans would have been able to withdraw in fairly good order to the Meuse, and that we should not have forced them to sign an armistice on November 11."[172]

Taking the broader view of the Great War on the Western Front, the French put more soldiers into the field and suffered the highest number of combat-related deaths, totaling almost 1.2 million, 40,000 of which were civilians. British combat deaths came to 744,000, but there can be no doubt that the British single-handedly kept the Allies in the fight for a year following the French mutinies of April 1917. But in the end, the mighty German army fell to the overwhelming manpower superiority of the Allies—all the Allies. Considering that for most of the war the Germans also fought on the Eastern Front, it still took the French and the British and the Americans and the Belgians to defeat the kaiser's army on the Western Front. And as far as operational-level generalship, Foch—with significant input from Haig and Pétain—outgeneraled Ludendorff.

FOURTEEN

ARMISTICE AND OCCUPATION: 11 NOVEMBER 1918–28 JUNE 1919

Like Siegfried, stricken down by the treacherous spear of savage Hagen, our weary front collapsed. It was in vain that it had tried to drink in new vitality from the fountain in our Homeland which had run dry. It was now our task to save what was left of our army for the subsequent reconstruction of our Fatherland.

> *Field Marshal Paul von Hindenburg,* Out of My Life

Pétain spoke of taking a huge indemnity from Germany, so large that she will never be able to pay it. Meanwhile, French troops will hold the left bank of the Rhine as a pledge.

> *Field Marshal Sir Douglas Haig, in Gary Sheffield and John Bourne, eds.,*
> Douglas Haig: War Diaries and Letters, 1914–1918

WHEN GUNS FELL SILENT ON the Western Front at 1100 hours on 11 November 1918, the Armistice that went into effect had many confirmed critics and skeptics on both sides. Events of 1918, political and military, contributed incrementally to a final outcome that almost no one was happy with. Much of the peace process that played out during the last two months of the war was influenced by a speech delivered by President Woodrow Wilson to the U.S. Congress earlier that year on 18 January, outlining America's war aims and peace terms. Of all the countries that fought World War I, America was the only one that issued an explicit statement of war aims.[1] Wilson's Fourteen Points, resulting from that speech, were met with considerable skepticism by

British prime minister David Lloyd George, French premier Georges Clemenceau, and Italy's prime minister Vittorio Orlando. Not only were they suspicious of Wilson's unbridled idealism, but the European Allies also were concerned about direct threats to their colonial empires embedded in the Fourteen Points.

Germany initially ignored the Fourteen Points but started to pay more serious attention to Wilson's proposals when it became increasingly clear that Germany could not win the war on the battlefield or even achieve a strategic stalemate. The basic thought was that Wilson would be more flexible and lenient than the French or British because America had been in the war for such a short period of time and its homeland remained unscarred.

A few days after the previously mentioned 29 September meeting with Hindenburg, Ludendorff, Foreign Minister Paul von Hintze, and the kaiser, OHL's liaison officer to the Reichstag, Major Freiherr von der Bussche, told stunned party faction leaders that the war was lost. At a Crown Council meeting in Berlin that same day, 2 October, Hindenburg repeated OHL's demand for an immediate truce: "The Army cannot wait forty-eight hours."[2] The following day, Hindenburg sent a message to Prince Max von Baden, the new chancellor: "OHL insists on the immediate issue of a peace offer to our enemies in accordance with the decision of Monday, 29 September." Hindenburg went on to write, "There is no prospect, humanly speaking, of forcing our enemies to sue for peace."[3] By compelling the government in Berlin to make the first move in requesting peace negotiations, Hindenburg and Ludendorff gave OHL and the army "plausible deniability" for any responsibility in initiating Germany's surrender.[4]

On 6 October Prince Max sent the first German peace note, via neutral Switzerland, to Wilson asking the president to take the initiative to bring about the peace and invite the other Allies to participate in the negotiations. The key line in the note ran, "The German government accepts as the basis for peace negotiations the program stated by the President of the United States in his speech to Congress of January 8, 1918."[5] Neither Hindenburg nor Ludendorff nor virtually anyone else at OHL had at that point ever read the text of the Fourteen Points, and The Duo were deluding themselves into believing that Germany could still hold onto some of its conquered territories.[6] To the disappointment of OHL and the German government, Wilson's note of 8 October insisted that a precondition for any armistice was the withdrawal of all German forces from the territories of the Allies.[7]

After four years of fighting the war, the Allies were now faced with the problem of how to end it. In a series of exchanges between Foch and Clemenceau, the generalissimo repeatedly insisted that as commander in chief of the Allied armies, he, in coordination with the national commanders in chief, should be the one to frame the military requirements to be imposed upon Germany in the case of any armistice. The ambiguity of Foch's constitutional status muddied the waters. Clemenceau certainly had the authority to sack Foch as a general officer in the French army, but did he have the authority to remove or replace the Allied supreme commander? And if the prime minister of France did not, who did?[8] On 8 October Foch sent a note to Clemenceau insisting that following any German surrender, the French military had to control the Rhine bridgeheads at Breisach, Strasbourg, and Rastatt, which would give the French "the possibility of turning the defenses afforded by the central position of the Rhine, in case it should become necessary to take up arms again after a suspension of operations at this moment."[9] All three potential bridgeheads were anchored in Alsace.

The second German note was sent on 14 October from German state secretary of foreign affairs Wilhelm Solf to U.S. secretary of state Robert Lansing, again through neutral channels. It was a non-answer to the main point of Wilson's first note. Without ever mentioning a German withdrawal from occupied territory, Solf merely declared that the only purpose for starting discussions was to agree upon the practical details of a "permanent peace of justice."[10] In reply, President Wilson's second note dated that same day doubled down on his call for the withdrawal from Allied territory. He further added a demand for the cessation of all U-boat operations against Allied and neutral shipping, and he condemned the brutal destruction caused by the German forces that already had been pushed back by the Allies. Wilson hinted strongly that the abdication of the kaiser would facilitate the armistice negotiations.[11]

Ludendorff, meanwhile, continued to swing between extremes poles. At the 17 October meeting of the German War Cabinet in Berlin, Ludendorff had observed that the Allied attack was losing momentum, and he now argued that Germany could hold out well into 1919 by successively pulling back into prepared defensive positions. The chief of the naval staff, Admiral Reinhard Scheer, supported Ludendorff's overoptimistic assessment, and Lieutenant General Heinrich Scheuch, the new Prussian war minister, made the utterly unrealistic promise of being able to muster another 600,000 soldiers. As Ludendorff laconically noted in his memoirs, "I could not check his figures."[12]

Two days later the German navy mutinied at Kiel over Scheer's Operations Plan 19, a sortie by the High Seas Fleet for a head-on clash with the Royal Navy. It would have been a virtual act of suicide to salvage the German navy's honor in defeat.[13]

In the third German peace note of 20 October, Solf disingenuously claimed that only German military commanders in the field could decide on any withdrawals from occupied territory. The note also insisted that neither the German army nor the navy had violated any of the laws of warfare. Solf concluded that Germany was then undergoing internal political changes that ultimately would result in the country becoming a constitutional democracy. The implication, of course, was that Germany subsequently deserved more lenient treatment from its democratic opponents.[14]

Replying on 23 October, President Wilson in his third note hardened his stance even more. Much to the relief of the Allies, Wilson made it bluntly clear that no armistice agreement could be reached without the full concurrence of the other Allies. The key lines in Wilson's note emphasized that the necessary terms of any armistice "will fully protect the interests of the peoples involved and ensure to the associated governments the unrestricted power to safeguard and enforce the details of the peace to which the German Government has agreed." And, if the U.S. Government "must deal with the military masters and monarchical autocrats of Germany now, or if it is likely to have to deal with them later in regard to the international obligations of the German Empire, it must demand not peace negotiations, but surrender."[15] It was this last line that so enraged Hindenburg and Ludendorff and resulted in the 24 October message to the troops that finally got Ludendorff relieved.

Still equivocating, the fourth German note of 27 October avoided all the main issues and continued to try to impress Wilson with Germany's constitutional changes, assuring the president that the peace negotiations were now being conducted by "a government of the people, in whose hands rests, both actually and constitutionally, the authority to make decisions."[16] The kaiser, however, was still on his throne.

On 25 October Pershing, Haig, Pétain, and Vice Admiral Ferdinand-Jean-Jacques de Bon, chief of staff of the French navy, met at Foch's headquarters in Senlis to discuss military terms of an armistice. Ironically, Haig at that point was starting to lose his earlier confidence in a German collapse before the end of the year. He now argued that the German army would still be able to put up a significant fight once it withdrew behind its own borders, and it was therefore in the interest of the Allies for the Germans to come to terms sooner than later. Pétain insisted that the armistice terms should make it impossible for the Germans to resume hostilities. The German army must withdraw to Germany without a single gun or a tank, and the Allies should occupy a zone of Germany on the east bank of the Rhine. Pershing also supported imposing severe restrictions on Germany. Citing comments once made by Moltke the Elder about the vulnerability of Germany to invasion, Foch said that the Allies at a minimum must establish three bridgeheads over the Rhine: at Cologne, Coblenz, and Mainz.[17] As opposed to the three Alsace bridgeheads designated by Foch on 8 October, these three were in the German Rhineland.

The following day Foch personally carried a memo of the consensus position reached during the commanders in chief meeting. It essentially was the same as his 8 October note to Clemenceau, with more details and the new list of bridgeheads:[18]

1. Evacuation of all previously annexed territory in Belgium, France, Alsace-Lorraine, and Luxembourg.
2. Surrender of 5,000 guns, 30,000 machine guns, and 3,000 trench mortars.
3. Evacuation of German forces to the right bank of the Rhine, with Allied bridgeheads on the right bank at Mainz, Coblenz, and Cologne to a depth of 18¾ miles and a 25-mile demilitarized zone along the right bank of the river.
4. No additional damage in the areas from which the German forces withdraw.
5. Surrender of 5,000 locomotives and 150,000 railway cars in good condition.
6. Surrender of 150 submarines, the withdrawal of the German surface fleet to the Baltic, and the Allied occupation of Cuxhaven and Heligoland.
7. Maintenance of the Allied maritime blockade until the above conditions are met.

Upon reading the draft terms, French president Raymond Poincaré privately told Foch's chief of staff, Maxime Weygand, "My dear general, they will never sign that."[19] Some of Foch's fellow generals, on the other hand, believed that the terms were far too lenient. Pétain and Pershing, in particular, thought that Germany should be forced to surrender unconditionally. Haig leaned more toward Foch's thinking. The debate continues to this day. If Germany had been given only the option of surrendering, would it have kept fighting?

Probably, but then what? If the Germans could have been forced into total surrender, could the extreme nationalists in the postwar years have claimed that the German army was never defeated on the battlefield? Probably not, but what difference would it have made, considering the draconian terms of the subsequent Versailles Treaty?

Pershing was far from satisfied. On 30 October, he broke ranks and directly advised the Allied political leaders that the military situation was then so favorable that the Allies should continue the offensive until Germany was forced to surrender unconditionally.[20] It was a very presumptuous action, considering the relatively low esteem with which the Allied political leaders held Pershing, and they were less than impressed with his outburst. Clemenceau and Lloyd George condemned Pershing's memo as a political rather than a military document. Secretary of War Newton Baker and U.S. Army Chief of Staff Peyton March criticized Pershing for stepping outside military lines. President Wilson's personal representative, Edward House, who was then in Europe himself, wrote in his diary, "Everyone believes it is a political document and a clear announcement of his intention to become a candidate for the Presidency in 1920."[21]

After Ludendorff's departure, Lieutenant General Wilhelm Groener had to try to hold the pieces together at OHL. The Germans then had some 80,000 wounded troops to be evacuated back to Germany, at the same time that their usable rail lines were being cut off one at a time. The political situation in Germany served only to complicate matters at OHL. As the pressures to abdicate mounted on the weak and vacillating Kaiser Wilhelm II, he decided to run away from the problems by leaving Berlin. Wilhelm and his entourage of royal camp followers arrived on 30 October at OHL headquarters in Spa, where the kaiser announced his intention to "lead his troops."[22] That was about the last thing Hindenburg and Groener needed.

When the eighth session of the Allied Supreme War Council met in Paris from 31 October to 4 November, the armistice was the main topic of discussion. Early on, House asked Foch point-blank why it would be better to grant an armistice now than to continue the war. For the deeply religious Foch, it was a moral conundrum as well as a strategic and political one. Prefacing his answer by paraphrasing Clausewitz, Foch responded, "I do not make war simply to make war, but to obtain results. If the Germans sign an armistice with the conditions necessary to guarantee those results, I am satisfied. No one has the right to prolong the bloodshed any further."[23] House's question and

Foch's answer in effect shielded the United States from any later criticism that America had pressured the Allies into agreeing to a premature armistice.

As prime minister of the world's greatest naval power, Lloyd George insisted that Germany be forced to surrender its entire High Seas Fleet. Concerned that the additional naval clause might force the Germans to reject the armistice and prolong the bloodletting, Foch tried to argue that the surrender of just their submarines would effectively neutralize the German navy. Foch never did rise above his limited understanding of the realities of sea power. Britain's First Lord of the Admiralty, Sir Eric Geddes, countered, "Marshal Foch has no idea how much trouble the High Seas Fleet has given us—because the [British] Grand Fleet has always held it in check. If these ships are not surrendered, the Grand Fleet during the armistice will be in the same state of tension as that of the two armies opposed to each other in the trenches."[24] Foch was told to insert the naval clause, and then if the Germans balked, it could be modified as a bargaining chip. What Britain demanded amounted to 10 battleships, 6 battle cruisers, 8 light cruisers, and 50 destroyers, in addition to all 176 of Germany's operational submarines. In any event, the Germans did surrender the High Seas Fleet, but then on 21 June 1919 the German skeleton crews scuttled almost all their surface ships that were being held at the British anchorage at Scapa Flow.

The Supreme War Council's 22nd Resolution reluctantly confirmed the lead that President Wilson had taken in the negotiations with Germany and accepted the Fourteen Points as the basis for the final peace settlement. The Allies did, however, register dissenting reservations about the American interpretation of freedom of the seas and the evacuation of invaded territories. Did that mean that Alsace and Lorraine would go back to Germany, as they had been before the war? The final resolution made it clear that these two particular points would be resolved during the formal peace negotiations after the armistice.[25] The following day, 5 November, Wilson sent his fourth and final peace note informing the German government that Foch was authorized by the Allies to deal with their representatives on the armistice.

By 7 November the internal situation in Germany was deteriorating rapidly. Strikes and organized violence were breaking out everywhere. Bavaria was on the verge of breaking away and declaring itself a free state (Freistaat Bayern). The kaiser decided that only he could restore order, and he intended to march back into Germany at the head of his troops. He ordered Groener to prepare the necessary plans immediately. Groener in turn had to convince a vacillating Hindenburg that the troops in Germany had already gone over to the revolution and that the army in the field would not follow the kaiser against them. Hindenburg finally accepted the reality of the situation.[26]

The German government, meanwhile, transmitted the names of its armistice delegation, and Foch issued the orders to make sure they were escorted through the Allied lines properly. On the afternoon of 7 November, Foch in his special command train left Senlis for a rail siding in the Compiègne Forest, where the meeting was to take place. Arriving at 0800 hours the following morning, the members of the German delegation headed by special state secretary Matthias Erzberger presented their credentials issued by Prince Max. Once the formalities of the credentials were concluded, Foch asked the Germans the purpose of their visit. Somewhat at a loss for an answer to such an unexpected question, Erzberger replied to Foch that they had come to receive the Allied proposals. Foch replied curtly that he had no proposals to make and no conditions to offer. Falling back on the text of President Wilson's last note, Erzberger read out that Marshal Foch was authorized to make known the conditions of the armistice. Foch replied, "Do you ask for an armistice? If you do, I can inform you of the conditions to which it can be obtained."[27]

Erzberger replied in the affirmative, and then Weygand read out the key terms as the Supreme War Council had approved them. The members of the German delegation were shocked by the harshness of the terms, but they registered no immediate protest to any of the military clauses except for the 30,000 machine guns. They argued that because of the civil unrest then rampant in the country, the German army needed those machine guns to maintain internal order. Foch refused to budge, telling them that the state of things in their country was the cumulative result of their own actions over the course of the past four years. Erzberger then asked for an immediate cease-fire while he and his delegation returned to German lines and transmitted the terms to Berlin. Foch refused: "Hostilities cannot cease before the signing of the armistice." Foch told them they had seventy-two hours to accept the terms. Erzberger asked for an additional twenty-four hours because of the difficulties of getting the message to Berlin and the answer back to OHL at Spa. Foch refused, and the stunned Germans then left and made their way back through their own lines.[28]

Hindenburg and Groener met with the kaiser on the morning of 9 November. For once, the implacable Hindenburg was completely unnerved. As a Prussian officer he was psychologically incapable of telling his supreme warlord that the army was no longer loyal to him. Hindenburg asked Wilhelm for permission to resign, and the kaiser refused. Incapable of taking the next necessary step, the field marshal then ordered Groener to give the kaiser the considered opinion of OHL that the army was no longer behind him, and any attempt to use military force back in Germany would result in full-scale civil war. Thus, in later years Groener became the scapegoat for Hindenburg's inability to face up to his responsibility to the nation. As the field marshal after the war once blurted out to a group of nationalist political leaders, "You all blame me, but you should blame Groener."[29]

The dazed kaiser finally announced that he would abdicate as German emperor, but he would not give up the crown of the Kingdom of Prussia. He also said that he formally would transfer command of the German armies to Hindenburg. But the march of history had already left the House of Hohenzollern behind. Shortly after 1400 hours the government of Chancellor Prince Max, without consulting with the kaiser, announced in Berlin the abdication of Wilhelm II.[30] Prince Max then resigned and was replaced as chancellor by Friedrich Ebert, the leader of the Social Democratic Party.

Foch knew that he had to keep the pressure on the German army. The same day that Berlin announced the kaiser's abdication, the generalissimo sent a message to all the Allied senior commanders: "The enemy, disorganized by our repeated attacks, is giving way all along the front. It is urgent to hasten and intensify our efforts. I appeal to the energy and initiative of commanders in chief and their armies to make the results achieved decisive."[31]

On the morning of 10 November, the kaiser boarded his private train and left OHL headquarters at Spa, never to return to Germany. He left without ever issuing a formal abdication, nor did he see Hindenburg on the day of his departure. The field marshal never saw his supreme warlord again, and for the remainder of his life he remained haunted by his failure as a Prussian officer to defend his king and kaiser. Ebert's new government, meanwhile, was struggling to maintain some semblance of control in Germany, and it was worried about the specter of a disintegrating German army and the chaos that would ensue. Ebert, therefore, was desperate for Hindenburg to remain in command of the army. That day, Groener and Ebert brokered an agreement for the army under Hindenburg to bring the troops home in an orderly manner. The new government, in turn, agreed to continue to recognize the authority of the German officer corps.[32] Only Hindenburg at that point had the stature to wield the necessary authority, and by remaining in command despite his reservations, he made a significant contribution, if not the decisive one, to the immediate survival of the new German Republic.

The German delegation returned to Foch's railcar in the early hours of 11 November and signed the armistice agreement at 0510 hours, although the actual time written on the document was 0500. Foch did allow the Germans to attach an addendum of protest to the armistice instrument: "Referring to their repeated oral and written statements, the undersigned plenipotentiaries also deem it their duty to strongly insist on the fact that the carrying out of this agreement may plunge the German people into anarchy and famine."[33]

The cease-fire was set for 1100 hours that morning, after which the Allied forces would advance no farther until 17 November. In the interim, the Germans were to start withdrawing back to Germany.[34] Foch sent the Allied commanders in chief instructions prescribing the conditions under which Allied territory evacuated by the enemy was to be occupied by their troops.[35] Later that day, the Third Army's General Karl von Einem issued a message to his troops: "Firing has ceased. Undefeated . . . you are terminating the war in enemy country."[36] It was one of the first foundation stones supporting the myth that the German army had never been defeated on the battlefield. But looking at it from the German perspective in November 1918, could the discipline and morale of the German army have been held together for an orderly withdrawal without such messages from the senior German commanders?

On 15 November OHL displaced back across the Rhine and established a new headquarters at Cassel, northeast of Frankfurt. The Allies' designated occupation forces started advancing toward the Rhine River two days later. In addition to the three key bridgeheads on the east bank of the river, the Allies occupied extensive amounts of German territory known as the Rhineland, on the west bank of the river from just south of Speyer, where the French-German border turns away from the Rhine, to the Dutch border. The AEF, on 7 November, had formally activated the U.S. Third Army to serve as the command and control headquarters of the American occupation force.[37] Initially commanded by Major General Joseph T. Dickman, General Hunter Liggett later assumed command.

Why did the AEF need another field army headquarters for the occupation force? Neither the French nor the British established new army headquarters for the occupation. The French, which had by far the largest occupation zone, moved their Eighth and Tenth Armies forward and later merged them into the French Army of the Rhine. The British Second Army became the British

Army of the Rhine.[38] Only the Americans stood up a completely new army headquarters for the occupation. It was an action that would puzzle any experienced staff officer. Establishing a senior-level headquarters from scratch and on the fly and trying to piece the staffs and forces together by taking them from the two existing armies made little sense. The Second Army already existed, it had been in action only a couple of days, and it was already the closest to the designated American occupation zone.

Pershing in his memoirs only mentions the Third Army in the AEF Order of Battle appendix, and Major General James Harbord in his book, *The American Army in France, 1917–1919*, mentions it only once in passing. Even Liggett in his memoirs mentions the Third Army only very briefly, offering no explanation as to why such an organization was necessary, except that it had "been planned before the Armistice."[39] None of the major memoirs offers any explanation as to why it was necessary to establish the Third Army when it was clear that the war would be over in a few days. And on the day that it was established on paper, it was far from being organized. George C. Marshall in his World War I memoirs does give some indication of what was involved in making it work. Among other things, a chronic shortage of horses complicated matters.[40] Without further explanation, and in light of Edward House's speculation about postwar political ambitions, it is all too easy to conclude that Pershing was engaging in empire building.

The French entered Metz on 24 November and Strasbourg the following day. By 30 November all the formerly occupied Allied territories were free of German forces. The Allies entered the German Rhineland on 1 December, closed to the west bank of the river eight days later, and had all their bridgeheads established on the east bank by the seventeenth. Still in overall Allied command, Foch established his headquarters at the Rhineland town of Kreuznach, in the center of the French zone. During the early stages of the war, Kreuznach had been OHL headquarters.

Between the armistice and the signing of the peace treaty at Versailles, many of the interallied frictions at the senior levels continued unabated. A secret British intelligence report in January 1919 commented on the continuing bad relations between Pershing and Foch and also between Foch and the Belgians over a possible annexation of Luxembourg by Belgium.[41] Pershing, on the other hand, suspected that it was the French who wanted to annex Luxembourg. Pershing and Foch also clashed over the number of American troops remaining in Europe. Pershing was furious over the generalissimo's insistence that the remaining Doughboys be used as laborers to clear away the war damage and rebuild France's shattered infrastructure.

Foch and Clemenceau too were in a constant state of conflict over issues of policy and strategy. Among other things, Foch kept insisting that for its future security, France had to cut the Rhineland off from Germany. In order to stop the fighting, Foch had supported armistice terms that allowed the German army in the field to withdraw to Germany without formally surrendering, but when it came to the actual peace treaty he believed passionately that Germany's future war-making capability had to be crippled permanently. And although Clemenceau had been willing to let the military commanders take the lead in brokering the armistice, he insisted to a resistant Foch that the actual peace treaty was a matter for the political leadership only. Some historians have concluded that Foch was in an actual state of rebellion against his own government, which leads to the question of why Foch was not sacked. Elizabeth Greenhalgh has suggested that Clemenceau was afraid that he might still need Foch if Germany balked at the last moment in signing the treaty.[42]

Clemenceau had ample cause for concern. The German government was in a state of shock over the draconian nature of the proposed terms of the Versailles Treaty. Internationally, however, there was little sympathy for Germany on that point, considering that the Treaty of Brest-Litvosk it had imposed on Russia in 1918 was harsher still. The German government was in a state of crisis over accepting the terms of the Versailles Treaty. Many wanted to reject it outright, even at the risk of the resumption of hostilities. Finally, the Allies on 22 June delivered an ultimatum: if Germany did not accept the treaty terms within forty-eight hours, hostilities would resume. Under extreme pressure, Chancellor Ebert told his cabinet that Germany would sign the treaty only if the German High Command assured him that there was no reasonable chance of an armed resistance.

The burden of a constitutional crisis was once again on Hindenburg's shoulders. He and Groener agonized over the answer, with Groener again acting as the voice of reality. Finally, with only fifteen minutes left until Ebert had to have an answer, Hindenburg left the room, telling Groener, "There is no need for me to stay. You can give the answer to the President as well as I can." As he had done in failing to tell the kaiser that the army was no longer behind him, Hindenburg again passed the buck to Groener. Afterward, Hindenburg told him, "The burden which you have undertaken is a terrible one." For a second time Groener had shouldered a responsibility that Hindenburg would not face, and once more he became the scapegoat.

The Versailles Treaty was signed on 28 June 1919. Foch was not present. "On that day, I took refuge in my quarters at Kreuznach," he recalled.[43] Two months earlier he had made a statement to the *Daily Mail* newspaper that proved prophetic: "The next time the Germans will make no mistake. They will break through into Northern France and will seize the Channel ports as a base of operations against England."[44]

FIFTEEN

THE FLUCTUATING VERDICT OF HISTORY

Any military historian worth his salt must recognize the risk that he will be beating his drum with the bones of the dead.

Richard Holmes, The Western Front

All very successful commanders are prima donnas and must be so treated.

General George S. Patton Jr., War as I Knew It

THE WARLORDS OF 1918 LIE today in very different sorts of resting places. In 1934 Hindenburg was interred at the massive monument complex at Tannenberg, the birthplace of his legend. He rested there a little more than ten years. As the Soviet army advanced across Poland in 1945, it reduced the memorial to rubble. Before it reached the site, however, the Wehrmacht removed the field marshal's remains and evacuated them to the west. After the war, Hindenburg was finally laid to rest again in St. Elizabeth's Church in Marburg an der Lahn. The church was built in the thirteenth century by the Teutonic Knights, who later were defeated by the Poles at the First Battle of Tannenberg in 1410. Ludendorff, to whom the field marshal owed virtually his entire military reputation, was buried in 1937 in the small town of Tutzing, Bavaria. Against his specific wishes, he was given a state funeral attended by Hitler. Despite its relatively obscure location, the grave marker is fairly large and impressive, but it is dark and somber in the German military tradition.

Foch is exactly where Clemenceau always suspected the generalissimo envisioned himself. In 1929, the marshal was laid to rest in a magnificent sarcophagus in Paris's Les Invalides. He lies close to the tomb of Napoleon. The German forces that occupied Paris from 1940 to 1944 respected Foch's grave. Nobody in November 1918 could have foreseen the final resting place of Pétain, who was both Foch's strategic partner and professional rival. Tried for treason following World War II for his leading role in the collaborationist Vichy government, Pétain was convicted and sentenced to death. Charles de Gaulle, Pétain's onetime military aide and protégé, commuted the sentence to life in prison. In 1951, the man who saved France from total collapse twice during the Great War was buried close to the prison where he died on the Île d'Yeu, off France's Atlantic coast. Successive French governments ever since have refused permission for his remains to be brought back to mainland France, where a gravesite is said to be reserved for him in the cemetery in front of the Douaumont Ossuary at Verdun. In 1973, nationalist extremists stole Pétain's coffin in an attempt to force the French government to allow the marshal's repatriation. French police recovered the coffin several days later, and it was reinterred in its original site.

Since 1948 Pershing has rested in the most appropriate of places, Arlington National Cemetery, the most hallowed piece of military ground in America. Within tight limits, the cemetery administration allows surviving families to purchase privately produced headstones that are slightly larger and more finely made than the government-issue markers. Pershing, however, rests under the standard plain marble headstone. Its only distinctive feature is his unique rank title, general of the armies, making him Arlington's senior-ranking resident. Haig's final resting place is very different from those of his Royal Navy counterparts during the Great War. Admirals of the Fleet Sir John Jellico and Sir David Beatty were interred in elaborate sarcophagi in the crypt of St. Paul's Cathedral in London. They lie close to other great British military leaders, including Admiral Nelson and the Duke of Wellington. Haig, at his own wish, was interred in the churchyard at Dryburgh Abbey in the Scottish Borders region. Similar to Pershing, Haig has a simple government-issue soldier's tombstone. But unlike Pershing, Haig's rank title of field marshal is not engraved on the headstone, nor is his nobility title of earl or his many knighthoods. In accordance with the standard British practice of including regimental badges on the marker, Haig's is that of the 7th (Queen's Own) Hussars, into which he was commissioned as a second lieutenant in 1885. British practice also allows a personalized epitaph at the base of each headstone. Haig's reads, "He Trusted in God and Tried to Do the Right."

Germans to this day remain widely divided on Hindenburg. To many, he is remembered as the personification of the German ultra-militarism that brought the country to the brink of destruction twice during the twentieth century and as the last president of the Weimar Republic that delivered Germany into Hitler's hands. A smaller grouping still considers him the last of Germany's great military heroes, who during World War I fought the good fight, nobly and honorably, and who kept the Weimar Republic alive until he finally was overcome by the ravages of old age and the surge of national socialism. The truth is most certainly somewhere in the middle, but that point has not yet become fixed. Some German towns to this day have streets named after Hindenburg, but that too remains contentious. During a recent controversy in the university town of Freiburg im Breisgau, an opinion piece by noted military historian Jürgen Förster appearing in the 19 October 2016 edition of the *Badische Zeitung* defended the retention of the name Hindenburgstrasse for one of the town's streets.[1]

After retiring from the army a second time in July 1919, Hindenburg intended to spend the rest of his life in peaceful retirement. It was not to be. That November he appeared before a special investigative committee of the Reichstag, where he testified that the German army had not been defeated on the battlefield. Invoking the story of the hero Siegfried, who in the Nibelungen saga had been struck down by the treacherous Hagen, the field marshal insisted that the German army too had been "stabbed in the back" by a cabal of Jews, Marxists, pacifists, and socialists in the homeland. Thus, he unwittingly gave credibility to the myth that the nationalists, especially Hitler and the Nazis, would use to destroy the Weimar Republic. In 1921 Hindenburg published his wartime memoirs, *Aus Meinem Leben* (*Out of My Life*). Like so many military memoirs, Hindenburg's are self-serving and are more interesting for what they do not say than for what they do say. The events of 11 November 1918, for example, are glossed over in a single paragraph. He did not actually write the book; the ghostwriters were staff officers on the team that compiled Germany's official history of the war. Thus, the memoirs offer little real insight into the mind of the Wooden Titan. And according to Holger Herwig, Hindenburg's papers have been so thoroughly cleansed by "patriotic self-censors" that they no longer contain anything of any real value.[2]

Germany in 1919 had little tradition of democracy and no institutions with any experience in the concept of government by the people. Hindenburg was no democrat. Even though he was personally disappointed in the weakness and incompetence of the ex-kaiser, the field marshal remained a monarchist until his dying day. When the French government demanded that the kaiser be extradited for trial as a war criminal, Hindenburg wrote to Foch asking him to intervene. Foch never answered, and Hindenburg never forgot what he considered to be the slight from his fellow marshal.[3]

Many if not most of the people of post–World War I Germany wanted order and stability far more than they wanted democracy and personal freedoms. The kaiser had been the symbol of that secure and more familiar world, but now he was gone. Germany, however, still had the field marshal, and Hindenburg during the final years of the war had already supplanted Wilhelm as the father figure of the nation. It was inevitable, then, that the "Hero of Tannenberg" would be called upon to play some major role in the life of the new Germany.

The Weimar Republic had three presidents in its first six years of existence. During the chaotic presidential election of March 1925, none of the seven candidates managed to garner more than 40 percent of the vote. Ludendorff, running for the ultra-right German Völkisch Freedom Party, came in dead last with only 1.1 percent. Most of the candidates, including Ludendorff, dropped out of the second round. A coalition of right-wing and nationalist parties then formed and persuaded a reluctant Hindenburg to run. The field marshal finally agreed, but only if he could run as a nonaligned candidate. In April, he won with a plurality of 48.3 percent.

In many ways, he was a figurehead chief of state. Otto Meissner, the state secretary of the office of the president—that is, the president's chief of staff—quickly became the politically oblivious Hindenburg's "new Ludendorff." As president, Hindenburg continued to display his lifelong sad weakness for signing anything that was put in front of him. As he advanced in age, Hindenburg increasingly was dominated by Meissner and by his own son, Colonel Oskar von Hindenburg, who tightly controlled access to the president.[4] He remained to the end of his life the popular symbol of the nation, but he contributed

294 | The Generals' War

almost nothing to stabilizing and strengthening the Weimar Republic. As Germany's internal political chaos lurched from crisis to crisis, Hindenburg spent most of the period from 1930 to 1933 ruling Germany by emergency presidential decrees.[5] How much he actually knew about what the executive orders he signed really said remains to this day a matter of conjecture. During one particularly nasty bout of political infighting in May 1932, Hindenburg did not lift a finger to support Wilhelm Groener, his old first quartermaster general who had carried so much water for the field marshal in late 1918 and early 1919. Groener, a staunch opponent of the Nazis, was unceremoniously dumped as minister of defense and minister of the interior.

Hindenburg despised Hitler personally, yet it was through the field marshal that the "Little Corporal" came to power in January 1933. A key member of the closed circle around the president in his last years was Franz von Papen, a wealthy nobleman, a former General Staff officer, and chancellor of Germany for a brief five-month period in 1932. After he was out of office, Papen, with the support of Oskar, was instrumental in convincing the president to appoint Hitler chancellor with a minority of Nazis in the cabinet as a way of keeping the political upstart under tight control. As the new vice chancellor, Papen himself would be the real political power. It did not quite work out that way, as Hitler quickly and methodically consolidated his hold on power. Less than a month in office, Hitler seized on the Reichstag fire of 27 February 1933 to maneuver Hindenburg into issuing a presidential decree that suspended most civil liberties in Germany. Less than a month after that, a staged ceremony on 21 March at the Potsdam Garrison Church gave the appearance to all the world that President Hindenburg had given his political blessing to Chancellor Hitler. Finally, Hitler seized virtually complete power during the brutal "Night of the Long Knives" (Nacht der langen Messer) blood purge of 30 June to 2 July 1934. After it was all over, Hindenburg sent Hitler a message of congratulations on his decisive actions to maintain public order. Most likely the telegram was sent in his name without even his knowledge. He was eighty-six and in rapidly failing health. A month later the president died at his East Prussian estate at Neudeck. Hitler immediately combined the offices of president and chancellor, declaring himself to be der Führer.

Field Marshal Paul von Hindenburg remains an enigma to this day. Historian Norman Stone wrote that Hindenburg was really a code name for a committee dominated by Ludendorff: "[Hindenburg] may not have been a great commander, but he was unquestionably a great chairman."[6] General Hermann von Kuhl, one of Germany's truly great battlefield chiefs of staff, dryly noted that Hindenburg "helped to see that OHL did not get slack in their work."[7] By the last year of the war, Hindenburg was little more than Ludendorff's top cover. The field marshal's principal British biographer, John W. Wheeler-Bennett, said that his greatest contribution was his "never-failing capacity and willingness to accept responsibility, a feature of his character which became less apparent in his later life."[8] Those cracks in his armor began to show at least as early as October 1918. Willian Astore and Dennis Showalter noted that Hindenburg "had strength and fortitude, but not dexterity and breadth of vision." He might have been a competent field army commander, but he was virtually lost as a coalition commander. Along with Ludendorff, he betrayed the trust of his soldiers in the trenches by shirking all responsibility for Germany's defeat, blaming scapegoats instead. According to Astore and Showalter, "He was a false icon."[9]

LUDENDORFF

There are no streets in Germany today named for Ludendorff. His place in German history is well established. In the Hindenburg-Ludendorff partnership, the field marshal got any benefit of the doubt, while the first quartermaster general got all the blame. Ludendorff was the high priest of German ultra-militarism and, even more than Hindenburg, the supporter of Hitler in his rise to power. *Meine Kriegserinnerungen 1914–1918*, Ludendorff's war memoirs published in 1919, paints a self-aggrandizing picture of a strong man surrounded by weaklings. In the book, he blames everyone but himself for Germany's defeat (as did Hindenburg) and carefully refrains from praising anyone, mentioning Foch only six times, Haig and Pétain only once each, and Pershing not at all.

After Ludendorff resigned—or was forced into retirement—things got hot for him in Germany once the revolution broke out. The former first quartermaster general slipped out of Germany wearing a preposterous disguise—including a false beard—and fled to Sweden. In February 1919 he returned to Germany after the Swedish government invited him to leave. He almost immediately dove into ultranationalist politics and right-wing conspiracies. In 1920 he supported the abortive Kapp-Lüttwitz Putsch, and in 1923 he marched at Hitler's side during the failed Munich Beer Hall Putsch. Had it succeeded,

Hitler promised to put Ludendorff in charge of the German army. All of the conspirators were later put on trial as a group. Hitler and others were convicted and sentenced to prison, but Ludendorff was acquitted.

The formerly "happy marriage" of The Duo was on rocky ground ever since the day in October 1918 that Ludendorff was fired. Ludendorff at the time made it quite clear to Hindenburg that he too should have resigned, despite the kaiser's rejection of the field marshal's offer.[10] It had always been an unbalanced partnership. Hindenburg could not have functioned without Ludendorff, but Ludendorff could have functioned quite well without Hindenburg. They both knew that. When describing their period of working together, Hindenburg always said "we"; Ludendorff always used "I."[11] During the controversy over the surrender of the kaiser for war crimes, both Crown Prince Wilhelm and Crown Prince Rupprecht offered to surrender themselves in the kaiser's place. When the distinguished sociologist Max Weber tried to persuade Ludendorff to offer himself as well, Ludendorff told him to suggest it instead to Hindenburg, who after all had been the superior officer. Weber replied that everyone knew that it was he and not Hindenburg who had been the real commander on the Western Front, to which Ludendorff replied, "Yes, thank goodness."[12]

Things got worse between Hindenburg and Ludendorff after Ludendorff's crushing defeat in the presidential election of 1925. They next met in September 1927, during the dedication ceremony for the monument at Tannenberg. The two old soldiers barely acknowledged each other. They did not shake hands, and Ludendorff refused to stand at the side of his old commander. Hindenburg spoke first and Ludendorff near the end of the ceremony. When Ludendorff rose to speak, the field marshal got up and left, leaving his former first quartermaster general almost alone on the platform. That episode effectively marked the point of Ludendorff's total ostracism from all of his former comrades.[13]

The rift only continued to grow. When in 1930 the president of the Reich gave his support to the acceptance of the Young Plan for the settlement of Germany's war debts, Ludendorff released a blistering statement that attacked Hindenburg's very identity as a German officer: "Field Marshal von Hindenburg has forfeited the right to wear the field-grey uniform of the army and to be buried in it. Herr Paul von Hindenburg has destroyed the very thing he fought for as Field Marshal."[14]

Although Ludendorff had been an early and ardent supporter of the national socialists, he later became a bitter and disillusioned critic of Hitler. After

Hindenburg appointed Hitler to the chancellery in 1933, Ludendorff fired off a telegram to the Reich president that was a salvo against two of his favorite targets: "This accursed man [Hitler] will cast our Reich into the abyss and bring our nation to inconceivable misery. Future generations will damn you in your grave for what you have done."[15] Hitler, nonetheless, made occasional efforts to reconcile with Ludendorff. In 1935, the Führer arrived unannounced at a party for Ludendorff's seventieth birthday, intending to promote him to field marshal on the retired list. An infuriated Ludendorff rejected the promotion, telling Hitler that field marshals were made on the battlefield, not at tea parties.

Ludendorff's final years were a spiraling descent into insanity, where he lived in a twilight world of conspiracies and ancient Nordic mysticism. He constantly railed against socialists, Jews, Catholics—especially Jesuits—and Freemasons. He continued to inveigh against the Nazis for not being Nazi enough. Along with his second wife, Mathilde, they published a number of bizarre books and essays and founded the cult-like Bund für Gotteserkenntnis (Union for God-Cognition). That organization still exists to this day, headquartered in the Bavarian town of Tutzing, where Ludendorff is buried. It possesses Ludendorff's papers, and despite the stipulation in Ludendorff's will to the contrary, those papers remain closed to scholars.

Ludendorff's slim 1935 book, *Der totale Krieg* (*The Total War*), summarized his brutal theory of the primacy of warfare. In it he wrote, "Warfare is the highest expression of the national will to live, and politics must, therefore, be subservient to the conduct of war."[16] As historian Elizabeth Hull has pointed out, total war as Ludendorff actually practiced it meant operations without limit, which is what he did for four years without codifying its principles. He did so only long after defeat.[17] But how clear was he on it all in his own mind at the time?

In many ways, the vaunted German General Staff system began to work against itself as the Great War progressed. Herbert Rosinski noted the tendency in the German army throughout the war for commanders to become marginalized, as the chiefs of staff and the General Staff officers in the subordinate units gained more real power through their own network. The commanders, on the other hand, tended to be far better in touch with actual conditions among their own troops. Thus, when the final breakdown came in the fall of 1918, Ludendorff and OHL were caught by surprise.[18] Ludendorff himself was one of the worst offenders, routinely interfering directly in the business of the armies over the heads of the army group commanders—usually in response to some communication from a junior General Staff officer down in the units. By 1918 many of the staff officers at OHL and the subordinate headquarters were complaining that Ludendorff combined total strategic indecision with endless interference over minor tactical details.[19]

Ludendorff's first wife, Margarethe, perhaps understood this brilliant but deeply flawed and haunted man best. Writing in 1929 she said, "Ludendorff never possessed any knowledge of human nature, otherwise he could never have been at the mercy of those influences which brought about his downfall."[20]

FOCH

Running southwest from the Arc de Triomphe, Avenue Foch is one of the grandest streets in Paris. Most French towns of any size have a street or a square named for the marshal, and Foch Streets are not uncommon in towns across the United States and the United Kingdom. Ferdinand Foch today is arguably the most honored of the Great War's senior commanders, although historians outside of France have long continued to debate and question his actual contribution to the Allied victory in 1918.

In 1919 Foch was made a British field marshal, an honor almost never accorded to a non-British subject who was not the head of state of a friendly nation. In his 21 December 1918 dispatch, his second-to-the-last to the British government, Haig wrote, "I should like to pay my tribute to the foresight and determination of the French Marshal [Foch] in whose hands the coordination of the action of the Allied Armies was placed."[21] Yet, not more than three weeks earlier Haig had refused to ride in the same carriage with Foch in a victory parade in London. Considering it an intentional snub from Prime Minister David Lloyd George, Haig bitterly wrote in his diary, "Now, the British Army has won the war in France in spite of LG, and I have no intention of taking part in any triumphal ride with Foch and a pack of foreigners through the streets of London, merely to add to LG's importance and help him win his election campaign."[22]

Foch, meanwhile, was engaged in his own internal political squabbles. Like Haig and Lloyd George, the feud between Foch and French prime minister Georges Clemenceau continued well into the postwar years, although it did not become quite as vitriolic. Also like Haig, Foch had no real political ambitions. In 1920, he declined Raymond Poincaré's suggestion that he stand for president of France when the latter's term expired that year.

Foch's wartime memoirs were published in 1931, two years after his death. The English edition was published that same year, translated by Colonel T. Bentley Mott, who had been Pershing's chief liaison officer at Foch's headquarters. The English version was generally not well received. Restrained and discrete, the memoirs sparingly mention persons by name. Foch instead refers more often to an individual by his functional position—such as the general commanding such-and-such corps. Yet, like most memoirs, the book is as interesting for what Foch omits as for what he says. One example is the organization of the book into two major sections: the first covers the period from July 1914 to April 1915; the second, from March 1918 through the end of the war. A forty-page preface to the second part, written by unidentified "military associates" of the marshal, summarizes the two-year gap in Foch's own writings, the period during which he was in internal exile, away from the center of the action. Foch also tended to understate his clashes with Pershing on the amalgamation controversy. Commenting on that issue shortly before his death, Foch rather disingenuously wrote, "None more than myself was convinced of the truth that a troop never fights better than under the folds of its own flags."[23] Undoubtedly, he believed that by the end of the war, but he did not start out thinking along those lines.

As the Allied supreme commander, Foch was the prototype, although not actually the model, for General Dwight D. Eisenhower in World War II. There were significant differences between the two command structures, and the World War II system was based in large part on the lessons learned from World War I. Eisenhower's Supreme Headquarters Allied Expeditionary Forces was a large (12,000 authorized strength), binational, and completely integrated staff, with liaison elements from the non-English-speaking allies. In contrast, Foch's very small staff consisted exclusively of French officers, with equally small liaison elements from the French, British, and Belgians. During World War II the British and Americans had adequate time to assemble and train an integrated staff, well before the landings in Normandy in June 1944. Not so Foch in late March 1918—he was forced to assemble his staff almost overnight, and in the middle of a major battle. And since neither Foch nor his chief of staff, General Maxime Weygand, spoke English, they had go with what they could pull together on the spot. Nor did the operations tempo of the remaining eight months of the war allow any time to build a more unified structure.[24]

Foch's actual command authority was nebulously defined, and in the end it was what he made of it through trial and error and the not-inconsiderable force of his personality. He could argue, cajole, and persuade, but he could not issue direct orders, except to the French army commanders. Eisenhower, on the other hand, had that authority from the start. But even then, Eisenhower had to deal with conflicts based on nationality and personality. Eisenhower's frictions with British field marshal Bernard Law Montgomery were similar to those of Foch's with Pershing, and within their own respective armies Eisenhower and General George S. Patton clashed almost as much as did Foch and Pétain.[25]

Elizabeth Greenhalgh is right when she argues that outside of France today, Foch does not get the credit he deserves. His tactical concepts never did catch up to the battlefield realities of the Great War, but by 1918 he was not a tactical-level commander. Any direct comparison with Eisenhower is unfair to Foch because of the vast differences in the scope and powers of the supreme commands and the nature of coalition warfare in both wars. Nonetheless, Foch's accomplishments as Allied supreme commander were significant, Greenhalgh points out several:

1. He made the right things happen.
2. He made Pétain and Haig coordinate in March 1918.
3. He never abandoned the principle of a contiguous British-French front.
4. He made the crucial decision to launch the counteroffensive on 18 July.
5. His 24 July 1918 directive to Haig, Pétain, and Pershing established the operational blueprint for the final Allied General Offensive.
6. He was always careful to husband a strategic reserve, he pushed the Allied governments to provide the necessary forces, and he used his own reserve as sparingly as possible, while simultaneously never losing sight of the German reserves.
7. He maintained a laser-like focus on the lines of communications, understanding that he first had to free the Allied lines and then attack the German lines of communication.[26]

From 18 July to the end of the war, Hindenburg and Ludendorff were forced to react to him, rather than the other way around. Greenhalgh does concede that Foch was lucky that by 1918 the Allies had both the technology and the resources necessary to achieve victory. But without the will and the strategic vision to seize the initiative at the decisive point, neither the technological nor the manpower superiority would have delivered victory in 1918, or possibly not even a year later.[27] Perhaps his old friend and sometimes critic Sir Henry Wilson summed up the generalissimo best when after the war he wrote, "Foch possesses qualities which are not possessed by any other soldier I have ever met. . . . He jumps over hills and valleys, but he always lands in the right place."[28]

PÉTAIN

Up until 1945, many French towns had streets named for Pétain. But his role as the chief of state of the Vichy government changed all that. Most of the streets were renamed following his trial and conviction for treason. Some smaller towns, however, held out for a very long time. The last was the small village of Belrain, close to Verdun, which finally changed the name of its Rue du Maréchal-Pétain in 2013. Curiously, some dozen towns in America, a few in Canada, and one in China still have Pétain Streets or Pétain Avenues.

History is still struggling to come to grips with the general who rescued his country from the brink of disaster twice and then was convicted of treason some thirty years later. Although dozens upon dozens of books have been written about Pétain, he alone among the six warlords of 1918 never wrote his memoirs or left a comprehensive war diary. His only book, *La bataille de Verdun*, appeared in 1929 but was never published in English. What exists of Pétain's papers are scattered. Some are in the French Military Archives at Vincennes, and some of his correspondence with other people is held by the Bibliothèque Nationale. It is hard to avoid the conclusion that the shadow of Vichy is the primary reason that there has never been a scholarly effort to compile and edit Pétain's papers.

Pétain far more than the other five continued to serve as a central figure in his country's national defense establishment for a long period following the Great War. In 1920 he became the vice president of the Supreme War Council, and two years later he was appointed inspector general of the French army. In 1924 he went to Morocco to assume command of the Rif Campaign. As France's preeminent proponent of defensive warfare, he was a major influence on the French army's adoption of a defensive tactical and strategic posture. He was a key supporter of the Maginot Line, but he also understood what military barriers can and cannot do. Writing in his book about Verdun, he said, "A fortification alone is not enough to check the enemy, but it greatly increases the resisting strength of troops who know how to use it."[29] The French generals of 1940 did not know how to use the Maginot Line. Pétain would have.

Pétain retired from active military service in 1931, at the age of seventy-five, but he continued to serve as a member of the Conseil Supérieur de la Guerre. For a ten-month period in 1934 he was minister of war. The French government tried to recall him to that post when World War II started in September 1939, but he declined. When Germany invaded France in May 1940, Premier Paul Reynaud brought the eighty-four-year-old marshal into the cabinet as deputy premier. France surrendered to Germany the following month, and Pétain, assuming the powers of chief of state, formed a new government based in the small town of Vichy, in the then-unoccupied sector of France.

Pétain was never a strong republican, and he always had far-right-wing leanings. He was convinced that the French Third Republic had collapsed from internal moral rot, and his new regime attempted to replace the traditional republican principles of "liberty, equality, and fraternity" with the conservative values of "work, family, and nation." Believing that he was saving his country from total destruction at the hands of the Nazis, Pétain agreed to collaborate with Germany, although Vichy France never declared itself to be an official military ally.

Pétain opposed the French Resistance movements, and he denounced as a hostile invasion the Allied Normandy landings in June 1944. As early as 1940 he declared Brigadier General Charles de Gaulle a traitor and sentenced him to death in absentia. A deep rift already had existed between Pétain and de Gaulle since 1925. As a young major assigned to the marshal's staff, de Gaulle was tasked with writing a history of the French army. They fell out when de Gaulle refused to make certain changes that Pétain demanded. After commuting Pétain's own death sentence in late 1945, de Gaulle quite accurately commented on his onetime mentor: "The facts cited, the testimonies given . . . made it clear that his had been a drama of a [senile man] lacking the strength necessary to lead men and control events."[30]

Writing in the later 1920s, Basil Liddell Hart noted that rather than being a commander of excess caution, Pétain was a commander who was extremely careful with lives: "While the motto of a brilliant fighting leader like Mangin was 'victory at any price,' Pétain's motto was 'victory at the smallest price.'"[31] As Alistair Horne wrote, "Pétain may not have had any original concepts on how the Great War should have been fought, but he understood better than either his colleagues or his opponents how it should *not* have been fought."[32] Actually,

Horne's assessment is somewhat parsimonious. Pétain's complete overhaul of French army tactics came a little after Ludendorff's initiatives, but they both drove that process in their respective armies from the top down. In the BEF under Haig and the AEF under Pershing, most tactical innovation trickled from the bottom up. History will never overlook Pétain's sad role in Vichy, but it may someday come to give greater weight to his role during the Great War.

PERSHING

There are literally hundreds of Pershing Streets in the United States. There are none in the United Kingdom, and the only one of any significance in France is the Rue du Général Pershing in Versailles. Pershing Park, in Washington, DC, is the site of America's new National World War I Memorial, planned for dedication in 2018.

In September 1919 Pershing was promoted to the rank of general of the armies, a unique rank specially created to honor him. He had been a full (four-star) general since October 1917. He continued to wear only four stars, but gold ones rather than the silver stars worn by all other general officers. When the rank of general of the army was created in late 1944, its insignia consisted of five silver stars, although it was recognized as being subordinate to Pershing's rank of general of the armies. No other U.S. Army officer held that rank until 1978, when George Washington was promoted posthumously to general of the armies, with an effective date of rank of 4 July 1776.

Like his wartime comrade Pétain, Pershing continued to play a significant role in his country's defense establishment in the years immediately following 1918. Pershing became chief of staff of the U.S. Army in 1921, and he immediately moved to solidify the position as the top of the chain of command—although during 1917 and 1918 he vigorously resisted General Peyton March's claim to just such authority. Pershing also completely revamped the U.S. Army's staff structure at all echelons, adopting the system the AEF had used in France, which Pershing originally had adopted from the French: G-1, personnel; G-2, intelligence; G-3, operations; G-4, logistics. When Pershing retired from active duty in 1924, he assumed the chairmanship of the American Battle Monuments Commission, responsible for the administration and maintenance of all of America's military cemeteries outside of the United States. Pershing held that position until his death in 1948.

As early as mid-1918, many suspected Pershing of having presidential aspirations. There was a movement to draft him during the 1920 election campaign,

and although he refused to campaign, he let it be known that he would not decline to serve if that proved to be the will of the American people. The movement, however, came to nothing, and Warren G. Harding succeeded Woodrow Wilson as president.

Pershing published his war memoirs, *My Experiences in the World War*, in
1931. It sold poorly. Inexplicably, the book was awarded the Pulitzer Prize,
despite a poor critical reception. Writing in the *American Historical Review*,
historian T. H. Thomas called the book "in every way disappointing," citing
its poor arrangement of subject matter, lack of adequate transitions between
topics within chapters, and excessive reliance on "swift generalizations, omis-
sions, sweeping claims, [and] well-rounded covering statements."[33] The book
also reopened many old wartime wounds. Peyton March was outraged by
Pershing's "damning with faint praise" treatment of his performance as army
chief of staff. The Pershing–March feud continued through World War II,
where many of the U.S. Army's senior-most generals still considered themselves "Pershing men" (for example, George Marshall) or "March men" (such
as Douglas MacArthur).

The overriding thrust of Pershing's memoirs was the validation of the claim
he made in his 19 November 1918 preliminary report to the secretary of the
army that the AEF under his command "had developed into a powerful and
smooth-running machine."[34] It was a claim largely unquestioned in America
for many years, until historians during the latter decades of the twentieth century began to examine it more critically, including Donald Smythe in *Pershing: General of the Armies*; David Trask in *The AEF and Coalition Warmaking,
1917–1918*; Robert Ferrell in *America's Deadliest Battle: Meuse Argonne, 1918*;
Edward Lengel in *To Conquer Hell: The Meuse-Argonne, 1918*; Mark Grotelueschen in *The AEF Way of War: The American Army and Combat in World War I*;
and Douglas Mastriano in *Thunder in the Argonne: A new History of America's
Greatest Battle*.

Pershing continued to insist that he was right and all the rest of the Allied leaders were wrong about the innate superiority of open warfare, rifle
marksmanship and the bayonet, "self-reliant" infantry, and of course vigorous
American manhood. As he wrote without a single shred of evidence to support it, "Ultimately, we had the satisfaction of hearing the French admit that
we were right, both in emphasizing training for open warfare and on insisting
on proficiency in the use of the rifle."[35]

By the end of the war many of Pershing's subordinate commanders and staff officers remained true believers in the Pershing doctrine, but some had come to understand that such thinking was the echo of the past rather than the wave of the future. Two of the AEF's divisional commanders who were the best practitioners of what is today called combined arms warfare were Major General Charles P. Summerall of the 1st Division and Marine major general John A. Lejeune of the 2nd Division. In fighting their divisions, they were able to get away with significant departures from the Pershing doctrine because they were successful on the battlefield.

Meeting in Europe immediately after the cessation of hostilities, the task of the AEF Superior Board on Organization and Tactics was to compile the lessons learned from the war. The members of the board were torn between support for the old dogma of the rifle and bayonet and recognition of the reality of massive firepower. Their final report, issued in 1920, tried to strike a middle ground by recommending increases of machine guns, automatic rifles, and mortars in the infantry units and even putting "auxiliary weapons," such as light guns and tanks, directly into the hands of the infantry commanders. Pershing was not pleased with the results. When he forwarded the report to the secretary of war, he attached his own criticism that the board's findings were too influenced by the experiences of stabilized warfare in Western Europe and should have focused instead on "the requirements of warfare of the character and the theater upon which we are most likely to be engaged."[36]

Despite his shortcomings, there most likely never would have been an AEF on the European battlefields of 1918 without "Black Jack" Pershing. He was a brilliant and tireless organizer who knew how to make things happen and had a talent for overcoming seemingly insurmountable obstacles. Nonetheless, his prejudices against modern weapons and his lack of understanding of firepower meant that his AEF units were trained and equipped inadequately for the war they had to fight. He was, however, right when he continued to insist that the AEF needed proper supply, transportation, medical, engineer, maintenance, and other support forces, as opposed to just the masses of infantrymen the Allies wanted to see arriving by the boatload. Pershing also was right in the amalgamation controversy with the Allies, but only to a point. The idea of putting American soldiers into French and British units as individual fillers was absurd, a demand the Allies made in desperation. At the higher echelons such as brigade or division, however, there was a great deal to be said for

American units training and operating with the Allies. General Tasker Bliss always thought that Pershing could have shown more flexibility at that level. And despite Pershing's general intransigence, a number of American divisions did wind up fighting and fighting well under French and British corps and field armies.

Pershing lived long enough to see his U.S. Army fighting on World War II battlefields that were far different from what he apparently had in mind when in 1920 he wrote his caveat to the AEF Superior Board report. The 1939–45 war was one in which the domination of mechanization and firepower went to far greater levels than in the war that ended a little more than twenty years earlier. Machine warfare was here to stay. Pershing also lived long enough to see the man he once called the greatest general of the war lead his country as a collaborationist vassal of the Germany they both had fought so hard to defeat in 1918. One can only wonder what the general of the armies thought about that in his final years.

HAIG

Despite the controversy that has surrounded Sir Douglas Haig for most of the last century, there remain today many streets named for the commander in chief of the World War I BEF. They exist not only in England and Scotland but also in Canada and the United States. There also is an Avenue du Maréchal Douglas Haig in Versailles, France. At least three equestrian statues of Haig exist: one in Montreuil, France (the location of BEF GHQ in 1916); one at Whitehall in London; and one at Edinburgh Castle. The two in the United Kingdom remain controversial. The one in Edinburgh originally stood in a prominent position on the esplanade outside the castle walls. In 2009 it was moved inside the walls, and even then not to the main courtyard. To this day there continue to be outraged demands to remove the statute in Whitehall, calling any honor of Haig an insult to Britain's dead of the Great War. Haig's record as BEF commander is certainly open to criticism on many levels, but does he really deserve this amount of opprobrium?

Haig was seen much differently during the first decade following the end of the Great War. In December 1918 he was welcomed back to London by cheering crowds. When offered a peerage, he refused to accept until Parliament passed pensions for disabled soldiers.[37] Declining another military command, he retired from the army and was instrumental in establishing the Royal British Legion, serving as its first president. His tireless work on behalf of British veterans only increased his popularity as a national hero. His premature death in 1928 triggered a wave of national mourning. Despite his modest final resting place, he was given a state funeral, and both Foch and Pétain were among his pallbearers.[38] But then things changed rapidly.

Following the war, the bitterness of the Haig–Lloyd George feud only got worse. Lloyd George fell from power as prime minister in 1922, in part over a scandal in which he was accused of selling honors, knighthoods, and peerages to wealthy businessmen in return for political contributions.[39] He nonetheless remained in Parliament and was the leader of the Liberal Party from 1926 to 1931. Haig's reputation started to plummet when Lloyd George began writing his own war memoirs in 1931; they were published in six volumes between 1933 and 1936. As Andrew Suttie has argued in his important 2005 book, *Rewriting the First World War: Lloyd George, Politics, and Strategy, 1914–18*, the former prime minister wanted to refurbish his reputation and refute the accusations made against him in the many already published memoirs by the war's military and political leaders that as secretary of state for war and then as prime minister he had been a mere dilettante, fiddling and interfering in strategic and military matters he did not understand and generally confounding the war effort.[40]

Although he held almost all British generals in contempt, Lloyd George's two special targets were Haig and Sir William Robertson, whom he accused of criminal incompetence that resulted in the needless slaughter of thousands of fine British soldiers on the fields of Flanders in 1917 while bringing the Allies no closer to victory. Lloyd George's discussion of the final "Hundred Days" gave all the credit to Foch while continuing to heap scorn on Haig. According to the former prime minister, Haig had been merely "fulfilling a role for which he was admirably adapted: that of a second-in-command to a strategist of unchallenged genius."[41] Although he was the head of the British government and ultimately responsible for the direction of the war effort, Lloyd George steadfastly refused to accept any direct personal responsibility for the tragic events at the Somme, Passchendaele, or British setbacks in March and April 1918.[42] In more contemporary terms, that would be the same thing as placing the entire blame for Vietnam on General William Westmoreland while letting President Lyndon Johnson and Secretary of Defense Robert McNamara completely off the hook.

Lloyd George's principal military adviser for his memoirs was the military historian Basil H. Liddell Hart, who by the early 1930s had become one of the most outspoken critics of British generalship in the Great War. But as Suttie has pointed out, Liddell Hart's ideas on the war had changed drastically during the previous fifteen years. In September 1916, Liddell Hart wrote that Haig was "the greatest general Britain had ever owned" and that Britain during the war had produced "fully a hundred first-rate generals."[43]

Many contemporary critics were not taken in by Lloyd George's war memoirs. A 27 September 1934 review in the *Times Literary Supplement* charged that Lloyd George's aim was self-vindication, achieved by blackening the reputations of his wartime colleagues who disagreed with his views.[44] A 7 September 1933 review in the *Morning Post* was even more blunt: "The reader is taught to conclude that if Mr. Lloyd George could only have been Captain-General of the Forces, Lord High Admiral of the Fleet, and absolute dictator in Downing Street, everything would have gone much better, because all the tragic blunders that prolonged the struggle were due to a perverse refusal to follow his advice."[45] Nonetheless, the *War Memoirs of David Lloyd George* struck into a deep vein of loss and anguish in the United Kingdom and claimed to focus a laser beam on the cause of it all. The pendulum of Haig's reputation swung from being a national hero and one of Britain's greatest generals to the opposite extreme of being the "butcher-and-bungler-in-chief."

To many, the portrait that Lloyd George painted of Haig remains vivid to this day. The 1960s play and subsequent movie *Oh What a Lovely War* faithfully reproduced the Douglas Haig of Lloyd George's memoirs. One particular passage in act 2 resurrects the argument of the peripheral front strategy:

> BRITISH GENERAL: Permission to speak, sir? I have been wondering, or rather the staff and I have been wondering, perhaps this policy of attrition might be a mistake. After all, it's wearing us down more than it is them. Couldn't we try a policy of manoeuvre on other fronts?
>
> HAIG: Nonsense. The Western Front is the only real front. We must grind them down. You see, our population is greater than theirs, and their losses are greater than ours.[46]

Except for a brief mention in passing, the head of the British government, Lloyd George himself, escapes criticism in the play, despite the fact that by starving the BEF of reinforcements in early 1918 he almost brought about its defeat in March and April. For all of its Monty Pythonesque biting satire, the play recycles the stereotypes, distortions, oversimplifications, and half-truths that continue to shape the image of the Great War held by far too many. The play really says more about popular attitudes about war in the 1960s than it does about 1914–18.

Haig's own writings about the war contain much self-justification. As Elizabeth Greenhalgh and others have pointed out, there is some evidence that Haig enhanced his own role in Foch's appointment on 26 March 1918.[47] Haig never published memoirs, but he kept by hand what grew to be a massive personal war diary. After the war he and his wife, Lady Dorothy Haig, produced a typewritten version, which with the addition of various official papers and memoranda came out to thirty-eight volumes. The National Library of Scotland has a copy of both the typed and the manuscript versions. The British National Archives has only the typed version. In 1952 *The Private Papers of Douglas Haig 1914–1919*, edited by Robert Blake, was published based on selected entries from the typed version. In 2005 *Douglas Haig: War Diaries and Letters, 1914–1918*, edited by Gary Sheffield and John Bourne, was published based on the original manuscript version. As Sheffield and Bourne note in their introduction, "The Ms diary is inevitably less well polished than the Ts diary, but what is lost in stylistic elegance is gained in accuracy, immediacy and authenticity."[48] The editors do indicate in footnotes any significant additions and differences between the two versions.

Earlier, *Dispatches: General Douglas Haig's Official Reports to the British Government* was published in 1919. The dispatches are full of tactical details, but he generally avoids direct mention of British casualties. In his final dispatch of 21 March 1919, Haig claimed for the BEF the decisive role in the final defeat of Germany. Writing about the "Hundred Days" he said, "In the decisive contests of this period, the strongest and most vital parts of the enemy's front were attacked by the British, his lateral communications were cut, and his best divisions fought to a standstill." He continued, "These results were achieved by 59 fighting British divisions, which in the course of three months of battle engaged and defeated 99 separate German divisions."[49] As previously noted, he failed to mention the American divisions that fought, and fought well, under his command, and he also included the four Canadian, five Australian, and one New Zealand divisions as "British divisions."

Like Pershing's writings, there is a strong element of tactical and operational self-justification in Haig's. While Pershing never stopped claiming that his ideas about open warfare and self-reliant infantry were right, Haig argued that the attritional campaigns of 1916 and 1917, what he called the "wearing-out battle," were the essential foundation for the successes of 1918:

The rapid collapse of Germany's military powers in the latter half of 1918 was the logical outcome of the fighting of the two previous years. It would not have taken place but for the period of ceaseless attrition which used up the reserves of the German armies, while the constant and growing pressure of the blockade sapped with more deadly insistence from year to year the strength and resolution of the German people. It is in the great battles of 1916 and 1917 that we have to seek the secret of our victory in 1918.[50]

Unquestionably, the Germans were weaker at the start of 1918 than they had been at any point in the war so far, but they still had plenty of fight left in them. Haig still has much to answer for in those attritional battles, especially Third Ypres, which culminated in the mud-drenched inferno of Passchendaele. Haig's few staunch supporters over the years have never been able to offer a reasonable defense for his attempt to achieve an operational breakthrough in 1917, when the same operational objective using the same tactics had failed so miserably on the Somme the previous year.

Many of Haig's criticisms of Pershing were unfair. Both the AEF and the BEF and their respective senior-level commanders went through much the same learning and evolutionary processes. The Americans, however, started almost three years after the British. By the end of 1918 they had not evolved as far, because the AEF was effectively in the war for only a quarter as long as the BEF. Pershing in 1918 committed his infantry much as the French did in 1915 and the British in 1916. Haig, however, was quite on solid ground in his criticisms of Pershing's obstinate rejection of the Allies' hard-learned battlefield lessons acquired over three years.

In his final dispatch, Haig defended the length of the war based on the long time that the BEF required to build up from six divisions to sixty trained, experienced, and equipped divisions: "The high-water mark of our fighting strength in infantry was only reached after two years of conflict, by which time heavy casualties had already been incurred."[51] Yet the Americans had a similar but even greater problem, because when they entered the war in April 1917 they had only a single division, and even that existed primarily on paper. And unlike the French and the Germans, both the British and Americans started the war with very few trained staff officers and were forced to develop their higher-level operational staffs through actual experience in the brutal and unforgiving school of combat. Finally, Haig could have been a little more understanding of Pershing on the amalgamation issue. When Haig assumed command of the BEF at the end of 1915, his instructions from Lord Herbert

Kitchener read, "I wish you distinctly to understand that your command is an independent one, and that you will in no case come under the orders of any Allied general further than the necessary cooperation with our Allies above referred to."[52] That is almost exactly what Secretary of War Baker told Pershing on 26 May 1917.

Haig and Robertson were right in the strategic debate between the Westerners and the Easterners. Especially after Russia dropped out of the war, the only place where the British and the French could defeat the Germans was on the Western Front. On the other hand, the war could not be fought there exclusively. The broader strategic imperatives of an empire fighting a global war required the defense of essential assets and economy of force operations in peripheral theaters. Haig's command was solely on the Western Front. He had the luxury of not being responsible for the overall global war, and as a result he frequently failed to recognize the importance and the interdependence of the other fronts.

Some of the way the BEF fought the Great War was beyond Haig's control. Perhaps the key factor was the social structure and internal institutions of the post-Edwardian British army. As discussed in Chapter 4, the British army, unlike the German army, had at the start of the war no formal system of capturing and analyzing lessons learned and modifying doctrine accordingly. The British officer corps regarded disagreement as something akin to disloyalty. Thus, through 1917 Haig was ill served by some of the most important members of his own staff. Nonetheless, a great deal of that was still his own fault. As Gary Sheffield has pointed out, one of Haig's most serious shortcomings as a commander was his tendency to believe what he wanted to believe about the Germans. His chief of intelligence, Brigadier General John Charteris, did his commander a grave disservice by constantly telling him the happy news that the Germans were on the verge of collapsing. We see much the same thing a little more than thirty years later when General Douglas MacArthur's intelligence chief, Major General Charles Willoughby, continually told his boss that there was no major threat of the Chinese intervening in Korea. Haig's first chief of staff, Lieutenant General Sir Launcelot Edward Kiggell, was also a major voice in the echo chamber at BEF GHQ. Kiggell consistently failed to stand up to Haig, who in any event had little appreciation of the concept of the loyal opposition.[53] Haig could not have tolerated working with an assertive chief of staff on the German model, such as a Lossberg or a Seeckt.

When Lloyd George exerted his political authority to have Charteris and Kiggell sacked in January 1917, he actually did Haig a great favor. Haig's new chief of staff, Lieutenant General Sir Herbert Lawrence, was a significant improvement and a definite influence on Haig's generalship in 1918—even though Lawrence was something of a Francophobe, who in the latter part of 1918 complained that the BEF was doing all the fighting and the French were doing nothing.

There can be little doubt that the key to the final Allied success was the difficult but ultimately effective partnership between Haig and Foch. The two met some sixty times between April and November 1918.[54] Regardless of any possible self-exaggeration of his role on 26 March, Haig's uncompromising support was essential to Foch's appointment to coordinate the Allied response to Operation MICHAEL and then to his final official designation as Allied supreme commander. Haig too was the first to see that the war could be ended in 1918, and he convinced Foch that the AEF's main effort should be toward Mézières, turning the Allied General Offensive into a gigantic, sequential, and converging pincer attack.

Assessments of Haig have been changing slowly over the last thirty years, but British historians are still split. As Gary Sheffield has noted, many historians have yet to break out completely from the prison that Lloyd George constructed with the help of Liddell Hart. Between the 1950s and the 1990s, British historian John Terraine was virtually Haig's only defender, arguing that there was no shortcut to victory on the Western Front and that Haig was a "Great Captain, fit to stand alongside Marlborough and Wellington."[55]

Historian Tim Travers remains a Haig critic, arguing that he was largely irrelevant to the final victory, because by the Hundred Days his power had been constrained significantly by the appointment of Foch as generalissimo and of Sir Henry Wilson as chief of the Imperial General Staff. "Haig did not really contribute to strategy in mid- to late-1918, apart from refusing to follow some of Foch's more foolishly conceived aggressive plans, such as the desire to keep attacking after 14 August," Travers contends.[56]

There have been definite indicators over the last twenty years that Haig's military reputation is recovering. In 2008 J. P. Harris wrote of Haig during the Hundred Days, "He commanded the most combat effective of the Allied Armies at this period in the war and there were few, if any, others who had the authority and determination to use the instrument with such vigor."[57] And as Major General Mungo Melvin, the past president of the British Commission on Military History, recently wrote, "According to the audience at a National Army Museum celebrity speaker event on 9 April 2011, the joint winners of the accolade of 'Britain's Greatest General' were the Duke of Wellington and Field Marshal Sir William Slim. Rather surprisingly, however, the runner-up was Haig, rather than Montgomery, as might otherwise be expected."[58] Haig's pendulum is still in motion.

IF NOT . . . THEN WHO?

These, then, were the six general officers who for better or worse shaped the way the last year of the Great War played out on the battlefields of the Western Front. None of them will ever go down in history as "Great Captains." But then, it is doubtful that we ever again will see a great captain in the mold of Scipio Africanus or Marlborough. Modern warfare has become far too complex for a single commander to grasp all the reins. It is not that the nature of warfare has changed, as so many of today's pundits are fond of telling us. It has not changed. It is still as Carl von Clausewitz defined it, an act of force to compel an enemy to our will. It is still a brutal, savage, and bloody business that consists of killing people and destroying things, or creditably threatening to do so. What has changed, as discussed in Chapter 2, are the mechanics, the speed, the destructiveness, and the lethality of warfare, and with them the second- and third-order effects for the world at large. Those changes have continued unabated and at an ever-increasing pace since 1918.

None of the Big Six of 1918 was equally skilled at both the tactical and operational levels. Any such general is an extreme rarity, indeed. Were there other general officers of the Great War who could have done better, or at least as well? Any answer to such a question can be only pure speculation. There is no way to predict how a commander will perform in combat, no matter how sterling his background before the shooting starts. Who in 1861 would have thought that an obscure captain of volunteers with a drinking problem named Ulysses S. Grant would shortly become one of America's greatest battlefield generals? Nonetheless, there are some intriguing "what ifs" among the generals of the Great War.

The Germans had the widest range of possible options. After all, Hindenburg and Ludendorff lost. Other German generals by 1918 might not have been able to deliver battlefield victory, but they might have managed a less catastrophic defeat. They also might have been able to stay better focused on managing the fight on the battlefield rather than on meddling in diplomacy, internal politics, and the economy. Although by 1918 Hindenburg had become almost irreplaceable as Germany's father figure, there were other generals who could have been at least as effective as the chief of the General Staff of the German Field Army. Crown Prince Wilhelm certainly was not one of them. Crown Prince Rupprecht of Bavaria had the experience and the skill, but for internal political reasons only a Prussian officer could have filled Hindenburg's slot. Field Marshal August von Mackensen was arguably Germany's best field commander of the war. He is little remembered today because he fought almost the entire war on the Eastern Front, but his reputation and stature within the German army were unimpeachable. Furthermore, he and his chief of staff, the brilliant Major General Hans von Seeckt, made up another of history's great commander/chief teams. They, in fact, worked together more effectively than The Duo.

There were other potential substitutes for Ludendorff. Seeckt, Hermann von Kuhl, Fritz von Lossberg, and Max Hoffmann come immediately to mind, and Wilhelm Groener did replace Ludendorff to pick up the pieces at the end. Kuhl, who had a doctorate in history, was one of the intellectual leading lights of the General Staff, and as noted in Chapter 13, Ludendorff actually recommended him as his replacement. After the war Kuhl, along with the distinguished military historian Hans Delbrück, was appointed by the Reichstag to write a study of the German military collapse in 1918. Georg Wetzell, who became Ludendorff's chief whipping boy at OHL, had his own rather definite thoughts on the matter. In a July 1919 letter to Seeckt, Wetzell speculated that Ludendorff might have been talked into a more logical and rational approach if only Seeckt had been at OHL.[59]

There were not many alternatives to Foch or Pétain. At the start of the war General Joseph Gallieni was one of France's most distinguished retired soldiers. Recalled to active duty in 1914 as military governor of Paris, he played a key role—arguably *the* key role—in the French victory at the Marne. Gallieni then became French secretary of war and a critic of General Joseph Joffre, his onetime subordinate, for the latter's handling of Verdun. Had he not been in poor health and died in 1916, Gallieni quite likely would have become Joffre's successor. He almost certainly would have performed better than Robert Nivelle, but then Pétain might never have come to power. Charles Mangin was France's best fighting general, but he was too rough-edged and controversial for the highest levels of command. He was France's Patton. Notorious for his disregard for casualties, Mangin's nickname was "The Butcher." General

Marie Émile Fayolle was Pétain's best army group commander in 1918. He might have been able to replace Pétain as an operational commander that year, but could he have rescued the French army from the mutinies of 1917? Could anyone other than Pétain have done so? Foch and Pétain were the two right generals in the right positions at the right time.

As previously noted, there never would have been an AEF on the 1918 battlefield without Pershing, despite his lack of understanding of the war's tactical realties and his blind refusal to learn anything from the Allies. As a former U.S. Army chief of staff, Tasker Bliss had the necessary stature and experience to lead the AEF, but did he have the energy and drive to create it almost out of thin air? Peyton March, the U.S. Army chief of staff from May 1918 on, was irreplaceable in that position. Despite the bitter animosity between the two, the AEF owed almost as much to March's "push" as it did to Pershing's "pull." Unfortunately, Pershing was a mediocre battlefield commander at best, and his decision to attempt to command both the AEF and the U.S. First Army simultaneously was a grave error. When Hunter Liggett took command of the First Army for the final phase of the Meuse-Argonne battle, the Americans started making far better use of combined arms, and especially firepower carefully integrated with infantry maneuver. Liggett had none of Pershing's blind prejudice against the Allies' experience. As Liggett later wrote of his early activities upon arriving in France in 1917, "When we had paid our visits to [the French] corps and division commanders, we enrolled as students and went at the job of learning all we could."[60]

If Lloyd George really believed that Haig was such an incompetent bungler, then why did the prime minister not fulfill his constitutional responsibility by replacing him? If, as Lloyd George later claimed, he was forced to conclude that by early 1918 there was no alternative to Haig, then did not the head of the British government have a moral as well as a constitutional responsibility to support his senior field commander rather than work constantly to undermine him?

A more intriguing question is whether Haig was the best possible replacement in late 1915 as commander of the BEF. As J. P. Harris has written, "Haig almost certainly was not the most suitable officer in the British Army to take over from Sir John French as commander-in-chief in December 1915. Robertson, despite his lack of command experience, might have done better."[61] Secretary of War Sir Herbert Kitchener initially intended to make Robertson the BEF commander. But despite his widely acknowledged competence and strategic insight, "Wully" faced a significant social barrier that he never quite overcame. He was a "ranker," an officer who had worked his way up the ladder from private, and all his life he spoke with a slightly Cockney accent and had a tendency to drop his "haches." Chief of the Imperial General Staff, which had no direct command authority, was one thing. But direct command in the field over senior generals of a much different social background would have been almost impossible in an army still very much rooted in the late Victorian and Edwardian eras. Besides, by 1918 Robertson had supported Haig from the War Office for more than two years to the point where he never would have been acceptable to Lloyd George and other members of the government.

The BEF in late 1917 did have some very talented generals. Sir Arthur Currie and Sir John Monash were two of the BEF's best and most innovative corps commanders. But as Dominion officers, Canadian and Australian respectively, it would have been politically impossible to place them in command of the BEF. Despite the fact that he looked a bit like David Low's famous cartoon character Colonel Blimp, Sir Herbert Plumer arguably was the BEF's best field army commander. After Sir John French was sacked in late 1915, the former BEF commander lost no opportunity to intrigue against Haig, at one point suggesting that he be replaced by Plumer. Quite possibly Plumer could have been the one to replace Haig, but there is some doubt that Plumer would have wanted the job. Plumer, in fact, had turned down an offer from Lloyd George to succeed Robertson as chief of the Imperial General Staff.[62] General Sir Henry Rawlinson was another of the BEF's more competent field army commanders; but by the last year of the war he was carrying too much personal baggage to assume command of the BEF. For one thing, he was too closely associated with Haig, and Rawlinson forever will be linked with the 60,000 British casualties suffered on 1 July 1916, the first day of the Battle of the Somme. And much like General Sir Henry Wilson, many of Rawlinson's general officer colleagues considered him an intriguer and were suspicious of his driving ambition. Among his various uncomplimentary nicknames were "The Cad" and "Rawly the Fox."[63]

As one of the war's leading Easterners, Winston Churchill had been among Haig's foremost critics. The future World War II prime minister, however, came to see Haig differently in later years, writing in 1926, "[My] subsequent study of the war has led me to think a good deal better of Haig than I did at the time. It is absolutely certain there was no one who could have taken his place."[64]

BIOGRAPHICAL CHRONOLOGIES

FERDINAND FOCH

1851	Born in Tarbes, Hautes-Pyrénées Department (2 October).
1870–71	Service in 4th Infantry Regiment during Franco-Prussian War; did not see action.
1871	Entered the École Polytechnique.
1873	Commissioned second lieutenant.
1874	Assigned to 4th Artillery Regiment.
1885–87	Student, École Supérieure de la Guerre.
1887	Assigned to the General Staff Operations Bureau.
1895	Instructor, École Supérieure de la Guerre.
1898	Lieutenant colonel, 29th Artillery Regiment.
1903	Colonel; commander, 35th Artillery Regiment.
	Des Principes de la Guerre (*The Principles of War*) published.
1904	*Conduite de Guerre* (*Conduct of War*) published.
1905	Chief of staff, V Army Corps, at Orleans.
1907	General of brigade; commander, V Corps Artillery.
1908	Commandant, École Supérieure de la Guerre.
1911	Commanding general, 13th Division.

1912   General of division; commanding general, VIII Corps.

1913   Commanding general, XX Corps, in Lorraine.

            Foch's son Germain and son-in-law Charles Bècourt both killed
            in action near Joppécourt on the Belgian border (22 August).

            Assumed command of Ninth Army (4 September); led it during
            the Battle of the Marne (5–12 September).

            Designated General Joseph Joffre's deputy to the commander in
            chief (24 September).

            Assumed command of an ad hoc army group on the Allied left
            wing (4 October).

1915   Awarded the Grand Cross of the Order of the Bath by King
            George V personally.

            Given the title commander of the Armies of the North by the
            Allies.

1916   Suffered head injuries in a car crash.

            Commanded French forces supporting the British right flank
            during the Battle of the Somme (July).

            Relieved of command of Northern Army Group and assigned to
            plan potential operations if Germany violated Swiss neutrality
            (27 December).

1917   Awarded Médaille Militaire (20 February).

            Ordered to Italy to coordinate plans for reinforcing the Italians
            against a German-Austrian attack (April).

            Designated chief of the general staff of the French army as part
            of the political and military shake-up following the disastrous
            Nivelle Offensive (17 May).

            General Robert Nivelle replaced as general-in-chief of the French
            Armies of the North and Northeast by Pétain (17 May).

            Personally organized and directed the rapid relief force of eleven
            French and British divisions sent to Italy after the Austro-
            German breakthrough in the Battle of Caporetto (14 October–9
            November).

Rapallo Conference; Foch appointed France's permanent military representative to the newly established Allied Supreme War Council; forced to relinquish chief of staff position (7 November).

Replaced on the Supreme War Council with Maxime Weygand by order of Prime Minister Georges Clemenceau; reassumed position as chief of the French general staff (19 November).

1918   Doullens Conference; Foch given the authority to "coordinate the actions of the Allied Armies on the Western Front" (26 March).

Beauvais Conference; Foch charged with "the strategic direction of military operations" on the Western Front (3 April).

Given the official title of commander in chief of the Allied armies in France (14 April).

Foch's coordinating authority extended to the Italian Front by the Supreme War Council (2 May).

Pétain ordered by the French War Committee to follow Foch's directives without appealing to the French government (26 June).

Promoted to marshal of France, solidifying his position over Pétain (7 August).

Dictated armistice terms to the Germans at Compiègne and oversaw its signing (11 November).

Elected to the Académie Française (11 November).

1919   Boycotted signing of Treaty of Versailles, proclaiming, "This is not peace. It is an armistice for 20 years" (28 June).[1]

Made a British field marshal, the only French officer to have been so honored.

Appointed president of the Conseil Supérieur de la Guerre.

---

1. Neiberg, *Foch*, 101.

1920   Declined President Raymond Poincairé's suggestion that he stand for president of France when Poincaré's term expired that year.

1923   Made a marshal of Poland.

1929   Died in Paris on 20 March and interred at Les Invalides, near Napoleon's tomb.

1931   *Mémoire pour servir à l'histoire de la guerre 1914–1918* published.

   English translation of Foch's memoirs poorly received.

HENRI PHILIPPE PÉTAIN

1856   Born to a farming family at Cauchy-à-la Tour, Pas de Calais (24 April).

   Attended a Jesuit boarding school in St. Omer, then the Dominican school at Arcueil.

1876   Entered French Military Academy at St. Cyr.

1878   Assigned to the 24th Battalion of Light Infantry in Villefranche.

1883   Assigned to 3rd Light Infantry Battalion at Besançon.

1888   Student, École Supérieure de la Guerre.

1900   Instructor, École de Tir (School of Fire) at Châlons-sur-Marne.

   Conflict with his superiors because he emphasized aimed individual fire by infantrymen rather than the prevailing doctrine of high-volume mass firing.

1910   Professor of applied infantry tactics, École Supérieure de la Guerre.

   Challenged the prevailing cult of the offensive in the French army by advocating defensive tactics: *"Le feu tue"* ("Firepower kills").

1911   Instructor of tactics, Cavalry School at Saumur.

   Command of the 33rd Infantry Regiment at Arras.

1913   Command of the 4th Infantry Brigade, 6th Infantry Division.

1914   Upon mobilization promoted to general of brigade (August).

Assumed command of 6th Infantry Division (29 August).

Served as commanding general of 6th Infantry Division during the Battle of the Marne (5–12 September)

Assumed command of XXXIII Corps in Alsace (October).

Awarded Legion of Honor (October).

1915   Promoted to general of division.

Served as commanding general of XXXIII Corps at battle for Vimy Ridge (May).

Awarded Commander of the Legion of Honor (May).

Assumed command of Second Army in Champagne (22 June).

Second Army failed to crack the German defenses-in-depth during the Second Champagne Offensive (15 September–6 October).

1916   In the midst of crisis, assumed command of and then stabilized the defense of Verdun (25 February).

After saving Verdun, "kicked upstairs" to assume command of Army Group Center (1 May).

Joffre relieved as commander of the French army, but Premier Aristide Briand bypasses Pétain in favor of the more charismatic, offensive-minded Nivelle, who promised an end to the war with a great offensive (December).

1917   To save face and avoid having to relieve Nivelle, French political leaders proposed naming Pétain his chief of staff and designated successor; Nivelle agreed, but Petain refused (29 April).

Much of the French army mutinied following failure of Nivelle Offensive.

Pétain replaced Nivelle as general-in-chief of the French Armies of the North and Northeast (17 May).

Foch became chief of the general staff of the French army (17 May).

Pétain methodically and skillfully rebuilt the French army and restored its morale (remainder of 1917).

Awarded Grand Cross of the Legion of Honor (25 August).

1918 Pétain and Foch increasingly clash after Allies at Beauvais Conference gave Foch authority to coordinate the battles on the Western Front (3 April).

Pétain's position vis-à-vis Foch weakened when Clemenceau removed his chief of staff, General François Anthoine, who was an old antagonist of Foch (May).

Clemenceau rejected Pétain's offer to step down to command an army corps (May).

Promoted to marshal of France (8 December).

1920 Vice president, Conseil Supérieur de la Guerre (January).

1922 Appointed inspector general of the French army.

1924 Sent to Morocco to oversee the Rif Campaign.

1925 Charles de Gaulle assigned to Pétain's staff and tasked with writing a history of the French army; they fell out when de Gaulle refused to make changes that Pétain wanted.

1929 Assumed Foch's chair at the Académie Française.

La bataille de Verdun published.

As the French army's elder statesman, Pétain played a major role in encouraging the army to adopt a defensive tactical and strategic posture.

Supporter of the Maginot Line.

1931 Retired from active military service at the age of seventy-five but continued to serve as a member of the Conseil Supérieur de la Guerre.

1934 Minister of war (February–November).

1936 Appointed member of the Permanent Committee for National Defense (June).

1939 Refused to run for president.

Recalled as minister of war; refused (September).

Ambassador to Spain.

1940   Premier Paul Reynaud recalled Pétain from Spain and brought him into the cabinet as deputy premier to strengthen the French defense against the Germans (18 May).

Following the defeat by Germany, Pétain formed a new government in Vichy as chief of state (16 June).

National Assembly voted to give Pétain full political powers (10 July).

Convinced that the Third Republic had collapsed from internal moral rot, he implemented the controversial Vichy regime, which governed France under principles of collaboration with Nazi Germany until the liberation in 1944.

Pétain's right-wing "national revolution" wished to replace the republican principles of "liberty, equality, and fraternity" with the conservative values of "work, family, and nation."

Met with Hitler at Montoire; agreed to collaborate with Germany but not become an official military ally (24 October).

Vichy government passed the Statut des Juifs (Anti-Jewish Laws) (30 October).

Declared Free French leader Charles de Gaulle a traitor and sentenced him to death in absentia (October).

1941   Opposed to the French Resistance, which was overwhelmingly left-wing.

Germans moved into the remainder of unoccupied (Vichy) France (November).

1943   Pierre Leval took the effective reins of day-to-day leadership from Pétain's hands.

1944   Denounced Operation OVERLORD as an invasion.

Removed to Germany by the Gestapo, where he formed a "government-in-exile" (July).

1945   Put on trial in Paris for treason (23 July).

Convicted, but death sentence commuted by de Gaulle because of his prestige from the First World War and his extreme age (15 August).

1951   Died in prison on the Île d'Yeu (23 July).

Buried on the Île d'Yeu, despite several unsuccessful attempts over the years to have the French government allow him to be reburied at Verdun.

SIR DOUGLAS HAIG

1861   Born in Edinburgh (19 June).

1880–83   Studied at Brasenose College, Oxford, but did not graduate.

1884   Graduated from the Royal Military College, Sandhurst.

Passed out first in order of merit of a class of 129 with the Sanson Memorial Sword.

Assigned to the 7th (Queen's Own) Hussars.

1885–93   Served as a cavalry regimental officer, chiefly in India.

1895   Graduated from the Staff College.

1897–98   Served in the Omdurman Campaign.

Squadron commander in the Nile Expedition of 1897.

1899   Served in the Boer War.

Chief of staff to Major General John French, commander of the Cavalry Corps.

1901   Promoted to colonel and assigned command of the 17th Lancers.

Companion of the Order of the Bath (27 September).

1903–6   Inspector general of cavalry in India.

1906   Director of military training, War Office.

1907   Director of staff duties, general staff.

1909   Chief of staff of the Indian army.

Knight Commander of the Royal Victorian Order (25 June).

Knight Commander of the Order of the Indian Empire (12 December).

1912   Command of the corps at Aldershot designated as the BEF's I Corps upon mobilization.

1913	Knight Commander of the Order of the Bath (3 June).
1914	Command of the BEF's I Army Corps as a lieutenant general (August).
	Command of First Army (26 December).
1915	Knight Grand Cross of the Order of the Bath (3 June).
	Replaced Field Marshal Sir John French as commander in chief of the BEF (19 December).
1916	Grand Cross of the Legion of Honor (24 February).
	Knight Grand Cross of the Royal Victorian Order (5 August).
1917	Knight of the Thistle.
1918	Agreed to the appointment of Foch at the Doullens Conference (26 March).
	"Backs to the Wall" message during the German GEORGETTE Offensive (11 April).
	British attack at Amiens; Ludendorff's "Black Day of the German Army" (8 August).
	Refused Prime Minister David Lloyd George's offer of a viscountcy.
1919–21	Commander in chief, British Home Forces.
1919	Created an earl (March).
	Dispatches published.
1921	Retired from the British army.
	Created Baron Haig of Bemersyde.
1921–28	Helped to establish and served as first president of the Royal British Legion.
1928	Died in London (28 January).
	Buried at Dryburgh Abbey, Scotland.

JOHN J. PERSHING

1860	Born in Laclede, Missouri (13 September).

1882–86   Cadet, U.S. Military Academy, West Point.

1886   Commissioned a second lieutenant of cavalry.

1886–90   Served in operations against the Indians in the southwest and northern Plains.

1890   Participated in Battle of Wounded Knee (29 December).

1891–95   Professor of military science and tactics, University of Nebraska.

1893   Law degree from the University of Nebraska.

1895–96   Frontier service in Montana.

1897–98   Assistant instructor of tactics at West Point.

1898   Troop commander with the 10th Cavalry (Buffalo Soldiers) during the Spanish-American War.

           Participated in Battle of San Juan Hill in Cuba (1 July).

1899–1903 Service in the Philippines.

           Participated in actions against the Moros.

1903–4   Service on the War Department general staff.

1904–5   Student, U.S. Army War College.

1905–6   Military attaché to Japan and military observer in the Russo-Japanese War. (Other observers included First Lieutenant Douglas MacArthur, Captain Peyton C. March, and Captain Max Hoffmann.)

1906   Promoted from captain to brigadier general over 835 more senior-ranking officers (20 September).

           Commanded the Department of California.

1907–8   Commanded Fort McKinley, Philippines.

1908–9   Assigned to the Office of the Chief of Staff of the U.S. Army.

1909–13   Governor of Moro Province, Philippines, and commander of the Department of Mindanao.

1914–16   Commanding general, 8th Infantry Brigade, Presidio of San Francisco.

1915	Wife and three daughters killed in a house fire at the Presidio (26 August); son Warren was the only survivor.
1916–17	Commanding general, Mexican Punitive Expedition.
1916	Promoted to major general (25 September).
1917–19	Commander in chief, American Expeditionary Force.
1917	Arrived in Paris (13 June).
	Pershing and Pétain met (16 June).
	Agreed for the AEF to occupy positions in Lorraine and use Atlantic ports (26 June).
	Promoted to full general (9 October 1917).
1918	U.S. First Army activated (10 August 1918).
	Exercised dual command of the First Army and the AEF.
	U.S. Second Army activated (10 October 1918).
	Relinquished command of First Army when the AEF became an army group.
1919	Departed Europe on the SS *Leviathan* (1 September).
	Promoted to the special rank of general of the armies (3 September).
	Testified on the Army Reorganization Bill before a House and Senate Joint Committee (31 October–2 November).
1921	Chief of staff, U.S. Army (13 May 1921).
1924	Retired from active duty (13 September).
1924–48	Chairman, American Battle Monuments Commission.
1931	*My Experiences in the World War* published.
	Awarded Pulitzer Prize, but initial sales poor.
1948	Died in Washington (15 July).
	Buried in Arlington National Cemetery.

PAUL VON BENECKENDORFF UND VON HINDENBURG

1847	Born in Posen, Prussia (now Poznan, Poland) (2 October).

1859   Entered the Prussian Military Institute at Wahlstatt, Silesia (1 April).

1863   Transferred to the Senior Cadet School in Berlin.

1865   Officer candidate (*Fahnenjunker*), 3rd Regiment of Foot Guards.

1866   Commissioned in 3rd Guards Infantry Regiment (7 April).

           Served in the Austro-Prussian War.

           Slightly wounded at the Battle of Königgratz (3 July).

1870–71   Served in Franco-Prussian War.

1871   As the representative of his regiment, present in the Hall of Mirrors at Versailles when Prussian king Wilhelm was crowned German kaiser (18 January).

1873–76   Attended the Kriegsakademie in Berlin, graduating with honors.

1877   Appointed a full member of the General Staff after completing the standard probationary period.

1878   Promoted to captain and assigned to the Great General Staff in Berlin (April).

1881   General Staff officer, 1a (operations), 1st Infantry Division in Stettin.

1884   Company commander, 58th Infantry Regiment.

1885   Reassigned to the Great General Staff and served under Colonel Alfred von Schlieffen.

1888   Assigned a General Staff officer of III Army Corps in Berlin.

1889   Promoted to lieutenant colonel and assigned as bureau chief in the Prussian Ministry of War (July).

1893   Promoted to colonel and assigned command of the 91st Infantry Regiment in Oldenburg (April).

1896   Promoted to major general and assigned as chief of staff of VIII Army Corps (15 August).

1901   Promoted to lieutenant general and assigned command of the 28th Infantry Division at Karlsruhe (1 July).

1903   Promoted to general of infantry and assigned command of IV Army Corps at Magdeburg (27 January).

1912   Retired from active duty and took up residence in Hanover (31 December).

1914   Recalled to active duty and assigned command of the Eighth Army in East Prussia (22 August).

        Promoted to colonel general (26 August).

        Awarded the Ordern Pour le Mérite (2 September).

        Assigned command of the newly formed Ninth Army (18 September).

        Appointed commander in chief of the German Army in the East (Ostheer) (1 November).

        Promoted to field marshal (27 November).

1915   Wooden statues (*Nagelsäulen*) of Hindenburg start appearing in German cities.

        Awarded the Ordern Pour le Mérite mit Eichenlaub (23 February).

1916   Replaced General Erich von Falkenhayn as chief of the General Staff of the German Field Army (Feldheer) (26 August).

        Awarded the Grand Cross of the Iron Cross (9 December).

1918   Awarded Star of the Grand Cross of the Iron Cross, aka the Blücher Star (25 March).

        Hindenburg and Ludendorff offered their resignation. The kaiser accepted Ludendorff's but refused Hindenburg's (26 October).

1919   Retired again from the German army (4 July).

        During his testimony in front of the Reichstag's Investigation Committee, Hindenburg first gave voice to the *Dolchstosslegende*—the "stab-in-the-back myth" (18 November).

1921   *Aus Meinem Leben* (*Out of My Life*) published.

1925   Elected president of the Weimar Republic (26 April).

1932   Won reelection and defeated Hitler for the presidency (10 April).

1933   Appointed Adolf Hitler chancellor of Germany (30 January).

1934   Died in office while at his estate in Neudeck (2 August).

          Interred at the Tannenberg Memorial (6 August).

1945   Hindenburg's coffin removed and the Tannenberg Memorial destroyed by the Germans to prevent its capture by the Russians (January).

1946   Reinterred in the Elizabethkirche at Marburg an der Lahn (August).

ERICH LUDENDORFF

1865   Born in Kruszczewina, Posen, East Prussia (now Poznan, Poland) (9 April).

1877   Cadet, Ploen Cadet School.

1879   Cadet, Lichterfelde Senior Cadet School.

1882   Commissioned second lieutenant, 57th Infantry Regiment (15 April).

1889   Assigned to the Marine Infantry, 2nd Sea Battalion (1 April).

1890   Promoted to first lieutenant (24 March).

          Assigned to the 8th Grenadier Regiment (12 August).

          Student, Kriegsakademie (1 October).

1894   Probationary member, General Staff (17 March).

1895   Promoted to captain and appointed full member of the General Staff (22 March).

1896   Assigned to the General Staff of IV Corps (19 March).

1898   Company commander, 61st Infantry Regiment (22 March).

1900   Assigned to the General Staff of the 9th Division (22 July).

1901   Promoted to major (19 September).

1902   Assigned to the General Staff of V Corps (18 October).

1904   Assigned to the Great General Staff, Berlin (10 March).

1906–8   Instructor, Kriegsakademie (13 September).

1908	Assistant department chief, Great General Staff (10 April).
	Promoted to lieutenant colonel and assigned as department chief, Great General Staff (18 May).
1909–13	Lived in the same building in Berlin as Max Hoffmann.
1911	Promoted to colonel (21 April).
1913	Assigned as commander, 39th Fusilier Regiment (27 January).
1914	Promoted to major general and assigned as commander, 85th Infantry Brigade (22 March).
	Assigned as assistant chief of staff, Second Army (1 August).
	Acting commander, 14th Infantry Brigade (6–7 August).
	Awarded the Pour le Mérite (8 August).
	Assigned as chief of General Staff, Eighth Army (22 August).
	Assigned as chief of General Staff, Ninth Army (15 September).
	Assigned as chief of the General Staff, Supreme Command East (11 November).
	Promoted to lieutenant general (27 November).
1915	Awarded the Pour le Mérite mit Eichenlaub (23 February).
1916	Promoted to general of infantry and assigned as first quartermaster general of the German army (29 August).
1918	Awarded the Grand Cross of the Iron Cross (24 March).
	Forced into retirement from the German army (26 October).
1919	*Meine Kriegserinnerungen 1914–1918* (*My War Memories, 1914–1918*) published.
1920	Supported the Kapp-Lüttwiz Putsch (13–17 March).
1921	*Urkunden der Obersten Heeresleitung über ihre Tätigkeit 1916–1918* (*The General Staff and Its Problems, 1916–1918*) published.
1922	*Kriegführung und Politik* (*War Leadership and Politics*) published.
1923	Participated in Hitler's Beer Hall Putsch (8 November).
1924	Acquitted for his role in the Beer Hall Putsch (1 April).
1924–28	Served as a Nazi delegate to the Reichstag.

1925   Unsuccessfully ran against Hindenburg in the German presidential elections.

1935   *Der totale Krieg (The Total War)* published.

Rejected Hitler's offer of a promotion to field marshal on his seventieth birthday (9 April).

1937   Died in Munich (20 December).

Buried in the Neuer Friedhof in Tutzing, Bavaria.

A NOTE ON GENERAL OFFICER RANKS

ABOVE THE LEVEL OF COLONEL, there were some significant variations in the rank titles of the general officer corps of the armies of the Great War. Below the level of general officer, the rank titles and functions of officers were essentially the same in most armies. Lieutenants commanded platoons; captains commanded companies; majors were primarily staff officers; lieutenant colonels commanded battalions; and colonels commanded regiments. Most officers spent the majority of their careers as staff officers, interspersed with command assignments. The rank of major, however, was generally the only one for which there was no standard echelon of command. During crisis situations in wartime, officers frequently were called upon to assume command at echelons above the levels of their actual ranks. Hence, it was not uncommon for a captain to find himself in command of a battalion or a major in command of a regiment.

GREAT BRITAIN

In the British army, commanders of brigades held the rank of brigadier general. After the war, the rank title was changed to brigadier, and the insignia of rank was modified to indicate that a British brigadier was more like a senior colonel than a proper general officer. The rank remains brigadier in the British army today, although in most other armies the rank immediately above colonel is brigadier general. Departing from British practice, the Canadian army today still uses the rank title of brigadier general. And despite the absence of the word "general" in their rank titles, British brigadiers today are regarded as general officers in all combined North Atlantic Treaty Organization headquarters. Divisions during World War I were (and still are) commanded by major generals, corps by lieutenant generals, and numbered field armies by generals. The highest British military rank was field marshal, usually awarded to commanders of theaters and army groups and also to distinguished senior generals in retirement. During the war, British field marshals included Sir John French, Sir Douglas Haig, and Sir Herbert Kitchener, a retired field marshal who served as secretary of state for war until his death in 1916. Sir Charles Egerton, a retired officer of the British Indian army, also was promoted to field marshal in 1917. Following the war, Sir Herbert Plumer, Sir Edward Allenby, and Sir Henry Wilson were promoted to field marshal in 1919; Sir William Robertson in 1920; and Sir William Birdwood in 1925.

UNITED STATES

Prior to the Great War, major general (two stars) was the highest permanent rank in the U.S. Army. In October 1917, Tasker Bliss as chief of staff of the U.S. Army and John Pershing as commander of the AEF were promoted to the temporary rank of general (four stars). They were the fourth and fifth American officers to hold that rank, following Ulysses S. Grant, William T. Sherman, and Philip Sheridan. Peyton C. March also received four stars when he became chief of staff of the army in early 1918. As the war progressed, American corps commanders were promoted to lieutenant general (three stars), Hunter Liggett being among the first. As noted in Chapter 15, Pershing in September 1919 was promoted to the special rank of general of the armies. He continued to wear only four stars, but gold ones rather than the silver stars worn by all other general officers. When the rank of general of the army (five stars) was created in late 1944, it was considered as subordinate to Pershing's general of the armies. No other U.S. Army officer held that rank until 1978, when George Washington pursuant to an act of the U.S. Congress passed in 1976 was promoted posthumously to general of the armies, with an effective date of rank of 4 July 1776.

FRANCE

At the start of the Great War, France had only three general officer ranks: general of brigade (*général de brigade*), general of division (*général de division*), and marshal of France (*maréchal de France*). A general of brigade wore two stars; a general of division, three; and a marshal of France, seven. No officer had been promoted to marshal since the fall of the Second Empire in 1870.

Joseph Joffre became the Third Republic's first marshal in 1916, as something of a consolation prize following his relief from command. Foch and Pétain were promoted to marshal in August and December 1918, respectively. In 1921 Joseph Gallieni (posthumously), Louis Franchet d'Esperey, and Marie Émile Fayolle were all raised to the dignity of marshal of France. Although general of division was the highest nominal rank, officers commanding field armies were distinguished by an additional horizontal row of silver braid on their kepis. There was never any confusion among the French themselves as to who was the senior general. Following the war, the French added the ranks of general of corps (*général de corps*), wearing four stars, and general of army (*général d'armée*), wearing five stars. Thus, French generals today wear one star more than their American counterparts of the same rank The mismatch continues to cause minor confusion at times in NATO combined staffs.

GERMANY

Until 1945, the lowest general officer rank in the German army was major general (*Generalmajor*), who typically commanded a brigade. A lieutenant general (*Generalleutnant*) commanded a division, which was commanded by a major general in the British and American armies. At the next level up, the general's rank title was based on his branch of service; hence, general of infantry (*General der Infantrie*), general of artillery (*General der Artillerie*), general of engineers (*General der Pioniere*), and so on. These officers typically command corps. Colonel general (*Generaloberst*) was the equivalent of a British or American full general. The highest German rank was general field marshal (*Generalfeldmarschall*), typically translated into English simply as field marshal. By tradition, a *Generalfeldmarschall* had *Immediatrecht*, the right of direct access to the kaiser, or during World War II to the Führer. To a much greater extent than in the other armies, German generals were often found in command of echelons above their actual ranks. Erich von Falkenhayn, for example, was only a lieutenant general when he became the chief of the German General Staff in September 1914. In today's German Bundeswehr the general officer rank structure mirrors that of the British and Americans, starting with brigadier general (*Brigadegeneral*) and culminating at general. During World War I a fairly large number of German officers held the rank of field marshal. In addition to Hindenburg, who was promoted in 1914, they included Colmar von der Goltz (1911); Friedrich Augustus III von Sachsen (1912); Karl von Bülow (1915); August von Mackensen (1915); Ludwig III von Bayern (1915); Wilhelm II von

Württemberg (1916); Crown Prince Rupprecht von Bayern (1916); Leopold von Bayern (1916); Albrecht von Württemberg (1916); Hermann von Eichhorn (1917); and Remus von Woyrsch (1917). No other German officer was promoted to field marshal until Hermann Göring in 1938.

MARSHALS

In Germany, France, and Britain, marshals also were distinguished by a marshal's baton. Britain and Germany frequently conferred the honorific title on high-ranking noblemen and the heads of state of friendly foreign nations. After the war, Foch was made a British field marshal and a marshal of Poland. The United States never had a marshal rank, although general of the army introduced in late 1944 was supposed to be the U.S. equivalent. By extension, then, Pershing's special rank of general of the armies would be too. No American officer has held the rank of general of the army since 1950, although it still exists officially on the books. Likewise, the last three French officers promoted to marshal of France were in 1952, with the special exception of Marie-Pierre Koenig, who was promoted posthumously in 1984, fourteen years after his death. The United Kingdom today confers the rank of field marshal only on distinguished officers in retirement. In 1940 Hitler promoted Göring to the theoretically higher rank of marshal of the Reich (*Reichsmarschall*), based on a rank resurrected from the Holy Roman Empire. The Bundeswehr today does not have a rank above general.

NOTES

1. GENERALSHIP IN THE GREAT WAR

1. Travers, *Killing Ground*, xvii–xviii.
2. Bidwell and Graham, *Fire-Power*, 1–4.
3. Travers, *Killing Ground*, 252.
4. Strachan, *First World War*, 172. Two American generals were killed in World War I, but neither of them was functioning in a general officer's position at the time. Colonel Edward Sigerfoos was mortally wounded at the front on 29 September 1918 and died in the base hospital eight days afterward. Just prior to his death the U.S. Congress confirmed his promotion to brigadier general, making him the most senior American killed during the war. Brigadier General Henry Root Hill was sacked by Pershing on 31 August 1918. He remained in the AEF as a major and was killed in action on 16 October while commanding a battalion near Romange.
5. Holmes, *Tommy*, 212.
6. Clausewitz, *On War*, book 2, 131–32.
7. Will Durant and Ariel Durant, *The Lessons of History* (New York: Simon and Schuster, 1968), 97.
8. A quartermaster was not necessarily a logistics officer in the German army. A German General Staff officer who was an *Oberquartiermeister* (senior quartermaster) was a deputy chief of staff. Ludendorff as first quartermaster general of the German army was what we today would call the vice chief of staff.
9. Travers, *How the War Was Won*, 179.
10. Greenhalgh, *Foch in Command*, 3.
11. Bailey, *First World War*, 3.

2. FUTURE SHOCK ON THE 1914–1918 BATTLEFIELD

1. Bailey, *First World War*, 3.
2. Travers, *Killing Ground*, xix, 250, 253.
3. *Cambridge Advanced Learner's Dictionary and Thesaurus* online, s.v. "paradigm shift."

337

4. Strachan, *First World War*, 163.

5. The terms "close," "deep," and "rear battle" came into use only during the final decades of the twentieth century, but they nonetheless describe accurately the new complexities the World War I commanders had to face.

6. Holmes, *Western Front*, 214.

7. Timothy K. Nenninger, "American Military Effectiveness in the First World War," in Millett and Murray, *Military Effectiveness*, 117.

8. Herwig, *First World War*, 48.

9. Quoted in Asprey, *German High Command at War*, 35.

10. Lucas, *Evolution of Tactical Ideas*, 6.

11. Holmes, *Western Front*, 30–35.

12. Travers, *Killing Ground*, 48–55, 62–78.

13. Lucas, *Evolution of Tactical Ideas*, 87.

14. Terraine, *White Heat*, 286.

15. Thaer, *Generalstabsdienst an der Front und in der O.H.L.*, 220.

16. Fuller, *Tanks in the Great War*, 171.

17. Kuhl, *Entstehung, Durchführung und Zusammenbruch der Offensive von 1918*, 70.

18. Essame, *Battle for Europe 1918*, 2.

19. Terraine, *White Heat*, 303.

20. The few tanks the Germans did have were captured Allied tanks that the Germans put back into action.

21. Strachan, *First World War*, 305.

22. Hogg, *Guns*, 8.

23. Brooke, "Evolution of Artillery in the Great War," Part 1, November 1924, 250–67.

24. Ząbecki, *Steel Wind*, 8–9.

25. Lucas, *Evolution of Tactical Ideas*, 9–10, 26, 39–40.

26. This quote is frequently attributed to Pétain.

27. Hoffmann, *War of Lost Opportunities*, 135.

28. Ludendorff, *My War Memories*, 2:606.

29. Bruchmüller, *Die deutsche Artillerie in den Durchbruchschlachten des Weltkriegs*, 2nd ed., 80.

30. For a detailed discussion of Bruchmüller and his tactical system, see Ząbecki, *Steel Wind*.

31. Quoted in Oberkommando des Heeres, *Der Weltkrieg 1914 bis 1918*, 12:53–54.

32. Erich Ludendorff, "Der Angriff im Stellungskrieg," in *Urkunden der Obersten Heeresleitung über ihre Tätigkeit 1916/18*, 641–66.

33. Griffith, *Forward into Battle*, 98; W. Balck, *Development of Tactics*, 153–60.

34. Gudmundsson, *Stormtroop Tactics*, 151–52.

35. Paul Kennedy, "Britain in the First World War," in Millett and Murray, *Military Effectiveness*, 63.

36. Wynne, *If Germany Attacks*, 57–58; Lucas, *Evolution of Tactical Ideas*, 38, 109.

37. Gudmundsson, *Stormtroop Tactics*, 47–53.

38. Gudmundsson, 77–79, 96.

39. House, *Combined Arms Warfare in the Twentieth Century*, 35.

40. Wynne, *If Germany Attacks*, 295.

41. Lucas, *Evolution of Tactical Ideas*, 132–38; W. Balck, *Development of Tactics*, 266.
42. Travers, *Killing Ground*, 260; W. Balck, *Development of Tactics*, 264.
43. Lucas, *Evolution of Tactical Ideas*, 43, 102; W. Balck, *Development of Tactics*, 62, 81, 91.
44. Oberkommando des Heeres, *Der Weltkrieg 1914 bis 1918*, 14:41–42.
45. Oberkommando des Heeres, 59.
46. Ludendorff, *My War Memories*, 2:583.
47. Howard, "Military Science in an Age of Peace," 6–7.

3. THE STRATEGIC SITUATION AT THE END OF 1917

1. Barnett, *Swordbearers*, 277.
2. Gross, *Myth and Reality of German Warfare*, 130.
3. See Jessen, *Verdun 1916*.
4. Ironically, what the Allies in World War II called the Siegfried Line was called the West Wall by the Germans.
5. Herwig, *First World War*, 250.
6. Holger H. Herwig, "The Dynamics of Necessity: German Military Policy During the First World War," in Millett and Murray, *Military Effectiveness*, 97.
7. Hindenburg, *Out of My Life*, 2:33.
8. Holmes, *Tommy*, 69.
9. Doughty, *Pyrrhic Victory*, 37–42.
10. Neiberg, *Fighting the Great War*, 15.
11. Douglas Porch, "The French Army in the First World War," in Millett and Murray, *Military Effectiveness*, 215.
12. Doughty, *Pyrrhic Victory*, 54.
13. Doughty, 277.
14. Quoted in Ryan, *Pétain the Soldier*, 137.
15. Doughty, *Pyrrhic Victory*, 369.
16. Herwig, *Marne, 1914*, 241–54.
17. Sheffield, *Chief*, 82–86.
18. Neiberg, *Fighting the Great War*, 20–25.
19. Holmes, *Tommy*, 225.
20. Kuhl, *Der Weltkrieg 1914–1918*, 2:126.
21. Sheffield and Bourne, *Douglas Haig*, 317.

4. THE COMMANDERS IN CHIEF

1. Quoted in Holmes, *Western Front*, 35.
2. Keegan, *Face of Battle*, 29, 75.
3. Longstreet, *From Manassas to Appomattox*, 551.
4. Fuller, *Foundations of the Science of War*, 334.
5. Keegan, *Face of Battle*, 51.
6. The U.S. 1st Division attacked at Cantigny in May 1918; the U.S. 2nd Division (including the 4th Marine Brigade) counterattacked at Belleau Wood in June, and the U.S. 3rd Division defended at Château-Thierry in July. Along with the American divisions that participated in the French counterattack from 18 July to 6 August, they all operated under overall French command.

7. Several German cities conducted fund-raising drives for the war by erecting a huge wooden statue of Hindenburg in the town square. Citizens were given the opportunity to purchase nails to drive into the statue, with the proceeds going to the war effort—the prices varied for iron, brass, and gold-coated nails.

8. Sheffield, *Chief*, 141.

9. Wheeler-Bennett, *Hindenburg*, 84.

10. Clayton, *Paths of Glory*, 151–54.

11. Douglas Porch, "The French Army in the First World War," in Millett and Murray, *Military Effectiveness*, 213–20.

12. Astore and Showalter, *Hindenburg*, 80.

13. Clayton, *Paths of Glory*, 178.

14. Greenhalgh, *Foch in Command*, 236.

15. Harris, *Douglas Haig and the First World War*, 2.

16. Travers, *Killing Ground*, 138–39.

17. Paul Kennedy, "Britain in the First World War," in Millett and Murray, *Military Effectiveness*, 51, 52–53, 68.

18. Smythe, *Pershing*, 68; Paschall, *Defeat of Imperial Germany*, 210; Ferrell, Robert *America's Deadliest Battle*, 113–14.

19. Quoted in Rupprecht, *In Treue Fest*, 2:372.

20. Quoted in Greenhalgh, *Foch in Command*, 516.

21. Sheffield and Bourne, *Douglas Haig*, 384.

22. Ząbecki, *Chief of Staff*, 10.

23. Herwig, *First World War*, 420.

24. Liddell Hart, *Reputation*, 212.

25. Sheffield and Bourne. *Douglas Haig*, 11.

26. Wilhelm II, *Kaiser's Memoirs*, 273–74.

27. Görlitz, *History of the German General Staff*, 183.

28. Ludendorff, *My War Memories*, 550.

29. Rupprecht, *In Treue Fest*, 2:178.

30. Doughty, *Pyrrhic Victory*, 151.

31. Porch, "French Army in the First World War," 210.

32. Neiberg, *Foch*, 68; Doughty, *Pyrrhic Victory*, 455.

33. Quoted in Liddell Hart, *Foch*, 322.

34. Clayton, *Paths of Glory*, 177.

35. Quoted in Doughty, *Pyrrhic Victory*, 456.

36. Greenhalgh, *Foch in Command*, 503–4.

37. Sheffield, *Chief*, 154.

38. Sheffield, 316–17.

39. Sheffield and Bourne, *Douglas Haig*, 11.

40. Sheffield. *Chief*, 205.

41. Suttie, *Rewriting the First World War*, 105, 111.

42. Pershing's wife and three daughters died in a house fire in August 1915.

43. Warren and Baker quotes cited in Smythe, *Pershing*, 4.

44. Cited in Smythe, 6.

45. Astore and Showalter, *Hindenburg*, 20.

46. Millotat, *Understanding the Prussian-German General Staff System*, 23–24.
47. Ludendorff, *My War Memories*, 1:239.
48. Quoted in Hastings, *Catastrophe*, 275.
49. Herwig, *First World War*, 134.
50. Rupprecht, *In Treue Fest*, 2:379–81.
51. Smythe, *Pershing*, 23–24.
52. Greenhalgh, *Foch in Command*, 2, 215
53. Bruce, *Pétain*, 61.
54. Quoted in Greenhalgh, *Foch in Command*, 503–4, 339.
55. Bruce, *Pétain*, 21.
56. Harris, *Douglas Haig and the First World War*, 112.
57. Sheffield, *Chief*, 264.
58. Harris, *Douglas Haig and the First World War*, 428–29, 538.

5. THE YANKS ARE COMING

1. Even a hundred years after World War I, more than 46 million Americans identify themselves as being of German descent, making them the largest national ancestry group in the United States (see the Census Bureau's 2010–15 American Community Survey online).
2. Reproduced in Ząbecki, *Germany at War*, 4:1546.
3. Quoted in Wheeler-Bennett, *Hindenburg*, 92.
4. Stevenson, *With Our Backs to the Wall*, 160–61.
5. Herwig, *First World War*, 320; Lengel, *To Conquer Hell*, 18.
6. Grotelueschen, *AEF Way of War*, 6, 8, 12–13, 15–16.
7. Timothy K. Nenninger, "American Military Effectiveness in the First World War," in Millett and Murray, *Military Effectiveness*, 134.
8. Ferrell, *America's Deadliest Battle*, 2.
9. See Trask, *AEF and Coalition Warmaking*.
10. Pershing, *My Experiences in the World War*, 1:38–39.
11. Ferrell, *America's Deadliest Battle*, 11–14.
12. Smythe, *Pershing*, 31.
13. Nenninger, "American Military Effectiveness in the First World War," 123.
14. Harbord, *American Army in France*, 107.
15. Nenninger, "American Military Effectiveness in the First World War," 149.
16. Pershing, *My Experiences in the World War*, 1:81, 86.
17. Pershing, 1:33–34.
18. Nenninger, "American Military Effectiveness in the First World War," 144.
19. Sheffield and Bourne, *Douglas Haig*, 290.
20. Smythe, *Pershing*, 27.
21. Pershing, *My Experiences in the World War*, 1:114.
22. Pershing, 1:153.
23. Smythe, *Pershing*, 82.
24. Pershing, *My Experiences in the World War*, 1:190–91.
25. Quoted in Pershing, 1:259.
26. Pershing, 1:265.

27. Quoted in Barnett, *Swordbearers*, 265.

28. Quoted in Smythe, *Pershing*, 70–71.

29. Smythe, 69–70.

30. Smythe, 75–78.

6. TWO CONFERENCES IN NOVEMBER 1917

1. Doughty, *Pyrrhic Victory*, 111.

2. Foch and Mott, *Memoirs of Marshall Foch*, 224.

3. Liddell Hart, *Foch*, 248.

4. Doughty, *Pyrrhic Victory*, 360.

5. Doughty, 398.

6. Greenhalgh, *Foch in Command*, 245.

7. Edmonds, *Military Operations*, 1:30.

8. Pershing, *My Experiences in the World War*, 1:214–16.

9. Doughty, *Pyrrhic Victory*, 400.

10. See Trask, *United States in the Supreme War Council*.

11. See Trask, *General Tasker Howard Bliss*.

12. Robertson, *From Private to Field Marshal*, 328–29.

13. Liddell Hart, *Foch*, 251.

14. Liddell Hart, 254.

15. Foch and Mott, *Memoirs of Marshall Foch*, 235.

16. Edmonds, *Military Operations*, 1:37.

17. Foch and Mott, *Memoirs of Marshall Foch*, 236; Greenhalgh, *Foch in Command*, 278–80.

18. Ludendorff, *My War Memories*, 2:539.

19. Ludendorff, 544.

20. Oberkommando des Heeres, *Der Weltkrieg 1914 bis 1918*, 14:51–55; Kuhl, *Entstehung, Durchführung und Zusammenbruch der Offensive von 1918*, 101–3.

21. Quoted in Kuhl, *Entstehung, Durchführung und Zusammenbruch der Offensive von 1918*, 103.

22. Quoted in Hermann von Kuhl, "Personal War Diary of General von Kuhl," 11 November 1917, File: RH 61/970., German Military Archives, Freiburg.

23. Barnett, *Swordbearers*, 278.

24. Georg Wetzell, "The Offensives in the West and Their Prospects of Success," 12 December 1917, File PH 3/267, German Military Archives.

25. Edmonds, *Military Operations*, 1:142.

26. Oberkommando des Heeres, *Der Weltkrieg 1914 bis 1918*, 14:68–69; Rupprecht, *In Treue Fest*, 2:305–9; Kuhl, *Entstehung, Durchführung und Zusammenbruch der Offensive von 1918*, 115.

27. OHL, Ia 5905, "1918 Operations in the West," 27 December 1917, File PH 3/278, German Military Archives.

28. Oberkommando des Heeres, *Der Weltkrieg 1914 bis 1918*, 14:76–77; Kuhl, *Entstehung, Durchführung und Zusammenbruch der Offensive von 1918*, 116.

29. Thilo, "Meeting Minutes with Excellency Ludendorff, 21 January 1918," 23 January 1918, File PH 5 I/45, German Military Archives.

30. Thilo, "Meeting Minutes with Excellency Ludendorff," 23 January 1918.

31. Ludendorff, *My War Memories*, 2:591–92.

32. Rupprecht, *In Treue Fest*, 2:372.

33. Lossberg, *Lossberg's War*, 318; Rupprecht, *In Treue Fest*, 2:321.

34. Oberkommando des Heeres, *Der Weltkrieg 1914 bis 1918*, 14:80–81.

7. THE GATHERING STORM

1. See Showalter, *Railroads and Rifles*.

2. Gross, *Myth and Reality of German Warfare*, 131.

3. Brown, *British Logistics on the Western Front*, 184.

4. Brown, 191.

5. Henniker, *Transportation on the Western Front*, 398.

6. Henniker, 157.

7. Brown, *British Logistics on the Western Front*, 109–34; Henniker, *Transportation on the Western Front*, 398–400.

8. For a detailed discussion of the BEF's rail system in March 1918, see Ząbecki, *German 1918 Offensives*, 85–88.

9. Porter, "German Supply System," 1.

10. Strachan, *First World War*, 178; Henniker, *Transportation on the Western Front*, 438.

11. Georges-Henri Soutou, "French Strategy in 1916 and the Battle of the Somme," in Strohn, *Battle of the Somme*, 64.

12. Stevenson, *With Our Backs to the Wall*, 223, 176.

13. Greenhalgh, *Foch in Command*, 443.

14. Clayton, *Paths of Glory*, 181–82.

15. Alistair Horne, "Pétain," in Carver, *War Lords*, 69.

16. Quoted in Carver, *War Lords*, 152–53.

17. Henri Pétain, "Plans for the Campaign of 1918," 3rd Section, General Staff, No. 3858, 8 January 1918, in Department of the Army, *United States Army in the World War 1917–1919*, 2:151–52.

18. Neiberg, *Second Battle of the Marne*, 107–8.

19. Edmonds, *Military Operations*, 1:43; Doughty, *Pyrrhic Victory*, 393, 417.

20. Quoted in Edmonds, *Military Operations*, 1:258.

21. Sheffield and Bourne, *Douglas Haig*, 367, 370–71.

22. Sheffield and Bourne, 371.

23. Suttie, *Rewriting the First World War*, 161.

24. Doughty, *Pyrrhic Victory*, 420.

25. Pershing, *My Experiences in the World War*, 1:309–10; Edmonds, *Military Operations*, 1:64.

26. Pershing, *My Experiences in the World War*, 1:323.

27. Supreme War Council, Joint Note 13, Joint Note 14, 2 February 1918, in Department of the Army, *United States Army in the World War 1917–1919*, 2:189–90.

28. Foch and Mott, *Memoirs of Marshall Foch*, 241; Liddell Hart, *Foch*, 257.

29. Doughty, *Pyrrhic Victory*, 412; Liddell Hart, *Foch*, 260; Edmonds, *Military Operations*, 1:80–86.

30. Sheffield and Bourne, *Douglas Haig*, 378.

31. Holmes, *Western Front*, 205.

32. Maxime Weygand, "Memorandum for the Commanders-in-Chief of the British, French, and Italian Armies," 6 February 1918, in Department of the Army, *United States Army in the World War 1917–1919*, 2:194–95.

33. Edmonds, *Military Operations*, 1:101–2; Doughty, *Pyrrhic Victory*, 413.

34. Douglas Haig, "To the British Military Representative, Supreme War Council, Versailles," 2 March 1918, in Department of the Army, *United States Army in the World War 1917–1919*, 2:227–28; Edmonds, *Military Operations*, 1:83.

35. Executive War Board, "Interallied General Reserve," 7 March 1918, in Department of the Army, *United States Army in the World War 1917–1919*, 2:238–39; Foch and Mott, *Memoirs of Marshall Foch*, 242.

36. Tasker Bliss, "Memorandum for Secretary of State and Secretary of War," 14 March 1918, in Department of the Army, *United States Army in the World War 1917–1919*, 2:240–42.

37. Edmonds, *Military Operations*, 1:95–100.

38. Haig, *Dispatches*, 217–18; Sheffield, *Chief*, 261.

39. Edmonds, *Military Operations*, 1:114–34; Travers, *Killing Ground*, 224, 226, 242.

40. Doughty, *Pyrrhic Victory*, 406.

41. OHL, Ia 6205, 24 January 1918, File PH 5 I/31, German Military Archives, Freiburg.

42. OHL, Ia 6213, 24 January 1918, File PH 2/278, German Military Archives.

43. Oberkommando des Heeres, *Der Weltkrieg 1914 bis 1918*, 14:82.

44. OHL, "Mons Conference Minutes by Major Thilo," 4 February 1918, File PH 5 I/45, German Military Archives.

45. Rupprecht, *In Treue Fest*, 2:326.

46. OHL, Ia 6405, 8 February 1918, File PH 5 I/50, German Military Archives.

47. OHL, Ia 7070, 10 March 1918, File PH 3/281, German Military Archives.

48. Kuhl, *Entstehung, Durchführung und Zusammenbruch der Offensive von 1918*, 118.

49. Army Group Crown Prince Rupprecht, Ia 4929, 25 December 1917, File PH 3/287, German Military Archives.

50. Oberkommando des Heeres, *Der Weltkrieg 1914 bis 1918*, 14:167–68.

51. Kuhl, *Entstehung, Durchführung und Zusammenbruch der Offensive von 1918*, 121–24; Oberkommando des Heeres, *Der Weltkrieg 1914 bis 1918*, 14:101.

52. Herwig, *First World War*, 392.

53. Sulzbach, *With the German Guns*, 146.

54. Ząbecki, *German 1918 Offensives*, 126–30.

55. OHL, Ia 7240, 20 March 1918, File PH 3/268, German Military Archives.

56. Rupprecht, *In Treue Fest*, 2:343; Kuhl, *Entstehung, Durchführung und Zusammenbruch der Offensive von 1918*, 132–33.

8. MICHAEL AND GEORGETTE

1. Oberkommando des Heeres, *Der Weltkrieg 1914 bis 1918*, vol. 14, appendix 39a.

2. Edmonds, *Military Operations: Belgium and France 1918*, 1:208.

3. Travers, *Killing Ground*, 227.

4. Harris, *Douglas Haig and the First World War*, 449.

5. Sheffield and Bourne, *Douglas Haig*, 390.

6. Stevenson, *With Our Backs to the Wall*, 267.

7. "Die deutsche Offensive im März 1918," 1291.

8. Kuhl, *Entstehung, Durchführung und Zusammenbruch der Offensive von 1918*, 130–32.

9. Foch and Mott, *Memoirs of Marshall Foch*, 266.

10. Oberkommando des Heeres, *Der Weltkrieg 1914 bis 1918*, 14:145.

11. AOK 18, Ia 1461, 22 March 1918, File PH 5 I/29, German Military Archives, Freiburg; *Der Weltkrieg 1914 bis 1918*, 14:145.

12. Sheffield and Bourne, *Douglas Haig*, 391.

13. Edmonds, *Military Operations*, 1:322.

14. Kuhl, *Entstehung, Durchführung und Zusammenbruch der Offensive von 1918*, 133.

15. Edmonds, *Military Operations*, 1:368.

16. Harris, *Douglas Haig and the First World War*, 453.

17. Hindenburg, *Out of My Life*, 2:160.

18. Travers, *Killing Ground*, 327.

19. Edmonds, *Military Operations*, 1:399.

20. Foch and Mott, *Memoirs of Marshall Foch*, 257.

21. "Pétain General Order of 24 March," quoted in Edmonds, *Military Operations*, 1:448–50.

22. Greenhalgh, *Foch in Command*, 298; Foch and Mott, *Memoirs of Marshall Foch*, 258.

23. Travers, *How the War Was Won*, 69.

24. Sheffield and Bourne, *Douglas Haig*, 391–92.

25. Oberkommando des Heeres, *Der Weltkrieg 1914 bis 1918*, 14:199.

26. Ludendorff, *My War Memories*, 2:600.

27. Travers, *Killing Ground*, 237.

28. Henniker, *Transportation on the Western Front*, 402; Brown, *British Logistics on the Western Front*, 186.

29. Foch and Mott, *Memoirs of Marshall Foch*, 257–58.

30. Sheffield and Bourne, *Douglas Haig*, 392–93.

31. Greenhalgh, "Myth and Memory."

32. Callwell, *Field Marshal Sir Henry Wilson*, 2:77.

33. Greenhalgh, "Myth and Memory," 793.

34. Travers, *How the War Was Won*, 67.

35. "Personal and Secret Orders to the Commander General of the Group of Reserve Armies, No.11 P.C.," 26 March 1918, in Viereck, *As They Saw Us*, 79.

36. Pitt, *1918*, 125–26.

37. Oberkommando des Heeres, *Der Weltkrieg 1914 bis 1918*, 14:201, 210–11, appendix 38e.

38. OHL, Ia 7341, 26 March 1918, File PH 3/268, German Military Archives; Army Group Crown Prince Rupprecht, Ia 6438, 26 March 1918, File PH 5 II/202, German Military Archives; Oberkommando des Heeres, *Der Weltkrieg 1914 bis 1918*, 14:199–202.

39. Kuhl, *Entstehung, Durchführung und Zusammenbruch der Offensive von 1918*, 135.

40. Edmonds, *Military Operations*, 1:537.

41. Ludendorff, *My War Memories*, 2:599.

42. Liddell Hart, *Foch*, 268.

43. Pershing, *My Experiences in the World War*, 1:363.

44. Barnett, *Swordbearers*, 325; Doughty, *Pyrrhic Victory*, 437.

45. Neiberg, *Foch*, 63.

46. Doughty, *Pyrrhic Victory*, 438; Foch and Mott, *Memoirs of Marshall Foch*, 263.

47. Liddell Hart, *Foch*, 275–77.

48. Sheffield and Bourne, *Douglas Haig*, 394; Foch, 263.

49. "Doullens Agreement," 26 March 1918, in Department of the Army, *United States Army in the World War 1917–1919*, 2:254.

50. Suttie, *Rewriting the First World War*, 168.

51. Foch and Mott, *Memoirs of Marshall Foch*, 264.

52. Doughty, *Pyrrhic Victory*, 438.

53. Foch and Mott, *Memoirs of Marshall Foch*, 265–66.

54. "General Order No. 104, (Headquarters No. 28277 T)," 27 March 1918, in Viereck, *As They Saw Us*, 81.

55. Doughty, *Pyrrhic Victory*, 439.

56. Smythe, *Pershing*, 100.

57. Henniker, *Transportation on the Western Front*, 374.

58. Oberkommando des Heeres, *Der Weltkrieg 1914 bis 1918*, 14:211–12.

59. Oberkommando des Heeres, 208.

60. Oberkommando des Heeres, 206–7.

61. Rupprecht, *In Treue Fest*, 2:359.

62. Doughty, *Pyrrhic Victory*, 439.

63. "Orders to Hold Ground at All Costs," 27 March 1918, in Department of the Army, *United States Army in the World War 1917–1919*, 2:260–61.

64. "Extract from Minutes of War Cabinet Meeting 374," 27 March 1918, in Department of the Army, *United States Army in the World War 1917–1919*, 2:258–59.

65. Greenhalgh, *Foch in Command*, 324.

66. Smythe, *Pershing*, 101.

67. Army Group German Crown Prince, War Diary Extracts, 28 March 1918, File PH 5 I/29, German Military Archives.

68. Rupprecht, *In Treue Fest*, 2:360.

69. Wetzell, "Michael, die Grosse Schlacht in Frankreich," 1946.

70. Oberkommando des Heeres, *Der Weltkrieg 1914 bis 1918*, 14:216–20.

71. Army Group Crown Prince Rupprecht, Ia 6483, 29 March 1918, File PH 3/281, German Military Archives.

72. Edmonds, *Military Operations*, 2:75.

73. Brown, *British Logistics on the Western Front*, 186.

74. "GHQ AEF War Diary, Book II, p. 446," 28 March 1918, in Department of the Army, *United States Army in the World War 1917–1919*, 2:260–61.

75. Rupprecht, *In Treue Fest*, 2:363.

76. Brown, *British Logistics on the Western Front*, 188–89.

77. Sheffield and Bourne, *Douglas Haig*, 395.

78. Foch and Mott, *Memoirs of Marshall Foch*, 270.

79. Edmonds, *Military Operations*, 2:118–19; Sheffield and Bourne, *Douglas Haig*, 396–98.

80. Edmonds, *Military Operations*, 2:458.

81. OHL, Ia 7408, 30 March 1918, File PH 3/268, German Military Archives.

82. AOK 2, War Diary, 30 March 1918, File PH 5 II/121, German Military Archives.

83. Sheffield and Bourne, *Douglas Haig*, 396.

84. "Supreme War Council Telegram 317–39," 29 March 1918, and "Supreme War Council Fldr. 316 Cablegram," 29 March 1918; and "Cable p-820-S," 30 March 1918, all in Department of the Army, *United States Army in the World War 1917–1919*, 2:263–64.

85. OHL, Ia 7414, 31 March 1918, File PH 3/268, German Military Archives.

86. OHL, Ia 7434, 1 April 1918, in Department of the Army, *United States Army in the World War 1917–1919*, 11:280.

87. Army Group German Crown Prince, War Diary extracts, "Notes of Discussion with Ludendorff," 1 April 1918, File PH 5 I/29, German Military Archives; Army Group Crown Prince Rupprecht, War Diary, 1 April 1918, File Hgr. Rupprecht, Bd. 80, Bavarian War Archives, Munich.

88. Army Group German Crown Prince, Ia 2406, 1 April 1918, File PH 5 I/31, German Military Archives.

89. OHL, Ia 7515, 5 April 1918, in Department of the Army, *United States Army in the World War 1917–1919*, 11:282.

90. Rupprecht, *In Treue Fest*, 2:359.

91. Kitchen, *German Offensives of 1918*, 79.

92. AOK 2, Ia/Art (no number), 7 April 1918, File Hgr. Rupprecht, Bd. 38, Bavarian War Archives.

93. OHL, II 82923, 8 April 1918, File Hgr. Rupprecht, Bd. 38, Bavarian War Archives.

94. Edmonds, *Military Operations*, 2:117, 506–8.

95. "General Staff Mp.34, General Foch to the Minister of War," 1 April 1918, in Department of the Army, *United States Army in the World War 1917–1919*, 2:270.

96. Pershing, *My Experiences in the World War*, 1:373–75.

97. "SWC: 376–1 Agreement. Minutes of a Conference held at the Hotel De Ville on Wednesday, April 3, 1918, at 3:15 p.m.," in Department of the Army, *United States Army in the World War 1917–1919*, 2:274–77.

98. Edmonds, *Military Operations*, 2:116–17.

99. Foch and Mott, *Memoirs of Marshall Foch*, 274.

100. Hoffmann, *War of Lost Opportunities*, 239–40.

101. The Oak Leaves indicated a higher level of the Pour le Mérite rather than a second award, as in the American system of military decorations.

102. Liddell Hart, *Foch*, 280.

103. Gray, *Kaisersschlacht 1918*, 76–77.

104. Doughty, *Pyrrhic Victory*, 416.

105. Edmonds, *Military Operations*, 1:486.

106. For a detailed assessment of Ludendorff's operational decisions during Operation MICHAEL, see Zabecki, *German 1918 Offensives*, 160–73.

107. Army Group Crown Prince Rupprecht, Ia 5243, 26 January 1918, File PH 3/278, German Military Archives.

108. Oberkommando des Heeres, *Der Weltkrieg 1914 bis 1918*, 14:273; Rupprecht, *In Treue Fest*, 2:371.

109. Georg Bruchmüller Papers, "Der Feldherr in meinem Blickfeld" (unpublished reminiscence of Ludendorff), File N275/2, German Military Archives.

110. Edmonds, *Military Operations*, 2:142–43.

111. "Letter Haig to Foch," 6 April 1918, in Department of the Army, *United States Army in the World War 1917–1919*, 2:285; Edmonds, *Military Operations*, 2:140–41.

112. Foch and Mott, *Memoirs of Marshall Foch*, 274, 278, 283.

113. "Headquarters, Allied Armies, General Staff No. 121," 7 April 1918, in Department of the Army, *United States Army in the World War 1917–1919*, 2:288–89.

114. Edmonds, *Military Operations*, 2:145.

115. Foch and Mott, *Memoirs of Marshall Foch*, 283.

116. Oberkommando des Heeres, *Der Weltkrieg 1914 bis 1918*, 14:272.

117. Rupprecht, *In Treue Fest*, 2:375–76; Oberkommando des Heeres, *Der Weltkrieg 1914 bis 1918*, 14:272–75.

118. Edmonds, *Military Operations*, 2:215–16; Foch and Mott, *Memoirs of Marshall Foch*, 284–85.

119. Lossberg, *Lossberg's War*, 323.

120. Foch and Mott, *Memoirs of Marshall Foch*, 285–86, 293.

121. "Headquarters Allied Armies. General Staff No. 133," 10 April 1918, in Department of the Army, *United States Army in the World War 1917–1919*, 2:314–15.

122. "General Headquarters British Armies in France, OAD 810," 10 April 1918, in Department of the Army, *United States Army in the World War 1917–1919*, 2:315.

123. Edmonds, *Military Operations*, 2:217.

124. Ludendorff, *My War Memories*, 2:607.

125. "General Headquarters British Armies in France. Support of British Troops by French Forces," 11 April 1918, in Department of the Army, *United States Army in the World War 1917–1919*, 2:315.

126. Foch and Mott, *Memoirs of Marshall Foch*, 291.

127. Edmonds, *Military Operations*, 2:248.

128. Edmonds, 2:512 (appendix 10).

129. Quoted in Keegan, *Mask of Command*, 100.

130. Army Group Crown Prince Rupprecht, War Diary, Ia 6738, 12 April 1918, File Hgr. Rupprecht, Bd. 80, Bavarian War Archives.

131. Edmonds, *Military Operations*, 2:277.

132. Foch and Mott, *Memoirs of Marshall Foch*, 288–90; Edmonds, *Military Operations*, 2:280.

133. Edmonds, *Military Operations*, 2:274–76.

134. Liddell Hart, *Reputations*, 118.

135. Foch and Mott, *Memoirs of Marshall Foch*, 290.

136. Kitchen, *German Offensives of 1918*, 111.

137. Doughty, *Pyrrhic Victory*, 443; Foch and Mott, *Memoirs of Marshall Foch*, 291–93.

138. Edmonds, *Military Operations*, 2:315.

139. "Headquarters, Allied Armies, Operations, General Staff, No. 176," 14 April 1918, in Department of the Army, *United States Army in the World War 1917–1919*, 2:323.

140. "Ministry of War, No. 149/H.R.," 14 April 1918, in Department of the Army, *United States Army in the World War 1917–1919*, 2:324.

141. Hermann von Kuhl, "Personal War Diary of General von Kuhl," 15 April 1918, File: RH 61/970, German Military Archives.

142. Liddell Hart, *Foch*, 299; Edmonds, *Military Operations*, 2:338.

143. Greenhalgh, *Foch in Command*, 319.

144. Lossberg, *Lossberg's War*, 332.

145. Rupprecht, *In Treue Fest*, 2:385–86; Lossberg, *Lossberg's War*, 332–33.

146. Foch and Mott, *Memoirs of Marshall Foch*, 294.

147. Callwell, *Field Marshal Sir Henry Wilson*, 2:92; Foch and Mott, *Memoirs of Marshall Foch*, 393.

148. Stevenson, *With Our Backs to the Wall*, 74–75.

149. Callwell, *Field Marshal Sir Henry Wilson*, 2:92.

150. Thaer, *Generalstabsdienst an der Front und in der O.H.L.*, 181–82.

151. Haig, *Dispatches*, 244; Edmonds. *Military Operations*, 2:367.

152. Army Group Crown Prince Rupprecht, War Diary, Ia 6852, 19 April 1918, File Hgr. Rupprecht, Bd. 80, Bavarian War Archives.

153. "Headquarters, Allied Armies. General Staff No. 261," 19 April 1918, in Department of the Army, *United States Army in the World War 1917–1919*, 2:332.

154. OHL, Ia 7777, 20 April 1918, Army Group Crown Prince Rupprecht, War Diary, File Hgr. Rupprecht, Bd. 80, Bavarian War Archives.

155. Kuhl, *Der Weltkrieg 1914–1918*, 2:348; Oberkommando des Heeres, *Der Weltkrieg 1914 bis 1918*, 14:289.

156. Hindenburg, *Out of My Life*, 2:169–70.

157. H. Balck, *Order in Chaos*, 84.

158. Edmonds, *Military Operations*, 2:437.

159. Liddell Hart, *Foch*, 301.

160. Army Group Crown Prince Rupprecht, War Diary, Ia 7010, 29 April 1918, File Hgr. Rupprecht, Bd. 80, Bavarian War Archives; Rupprecht, *In Treue Fest*, 2:392.

161. Oberkommando des Heeres, *Der Weltkrieg 1914 bis 1918*, 14:299.

162. Sheffield, *Forgotten Victory*, 193.

163. Doughty, *Pyrrhic Victory*, 444.

164. "General Headquarters. French Armies of the North and Northeast. 3rd Section General Staff. No. 25972," 24 April 1918, in Department of the Army, *United States Army in the World War 1917–1919*, 2:345–48.

165. Greenhalgh, *Foch in Command*, 325.

166. Cited in Stevenson, *With Our Backs to the Wall*, 249.

167. Pershing, *My Experiences in the World War*, 2:379.

168. Greenhalgh, *Foch in Command*, 324; Smythe, *Pershing*, 110.

169. Foch and Mott, *Memoirs of Marshall Foch*, 307.

170. Edmonds, *Military Operations*, 2:458.

171. Sheffield, *Chief*, 290.

172. Thaer, *Generalstabsdienst an der Front und in der O.H.L.*, 194–98.

9. BLÜCHER AND GNEISENAU

1. Hindenburg, *Out of My Life*, 327.

2. Quoted in Wheeler-Bennett, *Hindenburg*, 357.

3. Oberkommando des Heeres, *Der Weltkrieg 1914 bis 1918*, 14:317–18; Rupprecht, *In Treue Fest*, 3:318–19.

4. Ludendorff, *My War Memories*, 2:616.

5. AOK 7, Ia 371, 12 May 1918, File: Operations Documents (BLÜCHER-GNEISENAU-GOERZ) from 15 May to 26 May 1918, Part 2, U.S. Army Combat Arms Reference Library, Fort Leavenworth, KS.

6. Hindenburg, *Out of My Life*, 328.

7. Oberkommando des Heeres, *Der Weltkrieg 1914 bis 1918*, 14:317.

8. AOK 7, Ia 478, 23 May 1918, File: Operations Documents (BLÜCHER-GNEISENAU-GOERZ) from 15 May to 26 May 1918, Part 2, U.S. Army Combat Arms Reference Library.

9. Oberkommando des Heeres, *Der Weltkrieg 1914 bis 1918*, vol. 14, appendix 38h.

10. For a detailed discussion of the HAGEN plan, see Ząbecki, *German 1918 Offensives*, 280–310.

11. Oberkommando des Heeres, *Der Weltkrieg 1914 bis 1918*, vol. 14, appendix 38h, 39c.

12. "OAD 832. Notes of a Conference Held at Abbeville at 10:00 a.m., Saturday, April 27th, 1918," in Department of the Army, *United States Army in the World War 1917–1919*, 2:355–56.

13. Pershing, *My Experiences in the World War*, 2:28.

14. Pershing, 2:28.

15. Smythe, *Pershing*, 115.

16. Sheffield and Bourne, *Douglas Haig*, 409.

17. Sheffield and Bourne, 409.

18. "SWC 115, Resolution 2, Executive War Board," 2 May 1918, in Department of the Army, *United States Army in the World War 1917–1919*, 2:366–71.

19. Smythe, *Pershing*, 118.

20. Pershing, *My Experiences in the World War*, 2:35–36.

21. AEF GHQ, "Combat Instructions," 5 September 1918, quoted in Grotelueschen, *AEF Way of War*, 49.

22. Neiberg, *Fighting the Great War*, 322.

23. Edmonds, *Military Operations*, 3:39; Ryan, *Pétain the Soldier*, 167.

24. Greenhalgh, *Foch in Command*, 336.

25. Greenhalgh, 348.

26. Edmonds, *Military Operations*, 3:17–21.

27. Pershing, *My Experiences in the World War*, 2:61–62; Edmonds, *Military Operations*, 3:17–18.

28. Foch and Mott, *Memoirs of Marshall Foch*, 301.

29. Bruchmüller, *Die Artillerie beim Angriff im Stellungskrieg*, 71–94, appendix 4; Oberkommando des Heeres, *Der Weltkrieg 1914 bis 1918*, vol. 14, appendix 39c.

30. Army Group German Crown Prince, War Diary, 27 May 1918, File: Extracts from the War Diary of the Army Group German Crown Prince, 27 May to 15 June 1918, Combat Arms Reference Library; Oberkommando des Heeres, *Der Weltkrieg 1914 bis 1918*, 14:344.

31. Army Group German Crown Prince, War Diary, 28 May 1918, File: Extracts from the War Diary of the Army Group German Crown Prince, 27 May to 15 June 1918, Combat Arms Reference Library.

32. Army Group German Crown Prince, War Diary, 28 May 1918; Oberkommando des Heeres, *Der Weltkrieg 1914 bis 1918*, 14:351.

33. Edmonds, *Military Operations*, 3:116.

34. Edmonds, 3:24.

35. Pershing, *My Experiences in the World War*, 2:58–60.

36. Grotelueschen, *AEF War of War*, 73–79.

37. Bose, *Wachsende Schwierigkeiten*, 92.

38. Oberkommando des Heeres, *Der Weltkrieg 1914 bis 1918*, 14:360; Bose, *Deutsche Siege*, 135; Edmonds, *Military Operations*, 3:134.

39. Edmonds, *Military Operations*, 3:181–82; Foch and Mott, *Memoirs of Marshall Foch*, 317–18.

40. Sheffield and Bourne, *Douglas Haig*, 146.

41. OHL, Ia 8441, 30 May 1918, File: Operations Documents (BLÜCHER-GNEISENAU-GOERZ), 27 May to 9 June 1918, Combat Arms Reference Library; Oberkommando des Heeres, *Der Weltkrieg 1914 bis 1918*, 14:364.

42. Kuhl, *Entstehung, Durchführung und Zusammenbruch der Offensive von 1918*, 168.

43. Oberkommando des Heeres, *Der Weltkrieg 1914 bis 1918*, 14:325; Wilhelm, *My War Experiences*, 314.

44. Pershing, *My Experiences in the World War*, 2:62–65.

45. Foch and Mott, *Memoirs of Marshall Foch*, 319–20.

46. Edmonds, *Military Operations*, 3:141.

47. Oberkommando des Heeres, *Der Weltkrieg 1914 bis 1918*, 14:365–66.

48. Oberkommando des Heeres, 14:368.

49. Ząbecki, *German 1918 Offensives*, 228, table 8.8.

50. Edmonds, *Military Operations*, 3:146.

51. Oberkommando des Heeres, *Der Weltkrieg 1914 bis 1918*, 14:365.

52. Edmonds, *Military Operations*, 3:144–45.

53. Doughty, *Pyrrhic Victory*, 455; Foch and Mott, *Memoirs of Marshall Foch*, 320.

54. Kitchen, *German Offensives of 1918*, 143; Edmonds, *Military Operations*, 3:147.

55. OHL, Ia 8485, 1 June 1918, File: Operations Documents (BLÜCHER-GNEISENAU-GOERZ), 27 May to 9 June 1918, Combat Arms Reference Library.

56. Oberkommando des Heeres, *Der Weltkrieg 1914 bis 1918*, 14:373.

57. Oberkommando des Heeres, 14:374.

58. AOK 7, Ia 607, 2 June 1918, File: Extracts from the Diary of the Commander-in-Chief of the Seventh Army, 1 June to 21 August 1918, Combat Arms Reference Library.

59. "Memorandum, General-in-Chief Commanding the Allied Armies," 1 June 1918, in Department of the Army, *United States Army in the World War 1917–1919*, 2:435–38.

60. "Allied Supreme War Council, 6th Session," 2 June 1918, in Department of the Army, *United States Army in the World War 1917–1919*, 2:441–45.

61. Sheffield and Bourne, *Douglas Haig*, 417.

62. Smythe, *Pershing*, 135.

63. Pershing, *My Experiences in the World War*, 2:75.

64. Pershing, 2:82, 92.

65. "Memorandum, Commander-in-Chief of the Allied Forces," 2 June 1918, in Department of the Army, *United States Army in the World War 1917–1919*, 2:446.

66. Donald Smythe, "Pershing," in Carver, *War Lords*, 171.

67. Sheffield and Bourne, *Douglas Haig*, 418.

68. Smythe, "Pershing," 170–71.

69. Army Group German Crown Prince, War Diary, 3 June 1918, File: Extracts from the War Diary of the Army Group German Crown Prince, 27 May to 15 June 1918, Combat Arms Reference Library.

70. Sheffield and Bourne, *Douglas Haig*, 419.

71. Oberkommando des Heeres, *Der Weltkrieg 1914 bis 1918*, 14:381.

72. Quoted in Liddell Hart, *Foch*, 322.

73. Quoted in Doughty, *Pyrrhic Victory*, 455–56.

74. Army Group German Crown Prince, Ia 675, 5 June 1918, File: Army Group German Crown Prince, Operations Documents (BLÜCHER–GNEISENAU–GOERZ), 27 May to 9 June 1918, Combat Arms Reference Library.

75. Rupprecht, *In Treue Fest*, 2:407.

76. Hermann von Kuhl, "Personal War Diary of General von Kuhl," 5 June 1918, File: RH 61/970., German Military Archives, Freiburg.

77. Holmes, *Western Front*, 203.

78. Grotelueschen, *AEF Way of War*, 206–26.

79. Pershing, *My Experiences in the World War*, 2:64.

80. Quoted in Smythe, *Pershing*, 139.

81. OHL, Ia 8584, 8 June 1918, and AOK7, Ia 696, 8 June 1918, both in File: Army Group German Crown Prince, Operations Documents (BLÜCHER-GNEISENAU-GOERZ), 17 May to 9 June 1918, Combat Arms Reference Library.

82. Kuhl, *Entstehung, Durchführung und Zusammenbruch der Offensive von 1918*, 58.

83. Oberkommando des Heeres, *Der Weltkrieg 1914 bis 1918*, 14:300, appendix 42.

84. Oberkommando des Heeres, 14:666.

85. OHL, Ic 85444, 12 May 1918, File PH 5 II/295, German Military Archives.

86. Wilhelm, *My War Experiences*, 326.

87. Ludendorff, *My War Memories*, 620.

88. Army Group German Crown Prince, Ia 2466, 30 April 1918, and OHL, Ia 7736, 30 April 1918, File: Operations Documents (BLÜCHER-GNEISENAU-GOERZ) from 17 April to 20 May 1918, Part 1, Combat Arms Reference Library.

89. Oberkommando des Heeres, *Der Weltkrieg 1914 bis 1918*, 14:395–96.

90. Oskar von Hutier, *Diary*, 4 June 1918, File RH61-907, German Military Archives.

91. Oberkommando des Heeres, *Der Weltkrieg 1914 bis 1918*, 14:395–96.

92. OHL, Ia 8536, 5 June 1918, File: Army Group German Crown Prince, Operations Documents (BLÜCHER-GNEISENAU-GOERZ), 17 May to 9 June 1918, Combat Arms Reference Library.

93. Foch and Mott, *Memoirs of Marshall Foch*, 323–44.

94. Doughty, *Pyrrhic Victory*, 456; Foch and Mott, *Memoirs of Marshall Foch*, 324.

95. Liddell Hart, *Foch*, 321.

96. Sheffield and Bourne, *Douglas Haig*, 420; Edmonds, *Military Operations*, 3:167.

97. Liddell Hart, *Foch*, 323; Doughty, *Pyrrhic Victory*, 457; Foch and Mott, *Memoirs of Marshall Foch*, 325.

98. Army Group German Crown Prince, Ia 2545, 28 May 1918, File: Army Group German Crown Prince, Operations Documents (BLÜCHER-GNEISENAU-GOERZ), 17 May to 9 June 1918, Combat Arms Reference Library; Oberkommando des Heeres, *Der Weltkrieg 1914 bis 1918*, 14:344–48, 382.

99. Foch and Mott, *Memoirs of Marshall Foch*, 371; Edmonds, *Military Operations*, 3:172.

100. Edmonds, *Military Operations*, 3:172.

101. Edmonds, 3:165, 175.

102. Foch and Mott, *Memoirs of Marshall Foch*, 324.

103. Oberkommando des Heeres, *Der Weltkrieg 1914 bis 1918*, 14:388, 399–401.

104. Edmonds, *Military Operations*, 3:179; Oberkommando des Heeres, *Der Weltkrieg 1914 bis 1918*, 14:399.

105. Foch and Mott, *Memoirs of Marshall Foch*, 328.

106. Pershing, *My Experiences in the World War*, 2:95.

107. Army Group German Crown Prince, War Diary, 10 June 1918, File: Extracts from the War Diary of the Army Group German Crown Prince, 27 May to 15 June 1918, Combat Arms Reference Library.

108. "Cable P-1279-S for the Chief of Staff and the Secretary of War," 10 June 1918, in Department of the Army, *United States Army in the World War 1917–1919*, 2:460.

109. Pershing, *My Experiences in the World War*, 2:64.

110. Army Group German Crown Prince, Morning and Noon Reports, 11 June 1918, File: Extracts from the War Diary of the Army Group German Crown Prince, 27 May to 15 June 1918, Combat Arms Reference Library.

111. Army Group German Crown Prince, War Diary, 11 June 1918, File: Extracts from the War Diary of the Army Group German Crown Prince, 27 May to 15 June 1918, Combat Arms Reference Library.

112. Oberkommando des Heeres, *Der Weltkrieg 1914 bis 1918*, 14:404; Edmonds, *Military Operations*, 3:181.

113. Army Group German Crown Prince, Morning Reports, 13 June 1918, File: Extracts from the War Diary of the Army Group German Crown Prince, 27 May to 15 June 1918, Combat Arms Reference Library.

114. Edmonds, *Military Operations*, 3:183–85.

115. Doughty, *Pyrrhic Victory*, 459.

116. Edmonds, *Military Operations*, 3:170.

117. "H.S. Brit. File: 910–32.9. Telephone Message," 13 June 1918), Department of the Army, *United States Army in the World War 1917–1919*, 2:462.

118. Thaer, *Generalstabsdienst an der Front und in der O.H.L.*, 196–97.

10. OPERATION MARNESCHUTZ-REIMS AND THE SECOND BATTLE OF THE MARNE

1. Oberkommando des Heeres, *Der Weltkrieg 1914 bis 1918*, 14:466.

2. OHL, Ic 85444, 12 May 1918, File PH 5 II/295, German Military Archives, Freiburg.

3. Neiberg, *Fighting the Great War*, 86.

4. Hindenburg, *Out of My Life*, 2:188–89.

5. Wilhelm, *My War Experiences*, 322.

6. Wilhelm, 238.

7. Wilhelm, 330.

8. Hermann von Kuhl, "Personal War Diary of General von Kuhl," 14 June 1918, File RH 61/970, German Military Archives (hereafter Kuhl diary); OHL, Ia 8685, 14 June 1918, File: Operations Documents, Headquarters, Army Group German Crown Prince, 1918,

BLÜCHER-GNEISENAU-GOERZ, 14 June to 15 July 1918, Combat Arms Reference Library, Fort Leavenworth, KS.

9. Oberkommando des Heeres, *Der Weltkrieg 1914 bis 1918*, 14:334–35.

10. Kuhl diary, 19 June 1918.

11. OHL, Ia 8777, 18 June 1918, File: Operations Documents, Headquarters, Army Group German Crown Prince, 1918, BLÜCHER-GNEISENAU-GOERZ, 14 June to 15 July 1918, Combat Arms Reference Library.

12. Hindenburg, *Out of My Life*, 2:192.

13. Foch and Mott, *Memoirs of Marshall Foch*, 352.

14. Foch and Mott, 340.

15. Doughty, *Pyrrhic Victory*, 446.

16. Edmonds, Military *Operations*, 3:190; Foch and Mott, *Memoirs of Marshall Foch*, 310–11.

17. Greenhalgh, *Foch in Command*, 389.

18. Hunter, "Foch and Eisenhower," 84.

19. Greenhalgh, *Foch in Command*, 338.

20. Edmonds, *Military Operations*, 3:352–55.

21. Quoted in Doughty, *Pyrrhic Victory*, 460.

22. Greenhalgh. *Foch in Command*, 390.

23. Doughty, *Pyrrhic Victory*, 460.

24. Greenhalgh, *Foch in Command*, 377.

25. Smythe, *Pershing*, 145; Greenhalgh, *Foch in Command*, 392.

26. Pershing, *My Experiences in the World War*, 2:111.

27. Doughty, *Pyrrhic Victory*, 464–65; Foch and Mott, *Memoirs of Marshall Foch*, 345; Pershing, *My Experiences in the World War*, 2:123.

28. Pershing, *My Experiences in the World War*, 2:235; Smythe, *Pershing*, 172.

29. "Headquarters. General-in-Chief of the Allied Armies No. 1749. General Directive No. 4," 1 July 1918, Record Group WO 158/105, United Kingdom National Archives, Kew, Great Britain; Edmonds, *Military Operations*, 3:190–91, 217–19.

30. Greenhalgh, *Foch in Command*, 382–83; Foch and Mott, *Memoirs of Marshall Foch*, 356.

31. Edmonds, *Military Operations*, 3:221–23; Doughty, *Pyrrhic Victory*, 463–67.

32. "General Headquarters, French Armies of the North and Northeast. 3rd Section, General Staff, No. 5358. General Instructions," 5 July 1918, in Department of the Army, *United States Army in the World War 1917–1919*, 5:3.

33. Foch and Mott, *Memoirs of Marshall Foch*, 354–55; Edmonds, *Military Operations*, 3:215, 232, 238.

34. Foch and Mott, *Memoirs of Marshall Foch*, 353.

35. "General Headquarters, AEF, 3rd Section, General Staff, Fldr F-1, Conference Report," 10 July 1918, in Department of the Army, *United States Army in the World War 1917–1919*, 2:517–20, 527–31.

36. "Headquarters. General-in-Chief of the Allied Armies No. 2021. From General Foch to Marshal Haig," 12 July 1918, Record Group WO 158/105, United Kingdom National Archives; Edmonds, *Military Operations*, 3:222–23.

37. "French General Headquarters, Fldr G Notes. Notes on a Conversation at Provins Between General Pershing and General Pétain," 12 July 1918, in Department of the Army, *United States Army in the World War 1917–1919*, 2:523–24.

38. Edmonds, *Military Operations*, 3:280.

39. Oberkommando des Heeres, *Der Weltkrieg 1914 bis 1918*, vol. 14, appendixes 38i, 39e.

40. U.S. War Department, Document No. 905, *Histories of Two Hundred and Fifty-one Divisions of the German Army Which Participated in the War (1914–1918)*.

41.Wilhelm, *My War Experiences*, 332.

42. Army Group German Crown Prince, Ia/Art 12968, 26 June 1918, File PH 3/260, German Military Archives; Oberkommando des Heeres, *Der Weltkrieg 1914 bis 1918*, vol. 14, appendix 39e.

43. Lanza, "German XXIII Reserve Crosses the Marne," 308.

44. Lanza, "Five Decisive Days," *Field Artillery Journal*, 42.

45. Oberkommando des Heeres, *Der Weltkrieg 1914 bis 1918*, 14:449–50.

46. Army Group German Crown Prince, War Diary, 15 July 1918, File: Extracts from the War Diary, Army Group German Crown Prince, 15 July to 3 August 1918, Combat Arms Reference Library.

47. Army Group German Crown Prince, War Diary, 15 July 1918.

48. Hindenburg, *Out of My Life*, 2:196.

49. Kuhl diary, 16 July 1918.

50. AOK7, War Diary, 15 July 1918, File: Extracts from the Diary of the Commander-in-Chief of the Seventh Army, 1 June to 21 August 1918, Combat Arms Reference Library.

51. OHL, Ia 9304, 15 July 1918, File PH 3/264, German Military Archives.

52. Army Group German Crown Prince, War Diary, 15 July 1918.

53. Doughty, *Pyrrhic Victory*, 468.

54. Foch and Mott, *Memoirs of Marshall Foch*, 359; Edmonds, *Military Operations*, 3:233–34.

55. "Telephone Message, Foch to Pétain, 12:25 pm," 15 July 1918, in Department of the Army, *United States Army in the World War 1917–1919*, 5:242; Foch and Mott, *Memoirs of Marshall Foch*, 357.

56. Doughty, *Pyrrhic Victory*, 467.

57. Sheffield and Bourne, *Douglas Haig*, 429–30.

58. Army Group German Crown Prince, Ia 2670, 16 July 1918, File PH 5 II/409, German Military Archives; AOK7, Ia 1023, 16 July 1918, File PH 5 II/163, German Military Archives.

59. AOK3, Ia 7695, 16 July 1918, File: The Army Records, Army Group of the German Crown Prince, MARNE, 1918 Campaign, Combat Arms Reference Library.

60. AOK7, War Diary, 16 July 1918, File: Extracts from the Diary of the Commander-in-Chief of the Seventh Army, 1 June to 21 August 1918, Combat Arms Reference Library; Edmonds, *Military Operations*, 3:234.

61. Quoted in Neiberg, *Second Battle of the Marne*, 199.

62. Neiberg, 199.

63. Liggett, *A.E.F. Ten Years Ago in France*, 116–17.

64. Army Group German Crown Prince, Ia 2674, 17 July 1918, Document 411, in General Service Schools, *German Offensive of July 15, 1918 (Marne Source Book)*, 578.

65. Cited in Wolfgang Foerster, *Ludendorff*, 17.

66. AOK7, Ia 1039, 17 July 1918, File PH 5 II/163, German Military Archives.

67. Edmonds, *Military Operations*, 3:365–66; Sheffield, *Chief*, 292.

68. Pershing, *My Experiences in the World War*, 2:235.

69. Oberkommando des Heeres, *Der Weltkrieg 1914 bis 1918*, 14:478, appendix 39h; Edmonds, *Military Operations*, 3:239.

70. Quoted in Kuhl diary, 2 August 1918.

71. Ludendorff, *My War Memories*, 2:668.

72. Army Group German Crown Prince, Ia 2689, 18 July 1918, File PH 5 I/40, German Military Archives.

73. Rupprecht, *In Treue Fest*, 2:422; Oberkommando des Heeres, *Der Weltkrieg 1914 bis 1918*, 14:471.

74. Hindenburg, *Out of My Life*, 2:203–4.

75. "Special Directive No. 2168," 18 July 1918, Record Group WO 158/105, United Kingdom National Archives.

76. War Diary, Seventh Army, 18 July 1918, Document 441, in General Service Schools, *German Offensive of July 15, 1918*, 578.

77. Astore and Showalter, *Hindenburg*, 66; Oberkommando des Heeres, *Der Weltkrieg 1914 bis 1918*, 14:484.

78. "Personal and Secret Instruction for the General Commanding Army Chief of the North and Northeast, No. 2206," 19 July 1918, Record Group WO 158/105, United Kingdom National Archives.

79. AOK 7, War Diary, 19 July 1918, File: Extracts from the Diary of the Commander-in-Chief of the Seventh Army, 1 June to 21 August 1918, Combat Arms Reference Library.

80. Ząbecki, *German 1918 Offensives*, 280–95.

81. Liddell Hart, *Foch*, 337–38; Pitt, *1918*, 207.

82. Lossberg, *Lossberg's War*, 342.

83. Lossberg, 342–45; Oberkommando des Heeres, *Der Weltkrieg 1914 bis 1918*, 14:487–88.

84. Rupprecht, *In Treue Fest*, 2:424–27.

85. OHL, Ia 9388, 20 July 1918, File Hgr. Rupprecht, Bd. 105, Bavarian War Archives, Munich; Oberkommando des Heeres, *Der Weltkrieg 1914 bis 1918*, 14:534.

86. Kuhl diary, 20–21 July 1918; Oberkommando des Heeres, *Der Weltkrieg 1914 bis 1918*, 14:534.

87. Oberkommando des Heeres, *Der Weltkrieg 1914 bis 1918*, 14:487–88; Rupprecht, *In Treue Fest*, 2:424–27.

88. Oberkommando des Heeres, *Der Weltkrieg 1914 bis 1918*, 14:487–88.

89. Pershing, *My Experiences in the World War*, 2:157.

90. "Commander-in-Chief of the Allied Armies to Commander-in-Chief of the American Army, No. 2280," 22 July 1918, Record Group WO 158/105, United Kingdom National Archives.

91. Oberkommando des Heeres, *Der Weltkrieg 1914 bis 1918*, 14:490.

92. Neiberg, *Second Battle of the Marne*, 161.

93. "Memo Foch to Pétain," unnumbered, 23 July 1918, Record Group WO 158/105, United Kingdom National Archives; Foch and Mott, *Memoirs of Marshall Foch*, 366.

94. Stenger, *Schicksalswende*, 202–6; Oberkommando des Heeres, *Der Weltkrieg 1914 bis 1918*, 14:493.

95. Quoted in Foerster, *Ludendorff*, 28.

96. Stenger, *Schicksalswende*, 205; Oberkommando des Heeres, *Der Weltkrieg 1914 bis 1918*, 14:492.

97. Edmonds, *Military Operations*, 3:290.

98. OHL, Ia 9472, 25 July 1918, File: Extracts from Operations Documents from 1 July to 6 August 1918 Pertaining to Army Group German Crown Prince: The Defensive in July 1918, Combat Arms Reference Library.

99. Lossberg, *Lossberg's War*, 347–48; Kuhl diary, 26 July 1918.

100. Greenhalgh, *Foch in Command*, 411.

101. OHL, Ia 9536, 27 July 1918, File: Extracts from Operations Documents from 1 July to 6 August 1918 Pertaining to Army Group German Crown Prince: The Defensive in July 1918, Combat Arms Reference Library.

102. OHL, Ia 9541, 28 July 1918, in Department of the Army, *United States Army in the World War 1917–1919*, 11:348–49.

103. Rupprecht, *In Treue Fest*, 2:428–29.

104. Army Group German Crown Prince, Ia 2629, 26 June 1918, in General Service Schools, *German Offensive of July 15, 1918*, 172–74.

105. "Foch to the General of the Expeditionary American Forces, No. 2468," 28 July 1918, Record Group WO 158/105, United Kingdom National Archives.

106. Pershing, *My Experiences in the World War*, 2:189.

107. Army Group German Crown Prince, Ia 2751, 29 July 1918, File PH 5 II/189, German Military Archives.

108. Edmonds, *Military Operations*, 3:287.

109. Quoted in Doughty, *Pyrrhic Victory*, 474.

110. Foch and Mott, *Memoirs of Marshall Foch*, 367.

111. Oberkommando des Heeres, *Der Weltkrieg 1914 bis 1918*, 14:537.

112. Stenger, *Schicksalswende*, 218–19.

113. Foch and Mott, *Memoirs of Marshall Foch*, 393.

114. Hindenburg, *Out of My Life*, 2:205.

115. Kuhl, *Entstehung, Durchführung und Zusammenbruch der Offensive von 1918*, 185.

116. Waechter, "Das Artillerie-Angriffsverfahren beim Durchbruch im Weltkriege."

117. Oberkommando des Heeres, *Der Weltkrieg 1914 bis 1918*, 14:299.

118. Army Group German Crown Prince, Ia 2639, 29 June 1918, File: Extracts from Archives—Army Group German Crown Prince, 1918, First Army, 16 June to 31 July 1918, Combat Arms Reference Library.

119. AOK 7, Ia 893, 30 June 1918, File PH 5 II/163, German Military Archives.

120. Kuhl diary, 2 August 1918.

121. Walther Reinhardt, Chief of Staff of the Seventh Army, in Viereck, *As They Saw Us*, 98.

122. Ząbecki, *German 1918 Offensives*, 280–310.

123. Army Group Crown Prince Rupprecht, Ia 8082, 1 July 1918, File Hgr. Rupprecht, Bd. 112, Bavarian War Archives.

124. Gross, *Myth and Reality of German Warfare*, 128.

125. Travers, *How the War Was Won*, 108.

126. Doughty, *Pyrrhic Victory*, 472–73.

127. Doughty, 468.

128. Astore and Showalter, *Hindenburg*, 65.

11. HAMEL TO MONT ST. QUENTIN

1. Travers, *How the War Was Won*, 175–78.

2. Travers, 112–13.

3. Gary Sheffield and Dan Todman, "Command and Control in the British Army on the Western Front," in Sheffield and Todman, *Command and Control on the Western Front*, 8–9; Dan Todman, "The General Lamasery Revisited: General Headquarters on the Western Front, 1914–1918," in Sheffield and Todman, *Command and Control on the Western Front*, 51.

4. Peter Simpkins. "'Building Blocks,' Aspects of Command and Control at Brigade Level in the BEF's Offensive Operations, 1916–1918," in Sheffield and Todman, *Command and Control on the Western Front*, 162.

5. Greenhalgh, *Foch in Command*, 335.

6. Sheffield and Bourne, *Douglas Haig*, 425.

7. "Foch Instruction to Haig No. 2021," 12 July 1918, Record Group WO 158/105, United Kingdom National Archives, Kew, Great Britain.

8. Edmonds, Military *Operations*, 3:313–15, 356–66.

9. "Personal and Secret from General Foch to Marshal Haig, No. 2248," 20 July 1918, Record Group WO 158/105, United Kingdom National Archives.

10. Sheffield and Bourne, *Douglas Haig*, 433.

11. Henniker, *Transportation on the Western Front*, 422.

12. Quoted in Liddell Hart, *Foch*, 342.

13. "Memorandum from the Commanders-in-Chief Conference No. 2375," 24 July 1918, Record Group WO 158/105, United Kingdom National Archives.

14. "Memorandum from the Commanders-in-Chief Conference No. 2375."

15. "HS Secret Documents, Fldr F-1, Notes, Allied Conference at Château Bombon," July 24, 1918, in Department of the Army, *United States Army in the World War 1917–1919*, 2:549–50.

16. Foch and Mott, *Memoirs of Marshall Foch*, 373–74.

17. Sheffield and Bourne, *Douglas Haig*, 434.

18. Liggett, *A.E.F. Ten Years Ago in France*, 164.

19. Foch and Mott, *Memoirs of Marshall Foch*, 377.

20. "Special Directive. No. 2467," 28 July 1918, Record Group WO 158/105, United Kingdom National Archives.

21. "Foch to the British Commander-in-Chief, No. 2466," 28 July 1918, Record Group WO 158/105, United Kingdom National Archives.

22. Hindenburg, *Out of My Life*, 2:218–19.

23. Edmonds, *Military Operations*, 3:320–21.

24. Ludendorff, *My War Memories*, 2:679.

25. Quoted in Barnett, *Swordbearers*, 345–46.

26. Liddell Hart, *Foch*, 346.

27. Sheffield and Bourne, *Douglas Haig*, 438.

28. Doughty, *Pyrrhic Victory*, 477.

29. Ludendorff, *My War Memories*, 679.

30. Ludendorff, 680.

31. Ludendorff, 682.

32. Lossberg, *Lossberg's War*, 353–54.

33. Stevenson, *With Our Backs to the Wall*, 122.

34. Pitt, *1918*, 225.

35. Rupprecht, *In Treue Fest*, 2:436–36.

36. Travers, *How the War Was Won*, 127.

37. Doughty, *Pyrrhic Victory*, 477.

38. Foch and Mott, *Memoirs of Marshall Foch*, 382.

39. Stevenson, *With Our Backs to the Wall*, 124.

40. Sheffield and Bourne, *Douglas Haig*, 441.

41. Edmonds, *Military Operations*, 4:133–34.

42. Ludendorff, *My War Memories*, 2:682.

43. Kuhl diary, 10 August 1918.

44. Sheffield and Bourne, *Douglas Haig*, 442–43.

45. Ludendorff, *My War Memories*, 2:683.

46. Lossberg, *Lossberg's War*, 356–58.

47. Smythe, *Pershing*, 170–71; Sheffield and Bourne, *Douglas Haig*, 443.

48. "Foch to Haig, Pershing, and Pétain, No. 3035," 17 August 1918, Record Group WO 158/105, United Kingdom National Archives.

49. "Marshal Foch to Field Marshal Haig and General Pétain, No. 8/P.C.," 12 August 1918, Record Group WO 158/105, United Kingdom National Archives.

50. Edmonds, *Military Operations*, 4:154.

51. Lossberg, *Lossberg's War*, 354.

52. Ludendorff, *My War Memories*, 2:686–87.

53. Hindenburg, *Out of My Life*, 2:220.

54. Foch and Mott, *Memoirs of Marshall Foch*, 393.

55. Sheffield and Bourne, *Douglas Haig*, 445–46; Sheffield, *Chief*, 302.

56. Sheffield, *Chief*, 302; Edmonds, *Military Operations*, 4:169–70; "Marshal Foch to Field Marshal Haig, No.12/P.C.," 15 August 1918, Record Group WO 158/105, United Kingdom National Archives.

57. "Operations Priorities, No. 18/P.C.," 15 August 1918, Record Group WO 158/105, United Kingdom National Archives.

58. Foch and Mott, *Memoirs of Marshall Foch*, 388.

59. Lossberg, *Lossberg's War*, 354.

60. Haig, *Dispatches*, 261.

61. Sheffield and Bourne, *Douglas Haig*, 448.

62. Liggett, *A.E.F. Ten Years Ago in France*, 161.

63. Foch and Mott, *Memoirs of Marshall Foch*, 389.

64. Lossberg, *Lossberg's War*, 354.

65. "O.A.D. 911, Commander-in-Chief Telegram of 22nd August 1918," in Edmonds, *Military Operations*, 4:587–88, appendix 20.

66. Wilhelm, *My War Experiences*, 347–48.

67. Edmonds, *Military Operations*, 4:262.

68. Edmonds, 313.

69. Haig, *Dispatches*, 267.

70. Foch and Mott, *Memoirs of Marshall Foch*, 392.

71. Haig, *Dispatches*, 269.

72. Foch and Mott, *Memoirs of Marshall Foch*, 391–92.

73. Haig, *Dispatches*, 271.

74. Ludendorff, *My War Memories*, 696–98.

75. Lossberg, *Lossberg's War*, 355.

76. Edmonds, *Military Operations*, 4:335.

77. "Allied Commander-in-Chief to the Commanders-in-Chief of the Allied Armies," 30 August 1918, in Edmonds, *Military Operations*, 4:588–90, appendix 21.

78. Sheffield and Bourne, *Douglas Haig*, 451–52.

79. Edmonds, *Military Operations*, 4:389–95.

80. Sheffield and Bourne, *Douglas Haig*, 452.

81. Hindenburg, *Out of My Life*, 2:222; Foch and Mott, *Memoirs of Marshall Foch*, 403.

82. Greenhalgh, *Foch in Command*, 442.

83. Wilhelm, *My War Experiences*, 348.

84. Stevenson, *With Our Backs to the Wall*, 131.

85. Lossberg, *Lossberg's War*, 356.

86. Lossberg, 350.

87. Quoted in Doughty, *Pyrrhic Victory*, 487.

88. Lossberg, *Lossberg's War*, 356–57.

89. Foch and Mott, *Memoirs of Marshall Foch*, 403.

90. Quoted in W. Balck, *Development of Tactics*, 289.

91. Stülpnagel also was implicated in war crimes as the commander of the Seventeenth Army in Russia.

12. CLOSING TO THE HINDENBURG LINE

1. Ludendorff, *My War Memories*, 2:707.

2. Haig, *Dispatches*, 272.

3. Wilhelm, *My War Experiences*, 349–50.

4. Liddell Hart, *Foch*, 366.

5. Sheffield, *Forgotten Victory*, 206.

6. Pershing, *My Experiences in the World War*, 1:86.

7. Doughty, *Pyrrhic Victory*, 144.

8. Pitt, *1918*, 241.

9. Hindenburg, *Out of My Life*, 2:222.

10. "Fldr. F-1. Conference at Bombon on the Employment of American Troops," 10 July 1918, in Department of the Army, *United States Army in the World War 1917–1919*, 2:517–20, 527–31.

11. "Commander-in-Chief of the Allied Armies to Commander-in-Chief of the American Army, No. 2280," 22 July 1918, Record Group WO 158/05, United Kingdom National Archives.

12. "Foch to Pershing, No. 2307," 22 July 1918, Record Group WO 158/05, United Kingdom National Archives.

13. Edmonds, *Military Operations*, 3:315–17.

14. Smythe, *Pershing*, 161.

15. Greenhalgh, *Foch in Command*, 419.

16. "Foch to Pershing and Pétain, No. 1/P.C.," 9 August 1918, Record Group WO 158/05, United Kingdom National Archives; Pershing, *My Experiences in the World War*, 2:212.

17. "Addendum Note to No. 1/P.C.," 9 August 1918, Record Group WO 158/05, United Kingdom National Archives.

18. Greenhalgh, *Foch in Command*, 429.

19. "Foch to Pershing, No. 3201," 23 August 1918, and "Note: Personal and Secret, No. 3266," 23 August 1918, Record Group WO 158/05, United Kingdom National Archives.

20. Stevenson, *With Our Backs to the Wall*, 131; Doughty, *Pyrrhic Victory*, 482–83.

21. Sheffield and Bourne, *Douglas Haig*,. 450.

22. Sheffield and Bourne, 451.

23. Pershing, *My Experiences in the World War*, 2:243–47; Doughty, *Pyrrhic Victory*, 483.

24. Pershing, *My Experiences in the World War*, 2:244–47.

25. Pershing, 2:245–47; Foch and Mott, *Memoirs of Marshall Foch*, 399–402.

26. "Note to the Allied Commanders-in-Chief [unnumbered]," 30 August 1918, Record Group WO 158/05, United Kingdom National Archives.

27. Doughty, *Pyrrhic Victory*, 483; Pershing, *My Experiences in the World War*, 2:251–52; Greenhalgh, *Foch in Command*, 436; Smythe, *Pershing*, 177.

28. Pershing, *My Experiences in the World War*, 2:248–50.

29. "Foch to Pershing, No. 3480," 1 September 1918, Record Group WO 158/05, United Kingdom National Archives.

30. Pershing, *My Experiences in the World War*, 2:253–54.

31. Doughty, *Pyrrhic Victory*, 484; "Foch to Pershing, No. 3480."

32. Greenhalgh, *Foch in Command*, 452.

33. Holmes, *Western Front*, 204.

34. "Meeting Notes, Marshal Foch and Generals Pétain and Pershing, No. 3528," 2 September 1918, Record Group WO 158/05, United Kingdom National Archives.

35. "Directive, No. 3537," 3 September 1918, Record Group WO 158/05, United Kingdom National Archives.

36. Sheffield and Bourne, *Douglas Haig*, 456.

37. Pershing, *My Experiences in the World War*, 2:358.

38. Liddell Hart, *Foch*, 355; Foch and Mott, *Memoirs of Marshall Foch*, 397; Pershing, *My Experiences in the World War*, 2:264–66.

39. Grotelueschen, *AEF Way of War*, 109.

40. Ludendorff, *My War Memories*, 2:708.

41. General Otto von Ledebur, Chief of Staff of Army Detachment C, quoted in Viereck, *As They Saw Us*, 180–94.

42. Ludendorff, *My War Memories*, 2:709.

43. Pershing, *My Experiences in the World War*, 2:272.

44. Ferrell, *America's Deadliest Battle*, 33–36.

45. Ludendorff quoted in Viereck, *As They Saw Us*, 30.

46. Pershing, *My Experiences in the World War*, 2:272–73.

47. Pershing, 2:278.

48. Pershing, 2:273.

49. Pershing, 2:270.

50. Liggett, *A.E.F. Ten Years Ago in France*, 159.

51. Quoted in Viereck, *As They Saw Us*, 37.

52. Ludendorff, *My War Memories*, 2:711.

53. Ferrell, *America's Deadliest Battle*, 35.

54. Hindenburg, *Out of My Life*, 2:224.

55. Thaer, *Generalstabsdienst an der Front und in der O.H.L.*, 229.

56. Sheffield and Bourne, *Douglas Haig*, 458.

57. Haig, *Dispatches*, 227.

58. Boff, *Haig's Enemy*, 238.

59. Edmonds, *Military Operations*, 4:469–94.

13. THE ALLIED GENERAL OFFENSIVE

1. Henniker, *Transportation on the Western Front*, 433–37.

2. Oberkommando des Heeres, *Der Weltkrieg 1914 bis 1918*, vol. 14, appendix 35.

3. Lossberg, *Lossberg's War*, 314.

4. "Note on the Offensive North of the Lys, No. 3737," 9 September 1918, Record Group WO 158/105, United Kingdom National Archives.

5. Haig, *Dispatches*, 281.

6. Sheffield and Bourne, *Douglas Haig*, 463.

7. Callwell, *Field Marshal Sir Henry Wilson*, 2:126.

8. Foch and Mott, *Memoirs of Marshall Foch*, 408–9; "Instructions for the General Commanding the Group of Armies of the Reserve, No. 33479," 23 September 1918, in Department of the Army, *United States Army in the World War 1917–1919*, 2:609–10.

9. Liggett, *A.E.F. Ten Years Ago in France*, 172.

10. Terraine, *To Win a War*, 154.

11. Oberkommando des Heeres, *Der Weltkrieg 1914 bis 1918*, 14:605–9.

12. Edmonds, *Military Operations*, 5:11.

13. Pitt, *1918*, 251.

14. Hull, *Absolute Destruction*, 320.

15. Marshall, *Memoirs of My Services in the World War*, 139–50.

16. Pershing, *My Experiences in the World War*, 2:282.

17. Viereck, *As They Saw Us*, 293.

18. Department of the Army, *American Armies and Battlefields in Europe*, 170.

19. Pershing, *My Experiences in the World War*, 2:284.

20. Lengel, *To Conquer Hell*, 71.

21. Marshall, *Memoirs of My Services in the World War*, 162.

22. Lengel, *To Conquer Hell*, 60.

23. Pershing, *My Experiences in the World War*, 2:290.

24. "French Armies of the North and Northeast, 3rd Section, General Staff, No. 23976," 20 September 1918, in Department of the Army, *United States Army in the World War 1917–1919*, 2:607.

25. "Note on the Meuse-Argonne Offensive, No. 4179," 23 September 1918, Record Group WO 158/05, United Kingdom National Archives.

26. "First Army, AEF, Field Order No. 20," 20 September 1918, in Department of the Army, *United States Army in the World War 1917–1919*, 9:82–100.

27. Pershing, *My Experiences in the World War*, 2:292.

28. Marshall, *Memoirs of My Services in the World War*, 160.

29. Pershing, *My Experiences in the World War*, 2:293.

30. Pershing, 2:293.

31. "191.32.13 Letter," 27 September 1918, in Department of the Army, *United States Army in the World War 1917–1919*, 9:140.

32. Ludendorff, *My War Memories*, 721; Hindenburg, *Out of My Life*, 2:260.

33. Smythe, *Pershing*, 197–98.

34. Diary of Lieutenant Colonel P. L. Stackpole, A.D.C. to General Liggett, 25 January 1918 to 2 August 1919, p. 233, Library of Congress, Washington, DC (hereafter Stackpole diary).

35. Paschall, *Defeat of Imperial Germany*, 210.

36. Doughty, *Pyrrhic Victory*, 493.

37. "Pétain to Foch, General Staff No. 18775, bis/3," 30 September 1918, in Department of the Army, *United States Army in the World War 1917–1919*, 8:82.

38. "French Armies of the North and Northeast, 3rd Section, General Staff, No. 4353," 30 September 1918, in Department of the Army, *United States Army in the World War 1917–1919*, 2:617.

39. Foch and Mott, *Memoirs of Marshall Foch*, 412–13; Doughty, *Pyrrhic Victory*, 493–94.

40. OHL, Ia 10552, 30 September 1918, File Hgr. Rupprecht, Bd. 99/101, Bavarian War Archives, Munich.

41. Ludendorff, *My War Memories*, 2:725.

42. Grotelueschen, *AEF Way of War*, 277.

43. Sheffield and Bourne, *Douglas Haig*, 468.

44. Viereck, *As They Saw Us*, 250.

45. "Note: No. 22/PC GQGA," 27 September 1918, Record Group WO 158/05, United Kingdom National Archives.

46. Sheffield, *Chief*, 325.

47. Henniker, *Transportation on the Western Front*, 44–49, 439–40.

48. Rupprecht, *In Treue Fest*, 2:450.

49. Haig, *Dispatches*, 281.

50. Rupprecht, *In Treue Fest*, 2:452.

51. Oberkommando des Heeres, *Der Weltkrieg 1914 bis 1918*, 14:619.

52. Haig, *Dispatches*, 282.

53. Travers, *How the War Was Won*, 169.

54. Editorial note in Sheffield and Bourne, *Douglas Haig*, 467.

55. Edmonds, *Military Operations*, 5:186.

56. Edmonds, 5:95–111, 131–45.

57. Stevenson, *With Our Backs to the Wall*, 136.

58. "Precis Verbal of a Conference Held at the Villa Romaine, Versailles, on Monday, October 7, 1918, at 10:30 a.m., I.C.-78," Record Group WO 158/106, United Kingdom National Archives.

59. "Foch to the Chief North and Northeast, No. 4456," 4 October 1918, Record Group WO 158/106, United Kingdom National Archives.

60. Doughty, *Pyrrhic Victory*, 494.

61. Quoted in Doughty, 495.

62. Smythe, *Pershing*, 207.

63. Lengel, *To Conquer Hell*, 312.

64. Sheffield and Bourne, *Douglas Haig*, 470–71.

65. Pershing, *My Experiences in the World War*, 2:239.

66. Oberkommando des Heeres, *Der Weltkrieg 1914 bis 1918*, 14:648.

67. Smythe, *Pershing*, 208; Doughty, *Pyrrhic Victory*, 494.

68. "HS Ger, File: 810–33.5: Fldr. 1: War Diary. Group of Armies Gallwitz," 9 October 1918, in Department of the Army, *United States Army in the World War 1917–1919*, 9:547.

69. "HS Ger, File: 810–33.5: Fldr. 1: Order," 10 October 1918), in Department of the Army, *United States Army in the World War 1917–1919*, 9:549.

70. Wilhelm, *My War Experiences*, 353.

71. "Foch to Pershing, No. 4711," 12 October 1918, Record Group WO 158/106, United Kingdom National Archives.

72. Smythe, *Pershing*, 206, 218; Doughty, *Pyrrhic Victory*, 495.

73. "First Subsection, Third Section, General Staff, to the General Commander-in-Chief, Armies of the North and Northeast, No. 4844," 16 October 1918, Record Group WO 158/106, United Kingdom National Archives.

74. Viereck, *As They Saw Us*, 264.

75. "Operations Priority for Pershing, No. 4779," 14 October 1918, Record Group WO 158/106, United Kingdom National Archives.

76. Viereck, *As They Saw Us*, 268.

77. Stackpole diary, 259–60.

78. Stackpole diary, 261.

79. Stackpole diary, 265.

80. Pershing, *My Experiences in the World War*, 2:355.

81. "Note No. 4985," 21 October 1918, Record Group WO 158/106, United Kingdom National Archives.

82. Pershing, *My Experiences in the World War*, 2:356.

83. "Note No. 5174," 25 October 1918, Record Group WO 158/106, United Kingdom National Archives.

84. Foch and Mott, *Memoirs of Marshall Foch*, 440.

85. Doughty, *Pyrrhic Victory*, 504.

86. "Foch to Pershing, No. 5254," 27 October 1918, Record Group WO 158/106, United Kingdom National Archives.

87. Ferrell, *America's Deadliest Battle*, 115–17.

88. Foch and Mott, *Memoirs of Marshall Foch*, 434–36.

89. Quoted in Liddell Hart, *Foch*, 380.

90. Smythe, *Pershing*, 22.

91. Paschall, *Defeat of Imperial Germany*, 191.

92. Edmonds, *Military Operations*, 5:185.

93. Edmonds, 5:182–83.

94. Haig, *Dispatches*, 285.

95. Ludendorff, *My War Memories*, 2:742.

96. Lossberg, *Lossberg's War*, 359.

97. Greenhalgh, *Foch in Command*, 453.

98. "General Directive, No. 4627," 10 October 1918, Record Group WO 158/106, United Kingdom National Archives.

99. Sheffield and Bourne, *Douglas Haig*, 472.

100. Edmonds, *Military Operations*, 5:182–83.

101. Rupprecht, *In Treue Fest*, 2460–61.

102. Oberkommando des Heeres, *Der Weltkrieg 1914 bis 1918*, 14:690.

103. Ludendorff, *My War Memories*, 2:748–54.

104. Edmonds, *Military Operations*, 5:327–38.

105. Sheffield and Bourne, *Douglas Haig*, 479.

106. Ludendorff, *My War Memories*, 2:758.

107. Sheffield and Bourne, *Douglas Haig*, 481–82.

108. Doughty, *Pyrrhic Victory*, 499.

109. Edmonds, *Military Operations*, 5:212–28.

110. Oberkommando des Heeres, *Der Weltkrieg 1914 bis 1918*, 14:699.

111. "Foch to Haig, No. 5253," 27 October 1918, Record Group WO 158/106, United Kingdom National Archives.

112. "General Directive, No. 4925," 19 October 1918, Record Group WO 158/106, United Kingdom National Archives.

113. Clayton, *Paths of Glory*, 161–62.

114. Clayton, 180.

115. "Foch to Pétain, No. 4939," 20 October 1918, Record Group WO 158/106, United Kingdom National Archives.

116. Edmonds, *Military Operations*, 5:182–83.

117. "Foch to Pétain, No. 5060," 23 October 1918, Record Group WO 158/106, United Kingdom National Archives.

118. Foch and Mott, *Memoirs of Marshall Foch*, 445.

119. Quoted in Strachan, *First World War*, 321.

120. "Foch to Pétain, No. 5640," 5 November 1918, Record Group WO 158/106, United Kingdom National Archives.

121. Pershing, *My Experiences in the World War*, 2:386–87.

122. Liggett, *A.E.F. Ten Years Ago in France*, 129, 240.

123. Marshall, *Memoirs of My Services in the World War*, 203–4.

124. Wheeler-Bennett, *Hindenburg*, 85.

125. Ludendorff, *My War Memories*, 2:761.

126. Hindenburg, *Out of My Life*, 2:265.

127. Ludendorff, *My War Memories*, 2:762–63.

128. Kuhl diary, 27 October 1918.

129. Wilhelm, *My War Experiences*, 357.

130. Oberkommando des Heeres, *Der Weltkrieg 1914 bis 1918*, 14:693–94.

131. Edmonds, *Military Operations*, 5:455–62.

132. Herwig, *"Luxury" Fleet*, 246–57.

133. Oberkommando des Heeres, *Der Weltkrieg 1914 bis 1918*, 14:694, 699.

134. Haig, *Dispatches*, 293.

135. Wilhelm, *My War Experiences*, 362.

136. Doughty, *Pyrrhic Victory*, 506–7.

137. "Foch to Pershing and Maistre, No. 5471," 5 November 1918, Record Group WO 158/106, United Kingdom National Archives.

138. Smythe, *Pershing*, 219.

139. Stevenson, *With Our Backs to the Wall*, 245.

140. Oberkommando des Heeres, *Der Weltkrieg 1914 bis 1918*, 14:608–10.

141. Lengel, *To Conquer Hell*, 314.

142. Stackpole diary, 273.

143. Viereck, *As They Saw Us*, 275–76.

144. Liggett, *A.E.F. Ten Years Ago in France*, 222.

145. "Foch to Pershing and Maistre, No. 5471."

146. Viereck, *As They Saw Us*, 277–78.

147. Liddell Hart, *Foch*, 388.

148. Pershing, *My Experiences in the World War*, 2:378.

149. Viereck, *As They Saw Us*, 281.

150. Smythe, *Pershing*, 227–30.

151. Harbord, *American Army in France*, 455–56.

152. Harbord, 460.

153. Harbord, 549.

154. Summerall, *Way of Duty, Honor, Country*, 153.

155. Marshall, *Memoirs of My Services in the World War*, 191.

156. Some historians have questioned the story of MacArthur being "captured" by U.S. soldiers during the Race to Sedan. MacArthur himself says no such thing in his telling of the Race to Sedan in his 1964 memoirs, *Reminiscences* (69). But William Manchester does recount the capture story in his 1978 book, *American Caesar: Douglas MacArthur, 1880–1964* (109). The source he cites is Forrest Pogue's biography of George Marshall (1:187). Lengel recounts the capture story in *To Conquer Hell* (399). Ferrell, in *America's Deadliest Battle*, also recounts it but cites Clayton James, who says that it is "perhaps spurious" (141). This is an interesting problem, and there is enough evidence to raise questions about the authenticity of the story.

157. Liggett, *A.E.F. Ten Years Ago in France*, 229–30.

158. Smythe, *Pershing*, 230.

159. Stackpole diary, 227.

160. Pershing, *My Experiences in the World War*, 2:381.

161. Summerall, *Way of Duty, Honor, Country*, 152–54.

162. Ferrell, *America's Deadliest Battle*, 141.

163. Edmonds, *Military Operations*, 5:516,

164. Smythe, *Pershing*, 323.

165. Harbord, *American Army in France*, 401.

166. Haig, *Dispatches*, 295.

167. Holmes, *Tommy*, 71.

168. Liggett, *A.E.F. Ten Years Ago in France*, 137.

169. Liggett, 211.

170. Liggett, 4–5.

171. Lengel, *To Conquer Hell*, 419–20.

172. Quoted in Liggett, *A.E.F. Ten Years Ago in France*, 202–4.

14. ARMISTICE AND OCCUPATION

1. "President Woodrow Wilson. 'The Fourteen Points,' Address to Joint Session of the U.S. Congress," 8 January 1918, in Roberts, *Documents*, 2016–18.

2. Wheeler-Bennett, *Hindenburg*, 166.

3. "Message from Field Marshal Paul von Hindenburg to Imperial Chancellor Max von Baden," 3 October 1918, in Roberts, *Documents*, 2063.

4. Astore and Showalter, *Hindenburg*, 72.

5. "The First German Peace Note: Imperial Chancellor Prince Max von Baden to President Woodrow Wilson," 6 October 1918, in Roberts, *Documents*, 2064.

6. Herwig, *First World War*, 426.

7. "President Woodrow Wilson, First Reply to the German Request for an Armistice," 8 October 1918, in Roberts, *Documents*, 2064.

8. Greenhalgh, *Foch in Command*, 461.

9. Foch and Mott, *Memoirs of Marshall Foch*, 453.

10. "The Second German Note: German State Secretary of Foreign Affairs Wilhelm Solf to U.S. Secretary Robert Lansing," 14 October 1918, in Roberts, *Documents*, 2065.

11. "President Woodrow Wilson, Second Reply to the German Government," 14 October 1918, in Roberts, *Documents*, 2065–66.

12. Ludendorff, *My War Memories*, 2:748–51.

13. Herwig, *"Luxury" Fleet*, 247–51.

14. "The Third German Note: German State Secretary of Foreign Affairs Wilhelm Solf to U.S. Secretary Robert Lansing," 20 October 1918, in Roberts, *Documents*, 2067–68.

15. "President Woodrow Wilson, Third Reply to the German Government," 23 October 1918, in Roberts, *Documents*, 2068–69.

16. "The Fourth German Note: German State Secretary of Foreign Affairs Wilhelm Solf to U.S. Secretary Robert Lansing," 27 October 1918, in Roberts, *Documents*, 2074–75.

17. Foch and Mott, *Memoirs of Marshall Foch*, 459–61.

18. Foch and Mott, 461.

19. Greenhalgh, *Foch in Command*, 474.

20. "HS Secret File: Fldr. H-1: To the Allied Supreme War Council. Paris," 30 October 1918, in Department of the Army, *United States Army in the World War 1917–1919*, 10:28–30.

21. Quoted in Smythe, *Pershing*, 221.

22. Wheeler-Bennett, *Hindenburg*, 182–83.

23. Quoted in Greenhalgh, *Foch in Command*, 476.

24. Quoted in Liddell Hart, *Foch*, 398.

25. "Allied Supreme War Council, 22nd Resolution on the Armistice Terms," 4 November 1918, in Roberts, *Documents*, 2084.

26. Wheeler-Bennett, *Hindenburg*, 190–95.

27. Foch and Mott, *Memoirs of Marshall Foch*, 468–69.

28. Foch and Mott, 469–73.

29. Wheeler-Bennett, *Hindenburg*, 205.

30. Wheeler-Bennett, 200.

31. "Foch to the Commanders in Chief, Unnumbered," 9 November 1918, Record Group WO 158/106, United Kingdom National Archives, Kew, Great Britain.

32. Herwig, *First World War*, 446.

33. Foch and Mott, *Memoirs of Marshall Foch*, 487.

34. "Foch to the Commanders in Chief, Unnumbered," 11 November 1918, Record Group WO 158/106, United Kingdom National Archives.

35. Foch and Mott, *Memoirs of Marshall Foch*, 493.

36. "AOK 3, Ia 12257," 11 November 1918, in Department of the Army, *United States Army in the World War 1917–1919*, 11:427.

37. "AEF General Orders 198," 7 November 1918, in Department of the Army, *United States Army in the World War 1917–1919*, 11:2–4.

38. Edmonds, *Occupation of the Rhineland*, 145–46.

39. Liggett, *A.E.F. Ten Years Ago in France*, 243–44.

40. Marshall, *Memoirs of My Services in the World War*, 204.

41. "To Director of Military Operations, Nr. 1010/13/42," 17 January 1919, Record Group WO 158/106, United Kingdom National Archives.

42. Greenhalgh, *Foch in Command*, 503–4.

43. Liddell Hart, *Foch*, 427.

44. Greenhalgh, *Foch in Command*, 505.

15. THE FLUCTUATING VERDICT OF HISTORY

1. Jürgen Förster, "Eine neunzigjährige Geschichte, aus der man nicht einfach aussteigen kann," *Badische Zeitung*, 19 October 2016, 22.

2. Email message to author, 17 July 2017.

3. Wheeler-Bennett, *Hindenburg*, 227–28.

4. Wheeler-Bennett, 136, 268–70.

5. Astore and Showalter, *Hindenburg*, 89.

6. Norman Stone, "Hindenburg," in Carver, *War Lords*, 45.

7. Wheeler-Bennett, *Hindenburg*, 158.

8. Wheeler-Bennett, 27.

9. Astore and Showalter, *Hindenburg*, 102–3.

10. Wheeler-Bennett, *Hindenburg*, 179.

11. Wheeler-Bennett, 17.

12. Wheeler-Bennett, 232.

13. Astore and Showalter, *Hindenburg*, 87.

14. Quoted in Wheeler-Bennett, *Hindenburg*, 354.

15. Quoted in Astore and Showalter, *Hindenburg*, 95. Some historians have questioned the authenticity of this telegram.

16. Ludendorff, *Der totale Krieg*, 24.

17. Hull, *Absolute Destruction*, 330.

18. Rosinski, *German Army*, 145–46.

19. Lossberg, *Lossberg's War*, 323–24; Barnett, *Swordbearers*, 344.

20. Quoted in Barnett, *Swordbearers*, 283.

21. Haig, *Dispatches*, 246.

22. Sheffield and Bourne, *Douglas Haig*, 489.

23. Ferdinand Foch, "The American Soldier in the World War as Seen by a Friend," in Viereck, *As They Saw Us*, 16.

24. Hunter, "Foch and Eisenhower," 84–86.

25. Hunter, 84–86.

26. Greenhalgh, *Foch in Command*, 516.

27. Greenhalgh, 463.

28. Quoted in Greenhalgh, 517.

29. Pétain, *La bataille de Verdun*, 234.

30. Quoted in Bruce, *Pétain*, 111–12.

31. Liddell Hart, *Reputations*, 223.

32. Alistair Horne, "Pétain," in Carver, *War Lords*, 70.

33. Cited in Smythe, *Pershing*, 292.

34. "Preliminary Report of the Commander-in-Chief," G-3, GHQ, AEF: 1123, 19 November 1918, in Department of the Army, *United States Army in the World War 1917–1919*, 12:44.

35. Pershing, *My Experiences in the World War*, 1:153.

36. Grotelueschen, *AEF Way of War*, 353–54.

37. Sheffield and Bourne, *Douglas Haig*, 491–92.

38. Sheffield, *Chief*, 2, 367.

39. Suttie, *Rewriting the First World War*, 32.

40. Suttie, 15, 53.

41. Quoted in Suttie, 172–73.

42. Suttie, 4.

43. Quoted in Suttie, 22.

44. Suttie, 196.

45. Quoted in Suttie, 197.

46. Littlewood, *Oh What a Lovely War*, 73–74.

47. Greenhalgh, "Myth and Memory." 771–821.

48. Sheffield and Bourne, *Douglas Haig*, x.

49. Haig, *Dispatches*, 295.

50. Haig, 320.

51. Haig, 315.

52. Quoted in Hunter, "Foch and Eisenhower," 86.

53. Holmes, *Tommy*, 190.

54. Sheffield, *Chief*, 337.

55. Quoted in Sheffield, 3, 4.

56. Travers, *How the War Was Won*, 178.

57. Harris, *Douglas Haig and the First World War*, 516.

58. Mungo Melvin, "The Long Shadow of the Somme," in Strohn, *Battle of the Somme*, 226.

59. Georg Wetzell to Hans von Seeckt, 24 July 1919, Seeckt Papers, Folder N247/175, German Military Archives, Freiburg.

60. Liggett, *A.E.F. Ten Years Ago in France*, 21.

61. Harris, *Douglas Haig and the First World War*, 456.

62. Harris, 430.

63. Ian F. W. Beckett, "Henry Rawlinson," in Beckett and Corvi, *Haig's Generals*, 169.

64. Quoted in Sheffield, *Chief*, 365.

BIBLIOGRAPHY

GENERAL

Bailey, Jonathan. *The First World War and the Birth of the Modern Style of Warfare.* Camberly: Strategic and Combat Studies Institute, 1996.

Barnett, Correlli. *The Swordbearers: Studies in Supreme Command in the First World War.* London: Eyre and Spottiswoode, 1963.

Brooke, Alan F. "The Evolution of Artillery in the Great War." Pts. 1–8. *Journal of the Royal Artillery,* November 1924, 250–67; January 1925, 359–72; April 1925, 37–51; October 1925, 369–87; April 1926, 76–93; July 1926, 232–49; October 1926, 320–29; January 1927, 469–82.

Carver, Michael, ed. *The War Lords: Military Commanders of the Twentieth Century.* London: Weidenfeld and Nicholson, 1976.

Clausewitz, Carl von. *On War.* Translated and edited by Michael Howard and Peter Paret. Princeton, NJ: Princeton University Press, 1976.

Davis, Norman. *God's Playground: A History of Poland.* Vol. 2, *1795 to the Present.* New York: Columbia University Press, 1984.

Essame, Hubert. *The Battle for Europe 1918.* London: Batsford, 1972.

Fuller, J. F. C. *The Foundations of the Science of War.* London: Hutchinson and Co., 1926.

———. *Generalship: Its Diseases and Their Cure.* Harrisburg, PA: Military Service Publishing, 1936.

———. *Tanks in the Great War.* London: E. P. Dutton, 1920.

Hastings, Max. *Catastrophe: Europe Goes to War 1914.* London: HarperCollins, 2013.

Hogg, Ian V. *The Guns, 1914–1918.* New York: Ballantine, 1971.

Holmes, Richard. *The Western Front.* London: BBC Books, 1999.

House, Jonathan M. *Combined Arms Warfare in the Twentieth Century.* Lawrence: University Press of Kansas, 2001.

Howard, Michael. "Military Science in an Age of Peace." *RUSI Journal,* March 1974, 6–7.

Keegan, John. *The Face of Battle.* New York: Viking Press, 1976.

———. *The Mask of Command.* New York: Viking Press, 1987.

Kitchen, Martin. *The German Offensives of 1918*. Gloucestershire: Stroud, 2001.

Liddell Hart, Basil H. *The Real War, 1914–1918*. Boston: Little Brown, 1930.

———. *Reputations: Ten Years On*. London: John Murray, 1928.

Longstreet, James. *From Manassas to Appomattox*. 1896. Norwalk, CT: Easton Press, 1988.

Millett, Alan, and Williamson Murray, eds. *Military Effectiveness*. Vol. 1, *The First World War*. Boston: Unwin Hyman, 1988.

Neiberg, Michael. *Fighting the Great War: A Global History*. Cambridge, MA: Harvard University Press, 2005.

Pitt, Barrie. *1918: The Last Act*. New York: Ballantine Books, 1963.

Roberts, Priscilla, ed. *Documents*. Vol. 4 of *World War I: The Definitive Encyclopedia and Document Collection*, edited by Spencer Tucker. Santa Barbara: ABC-CLIO, 2014.

Sheffield, Gary. *Forgotten Victory: The First World War Myths and Realities*. London: Headline Book Publishing, 2001.

Stevenson, David. *With Our Backs to the Wall: Victory and Defeat in 1918*. London: Allen Lane, 2011.

Strachan. Hew. *The First World War*. London: Simon and Schuster, 2014.

Tuchman, Barbara. *The Proud Tower: A Portrait of the World Before the War, 1890–1914*. London: Hamish Hamilton, 1966.

Ząbecki, David T., ed. *Chief of Staff: The Principal Officers Behind History's Great Commanders*. Vol. 1, *Napoleonic Wars to World War I*. Annapolis, MD: Naval Institute Press, 2008.

AMERICAN

Allen, Henry T. *The Rhineland Occupation*. Indianapolis: Bobbs-Merrill, 1927.

Ferrell, Robert H. *America's Deadliest Battle: Meuse Argonne, 1918*. Lawrence: University Press of Kansas, 2007.

Grotelueschen, Mark E. *The AEF Way of War: The American Army and Combat in World War I*. Cambridge: Cambridge University Press, 2007.

Harbord, James G. *The American Army in France, 1917–1918*. Boston: Little Brown, 1936.

Lengel, Edward G. *To Conquer Hell: The Meuse-Argonne, 1918*. New York: Henry Holt, 2008.

Liggett, Hunter. *A.E.F. Ten Years Ago in France*. New York: Dodd, Mead, 1928.

Marshall, George C. *Memoirs of My Services in the World War, 1917–1918*. Boston: Houghton Mifflin, 1976.

Mastriano, Douglas V. *Thunder in the Argonne: A New History of America's Greatest Battle*. Lexington: University Press of Kentucky, 2018.

Pershing, John J. *My Experiences in the World War*. 2 vols. New York: Frederick A. Stokes, 1931.

Shipley, Thomas. *The History of the A.E.F.* New York: George H. Dolan, 1920.

Smythe, Donald. *Pershing: General of the Armies*. Bloomington: University of Indiana Press, 1986.

Summerall, Charles P. *The Way of Duty, Honor, Country: The Memoir of General Charles Pelot Summerall*. Edited by Timothy K. Nenninger. Lexington: University Press of Kentucky, 2010.

Trask, David F. *The AEF and Coalition Warmaking, 1917–1918*. Lawrence: University Press
    of Kansas, 1993.
———. *General Tasker Howard Bliss and the "Sessions of the World," 1919*. Philadelphia:
    American Philosophical Society, 1966.
———. *The United States in the Supreme War Council: American War Aims and Inter-Allied
    Strategy, 1917–1918*. Middletown, CT: Wesleyan University Press, 1961.
Viereck, George, ed. *As They Saw Us: Foch, Ludendorff, and Other Leaders Write Our War
    History*. New York: Doubleday, 1929.

BRITISH

Beckett, Ian F. W., and Steven J. Corvi. *Haig's Generals*. Barnsley, South Yorkshire: Pen and
    Sword, 2006.
Bidwell, Shelford, and Dominick Graham. *Fire-Power: British Armies and Theories of War,
    1904–1945*. London: Allen and Unwin, 1982.
Brown, Ian Malcolm. *British Logistics on the Western Front, 1914–1919*. Bridgeport, CT:
    Praeger, 1998.
Callwell, C. E., ed. *Field Marshal Sir Henry Wilson: His Life and Diaries*. 2 vols. New York:
    Scribner's, 1927.
Greenhalgh, Elizabeth. "Myth and Memory: Sir Douglas Haig and the Imposition of
    Allied Unified Command in March 1918." *Journal of Military History*, June 2004,
    771–821.
Griffith, Paddy. *Battle Tactics of the Western Front: The British Army's Art of the Attack,
    1916–1918*. New Haven, CT: Yale University Press, 1994.
———. *Forward into Battle: Fighting Tactics from Waterloo to the Near Future*. Novato, CA:
    Presidio, 1991.
Haig, Douglas. *Dispatches: General Douglas Haig's Official Reports to the British Govern-
    ment*. New York: J. M. Dent Sons, 1919.
Harris, J. P. *Douglas Haig and the First World War*. Cambridge: Cambridge University
    Press, 2008.
Holmes, Richard. *Tommy: The British Soldier on the Western Front, 1914–1918*. London:
    HarperCollins, 2004.
Littlewood, Joan, ed. *Oh What a Lovely War*. London: Methuen Drama, 1967.
McWilliams, James, and R. James Steel. *Amiens: Dawn of Victory*. Toronto: Dundern Press,
    2001.
Melvin, Mungo, ed. *The First World War Battlefield Guide*. Vol. 1, *The Western Front*. Ando-
    ver, UK: British Army Headquarters, 2015.
Messenger, Charles. *The Day We Won the War: Turning Point at Amiens, 8 August 1918*. Lon-
    don: Weidenfeld and Nicholson, 2008.
Robertson, William. *From Private to Field Marshal*. New York: Houghton Mifflin, 1921.
Sheffield, Gary. *The Chief: Douglas Haig and the British Army*. London: Aurum, 2011.
Sheffield, Gary, and John Bourne, eds. *Douglas Haig: War Diaries and Letters, 1914–1918*.
    London: Weidenfeld and Nicholson, 2005.
Sheffield, Gary, and Dan Todman, eds. *Command and Control on the Western Front: The
    British Army's Experience, 1914–1918*. Stroud, UK: Spellmount, 2004.

Suttie, Andrew. *Rewriting the First World War: Lloyd George, Politics, and Strategy, 1914–18.* Basingstoke: Palgrave Macmillan, 2005.

Terraine, John. *To Win a War: 1918, the Year of Victory.* London: Cassell, 1978.

———. *White Heat: The New Warfare, 1914–1918.* London: Sidgwick and Jackson, 1982.

Travers, Tim. *How the War Was Won: Command and Technology in the British Army on the Western Front, 1917–1918.* London: Allen and Unwin, 1992.

———. *The Killing Ground: The British Army, the Western Front and the Emergence of Modern Warfare, 1900–1918.* London: Allen and Unwin, 1987.

FRENCH

Bruce, Robert B. *Pétain: Verdun to Vichy.* Washington, D.C.: Potomac Books, 2008.

Clayton, Anthony. *Paths of Glory: The French Army, 1914–1918.* London: Cassell, 2003.

Doughty, Robert A. *Pyrrhic Victory: French Strategy and the Operations of the Great War.* Cambridge, MA: Belknap Press, 2005.

Foch, Ferdinand. *The Principles of War.* 1903. New Delhi: Reliance, 2002.

Foch, Ferdinand, and T. Bentley Mott. *The Memoirs of Marshall Foch.* Garden City, NY: Doubleday, 1931.

Goubard, J. "Defensive Employment of the French Artillery in 1918: The Artillery of the 21st Corps in the Battle of 15th July." *Field Artillery Journal*, November 1921, 565–75. (Translation of an article from *Revue d'Artillerie*, August 1921.)

Greenhalgh, Elizabeth. *Foch in Command: The Forging of a First World War General.* Cambridge: Cambridge University Press, 2014.

Herr, Frederic. *Die Artillerie in Vergangenheit, Gegenwart, und Zukunft.* Charlottenburg: Offene Worte, 1925. (Translation of *L'Artillerie, Ce Qu'Elle a Ete, Ce Qu'Elle Est, Ce Qu'Elle Doit Etre* [Paris, 1923]).

Hunter, T. M. "Foch and Eisenhower: A Study in Allied Supreme Command." *Canadian Army Journal* 17 (July 1963): 79–97.

Joffre, Joseph, and T. Bentley Mott. *The Personal Memoirs of Joffre: Marshal of the French Army.* New York: Harper Brothers, 1932.

King, Jere C. *Generals and Politicians: Conflict Between France's High Command, Parliament, and Government, 1914–1918.* Los Angles: University of California Press, 1951.

Liddell Hart, B. H. *Foch: Man of Orleans.* Boston: Little Brown, 1932.

Lucas, Pascal. *The Evolution of Tactical Ideas in France and Germany During the War of 1914–1918.* Paris: Berger-Levrault, 1923. (Manuscript translation in English by Major P. V. Kieffer, U.S. Army, 1925.)

Maitre, Colonel. "Evolution of Ideas in the Employment of Artillery During the War." *Field Artillery Journal*, January 1922, 1–18. (Translation of a lecture delivered at the Centre d'Etudes Tactiques d'Artillerie at Metz, France.)

Neiberg, Michael S. *Foch: Supreme Allied Commander in the Great War.* Dulles, VA: Potomac, 2004.

———. *The Second Battle of the Marne.* Bloomington: University of Indiana Press, 2008.

Pétain, Phillipe. *La bataille de Verdun.* Verdun: Les Editions Lorraines, 1929.

Philpott, William. "Ferdinand Foch: General in Chief." *Stand To! The Journal of the Western Front Association*, no. 111 (March 2018): 33–37.

Recouly, Raymond. *Foch: The Winner of the War.* New York: Charles Scribner's Sons, 1920.

Ryan, Stephen. *Pétain the Soldier*. London: Barnes and Company, 1969.

Smith, Leonard V., Stéphane Audoin-Rouzeau, and Ammette Becker. *France and the Great War, 1914–1918*. Cambridge: Cambridge University Press: 2003.

GERMAN

Asprey, Robert B. *The German High Command at War: Hindenburg and Ludendorff Conduct World War I*. New York: William Morrow, 1991.

Astore, William J., and Dennis E. Showalter. *Hindenburg: Icon of German Militarism*. Washington: Potomac Books, 2005.

Balck, Hermann. *Order in Chaos: The Memoirs of General of Panzer Troops Herman Balck*. Translated and edited by David T. Ząbecki and Dieter Biedekarken. Lexington: University Press of Kentucky, 2015.

Balck, William. *Development of Tactics: World War*. Fort Leavenworth, KS: General Service Schools Press, 1922.

Beck, Ludwig. "Der 29. September 1918." In *Studien*, edited by Hans Speidell, 191–225. Stuttgart: K. F. Koehler Verlag, 1955.

Bernhardi, Friederich von. *How Germany Makes War*. New York: George Doran, 1914.

———. *Von Kriege der Zukunft, nach den Erfahrungen des Weltkriegs*. Berlin: Mittler und Sohn, 1920.

Boff, Jonathan. *Haig's Enemy: Crown Prince Rupprecht and Germany's War on the Western Front*. Oxford: Oxford University Press, 2018.

Brose, Eric Dorn. *The Kaiser's Army: The Politics of Military Technology in Germany During the Machine Age, 1870–1918*. New York: Oxford University Press, 2001.

Bruchmüller, Georg. *Die Artillerie beim Angriff im Stellungskrieg*. Berlin: Verlag Offene Worte, 1926.

———. *Die deutsche Artillerie in den Durchbruchschlachten des Weltkriegs*. Berlin: Mittler und Sohn, 1921.

———. *Die deutsche Artillerie in den Durchbruchschlachten des Weltkriegs*. 2nd ed. Berlin: Mittler und Sohn, 1922.

Bull, G. V., and C. H. Murphy. *Paris Kanonen—The Paris Guns (Wilhelmgeschütze) and Project HARP*. Herford: E. S. Mittler and Sohn, 1988.

Cron, Hermann. *Geschichte des deutschen Heeres im Weltkriege 1914–1918*. Berlin: Militärverlag Karl Siegismund, 1937.

———. *The Imperial German Army, 1914–1918: Organization, Structure, Orders of Battle*. Solihull, Eng.: Helion, 2002.

"Die deutsche Offensive im März 1918." Part 4. *Militär-Wochenblatt*, 11 March 1928, 1289–95.

Dupuy, Trevor N. *A Genius for War: The German Army and the General Staff, 1807–1945*. Falls Church, VA: Nova, 1977.

Echevarria, Antulio J., II. *After Clausewitz: German Military Thinkers Before the Great War*. Lawrence: University Press of Kansas, 2000.

Ehlert, Hans, Michael Epkenhans, and Gerhard P. Gross, eds. *The Schlieffen Plan: International Perspectives on the German Strategy for World War I*. Lexington: University Press of Kentucky, 2014.

Fehr, Otto. *Die Märzoffensive 1918 an der Westfront: Strategie oder Taktik?* Leipzig: Verlag Koehler, 1921.

Foerster, Wolfgang. *Der deutsche Zusammenbruch 1918.* Berlin: Verlag Eisenschmidt, 1925.

———. *Ludendorff: Der Feldherr im Unglück.* Wiesbaden: Limes Verlag, 1952.

Gatzke, Hans W. *Germany's Drive to the West: A Study of Germany's Western War Aims During the First World War.* Baltimore: Johns Hopkins Press, 1950.

Gehre, Ludwig. *Die deutsche Kräfteverteilung während des Weltkrieges: Eine Clausewitzstudie.* Berlin: Mittler und Sohn, 1928.

General Service Schools. *The German Offensive of July 15, 1918 (Marne Source Book).* Fort Leavenworth, KS: General Service Schools Press, 1923.

Görlitz, Walter. *History of the German General Staff, 1657–1945.* New York: Praeger, 1953.

Gray, Randal. *Kaisersschlacht 1918: The Final German Offensive.* London: Osprey Campaign Series, 1991.

Great Britain War Office General Staff. *The German Forces in the Field: 7th Revision, 11th November 1918.* 1918; repr., Nashville, TN: Battery Press, 1995.

———. *Handbook of the German Army in the War, April 1918.* 1918; repr., London: Arms and Armour Press, 1977.

Gross, Gerhard. *The Myth and Reality of German Warfare: Operational Thinking from Moltke the Elder to Heusinger.* Lexington: University Press of Kentucky, 2016.

Gudmundsson, Bruce I. *Stormtroop Tactics: Innovation in the German Army, 1914–1918.* New York: Praeger, 1989.

Haeften, Hans von. *Hindenburg und Ludendorff als Feldherren.* Berlin: Mittler und Sohn, 1937.

Herwig, Holger H. *The First World War: Germany and Austria-Hungary, 1914–1918.* London: Arnold, 1997.

———. *"Luxury" Fleet: The Imperial German Navy, 1888–1918.* London: Allen and Unwin, 1980.

———. *The Marne, 1914: The Opening of World War I and the Battle That Changed the World.* New York: Random House, 2009.

Hindenburg, Paul von. *Out of My Life.* 2 vols. London: Harper, 1921.

Hoffmann, Max. *The War of Lost Opportunities.* Nashville, TN: Battery Press, 1995.

Hull, Isabel V. *Absolute Destruction: Military Culture and the Practices of War in Imperial Germany.* Ithaca, NY: Cornell University Press, 2005.

Jessen, Olaf. *Verdun 1916: Urschlacht des Jahrhunderts.* Munich: C. H. Beck Verlag, 2014.

Jünger, Ernst. *The Storm of Steel: From the Diary of a German Storm-Troop Officer on the Western Front.* New York: Zimmermann and Zimmermann, 1985.

Kabisch, Ernst. *Michael: Die grosse Schlacht in Frankreich.* Berlin: Vorhut-Verlag Otto Schlegel, 1936.

———. *Um Lys und Kemmel.* Berlin: Vorhut-Verlag Otto Schlegel, 1936.

Kuhl, Hermann von. *Entstehung, Durchführung und Zusammenbruch der Offensive von 1918.* Berlin: Deutsche Verlagsgesellschaft für Politik und Geschichte, 1927.

———. *Der Weltkrieg 1914–1918.* 2 vols. Berlin: Verlag Tradition Wilhelm Holt, 1929.

Lanza, Conrad H. "Five Decisive Days: The Germans in the Reims Offensive." *Field Artillery Journal* 27 (January 1937): 37–66.

———. "The German XXIII Reserve Crosses the Marne." *Field Artillery Journal* 27 (July 1937): 305–16.

Lossberg, Fritz von. *Lossberg's War: The World War I Memoirs of a German Chief of Staff*. Translated and edited by David T. Ząbecki and Dieter Biedekarken. Lexington: University Press of Kentucky, 2017.

Ludendorff, Erich. *The General Staff and Its Problems*. London: Hutchinson, 1922.

———. *Kriegsführung und Politik*. Berlin: Mittler und Sohn, 1922.

———. *My War Memories, 1914–1918*. 2 vols. London: Hutchinson, 1920.

———. *Der totale Krieg*. Munich: Ludendorff Verlag, 1935.

———. *Urkunden der Obersten Heeresleitung über ihre Tätigkeit 1916/18*. Berlin: Mittler und Sohn, 1922.

Lupfer, Timothy T. *The Dynamics of Doctrine: Changes in German Tactical Doctrine During the First World War*. Leavenworth Papers No. 4. Fort Leavenworth, KS: U.S. Army Combat Studies Institute, July 1981.

Millotat, Christian O. E. *Understanding the Prussian-German General Staff System*. Carlisle, PA: U.S. Army War College, 1992.

Moser, Otto von. *Kurzer strategischer Überblick über den Weltkrieg 1914–1918*. Berlin: Mittler und Sohn, 1921.

Paschall, Rod. *The Defeat of Imperial Germany, 1917–1918*. Chapel Hill, NC: Algonquin Books, 1989.

Pöhlmann, Markus, Harald Potempa, and Thomas Vogel, eds. *Der Erste Weltkrieg 1914–1918: Der deutsche Aufmarsch in ein kriegerisches Jahrhuntert*. Munich: Bucher Verlag, 2014.

Porter, J. A. "The German Supply System." Student paper. 3 June 1931. U.S. Army Command and General Staff School, Fort Leavenworth, KS.

Rosinski, Herbert. *The German Army*. New York: Praeger, 1966.

Rupprecht, Crown Prince of Bavaria. *In Treue Fest: Mein Kriegstagebuch*. 3 vols. Munich: Deutscher National Verlag, 1929.

Schlieffen, Alfred von. *Cannae*. Fort Leavenworth, KS: U.S. Army Command and General Staff College, 1992.

Seesselberg, Frederick. *Der Stellungskrieg 1914–1918*. Berlin: Mittler und Sohn, 1926.

Showalter, Dennis. *Instrument of War: The German Army, 1914–18*. Oxford: Osprey, 2016.

———. *Railroads and Rifles: Soldiers, Technology, and the Unification of Germany*. Hamden, CT: Archon Books, 1975.

Strohn, Matthias, ed. *The Battle of the Somme*. Oxford: Osprey, 2016.

Sulzbach, Herbert. *With the German Guns: Four Years on the Western Front, 1914–1918*. Hamden, CT: Archon, 1981.

Thaer, Albrecht von. *Generalstabsdienst an der Front und in der O.H.L.* Göttingen: Vandenhoeck and Ruprecht, 1958.

U.S. War Department. Document No. 905, *Histories of Two Hundred and Fifty-One Divisions of the German Army Which Participated in the War (1914–1918)*. 1920; repr., London: London Stamp Exchange, 1989.

Venohr, Wolfgang. *Ludendorff: Legende und Wirklichkeit*. Berlin: Ullstein Verlag, 1993.

Waechter, Hans. "Das Artillerie-Angriffsverfahren beim Durchbruch im Weltkriege." *Militär-Wochenblatt*, 11 June 1921, 1093–97.

Wallach, Jehuda L. *The Dogma of the Battle of Annihilation: The Theories of Clausewitz and Schlieffen and Their Impact on the German Conduct of Two World Wars*. Westport, CT: Greenwood Press, 1986.

Wetzell, Georg. *Der Bündniskrieg: Eine militärpolitisch operativ Studie des Weltkrieges*. Berlin: Mittler und Sohn, 1937.

———. "Michael, die Grosse Schlacht in Frankreich." *Militär-Wochenblatt*, 28 May 1935, 1944–46.

———. *Von Falkenhayn zu Hindenburg-Ludendorff*. Berlin: Mittler und Sohn, 1921.

Wheeler-Bennett, John W. *Hindenburg: The Wooden Titan*. New York: St. Martin's Press, 1967.

Wilhelm, Crown Prince of Germany. *My War Experiences*. New York: McBride, 1923.

Wilhelm II. *The Kaiser's Memoirs, 1888–1918*. London: Harper Brothers, 1922.

Wrisberg, Ernst von. *Wehr und Waffen, 1914–1918*. Leipzig: Koehler Verlag, 1922.

Wynne, Graeme. *If Germany Attacks: The Battle in Depth in the West*. London: Faber and Faber, 1940.

Zabecki, David T. *The German 1918 Offensives: A Case Study in the Operational Level of War*. London: Routledge, 2006.

———, ed. *Germany at War: 400 Years of Military History*. 4 vols. Santa Barbara, CA: ABC-Clio, 2014.

———. *Steel Wind: Colonel Georg Bruchmüller and the Birth of Modern Artillery*. Bridgeport, CT: Praeger, 1994.

———. "The U.S. Marines' Mythic Fight at Belleau Wood: Piercing the Fog of History to Separate Legend from Fact." *Military History*, March 2012, 40–49.

OFFICIAL HISTORIES

France

Ministre de la Guerre, État-major des armées. *Les armées francaises dans la grande guerre*. Paris: Imprimerie Nationale, 1921–38.

Tome VI: *L'hiver 1917–1918. L'offensive allemande (1er novembre 1917–3 avril 1918)*.
· Volume 1: *La préparation de la campagne de 1918. L'offensive allemande de l'Oise à la mer du Nord (1 novembre 1917–30 avril 1918)*. Text published 1931, 532 pages, 3 volumes of annexes, 1 volume of maps.
· Volume 2: *L'offensive allemande contre l'armée française (30 avril–17 juillet 1918)*. Text published 1935, 567 pages, 3 volumes of annexes, 1 volume of maps.

Tome VII: *La campagne offensive de 1918 et la marche au Rhin (18 juillet 1918–28 juin 1919)*.
· Volume 1: *Les offensives de dégagement et la préparation des Offensives générales (18 juillet–25 septembre 1918)*. Text published 1923, 405 pages, 2 volumes of annexes, 1 volume of maps.
· Volume 2: *La campagne offensive de 1918 et la marche au Rhin (26 septembre 1918–28 juin 1919)*. Text published 1938, 446 pages, 2 volumes of annexes, 1 volume of maps.

Germany

Bose, Theo von. *Deutsche Siege 1918, Das Vorbringen der 7. Armee über Ailette, Aisne, Vesle, und Ourcq bis zur Marne (27. Mai bis 13. Juni): Schlachten des Weltkriegs.* Vol. 32. Berlin: Gerhard Stalling, 1929.

———. *Die Katastrophe des 8. August 1918: Schlachten des Weltkriegs.* Vol. 36. Berlin: Gerhard Stalling, 1930.

———. *Wachsende Schwierigkeiten: Vergebliches Ringen vor Compiegne, Villers-Cotterets, und Reims: Schlachten des Weltkriegs.* Vol. 33. Berlin: Gerhard Stalling, 1930.

Deutschen Reichstages. *Die Ursachen des deutschen Zusammenbruchs im Jahre 1918.* Vol. 3, *Entstehung, Durchführung und Zusammenbruch der Offensive von 1918*, edited by Hermann von Kuhl and Hans Delbrück. Berlin: Deutsche Verlagsgesellschaft für Politik und Geschichte, 1925.

Oberkommando des Heeres. *Der Weltkrieg 1914 bis 1918.* Vol. 10, *Die Operationen des Jahres 1916 bis zum Wechsel in der Obersten Heeresleitung.* Berlin: Mittler und Sohn, 1936.

———. *Der Weltkrieg 1914 bis 1918.* Vol. 12, *Die Kriegsführung im Frühjahr 1917.* Berlin: Mittler und Sohn, 1939.

———. *Der Weltkrieg 1914 bis 1918.* Vol. 13, *Die Kriegsführung im Sommer und Herbst 1917.* Berlin: Mittler und Sohn, 1942.

———. *Der Weltkrieg 1914 bis 1918.* Vol. 14, *Die Kriegsführung an der Westfront im Jahre 1918.* Berlin: Mittler und Sohn, 1944.

Stenger, Alfred. *Der Letzte deutsche Angriff: Reims 1918: Schlachten des Weltkriegs.* Vol. 34. Berlin: Gerhard Stalling, 1930.

———. *Schicksalswende, von der Marne bis zur Vesle 1918: Schlachten des Weltkriegs.* Vol. 35. Berlin: Gerhard Stalling, 1930.

Strutz, Georg. *Die Tankschlacht bei Cambrai, 20.–29. November 1917: Schlachten des Weltkriegs.* Vol. 31. Berlin: Gerhard Stalling, 1929.

Great Britain

Edmonds, James E., ed. *Military Operations: Belgium and France 1918.* Vols. 1–5 and appendices. London: Macmillan, 1935–49.

———, ed. *The Occupation of the Rhineland, 1918–1929.* London: Her Majesty's Stationery Office, 1987.

Falls, Cyril. *Military Operations: Belgium and France 1917.* Vol. 1. London: Macmillan, 1940.

Henniker, A. M. *Transportation on the Western Front, 1914–1918.* London: Macmillan, 1937.

United States

Department of the Army. *American Armies and Battlefields in Europe.* 1938; repr., Washington, D.C.: Center of Military History, 1992.

———. *United States Army in the World War 1917–1919: Military Operations of the American Expeditionary Force*, vols. 2, 4, 5, 8–14. 1948; repr., Washington, D.C.: Center of Military History, 1989–91.

DOCUMENTS

Bavarian War Archives (Bayerisches Kriegsarchiv), Munich, Germany (arranged chronologically)

· Army Group Crown Prince Rupprecht, War Diary, 1 April 1918, File Hgr Rupprecht, Bd. 80.
· AOK 2, Ia/Art (no number), 7 April 1918, File Hgr Rupprecht, Bd. 38.
· OHL, II 82923, 8 April 1918, File Hgr Rupprecht, Bd. 38.
· Army Group Crown Prince Rupprecht, War Diary, Ia 6738, 12 April 1918, File Hgr. Rupprecht, Bd. 80.
· Army Group Crown Prince Rupprecht, War Diary, Ia 6852, 19 April 1918, File Hgr. Rupprecht, Bd. 80.
· OHL, Ia 7777, 20 April 1918, Army Group Crown Prince Rupprecht, War Diary, File Hgr. Rupprecht, Bd. 80.
· Army Group Crown Prince Rupprecht, War Diary, Ia 7010, 29 April 1918, File Hgr. Rupprecht, Bd. 80.
· Army Group Crown Prince Rupprecht, Ia 8082, 1 July 1918, File Hgr. Rupprecht, Bd. 4112.
· OHL, Ia 9388, 20 July 1918, File Hgr. Rupprecht, Bd. 105.
· OHL, Ia 10552, 30 September 1918, File Hgr. Rupprecht, Bd. 99/101.

Edmonds, James E., ed. Military Operations: Belgium and France 1918. Vol. 3. London: Macmillan, 1939 (arranged chronologically)

· "General Foch's Note of the 16th June 1918," appendix X, pp. 352–55.
· "Letter from Field-Marshal Sir Douglas Haig to General Foch, 17th July 1918. O.A.D. 895," appendix XVIII, pp. 365–66.
· "Letter from General Foch to Field-Marshal Sir Douglas Haig, 20th July 1918," Appendix XIX, pp. 366–67.

Edmonds, James E., ed. Military Operations: Belgium and France 1918. Vol. 4. London: Macmillan, 1947 (arranged chronologically)

· "O.A.D. 911, Commander-in-Chief Telegram of 22nd August 1918," appendix XX, pp. 587–88.
· "Allied Commander-in-Chief to the Commanders-in-Chief of the Allied Armies," 30 August 1918, appendix XXI, pp. 588–90.

General Service Schools. The German Offensive of July 15, 1918 (Marne Source Book). Fort Leavenworth, KS: General Service Schools Press, 1923 (arranged chronologically)

· Army Group German Crown Prince, Ia 2629, 26 June 1918, Document 126, pp. 172–74.
· Army Group German Crown Prince, Ia 2674, 17 July 1918, Document 411, p. 578.
· War Diary, Seventh Army, 18 July 1918, Document 441, p. 613.

German Military Archives (Bundesarchiv/Militärarchiv), Freiburg, Germany (arranged chronologically)

· Georg Wetzell, "The Offensives in the West and Their Prospects of Success," 12 December 1917, File PH 3/267.
· Army Group Crown Prince Rupprecht, Ia 4929, 25 December 1917, File PH 3/287.
· OHL, Ia 5905, "1918 Operations in the West," 27 December 1917, File PH 3/278.
· Thilo, "Meeting Minutes with Excellency Ludendorff, 21 January 1918," 23 January 1918, File PH 5 I/45.
· OHL Ia 6205, 24 January 1918, File PH 5 I/31.
· OHL Ia 6213, 24 January 1918, File PH 3/278.
· Army Group Crown Prince Rupprecht, Ia 5243, 26 January 1918, File PH 3/278.
· OHL Ia 6405, 8 February 1918, File PH 5 I/50.
· OHL 7070, 10 March 1918, File PH 3/281.
· OHL 7240, 20 March 1918, File PH 3/268.
· AOK 18, Ia 1461, 22 March 1918, File PH 5 I/29.
· Army Group Crown Prince Rupprecht, Ia 6438, 26 March 1918, File PH 5 II/202.
· OHL, Ia 7341, 26 March 1918, File PH 3/268.
· Army Group German Crown Prince, War Diary extracts, 28 March 1918, File PH 5 I/29.
· Army Group Crown Prince Rupprecht, Ia 6483, 29 March 1918, File PH 3/281.
· AOK 2, War Diary, 30 March 1918, File PH 5 II/121.
· OHL, Ia 7408, 30 March 1918, File PH 3/268.
· OHL, Ia 7414, 31 March 1918, File PH 3/268.
· Army Group German Crown Prince, Ia 2406, 1 April 1918, File PH 5 I/31.
· Army Group German Crown Prince, War Diary extracts, "Notes of Discussion with Ludendorff," 1 April 1918, File PH 5 I/29.
· OHL, Ic 85444, 12 May 1918, File PH 5 II/295.
· Army Group German Crown Prince, Ia/Art 12968, 26 June 1918, File PH 3/260.
· AOK 7, Ia 893, 30 June 1918, File PH 5 II/163.
· OHL, Ia 9304, 15 July 1918, File PH 3/264.
· AOK 7, Ia 1023, 16 July 1918, File PH 5 II/163.
· Army Group German Crown Prince, Ia 2670, 16 July 1918, File PH 5 II/409.
· AOK 7, Ia 1039, 17 July 1918, File PH 5 II/163.
· Army Group German Crown Prince, Ia 2689, 18 July 1918, File PH 5 I/40.
· Army Group German Crown Prince, Ia 2751, 29 July 1918, File PH 5 II/189.
· Georg Bruchmüller Papers, "Der Feldherr in meinem Blickfeld" (unpublished reminiscence of Ludendorff), File N275/2.
· "Mons Conference Minutes by Major Thilo," 4 February 1918, File PH 5 I/45.
· Oskar von Hutier, *Diary*, File RH 61/907.
· Hermann von Kuhl, "Personal War Diary of General von Kuhl," File RH 61/970.
· Hans von Seeckt, *Nachlass* (posthumous papers), Folder N247/175.

Library of Congress, Washington, D.C.

· Diary of Lieutenant Colonel P. L. Stackpole, A.D.C. to General Liggett: 25 January 1918 to 2 August 1919.

Roberts, Priscilla, ed. Documents. *Vol. 4 of* World War I: The Definitive Encyclopedia and Document Collection, *edited by Spencer Tucker. Santa Barbara: ABC-CLIO, 2014 (arranged chronologically)*

· "President Woodrow Wilson. 'The Fourteen Points,' Address to Joint Session of the U.S. Congress," 8 January 1918, pp. 2016–18.
· "Message from Field Marshal Paul von Hindenburg to Imperial Chancellor Max von Baden," 3 October 1918, p. 2063.
· "The First German Peace Note: Imperial Chancellor Prince Max von Baden to President Woodrow Wilson," 6 October 1918, p. 2064.
· "President Woodrow Wilson, First Reply to the German Request for an Armistice," 8 October 1918, p. 2064.
· "The Second German Note: German State Secretary of Foreign Affairs Wilhelm Solf to U.S. Secretary Robert Lansing," 14 October 1918, p. 2065.
· "President Woodrow Wilson, Second Reply to the German Government," 14 October 1918, pp. 2065–66.
· "The Third German Note: German State Secretary of Foreign Affairs Wilhelm Solf to U.S. Secretary Robert Lansing," 20 October 1918, pp. 2067–68.
· "President Woodrow Wilson, Third Reply to the German Government," 23 October 1918, pp. 2068–69.
· "The Fourth German Note: German State Secretary of Foreign Affairs Wilhelm Solf to U.S. Secretary Robert Lansing," 27 October 1918, pp. 2074–75.
· "Allied Supreme War Council, 22nd Resolution on the Armistice Terms," 4 November 1918, p. 2084.

United Kingdom National Archives, Kew, Great Britain

Record Group WO 158/105 358219 (arranged chronologically)

· "Headquarters. General-in-Chief of the Allied Armies No. 1749. General Directive No. 4," 1 July 1918.
· "Foch Instruction to Haig No. 2021," 12 July 1918
· "Headquarters. General-in-Chief of the Allied Armies No. 2021. From General Foch to Marshal Haig," 12 July 1918.
· "Special Directive No. 2168," 18 July 1918.
· "Personal and Secret Instruction for the General Commanding Army Chief of the North and Northeast, No. 2206," 19 July 1918.
· "Personal and Secret from General Foch to Marshal Haig, No. 2248," 20 July 1918.
· "Commander-in-Chief of the Allied Armies to Commander-in-Chief of the American Army, No. 2280." 22 July 1918.
· "Foch to Pershing, No. 2307," 22 July 1918.
· "Memo Foch to Pétain [unnumbered]," 23 July 1918.

· "Memorandum from the Commanders-in-Chief Conference No. 2375," 24 July 1918.
· "Foch to the British Commander-in-Chief, No. 2466," 28 July 1918.
· "Foch to the General of the Expeditionary American Forces, No. 2468," 28 July 1918.
· "Special Directive. No. 2467," 28 July 1918.
· "Addendum Note to No. 1/P.C.," 9 August 1918.
· "Foch to Pershing and Pétain, No. 1/P.C.," 9 August 1918.
· "Marshal Foch to Field Marshal Haig and General Pétain, No. 8/P.C.," 12 August 1918.
· "Marshal Foch to Field Marshal Haig, No. 12/P.C.," 15 August 1918.
· "Operations Priorities, No. 18/P.C.," 15 August 1918.
· "Foch to Haig, Pershing, and Pétain, No. 3035," 17 August 1918.
· "Foch to Pershing, No. 3201," 23 August 1918.
· "Note: Personal and Secret, No. 3266," 23 August 1918.
· "Note to the Allied Commanders-in-Chief [unnumbered]," 30 August 1918.
· "Foch to Pershing, No. 3480," 1 September 1918.
· "Meeting Notes, Marshal Foch and Generals Pétain and Pershing, No. 3528," 2 September 1918.
· "Directive, No. 3537," 3 September 1918.
· "Note on the Offensive North of the Lys, No. 3737," 9 September 1918.
· "Note on the Meuse-Argonne Offensive, No. 4179," 23 September 1918.
· "Note: No. 22/PC GQGA," 27 September 1918.
· "Foch to the Commanders in Chief, Unnumbered," 9 November 1918.
· "Foch to the Commanders in Chief, Unnumbered," 11 November 1918.

Record Group WO 158/106 358219 (arranged chronologically)

· "Foch to the Chief North and Northeast, No. 4456," 4 October 1918.
· "Precis Verbal of a Conference Held at the Villa Romaine, Versailles, on Monday, October 7, 1918, at 10:30 a.m., I.C.-78."
· "General Directive, No. 4627," 10 October 1918.
· "Foch to Pershing, No. 4711," 12 October 1918.
· "Operations Priority for Pershing, No. 4779," 14 October 1918.
· "First Subsection, Third Section, General Staff, To the General Commander-in-Chief, Armies of the North and Northeast, No. 4844," 16 October 1918.
· "General Directive, No. 4925," 19 October 1918.
· "Foch to Pétain, No. 4939," 20 October 1918.
· "Note No. 4985," 21 October 1918.
· "Foch to Pétain, No. 5060," 23 October 1918.
· "Note No. 5174," 25 October 1918.
· "Foch to Haig, No. 5253," 27 October 1918.
· "Foch to Pershing, No. 5254," 27 October 1918.
· "Foch to Pershing and Maistre, No. 5471," 5 November 1918.
· "Foch to Pétain, No. 5640," 5 November 1918.
· "To Director of Military Operations, Nr. 1010/13/42," 17 January 1919.

U.S. Army Combat Arms Reference Library, Fort Leavenworth, KS (arranged chronologically)

· Army Group German Crown Prince, Ia 2466, 30 April 1918, OHL, Ia 7736, 30 April 1918, File: Operations Documents (BLÜCHER-GNEISENAU-GOERZ), 17 April to 20 May 1918, Part 1.

· AOK 7, Ia 371, 12 May 1918, File: Operations Documents (BLÜCHER-GNEISENAU-GOERZ), 15 to 26 May 1918, Part 2.

· AOK 7, Ia 478, 23 May 1918, File: Operations Documents (BLÜCHER-GNEISENAU-GOERZ), 15 to 26 May 1918, Part 2.

· Army Group German Crown Prince, War Diary, 27 May 1918, File: Extracts from the War Diary of the Army Group German Crown Prince, 27 May to 15 June 1918.

· Army Group German Crown Prince, Ia 2545, 28 May 1918, File: Army Group German Crown Prince, Operations Documents (BLÜCHER-GNEISENAU-GOERZ), 17 May to 9 June 1918.

· Army Group German Crown Prince, War Diary, 28 May 1918, File: Extracts from the War Diary of the Army Group German Crown Prince, 27 May to 15 June 1918.

· OHL, Ia 8441, 30 May 1918, File: Operations Documents (BLÜCHER-GNEISENAU-GOERZ), 27 May to 9 June 1918.

· OHL, Ia 8485, 1 June 1918, File: Operations Documents (BLÜCHER-GNEISENAU-GOERZ), 27 May to 9 June 1918.

· AOK 7, Ia 607, 2 June 1918, File: Extracts from the Diary of the Commander-in-Chief of the Seventh Army, 1 June to 21 August 1918.

· Army Group German Crown Prince, War Diary, 3 June 1918, File: Extracts from the War Diary of the Army Group German Crown Prince, 27 May to 15 June 1918.

· Army Group German Crown Prince, Ia 675, 5 June 1918, File: Army Group German Crown Prince, Operations Documents (BLÜCHER-GNEISENAU-GOERZ), 27 May to 9 June 1918.

· OHL, Ia 8536, 5 June 1918, File: Army Group German Crown Prince, Operations Documents (BLÜCHER-GNEISENAU-GOERZ), 17 May to 9 June 1918.

· AOK7, Ia 696, 8 June 1918, File: Army Group German Crown Prince, Operations Documents (BLÜCHER-GNEISENAU-GOERZ), 17 May to 9 June 1918.

· OHL, Ia 8584, 8 June 1918, File: Army Group German Crown Prince, Operations Documents (BLÜCHER-GNEISENAU-GOERZ), 17 May to 9 June 1918.

· Army Group German Crown Prince, War Diary, 10 June 1918, File: Extracts from the War Diary of the Army Group German Crown Prince, 27 May to 15 June 1918.

· Army Group German Crown Prince, Morning and Noon Reports, 11 June 1918, File: Extracts from the War Diary of the Army Group German Crown Prince, 27 May to 15 June 1918.

· Army Group German Crown Prince, War Diary, 11 June 1918, File: Extracts from the War Diary of the Army Group German Crown Prince, 27 May to 15 June 1918

· Army Group German Crown Prince, Morning Reports, 13 June 1918, File: Extracts from the War Diary of the Army Group German Crown Prince, 27 May to 15 June 1918.

· OHL, Ia 8685, 14 June 1918, File: Operations Documents, Headquarters, Army
  Group German Crown Prince, (BLÜCHER-GNEISENAU-GOERZ), 14 June to 15
  July 1918.
· OHL, Ia 8777, 18 June 1918, File: Operations Documents, Headquarters, Army
  Group German Crown Prince, (BLÜCHER-GNEISENAU-GOERZ), 14 June to 15
  July 1918.
· Army Group German Crown Prince, Ia 2639, 29 June 1918, File: Extracts from
  Archives—Army Group German Crown Prince, 1918, First Army, 16 June to 31 July
  1918.
· AOK 7, War Diary, 15 July 1918, File: Extracts from the Diary of the Commander-in-
  Chief of the Seventh Army, 1 June to 21 August 1918.
· Army Group German Crown Prince, War Diary, 15 July 1918, File: Extracts from the
  War Diary, Army Group German Crown Prince, 15 July to 3 August 1918.
· AOK 3, Ia 7695, 16 July 1918, File: The Army Records, Army Group of the German
  Crown Prince, MARNE, 1918 Campaign.
· AOK 7, War Diary, 16 July 1918, File: Extracts from the Diary of the Commander-in-
  Chief of the Seventh Army, 1 June to 21 August 1918.
· AOK 7, War Diary, 19 July 1918, File: Extracts from the Diary of the Commander-in-
  Chief of the Seventh Army, 1 June to 21 August 1918.
· Army Group German Crown Prince, War Diary, 21 July 1918, File: Extracts from the
  War Diary, Army Group German Crown Prince, 15 July to 3 August 1918.
· OHL, Ia 9472, 25 July 1918, File: Extracts from Operations Documents from 1 July to
  6 August 1918 Pertaining to Army Group German Crown Prince: The Defensive in
  July 1918.
· OHL, Ia 9536, 27 July 1918, File: Extracts from Operations Documents from 1 July to
  6 August 1918 Pertaining to Army Group German Crown Prince: The Defensive in
  July 1918.

United States Department of the Army. United States Army in
the World War 1917–1919: Military Operations of the American
Expeditionary Force. *Vol. 2. 1948; repr., Washington, D.C.:
Center of Military History, 1989 (arranged chronologically)*

· "Doullens Agreement," 26 March 1918, p. 254.
· "Extract from Minutes of War Cabinet Meeting 374," 27 March 1918, pp. 258–59.
· "Orders to Hold Ground at All Costs," 27 March 1918, pp. 260–61.
· "GHQ AEF War Diary, Book II, p. 446," 28 March 1918, pp. 260–61.
· "Supreme War Council Telegram 317–39," 29 March 1918, and "Supreme War
  Council Fldr. 316 Cablegram," 29 March 1918, p. 265.
· "Cable p-820-S," 30 March 1918, p. 264.
· "General Staff Mp.34, General Foch to the Minister of War," 1 April 1918, p. 270.
· "SWC: 376–1 Agreement. Minutes of a Conference held at the Hotel De Ville on
  Wednesday, April 3, 1918, at 3:15 p.m.," pp. 274–77.
· "Letter Haig to Foch," 6 April 1918, p. 285.
· "Headquarters, Allied Armies, General Staff No. 121," 7 April 1918, pp. 288–89.

- "Headquarters Allied Armies. General Staff No. 133," 10 April 1918, pp. 314–15.
- "General Headquarters British Armies in France, OAD 810," 10 April 1918, p. 315.
- "General Headquarters British Armies in France. Support of British Troops by French Forces," 11 April 1918, p. 315.
- "Headquarters, Allied Armies, Operations, General Staff, No. 176," 14 April 1918, p. 323.
- "Ministry of War, No. 149/H.R," 14 April 1918, p. 324.
- "Headquarters, Allied Armies. General Staff No. 261," 19 April 1918, p. 332.
- "General Headquarters. French Armies of the North and Northeast. 3rd Section General Staff. No. 25972," 24 April 1918, pp. 345–48.
- "OAD 832. Notes of a Conference Held at Abbeville at 10:00 a.m., Saturday, April 27th, 1918," pp. 355–56.
- "SWC 115, Resolution 2, Executive War Board," 2 May 1918, pp. 366–71.
- "Memorandum, General-in-Chief Commanding the Allied Armies," 1 June 1918, pp. 435–38.
- "Allied Supreme War Council, 6th Session," 2 June 1918, pp. 441–45.
- "Memorandum, Commander-in-Chief of the Allied Forces," 2 June 1918, p. 446.
- "Cable P-1279-S for the Chief of Staff and the Secretary of War," 10 June 1918, p. 460.
- "H.S. Brit. File: 910–32.9. Telephone Message," 13 June 1918, p. 462.
- "Fldr. F-1. Conference at Bombon on the Employment of American Troops," 10 July 1918, pp. 517–20, 527–31.
- "French General Headquarters, Fldr G Notes. Notes on a Conversation at Provins Between General Pershing and General Pétain," 12 July 1918, pp. 523–24.
- "HS Secret Documents, Fldr F-1, Notes, Allied Conference at Chateau Bombon," 24 July 1918, pp. 549–50.
- "French Armies of the North and Northeast, 3rd Section, General Staff, No. 23976," 20 September 1918, p. 607.
- "Instructions for the General Commanding the Group of Armies of the Reserve, No. 33479," 23 September 1918, pp. 609–10.
- "French Armies of the North and Northeast, 3rd Section, General Staff, No. 4353," p. 617.

United States Department of the Army. United States Army in the World War 1917–1919: Military Operations of the American Expeditionary Force. *Vol. 5. 1948; repr., Washington, D.C.: Center of Military History, 1989 (arranged chronologically)*

- "General Headquarters, French Armies of the North and Northeast. 3rd Section, General Staff, No. 5358. General Instructions," 5 July 1918, p. 3.
- "Telephone Message, Foch to Pétain, 12:25 pm," 15 July 1918, p. 242.

United States Department of the Army. United States Army in the World War 1917–1919: Military Operations of the American Expeditionary Force. *Vol. 8. 1948; repr., Washington, D.C.: Center of Military History, 1989*

- "Pétain to Foch, General Staff No. 18775, bis/3," 30 September 1918, p. 82.

United States Department of the Army. United States Army in
the World War 1917–1919: Military Operations of the American
Expeditionary Force. *Vol. 9. 1948; repr., Washington, D.C.:*
Center of Military History, 1989 (arranged chronologically)

· "First Army, AEF, Field Order No. 20, 20 September 1918," pp. 82–88.
· "191.32.13 Letter," 27 September 1918, p. 140.
· "HS Ger, File: 810–33.5: Fldr. 1: War Diary. Group of Armies Gallwitz," 9 October 1918.
· "HS Ger, File: 810–33.5: Fldr. 1: Order," 10 October 1918.

United States Department of the Army. United States Army in the World
War 1917–1919: Military Operations of the American Expeditionary Force.
Vol. 10. 1948; repr., Washington, D.C.: Center of Military History, 1991

· "HS Secret File: Fldr. H-1: To the Allied Supreme War Council. Paris." 30 October
1918, pp. 28–30.

United States Department of the Army. United States Army in
the World War 1917–1919: Military Operations of the American
Expeditionary Force. *Vol. 11. 1948; repr., Washington, D.C.:*
Center of Military History, 1991 (arranged chronologically)

· OHL, Ia 7434, 1 April 1918, p. 280.
· OHL, Ia 7515, 5 April 1918, p. 282.
· OHL, Ia 9541, 28 July 1918, pp. 348–49.
· AEF General Orders 198, 7 November 1918, pp. 2–4.
· AOK 3, Ia 12257, 11 November 1918, p. 427.

United States Department of the Army. United States Army in
the World War 1917–1919: Military Operations of the American
Expeditionary Force. *Vol. 12. 1948; repr., Washington, D.C.:*
Center of Military History, 1991 (arranged chronologically)

· "Memorandum for the Chief of Staff. Subject: Training." AEF General
Headquarters, G-5 Section, 4 July 1918, pp. 303–5.
· "Preliminary Report of the Commander-in-Chief." G-3, GHQ, AEF: 1123, 19
November 1918, pp. 2–70.

Viereck, George, ed. As They Saw Us: Foch, Ludendorff, and Other Leaders
Write Our War History. *New York: Doubleday, 1929 (arranged chronologically)*

· "Personal and Secret Orders to the Commander General of the Group of Reserve
Armies, No.11 P.C.," 26 March 1918, p. 79.
· "General Order No. 104 (Headquarters No. 28277 T)," 27 March 1918, p. 81.

INDEX

DAVID T. ZĄBECKI retired from the U.S. Army in 2007 as a major general. He started his military career as an infantry rifleman in Vietnam in 1967 and 1968. In 1975 he was commissioned as a field artillery first lieutenant. He is a graduate of the U.S. Army War College and the U.S. Army Command and General Staff College, where in 1988 he received the General John J. Pershing Award as the distinguished honor graduate of his year group. From 1996 to 1998 he served extensively in Bosnia and former Yugoslavia. In 2003 he was attached to the U.S. State Department as the senior security adviser on the U.S. Coordinating and Monitoring Mission (Roadmap to Peace in the Middle East), where he negotiated between the Israeli Defense Force and the multiple Palestinian security organizations. In 2004 he was the commander of U.S. forces supporting the sixtieth anniversary commemorations of the D-Day landings, Operation MARKET-GARDEN, and the Battle of the Bulge. In 2005–6 he was the senior U.S. Army commander in Europe south of the Alps, based in Vicenza, Italy. Ząbecki holds a PhD in military history from the Royal Military College of Science, Cranfield University, where his supervisor was the late Professor Richard Holmes. In 2012 he served as the Dr. Leo A. Shifirn Distinguished Professor of Military History at the U.S. Naval Academy, Annapolis. Ząbecki is an Honorary Senior Research Fellow in the War Studies Programme at the University of Birmingham (UK) and is the author or editor of numerous military history books. In 2016 his encyclopedia, *Germany at War: 400 Years of Military History*, won a Society for Military History Distinguished Book Award. He is a Distinguished Member of the 47th Infantry Regiment. His military awards include the Distinguished Service Medal and the Combat Infantryman's Badge.